Dimensions. Journal of Architectural Knowledge
08/2024

Changing Spatial Practices: Alliances, Activism, and Networks

Issue Editors
Kadambari Baxi, Isabel Glogar, Gabu Heindl,
Bernadette Krejs, Tatjana Schneider

[transcript]

This journal is published bianually (in spring and autumn) and printed editions are available for annual subscription directly from the publisher. The retail price for an annual subscription to the print issue incl. shipment within Germany is 75,00 € and for international purchases 85,00 €. The electronic version is available free of charge (Open Access).

All information regarding notes for contributors, subscriptions, Open Access, back volume and orders is available online at:
https://www.transcript-publishing.com/dak

Additional information on upcoming issues, calls for contributions and the options for partaking as contributors, editors or members of the peer review procedure can be found at the journals website: www.dimensions-journal.eu
If you have any further questions please contact us, addressing Katharina Voigt, at: mail@dimensions-journal.eu

Bibliographic information published by the Deutsche Nationalbibliothek

The Deutsche Nationalbibliothek lists this publication in the Deutsche National-bibliografie; detailed bibliographic data are available in the Internet at http://dnb.de

Dimensions. Journal of Architectural Knowledge

Issue Editors
Kadambari Baxi, Columbia University, New York
Isabel Glogar, Technical University of Munich
Gabu Heindl, University of Kassel
Bernadette Krejs, Technical University of Vienna
Tatjana Schneider, TU Braunschweig

Lead Editorial Board
Ben Boucsein, Technical University of Munich
Uta Graff, Technical University of Munich
Ferdinand Ludwig, Technical University of Munich
Sandra Meireis, Technical University of Darmstadt
Jörg Schröder, Leibniz University Hannover
Katharina Voigt, Technical University of Munich

Advisory Board
Sonja Dümpelmann, Ludwig Maximilians University of Munich
Lidia Gasperoni, The Bartlett School of Architecture
Susanne Hauser, Berlin University of Arts
Wilfried Kühn, Technical University of Vienna

Dimensions. Journal of Architectural Knowledge was founded at the Technical University of Munich by Katharina Voigt, Uta Graff, and Ferdinand Ludwig.

The initial funding to this journal is provided by the Department of Architecture at the TUM School of Engineering and Design in Munich, Germany.

Additional funding for this issue is provided by the Institute for History and Theory of Architecture and the City, TU Braunschweig, and the Department ARCHITECTURE CITIES ECONOMIES | Building Economy & Project Development, University of Kassel.

First published 2025 by transcript Verlag, Bielefeld
© Kadambari Baxi, Isabel Glogar, Gabu Heindl, Bernadette Krejs, Tatjana Schneider
(eds.)

transcript Verlag | Hermannstraße 26 | D-33602 Bielefeld | live@transcript-verlag.de

Cover layout: Katharina Voigt (Technical University of Munich)
Copy-editing: Isabel Glogar (Technical University of Munich),
Bernadette Krejs (Technical University of Vienna)
Proofreading: Lumi Kirk (Technical University of Munich)
Typeset: Victoria Fricker (Vienna)
Printed by Druckhaus Bechstein GmbH, Wetzlar
ISSN 2747-5085
eISSN 2747-5093
Print-ISBN 978-3-8376-7349-4
PDF-ISBN 978-3-8394-7349-8

Printed on permanent acid-free text paper.

Contents

ACTIVISM

NETWORKS

CONTRIBUTORS

EDITORIAL

I.
Editorial Meeting, Vienna. Photograph by Isabel Glogar, 2025.

Dimensions of Architectural Knowledge, 2024–08
https://doi.org/10.14361/dak-2024-0801

Changing Spatial Practices:
Alliances, Activism, and Networks

Kadambari Baxi, Isabel Glogar, Gabu Heindl, Bernadette Krejs, Tatjana Schneider

Changing Spatial Practices

Architecture is always political. It produces space – and thus relations, exclusions, possibilities. At a time of overlapping crises – ecological, social, and political – we must ask not *whether* architecture can change, but *how* it must change. As change is urgent. Not as an esthetic shift or a technical update, but as a political realignment of our tools, methods, and modes of operating. The myth of the solitary genius will have to give way to practices rooted in collective processes and situated knowledges. If space is central to architecture, then spatial practice must be redefined through the lens of solidarity and struggle.

In this book, we argue for a shift: from architecture as product to architecture as practice. Drawing, building, teaching, writing, and resisting – all these form part of the architectural field, none superior to the other. To address the demands of our time, we propose architecture as an act of alliance, of activism, of networks, not for the sake of collaboration itself, but as a political project. With our call for papers we searched not for high moral ground but for concrete ideas, meaningful measures, inclusive cultural shifts, and creative collaborations. The practices of collectivity portrayed here are self-critical, aware of their limits, and conscious of their position within power structures.

Because alliances can be co-opted, activism can serve reactionary goals, and networks can just as well entrench inequality as dismantle it, we need

Corresponding authors: Kadambari Baxi (Columbia University, New York, USA), Isabel Glogar (Technical University of Munich, Germany), Gabu Heindl (University of Kassel, Germany), Bernadette Krejs (Technical University of Vienna, Austria), Tatjana Schneider (TU Braunschweig, Germany); kbaxi@barnard.edu; https://orcid.org/0009-0002-0371-7720; isabel.glogar@tum.de; https://orcid.org/0000-0002-9831-6286; gabu.heindl@uni-kassel.de; https://orcid.org/0009-0007-4436-4008; krejs@wohnbau.tuwien.ac.at; https://orcid.org/0009-0007-4601-9566; tatjana.schneider@tu-braunschweig.de; https://orcid.org/0000-0003-2372-0919

to position ourselves. This is why this book centers practices that seek transformation across the following interconnected fields, which seem equally urgent. There is the intricate relationship of architecture with climate, especially obvious in the destructive ways the building industry hungrily extracts for excessive material use and is responsible for heavy CO_2 emissions. Yet, within architectural history there is an alternative thread of diverse and solidarity economies that aspire to more social and climate justice. Also, a central thread running throughout this book is a focus on collaborative and feminist spatial practices, which provided the starting point for our editorial work. Working within academia and professional practice, we wanted to bring to the fore practices and modes of operating that have been seminal for and in our own work: Practices that challenge hierarchies, foreground collective agency, embrace non-linear processes of making and knowing, and demand that we rethink the role of the professional (that is: the expert) in today's complex networks of relations. This of course relates just as much to education and research.

Architecture is based on established forms of knowledge. When we consider the current implications of spatial production, we must think about who produces knowledge for whom, and who is included or excluded, both now and historically. You can observe such empowering practices combining research and education in Alissa Diesch's contribution »*Mapping Territorial Resistance – Transformative Heritage in Bogotá*« examining and mapping Bogotá's urban transformation through overlapping crises, showing how indigenous practices, colonial structures, and urbanization shape the city. Using decolonial theory and participatory research, it reframes crisis as a catalyst and proposes transformative heritage as a resource for community-based urban renewal.

Looking towards architectural education, Changing Spatial Practices builds on inclusive and intersectional practices and on forms of teaching that empower and build up decolonization or rethink power relations. It involves not only rethinking teaching formats, but also knowledge production where the architectural canon, references, images, and curricula, integrate diverse voices, such as those of non-Western, queer, and feminist practitioners, researchers, and thinkers. In »*Spatial Activist Research as Embodied Praxis*,« Esra Can, Maria Alexandrescu, Andrew Belfield, Jakleen Al-Dalal'a, Lara Scharf, and Doina Petrescu examine how activist research generates embodied knowledge that informs architectural and spatial practice. Using feminist and decolonial perspectives, their contribution introduces

»embodied praxis« as a reflexive method for socio-spatial transformation. In their contribution »*Transing Space(s)*« Vio:la Wagner and Alvie Augustin describe how cisnormative frameworks inscribe binary gender norms into space, marginalizing non-binary identities. Drawing on trans studies, architecture theory, disability studies, and interviews with trans activists, it proposes trans-informed understandings and practices of space to challenge cissexist structures through an interdisciplinary and intersectional lens. In »*Staying with the Trouble: Feminist Spatial Practices and Hybrid Agency in Slovakia and the Czech Republic*,« Lýdia Grešáková explores how collaborations with marginalized communities and non-human actors challenge top-down planning and promote more just, responsive approaches to design.

In architecture, both working modes and working models are changing due to economic, technological and societal transformations. Thus, challenging the overall framework around architectural production with evolving practices that question competitions, briefs and commissions, or that create their own clients, or start new types of civic collaborations. The forms of representation we produce as spatial designers create visions and impact society. The contribution »*Counterproposals in Zurich: Constructive Criticism of Destructive Practices*« traces the history of Zurich's ZAS / ZAS* collective, and shows the groups' use of counterproposals to participate in urban planning. By combining professional expertise with civic activism, they demonstrate how architects can cooperate and reshape democratic processes, resist destructive practices, and foster transformative approaches to urban life amid ecological and social crises. This involves preserving and activating as many resources as possible, using less material and leaving a smaller impact on an architectural, urban, and global scale. In »*Entangled Thresholds: Building Multispecies Envelopes Beyond Human Comfort in the Philippines and Japan*,« Natalya Dikhanov-Juswigg and Sadie Imae examine the building envelope as a threshold where human and non-human collaborations can reshape architecture beyond comfort-centered design. Drawing on symbiotic models, it argues for porous, multispecies, and community-oriented approaches that dismantle extractive practices, expand notions of comfort, and reposition architects as facilitators of ecological and social repair.

In the contribution »*Repair as Practice: Expanding Architectural Approaches to Climate Justice in Southern Africa*,« Jhono Bennett proposes reparative urbanism as an approach to climate justice that challenges Western, extractive paradigms. It frames repair as a continuous material and relational practice – centered on care, justice, and long-term community partnerships – that redefines architectural agency through the relationships and systems it sustains.

Thus, by looking closer at alliances, activism, and networks we take these questions along: What are we allying for? What do we activate? Whom do we connect – and who remains excluded? Alliances, Activism and Networks are interwoven concepts – terms that reflect not fixed categories, but fluid orientations for understanding diverse spatial and organizational practices. Rather than rigidly compartmentalizing contributions, we use them as overlapping, interdependent clusters that offer a framework for navigation or points of entry into the rich terrain of spatial and social practices in this book. Collectively, the contributions respond to urgent socio-ecological questions and challenge dominant narratives by proposing alternative models grounded in care, collaboration, and situated practice.

Alliances

The first section of this book addresses these questions: How can architecture participate in building alliances, how can it enter co-working with unexpected partners? What makes an alliance? Political theory – especially the Marxist kind – defines alliances as collective actions of groups that don't lose their identity in the cooperation, which is not based on habitual sameness of interests or similarity of habitus, but serves a temporal strategic goal.

Alliances do not come »natural.« They have to be built; either around moral altruism, which makes one group take a stance for another one. Or, quite differently, around a shared project goal, which can be a common goal but also a common enemy. More soberly explained by use of the »chain of equivalence« concept within hegemony politics theory: A big difference to a shared external adversary can level and relativize smaller interior differences between groups (or interests) entering into an alliance. We encounter such alliances in many cases, of course with neither only left, or radical-democratic projects, nor exclusively with anti-hegemonic projects: Examples include alliances between architects and other spatial practitioners, climate institutions, activists, politicians, government bodies, entrepreneurs and academia, as well as wider society, to address climate breakdown through new policies, just building practices and processes that put an end to extractivist ways of doing.

Hence, alliances compel us to attend equally to the what of political action as to the how – the process, the composition, the labor of building coalitional structures. As a form of co-working, alliances allow actors to contribute specific expertise, tactics, and forms of knowledge toward a shared undertaking. The alliance, then, becomes a space where contradiction is not eliminated but negotiated – held in tension by a unifying vision, antagonism, or necessity.

Alliances are neither natural nor habitual, but rather built. Therefore, unforeseen, unexpected allies with different backgrounds and typical group interests enter the picture. Yet, when the structural role and embeddedness of architects within capitalist production remains unchallenged, the alliance-building with architects is discouraged. To become an ally architect requires more than ethical positioning; it demands structural realignment. It requires seeing architecture not as an end in itself, but as part of broader social and political struggles.

The contribution »Becoming Architect-as-Ally: A Conversation on Practice, Definitions, and Privilege with Nature of Hope Participants« by Alina Paias, public works, Karin Reisinger, Lis-Mari Gurák Hjortfors, and Husos arquitecturas, portrays a group of exhibitors at the International Architecture Biennale in Rotterdam 2014 entitled »Nature of Hope.« It highlights common cause-alliances between anti-extractivism activists and anti-colonially minded architects supporting them by contributing what they do well: e.g., mapping, unveiling, exhibiting – in this particular case with regards to systems that displace people, deplete ecosystems, and export environmental harm under the banner of »development.« An alliance and a network at the same time it is calling for a shift from doing-for to doing-with – a redefinition of practice that is grounded in accountability rather than authorship. Beverly Engelbrecht´s contribution »Counter Architectures of Sex Work: Collective Care Networks and their Spatial Productions along Potsdamer Straße in West Berlin in the 1980s,« highlights, first, alliances between sex-workers, which resembles the classical class example, i.e., the development of a sense of shared experience and belonging between exploited workers, resulting in something akin to class consciousness and solidarity vis-à-vis pimps, clients, and the authorities. Secondly, there are researchers allying themselves with the sex workers over a temporal and social distance. Lindsay Harkema´s contribution »Self, Standpoint, Network: Learning from the Autoethnographic Methods of Reproductive Justice,« shows how reproductive justice activists find unexpected allies in architects. These groups fight common adversaries:

patriarchy, neo-authoritarian legislature, and agents of an anti-feminist backlash. Ultimately, this alliance allows architects to also clarify their own position regarding notoriously hetero-male normative bias in their practice and its history. In seizing the cooperation as an opportunity to confront their discipline's inherent misogyny, an advance in anti-sexist critical self-enlightenment becomes their proto-political gain from this alliance.

Activism

Activism activates new trajectories of change. It often promotes collective actions that aim to disrupt or change existing paradigms. Eager to explore the potential of activism in our field at large – our call invited views on what activism might mean or make possible today. We sought activist practices that integrated not just mild resistance against certain hegemonic influences, but also offered proactive and projective actions.

The contributions we received begin to outline some possibilities. Participating in mass protests and civic disobedience, as climate activists; lobbying city agencies or trade organizations, as professional architects; advocating participatory design or industrial and legal reforms, as urban and building experts; redefining disciplinary lexicons and pedagogies, as designers and educators, among others. With local case studies and site-specific research, the authors draw attention to depleted rural and urban landscapes, sites of extraction and exploitation, and architectures of urban and social inequalities. To address such pervasive problems, they deploy anti-development schemes, counter-design proposals, and community-engaged design and planning initiatives. Some use their architectural skills to aid public protests, direct actions, or performative campaigns, and bring design agencies to grassroots activism. Looking inward within the discipline, other authors challenge foundational architectural concepts and ingrained knowledge, and mobilize a new language of design, especially one that is based on gender, trans, and decolonial frameworks.

At another level, the essays reframe spatial practices through historic or current geopolitical inequalities. Any scale of architectural practice must negotiate the material, labor and political relations dispersed worldwide. Consider this powerful illustration included in the article »Reimagining Architectural Practice through Relation: Notes from the In-Between« by Ana Bisbicus and Sarah Hachem – [habi practice], where the authors describe an image, posted on Instagram by the Palestinian Youth Movement, of a drone moments before it struck a building. The image caption, in part, states: »*Every building is a planet.*« That every physical or imagined object or space is simultaneously linked to an elsewhere, is poignantly understood by the youth activists. To make these relations visible, and to make them actionable, remains an ongoing challenge. In »*Architects as Climate-Activists*,« Armelle Breuil foregrounds three spatial practitioners participating in the climate movement in different ways. Analyzing the work of Nick Newman, Tom Bennett, and Léa Hobson, and their practices that range from design work to civil disobedience, the article redefines architecture's role in addressing systemic crises, highlighting new pathways for collective action, spatial justice, and planetary care. Collaboration as a powerful but also sometimes critical and fragile process can be observed in Rui Ferreira dos Santos' personal narration »*Toward Poetopolitics: Attempts at Landing as a Collective in Portugal.*« The article reflects on the rise and dissolution of an intentional collective and proposes poetopolitics – a practice attentive to legality, infrastructure, and reciprocity.

To bring about the necessary change in architectural practices today, insurgent, interconnected, and organized activism is essential. To steer spatial practices towards inclusive climate, social, and political ecosystems, unlearning, relearning, and co-learning is required, by one and all. No tactic, method, or solution is sufficient on its own. Scaling up and speeding up any and all actions is increasingly evident. However, change is a process – it is inherently slow and often incremental. When enacted through planned actions, plural or molecular – collective and organized – it can lead to genuine transformation.

Networks

We understand networks as a particular form of mesh, or web, of different types and forms of organisations, human and beyond-human – more or less structured, more or less connected, more or less defined —, yet constructs that share issues of concern. They are threaded and interwoven accumulations and tangles of allies, held together by thoughts, ideas, and actions, sharing not necessarily a common goal, but an idea of a direction: environmental justice, ecological solidarity, the deflation of persisting myths of modernity and patriarchal strongholds, or the shattering of dominant narratives of heroes and heroines. Instead, they are tools of resistance, trapping mechanisms, instruments of solidarity, comfort blankets, powerful vehicles, beautiful, repairable, soft landings, catchers and keepers of dreams – and anything but made of rigid hierarchies.

This third section of our book therefore, draws attention to those works of intentional netting (or: net-making) that emphasize those powers and capabilities that rest in a net's inherent configuration of decentralization, mutuality, but also interdependence: You pull at one node and others will feel the effect. Offering a vision of a cosmos that resists the cascade of concentrated top-down decision-making, the stories that we have collated here focus on types of relations that are fierce because they are horizontal, on powers that are distributed and responsive, and on practices that are rooted in cooperation. What emerges are accounts that shift, sometimes ever so slightly but always decidedly; strongholds of capital and political might, as well as texts that tell different stories through different voices.

The nets that sit at the center of our interest are those that understand a network not as a schematic, anonymous organizational structure or mere matter of pragmatism to ensure, for example, the smooth operation of a system. Instead, the nets are strategic acts of crafting connections between previously independent nodes to build strength (and power) through a deliberate stitching together of alternative economic and social relations. In doing so, these practices contribute with their work to imaginaries that illustrate how other worlds and other futures are not the stuff of distant dreams but are already in the making.

Networks can be material and immaterial and they include actors and actants such as land and rubble. Robin V Hueppe describes such networks in »*From Companion Mounds to Ruderal Ecologies. Reconstructing Land as a Medium of Resistance in Berlin's Housing Estates.*« It explores how former rubble landfills have been transformed into ruderal ecologies that resist institutional control. It argues for a land-centered perspective that highlights how human and non-human actors co-create counter-spaces, fostering social encounters and supporting just climate futures. With »*Urban Mediations and Collective Architecture: Zuloark and the Case of Campo de Cebada, Madrid,*« Enrique Espinosa and Enrique Nieto show how practices of mediation decenter architecture and foster networks with civil society, public institutions, and citizen movements. These processes mobilize »minor knowledges« and participatory practices, opening possibilities for more ecological, inclusive urban futures.

To make the net of the network *is* work. Recognising work (i.e. labour) as a constituent part of the network, it becomes clear that making that net is as much about those who forge the connections between nodes as it is about the connections and relations between them, which have to be tended to, maintained, and cared for.

Are we doing the work?

Audre Lorde leads us to the question *Are we doing the work?*[1], that has been a guide and lens for our work on the publication, but also about what the work is that is being done and how it is being done. A radical rethinking of the network as net-work, of alliances as co-work and activism as counter-work accompanies the wider radical rethinking of ethics, politics, and kinship in times of stubbornly persisting narratives of mastery and control. It reshapes how action is conceptualized: No longer as heroic intervention by individual saviours, but as collaborative world-making enacted across scales to create impacts that resist: colonialisms, capitalisms, or heteropatriarchy; while also opening space for something quieter, more enduring: a collective orientation towards interdependence, and transformation.

For all these essential questions, this publication does not intent to offer answers, it rather offers propositions, tools, and reflections – invitations to act. Because practice is not only what we do, but how we position ourselves while doing it. The diverse approaches in this book are not necessarily new, but operate in specific local, regional, and cultural contexts. This is key to their overall arguments. The range of work, while not exhaustive, is multi-dimensional and collaborative. A number of contributions are co-authored or written by collectives. As readers, our task is to reinterpret these situated practices, and to consider how to adapt them to other circumstances, maximizing their potential – to connect them to larger discourses and practices, and to build alliances and networks, as integral to any practice of activism.

The contributions are offerings that differ in strategies, stories, and actions, yet they form powerful connections despite an existing racist, extractive, and patriarchal architecture that seeks to keep us separated. They compellingly demonstrate ways of sharing knowledge and caring for one

---

1 »Each of us must find our work and do it. [...] It means actively working for change, sometimes in the absence of any surety that change is coming. It means doing the unromantic and tedious work necessary to forge meaningful coalitions, and it means recognizing which coalitions are possible and which coalitions are not. [...] It means fighting despair.« (Lorde, Audre (1984): *Sister Outsider: Essays and Speeches*, New York: Crossing Press, 135.)

another, attending to our histories while also providing feminist imaginations that make space for other stories, bodies, and spaces. We end here, but the work is of course not done, we leave the work open to us all, to a diversity of forms of collaborations to continue the path toward just, joyful, empowering, and non-extractive architectural practices.

Acknowledgement

We, the editors – Kadambari Baxi, Isabel Glogar, Gabu Heindl, Bernadette Krejs, and Tatjana Schneider – are deeply grateful to Esra Akcan, Anamarija Batista, Gauri Bharat, Lori A. Brown, Cristina Cerulli, Peggy Deamer, Jigna Desai, Victoria Fricker, Lidia Gasperoni, Uta Graff, Monika Grubbauer, Sabine Hansmann, Lumi Kirk, Elke Krasny, Uta Laconte, Ferdinand Ludwig, Catalina Mejia Moreno, Peter Mörtenböck, Gabrielle Schaad, Meike Schalk, Rosario Talevi, Renée Tribble, Brittany Utting, Katharina Voigt, Alla Vronskaya, and Lennart Wolff.

ALLIANCES ALLIANCES ALLIANCES ALLIANCES ALLIANCES ALLIANCES ALLIANCES ALLIANCES ALLIANCES

ACTIVISM ACTIVISM ACTIVISM ACTIVISM ACTIVISM ACTIVISM ACTIVISM ACTIVISM ACTIVISM

Staying with the Trouble

Counter Architectures of Sex Work

Becoming Architect-as-Ally

Self, Standpoint, Network

Toward Poetopolitics

Counterproposals in Zurich

Reimagining Architectu

Transing Space

Architects

2.
Editorial Concept Diagram by Kadambari Baxi.

ALLIANCES

Dimensions of Architectural Knowledge, 2024-08 ∂
https://doi.org/10.14361/dak-2024-0802

Self, Standpoint, Network:
Learning from the Autoethnographic Methods
of Reproductive Justice

Lindsay Harkema

Abstract: »*Revealing one's subjective self and standpoint increasingly is treasured in ethnography as well as the reproductive justice movement because we actually challenge the omnipresent, allegedly neutral voice that distances itself from the objects of the discourse*« *(Ross 2017: 207).*
This essay addresses political threats to reproductive bodily autonomy vis-à-vis the built environment and speculates how the intersectional, feminist perspective of Reproductive Justice (SisterSong 2025), a human rights framework calling for bodily autonomy, reproductive freedom, and sustainable communities founded by a coalition of Black women in 1994, could transform architecture into a more politically engaged and socially imaginative discipline. In contrast to the objective neutrality of conventional design practice, this framework draws from self-awareness of individual needs in collective contexts to care for others and build sustainable futures. To become more supportive of real, diverse human bodies and lived experiences, architecture could adopt autoethnographic methods, which draw from personal experience to address oppression and build common grounds.
The autoethnography of Reproductive Justice is explored through the lenses of *self* (an individual's immediate, personal experience), *standpoint* (the perspective shaped in relation to larger societal contexts), and *network* (the broader interconnected social and environmental relationships). A case study of recent academic design studios addressing Reproductive Justice and the built environment amid increasing threats and restrictions to reproductive healthcare in the US demonstrates how designers could draw from their own experiences to establish compassion for others and embrace the interconnectedness of all three scales in imagining alternative futures. Countering the status quo of abstraction from real, embodied experiences in design, RJ offers a model of engaging situated lives and perspectives in building just futures.

Keywords: Reproductive Justice; Autoethnography; Embodiment; Feminist Practice; Pedagogy.

Corresponding author: Lindsay Harkema (WIP Collaborative (WBE)/Columbia University, New York, USA); lindsay@wip-studio.org; https://orcid.org/0009-0004-6216-2133

Introduction

One of the most pervasive tools in architecture is the generic »user.« As a stand-in for real human bodies, the abstract scale figure distances designers from the actual, lived experiences of the built environments they create. Experiences that are shaped by forces other than spatial composition, like social, political, and cultural dynamics, as well as individual human characteristics, e.g., race, gender, ethnicity, sexuality, health, physical and intellectual abilities, and economic status. Instead of addressing the intersectional complexity of embodied human identities, the assumption of objective neutrality enables architects to avoid the political implications of their work. Conventional design methods often apply this kind of false neutrality to the built environment in ways that ignore interpersonal differences in favor of a one-size-fits-all approach, thus perpetuating the systemic exclusion of marginalized bodies. In this way, they avoid addressing societal constraints that often exercise more control over bodies than their immediate physical surroundings.

Alternatively, feminist methods focus on the ways in which individual, lived experiences are impacted by societal contexts, recognizing diverse embodied realities and challenging existing power hierarchies that negate difference. This undermines the notion of a generic user by foregrounding the entanglement of personal identity and the surrounding environment. For example, an individual's ability to access abortion in the US is compounded by their gender, race, and class, as well as their geographic location and legal setting. In the contemporary political context of the US over the past decade, where right-wing extremism has gained mainstream tolerance despite its existential threats against marginalized groups e.g., women, people of color, immigrants, people with disabilities, disciplinary neutrality proves complicit in perpetuating an anti-liberal status quo. New applications of methods that center real and diverse human bodies and experiences are urgently necessary to affirm and protect individual freedoms from threats to take them away.

This essay addresses political threats to reproductive bodily autonomy vis-à-vis the built environment and speculates how the intersectional, feminist perspective of Reproductive Justice (RJ), a human rights framework calling for bodily autonomy, reproductive freedom, and sustainable communities founded by a coalition of Black women in 1994, could transform architecture into a more politically engaged and socially imaginative discipline. The RJ movement altered reproductive rights advocacy through autoethnographic methods centering the specific experiences and needs of marginalized groups who were not properly represented in mainstream feminist activism at the time. Countering the status quo of abstraction from real, embodied experiences in design, RJ offers a model of engaging situated lives and perspectives in building just futures.

Architecture's failure to address the needs of specific groups perpetuates inequality in the built environment. Conventional design neutrality often produces built environments in which human bodies that do not conform to assumed norms are made more vulnerable, and perpetuate the discipline's detachment from political realities.[1] Instead, autoethnographic methods that draw from personal experiences could foster mutual understanding and address inequity and oppression – »an active demonstration of the ›personal is political«« (Ettore 2017: 3). The distinct yet interconnected positions of *self*, *standpoint*, and *network* found in the RJ framework offer multiscale application for spatial practice. First, the *self*-experience and knowledge of user(s) and designer(s) could overcome disciplinary abstraction from politics. Second, an understanding of *standpoint* situates individual lives in relation to systemic inequalities. Third, an international *network* of action demonstrates how interrelationships connect individuals to each other and to broader systems of care, instigating transformative political action across scales.

Considering these three scales offers insights for reimagining design as political advocacy and action. A case study at the end of the chapter considers the work of recent academic design studios addressing Reproductive Justice and the built environment after the overturn of Roe v. Wade.[2] The studio

---

1 Architectural critics and spatial practitioners have investigated ways that women and other marginalized groups are adversely impacted by power hierarchies in the design of the built environment, in such books as: Cheng, Irene/Davis II, Charles L./ Wilson, Mabel O. (2020): *Race and Modern Architecture: A Critical History from the Enlightenment to the Present* (Culture Politics & the Built Environment), Pittsburgh: University of Pittsburgh Press; Matrix Feminist Design Co-operative, (1994) *Making Space: Women and the Man-made Environment*, London: Pluto Press; Kern, Leslie (2020): *Feminist City: Claiming Space In A Man Made World*, London/New York: Verso Books; Weisman, Leslie Kanes (1994): *Discrimination by Design*, Champaign: University of Illinois Press.

2 Roe v. Wade is a landmark US Supreme Court decision in 1973 that established constitutional protection for an individual's legal right to abortion in the US. Under Roe, state laws were allowed to regulate abortion access, for example according to the gestational duration of pregnancy, but could not ban it entirely. The 2022 decision in Dobbs v. Jackson Women's Health Organization overturned Roe v. Wade, ending federal protection of abortion rights, enabling states to fully restrict abortion access for the first time in nearly 50 years.

outcomes encompass comprehensive, multiscale research and design proposals for enabling access to reproductive healthcare despite increasing legal uncertainties and spatial challenges caused by state-by-state disparities in the US since the overturn of Roe ended constitutional protection of reproductive rights, returning abortion legislation to individual states. Culminating in a traveling exhibition entitled »Spatializing Reproductive Justice« (Brown et al. 2024), the work showcases how the tools of architecture (spatial mapping, critical reasoning, graphic narration, building and environmental design, and site planning) can engage activist and feminist frameworks, and contribute toward just and sustainable reproductive futures for all. Understanding personal experiences as windows into larger structural challenges, architecture could embrace situatedness and discard neutrality, for good.

Personal is Political

Reproductive Justice efforts combine practices of personal storytelling, self-advocacy, and collective activism in pursuit of systemic change to ensure reproductive self-determination and sustainability for all. Coined in 1994 by the Women of African Descent for Reproductive Justice (WADRJ),[3] Reproductive Justice is the right »to maintain personal bodily autonomy, have children, not have children, and parent the children we have in safe and sustainable communities« (Sister Song, 2025). As a human rights framework, it addresses how the intersections of gender, race, class, and sexuality produce »a complicated matrix of reproductive oppression« (Ross 2017b: 62). Concerned by how the reproductive lives and decision-making of Black and low-income women were shaped by broader social inequality in the US and the failure of healthcare policy to address these disparities, the WADRJ identified a need for advocacy by and for those most at risk.

---

3 The WADRJ was a group of 12 Black women who came together in Chicago amid national healthcare debates. The group felt that the reform proposed by the Clinton administration at the time did not sufficiently address women's reproductive health, and in particular, the specific issues faced by Black and low-income women whose reproductive lives and choices were impacted by systemic inequality beyond abortion access (e.g., housing, labor, criminal justice, and education). Separating from the mainstream pro-choice movement, the WADRJ focused on advocating for a more holistic approach that considered a broader set of issues impacting the reproductive decision-making and well-being of marginalized groups.

In the US, Black women face higher risks of sexual and domestic abuse and higher rates of maternal health complications and mortality due to systemic racism. The RJ founders were disillusioned by the white feminist movement's narrow focus and »frustrated by the individualist approach of the pro-choice framework« (Price 2020: 340), instead they expanded reproductive rights advocacy to encompass more aspects of an individual's reproductive life, like poverty, violence, welfare reform, drug policy, sex education, and other specific factors impacting the health and safety of Black women. This enabled a more holistically inclusive activist movement working toward reproductive freedom for all, more capable of embracing individual needs rather than clinging to generic assumptions. While the white feminist movement emphasized broad claims of equality, Black women demanded justice (Cooper 2014) (fig. 1).

Individual experiences of marginalization, vulnerability, and precarity can be traced to broader societal inequalities. Practices of ethnography examine subjective human perspectives within their broader social and political contexts. *Autoethnography* uniquely situates this research through the author's personal lens, reflecting on their own lived experiences in relation to larger systems. As a feminist research method, autoethnography enables »personal ›truths‹ and speaking about oneself to transform into narrative representations of political responsibility« (Ettore 2017: 3). This approach scales political agency from the self to the collective, gathering multiple perspectives to illuminate shared oppression and building common grounds that are strengthened by diversity.

For architects, designing environments for multiple subjectivities is not so straightforward. The complexity and contradiction of individual needs, inconsistent from one person to the next and increasingly nuanced the more political factors considered, pose challenges to the tools of the trade that lean on broad generalization – standards, conventions, codes, and other regulatory mechanisms. The personal experience of a designer is inconsistently valued – sometimes celebrated and others, unwanted. Still, personal and professional biases, ignorance, and blind spots crop up, often perpetuating inequity or exclusion in design practices and built outcomes.

Matters typically gendered as female, such as embodiment, care, maintenance, and reproductive labor, are marginalized in architectural discourse and absent from its disciplinary tools. Consider Architecture's most

1.
»African-American Women Are for Reproductive Freedom: We Remember,«
pamphlet, 1994. Courtesy of the National Council of Negro Women (NCNW).
A printed pamphlet and joint statement issued by leaders of Black women's
organizations to exert pressure on public policy and denounce racist and sexist
oppression.

celebrated generic user: Le Corbusier's »Modulor,«[4] a universal bodily standard derived from rationalized geometric proportions overlaid on a human figure and interpreted through a patriarchal lens. The resultant graphic has »more to do with the schemes of domination of a given society, than with an objective statistic of physical average« (Failed Architecture 2017). Idealizing the white, able-bodied, masculine form, it negates the existence of other body types. Modulor has no variable characteristics, e.g., race, gender, sexuality, socioeconomic status, political context, or other condition that would impact an individual's spatial experience, mobility, and vulnerability. »Every time that the issue of sexual identity obtruded into Le Corbusier's discussion of the Modulor, the male principle won over the female« (Evans 1995: 285). Le Modular could not get pregnant (neither could his author). As a result, the iconic scale figure remains a symbol of disciplinary misogyny and preference for false abstraction over embodied reality.

Feminist discourse[5] critically examines and challenges the ways environments are constructed and experienced according to systems of power. Scholar Donna Haraway developed the concept of situated knowledges to describe how human perception and knowledge are shaped by individual circumstances and perspective. The notion of a supposedly neutral, objective stance only perpetuates existing power hierarchies – the »conquering gaze from nowhere« (Haraway 1988: 581). In the built environment, generically designed spaces often support dominant groups while contributing to the marginalization of others. This is caused by avoiding the self-specificity of both designer and user. The architect who designs for others without drawing from their own personal experience risks failing to consider the nuanced lived experiences of people who are different from them. Alternatively, autoethnographic methods enable designers to consider their own situated

---

4 The Modulor is a system of proportional measurements created by Le Corbusier (Charles Edouard Jeanneret) intended to reconcile the scale of a human body within a Euclidean geometry framework. Modulor was developed between 1943 and 1955 in an era of »fascination with mathematics as a potential source of universal truths« (Ostwald 2001). Its recognizable graphic is composed of an abstract illustration of a six-foot English male body with one arm upraised overlayed with a series of Golden Section rectangles. The validity of Modulor as a useful tool is undermined by its »blatant ignorance of actual human proportions,« as well as its ignorance of embodied differences from individual to individual.

5 Feminist discourse explores the interplay of gender, power, and inequality within society, with a focus on how social systems and exchange uphold patriarchal norms.

knowledge as a means of understanding their self »in relation to others« and society as a highly diverse yet interconnected whole (Ettore 2017: 112).

In addition to designing functional spaces and buildings, architects must increasingly contend with multiple social, political, and environmental crises at once. This demands a sense of empathy for human experiences that are different from one's own. An activist design framework incorporates situated awareness and capacity for nuance in understanding individual livelihoods and broader societal contexts. Adopting autoethnographic methods in design addresses the personal and political conditions of the built environment. The Reproductive Justice framework offers a model for a multiscale perspective, operating through the lenses of self, standpoint, and network, that could shape a more politically engaged and social justice-oriented discipline.

Self

Feminist authors like Audre Lorde[6] and bell hooks[7] transformed their discourse by weaving lived experiences as Black women into their theoretical work. Each used personal storytelling as a powerful tool of self-reflection and political analysis, revealing how personal struggles reflect broader systems of oppression. As a Black lesbian woman, Lorde articulated the intersectionality of race, gender, sexuality, and class in her life, describing self-knowledge as »a lens through which we scrutinize all aspects of our existence, forcing ourselves to evaluate those aspects honestly in terms of their relative meaning within our lives« (Lorde 1978: 7). Similarly bell hooks used personal narrative to illuminate Black women's critical perspective from the margins of a patriarchal, white supremacist society: »Living as we did – on the edge – we developed a particular way of seeing reality. We looked from both the outside in and the inside out« (hooks 1984: ix).

hooks described social marginalization as being »part of the whole but outside the main body« (ibid.), both entangled within and excluded from

---

6 Audre Lorde (1934–1992) was a writer, professor and activist whose poetry and prose addressed civil rights issues from an intersectional feminist perspective drawn from her own lived experiences.

7 bell hooks, born Gloria Jean Watkins, (1952–2021) was an author and social critic best known for her writings on race, feminism, and class.

society at once. Without acknowledging the underlying disparities (e.g., racism, sexism, classism) that produce marginalization, feminist movements cannot adequately advocate for shared and diverse needs. As hooks wrote of her white feminist contemporaries, they »rarely question whether or not their perspective on women's reality is true to the lived experiences of women as a collective group« (hooks 1984: 3). Thus they operate from the position of self but without self-awareness in relation to others, especially those whose experiences differ significantly from their own.

Social justice isn't achieved by assuming commonality, but by recognizing difference. Intersectional subordination, as articulated by civil rights advocate Kimberly Crenshaw, recognizes the ways that »the imposition of one burden that interacts with preexisting vulnerabilities to create yet another dimension of disempowerment« (Crenshaw 1991: 1249). Intersectional feminism acknowledges that while sexism is experienced by many women, their experiences are distinguished by other compounding forms of oppression affecting individual women in different ways. hooks and Lorde's autoethnography resists generalizing oppression by emphasizing subjective experience, reframing broader political contexts through their personal lenses.

What Lorde and hooks did for feminist discourse, the RJ framework did for reproductive rights, centering marginalized groups' experiences of reproductive injustice tied to broader systemic racial inequality. Activist and WADRJ co-founder Loretta Ross described: »Instead of working together based on shared victimization, we acknowledge that we all suffer in some way from white supremacy and population control, but we do not suffer in the same way, nor are we all equally oppressed« (Ross 2017a: 207). Published in the Washington Post on August 16,1994, the WADRJ 's introductory statement articulated concerns for the unique health problems of Black women, describing reproductive freedom as »a life and death issue« (WADRJ 1994). Addressing their intersectional vulnerabilities, they called for anti-discriminatory policies and Black women's representation in decision-making bodies. They emphasized various forms of reproductive oppression, including the lack of access to abortion as well as the lack of support for improving sex education and prenatal and postnatal healthcare and preventing sexual and domestic abuse, sexually transmitted diseases, and teenage pregnancy in communities of color. »When we centered ourselves in our lens, we understood how intersectional paradigms could reframe historical inequalities and differences in power and opportunities« (Ross 2017a: 173).

Reproductive justice calls for the human right to safe and sustainable communities, but there is no universal definition for what that requires – it is specific to context and individual circumstances. The right to healthy, resilient environments goes hand in hand with the right to live without restrictions against personal freedom and well-being. Ensuring safety, feeling unthreatened and protected from danger, and sustainability – the ability to endure with resources not being depleted – demands both forward-looking political liberation and retrospective healing and repair. Ross describes the RJ movement as an ongoing »synthesis of theory, strategy, and practice« (Ross 2017 a: 171). She had her WADRJ co-founders comingled their individual experiences, describing Reproductive Justice as an ongoing, collective process of »introspective storytelling,« cultivating self-knowledge, self-preservation and self-determination in the face of shared, systemic oppression (ibid.: 207).

Standpoint

Expanding from the self, one's standpoint describes their position in relation to broader societal systems. This frame of reference emphasizes how personal experiences are shaped by individual circumstances within larger social and political contexts. Standpoint is both a unique way of seeing, a mechanism for connection and mutual understanding between individuals, and a locus of gravity that can shift public perception. The RJ movement positioned its advocacy from the standpoint of Black women, diverging from the mainstream feminist movement that largely defaulted to the perspective of white women. RJ's origins preceded its public launch in 1994 through earlier organized efforts to raise awareness of and support for the unique reproductive experiences of women of color vis-à-vis the healthcare system in the US.

In 1983, activist and healthcare advocate Byllye Avery[8] organized the First National Conference on Black Women's Health Issues at Spelman College in Atlanta, GA.[9] The event drew nearly 2,000 attendees for a weekend of panels and workshops on specific health issues uniquely faced by Black women, as

---

8 Byllye Avery (1937b) is an American healthcare activist and proponent of reproductive justice who works to expand access to healthcare services and education for Black women. She is the founder of the National Black Women's Health Project (est. 1983), the first national organization to focus on Black women's reproductive health issues.

9 https://www.nytimes.com/2023/11/11/headway/black-women-health.html, accessed October 20, 2024.

well as the opportunity to exchange personal experiences and information freely amongst themselves. Avery organized the event after noticing in her research statistics a disproportionate occurrence of disease and distress amongst Black women. The conference encouraged participants to consider and discuss »how oppression affected their interactions with the health system [...] refram[ing] health as inextricable from racism« (Mathis 2023). After the conference, Avery founded the National Black Women's Health Project[10] and established chapters in private homes across the southern US. In these spaces, Black women could gather in small groups and share their concerns often ignored or dismissed by the medical establishment.

At the same time, local community-based healthcare initiatives emerged to meet unserved needs for individuals estranged them from the healthcare system altogether. In Harlem during the 1990s, a program called First Steps[11] provided counseling and outpatient drug treatment for mothers who used substances. As one of the program directors, Lynn Roberts, activist and professor at the CUNY School of Public Health, described: »While the mainstream media was busy demonizing mothers and labeling their children »crack babies,« we were busy engaging in the revolutionary act of »mothering – creating, nurturing, affirming, and supporting life« (Roberts 2017: 129). The program was unique in its offering of »support rather than punishment« (ibid.: 129) to the individuals and families it served, demonstrating the need for non-judgmental, unconditional care for childbearing and caretaking people alongside their families and communities. To provide these services required compassion and understanding about and from the standpoint of individuals struggling against the odds »to become mothers, to not become mothers, to mother the children we birthed, to mother the children other mothers were denied their right to mother, and to mother other mothers« (Roberts 2017: 133).

Reproductive Justice demands awareness of the entanglement of personal experience and systemic marginalization and its impact on individual lives and communities. Individual reproductive choices depend on a multiplicity of aspects of person and place. The right to make one's own decisions in these

---

10 https://bwhi.org/, accessed October 20, 2024.

11 First Steps was part of a larger initiative known as the Family Rehabilitation Program (FRP) that operated from 1990 to 1995 and focused on the needs of low-income Black and Latina women who used substances. City funding for the program was entirely cut in the first year of the Giuliani administration. (Roberts 2017, 129)

matters must be unconditionally affirmed, without qualifications based on someone else's judgment. Awareness of standpoint is key to avoiding objective assumptions or moralistic prejudice. Ensuring reproductive freedom for all means respecting difference and individual self-determination amid the »competing ideals of equality and the social reality of inequality [caused by] disparity in opportunities to determine our reproductive destinies« (Ross 2017a: 212).

Network

The third scale of reference is that of the network, or the set of relationships that connect individuals to each other and to broader systems of care. Networks »play an essential role in the emergence and ongoing work of social movements« (Brain 2023: 120). Throughout the history of struggle for reproductive freedom in the US and globally, underground networks have established and protected care access, distributed resources and information, and assisted individuals in overcoming barriers to receive the care they need. Before abortion was legalized in the US in 1973, an underground group called The Jane Collective[12] facilitated safe abortions for thousands of individuals in Chicago through a robust grassroots collective that operated outside official healthcare systems and under the radar of law enforcement. After Roe v. Wade enshrined constitutional protection for abortion in the US, The Jane Collective disbanded, and with it, a false sense of security took hold that reproductive care access would always be available through official channels, despite some hoop-jumping. But the lived realities of many proved otherwise. Even while Roe was upheld, the multitude of barriers to care access – time-based state abortion bans, long travel distances to clinics, financial burden, lengthy time requirements, social stigma, targeted misinformation – were insurmountable for many.

In the US, reproductive rights efforts since Roe v. Wade have focused on protecting legal access to abortion via healthcare providers and formal medical systems, even as the venues for this care were pushed outside hospitals to independent clinics. After the overturn of Roe, practices of

---

12 The Jane Collective was an underground network of pro-abortion and women's liberation activists that assisted more than 11,000 individuals in procuring safe, secret abortions in Chicago from 1969 to 1973.

self-managed abortion (SMA), or ending pregnancy via methods outside formal healthcare systems, surged in the US with increased use of abortion pills. Centuries-old SMA practices like herbal remedies involving plants with abortive properties have been practiced around the world since long before Western medicine emerged. In the US, medication abortion (abortion pills) became the most common method after its USFDA approval in 2000 and the expansion of telemedical services in 2020 (Friedrich-Karnik 2024). This was preceded in the Global South – in countries where abortion rights were never guaranteed – where robust underground SMA networks expanded medical abortion access and changed its public perception over time, in some cases instigating momentum for legalization.

In Latin America, where until recently abortion was mostly banned, an international network of activist groups created hotline accompaniment models beginning in the 1980s to provide individuals with the resources for self-induced medical abortion (Yanow 2024). Accompaniment networks train volunteers to offer one-on-one abortion support while »building a sense of community and dismantling stigma« more broadly (ibid.). Linking between hotlines in various countries enabled widespread, safe practice of SMA across Latin America, changing public opinion over time and contributing to the recent decriminalization of abortion in Mexico, Argentina, and Columbia. Known as the »green wave« of changing abortion laws, these achievements are the products of decades-long collaboration between feminist individuals, groups, and organizations, that persisted with or without the support of local healthcare providers and politicians (ibid.).

On a global scale, SMA movement networks create bridges between countries and regions by linking individuals and groups, particularly in locally criminalized contexts. The reciprocity between »formal, named networks that link organizations nationally [and] densely woven informal networks amongst activists« can enable structural change over time (Brain 2023: 122). City or country-specific movements emerge in dialogue with those in other places, cultivating international reciprocity between locations, contexts, and scales – »interpersonal and interorganizational ties« (ibid.). Common hardships like governmental dictatorship and gender-based violence amongst countries on different continents can be sources of mutual understanding and information exchange that build international solidarity. This transnational autoethnography empowers situated activist efforts to build upon one another in geographically disparate places.

The autoethnographic specificity of people and place that underpins the global Reproductive Justice movements offers a counternarrative to conventional neutrality in the design of built environments. As Loretta Ross declared, »revealing one's subjective self and standpoint« challenges the »omnipresent, allegedly neutral voice that distances itself from the objects of the discourse« (Ross 2017a: 207). Architects could learn from RJ's intersectional activism and self- awareness as a genesis for sustainable built futures supporting holistic individual and collective well-being.

Reproductive Justice in Pedagogy

Amid compounding political and environmental crises, feminist methods centering interconnectivity and community care offer necessary alternatives to autonomy in architecture pedagogy and practice. The autoethnographic lenses of self, standpoint, and network could shape a critical framework, pushing design considerations beyond form, aesthetic, and program, to engage issues of identity, place, and politics. Centering human subjectivity in design requires an understanding of diverse communities gained through listening to their lived experiences, learning from their situated knowledges, and investigating how environments are experienced differently by different bodies.

The future of a more socially and politically engaged discipline begins in its pedagogy, where meaningful engagement with different human experiences and perspectives is complemented by the agility to adapt or even reject outdated disciplinary conventions. To push back against default neutrality, architecture education could better establish designers' self-awareness in relation to the individuals and communities they serve, and the ability to draw from other disciplinary frameworks as needed. Incorporating autoethnographic methods in design teaching encourages students to reflect on their own experiences as sources of empathy and awareness to better understand and prioritize human needs, including those that are very different from their own. These methods inspire agency to respond to the complex, personal and political experiences of human bodies in the design of shared environments. For academic instruction, this demands more politically engaged subject matter in design studio courses, new forms of collaborative teaching methods, and continuous seeking of opportunities for transdisciplinary exchange.

A case study of implementing these demands in design education took place after the Dobbs vs. Jackson Women's Health Organization Supreme Court decision[13] in three academic architecture studios taught in the fall of 2022. The studios formed an interinstitutional coalition addressing the past, present, and future precarity of reproductive care in the US through the lens of the built environment. They were taught at the City College of New York (CCNY), Columbia University, and Syracuse University by architects and professors Lindsay Harkema, Bryony Roberts, and Lori Brown, respectively. This experimental, collaborative teaching format formed a supportive network – sharing resources, instruction methods, and a series of guest lectures, and enabling exchange between students and faculty beyond their respective institutional walls. The studios focused on a research-based approach to Reproductive Justice in the built environment, investigating the spatial, legal, and social logistics of reproductive healthcare after Dobbs. To do so, students documented the geographic disparity of care access amid a changing landscape of state abortion bans, restrictions and protections. This analysis complemented research about sexual and reproductive healthcare types, formats, procedures, and the critical underground networks past and present that have worked to enable access despite political adversity and legal uncertainty.

Underpinning the studios' design and research efforts were a robust historical survey and an active discussion of the Reproductive Justice framework and its activist network. Students read foundational texts by key RJ authors and heard guest lectures by a series of experts in the fields of public health, social justice, reproductive healthcare, law, and design. Equipped with these perspectives, students considered the individual experiences of reproductive care-seekers in various locations and circumstances across the country. How would an individual in a state with legal restrictions travel across borders to access essential care? What would their journey entail? How much would it cost? Which networks of support would be needed? How would environmental conditions shape their experience and impact their journey to care? Visualizations of this research through national and regional-scale maps revealed the constantly changing landscape of reproductive healthcare access and demystified the realities of care procedures and their often contradictory

---

13 The 2022 Supreme Court decision in Dobbs vs. Jackson Women's Health Organization changed reproductive rights in the US by overturning Roe v. Wade and Planned Parenthood v. Casey. Dobbs removed constitutional protection of abortion, returning its legal regulation to individual states.

2.
»Carewear,« transformed hospital gown, Student work by Valeska Abarca (CCNY), Fall 2022.

medical and legal timelines. Students considered environmental characteristics that would support individuals through difficult physical and emotional experiences by drawing from their personal healthcare experiences. This foundational work shaped their final design proposals for facilities, systems, and networks, enabling access to reproductive care in diverse contexts.

Teaching Self, Standpoint, Network

At the outset of the studios, initial exercises encouraged students to find a personal connection to Reproductive Justice, establishing a sense of self in relation to the studio topic. While most found the subject matter important and valuable, not all found it relevant in their own lives at the start of the semester. Introductory assignments invited students to reflect on past healthcare experiences and identify positive and negative aspects, as well as how they made them feel. At Columbia, students depicted care experiences in narrative sectional drawings, highlighting themes of misunderstanding and miscommunication between patients and care providers. At CCNY, students considered feelings of discomfort or vulnerability and channeled their memory of those experiences into the creation of reimagined paper hospital gowns, designed to empower the wearer (themselves) (fig. 2).

Shifting into research, students delved into understanding and visualizing the lived realities of restricted access to reproductive healthcare and establishing critical standpoints across scales through drawing and mapping. National maps revealed the rapidly evolving landscape of abortion access considering changing state legal circumstances (fig. 3). At the regional scale, students traced travel routes, itineraries, and associated costs for those seeking care across state borders, and outlined the associated barriers and challenges faced along the way (fig. 5). From an architectural perspective, students drew the intimate environments of private homes and clinical environments where medical and surgical abortions occur. As the studio's design outcomes, students developed architectural proposals for clinics, facilities, and infrastructures enabling access to care, conceived as prototypical nodes within larger networks of care. Each studio had its own project framing, within which students determined the locations, site contexts, programs, and typologies of their projects according to their research narratives and how they felt compelled to respond.

Their projects imagined environments and systems aiming to improve patient experiences and health outcomes, fostering individual comfort and

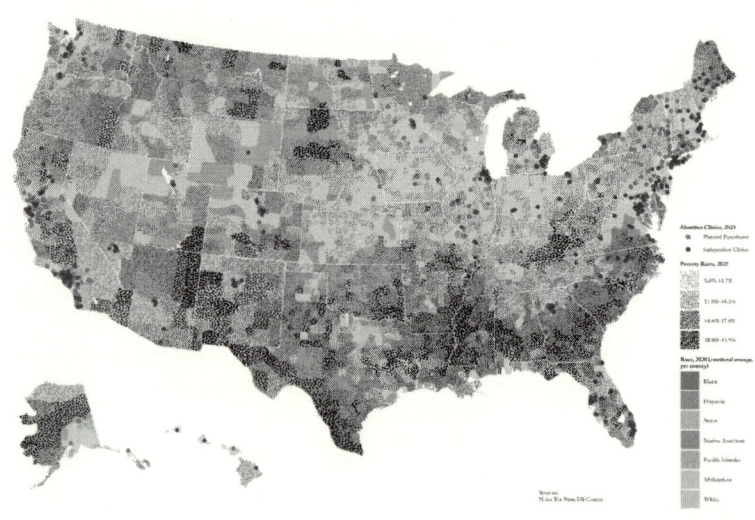

3.
Map by Sadie Imae and Lindsay Harkema, based on work created by students of
The City College of New York. Drawing updated by the curatorial team, May 2022.

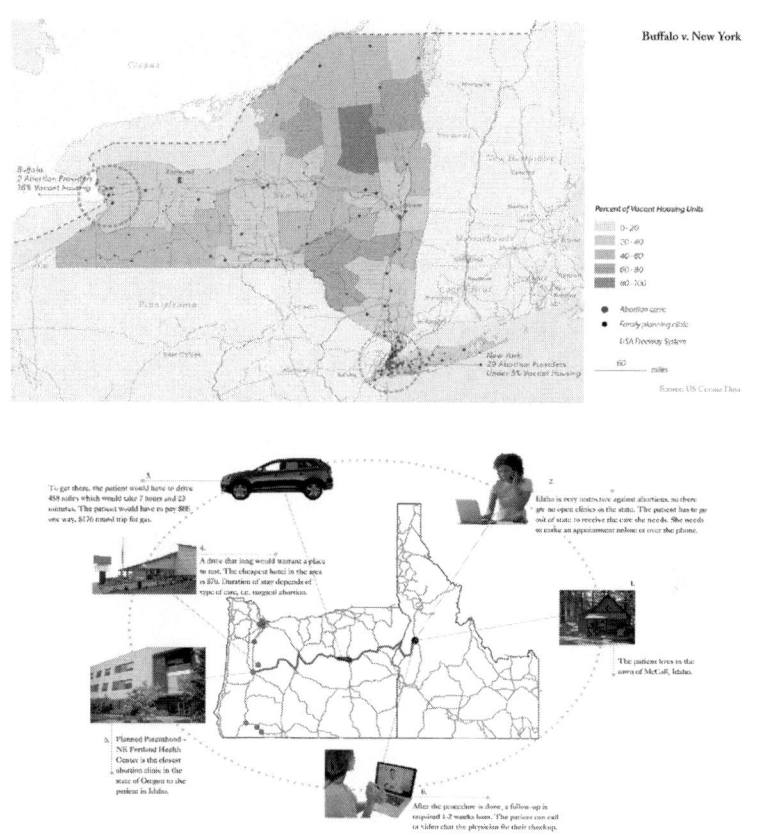

4.

Maps of travel distances and associated costs to access abortion care in various locations. Student work by Valeska Abarca, Nathaly Castillo, Mauricio Guidos (CCNY).

community support, and, where necessary, offering spatial and programmatic tactics to circumvent local state restrictions. Amid an increasingly hostile political context, the projects slipped between judicial boundaries and nestled within spaces of exception. They occupied ambiguous legal zones, repurposed decommissioned buildings, and activated existing care networks with new spatial and operational strategies. Rooted in intersectional feminism, the projects consider the whole journey of a care-seeking individual. They tested programmatic hybrids, infrastructural systems, and inventive site planning to counter restrictions and enable access to care. In restrictive state contexts, proposals were focused on resource sharing, education, and spatial tactics like mobile clinics to support individuals needing to travel for legal access to care. In protective state contexts, they expanded capacity of existing facilities, reimagined care programs to provide more holistic support, and integrated robust systems of reproductive care into public landscapes. The resulting body of work makes visible issues that are often private, unseen, and ignored within the architectural discipline.

The students' projects incorporated strategies of landscape design, adaptive reuse, public/private partnerships, telehealth systems, and mobile clinic networks to broaden access and transit to care beyond site limits. Considering care sequences and various durations of stay, one student group distributed facilities throughout a federally owned site to provide medical and surgical abortion care, abortion pill distribution, telehealth, therapy, short and long-term recovery stay, and childcare services embedded within national recreation areas. The design scope encompassed both the intangible, lived experiences of care seekers and the technical and functional performance of the structures proposed. Flexible spatial sequences, sensory-based material selections, and accessible design conveyed the intent for the architecture to feel as if it were tailored to each user's unique needs and circumstances (fig. 5).

»Spatializing Reproductive Justice«

The studio outcomes are now the content of a traveling exhibition entitled *Spatializing Reproductive Justice*, which opened at the Center for Architecture in New York in 2024[14] and aims to raise awareness about the disparity

---

14 https://www.centerforarchitecture.org/exhibitions/spatializing-reproductive-justice/, accessed October 20, 2024.

of reproductive healthcare access in the US after Roe and the agency of designers to respond. The exhibition showcases the student projects along-side professional works, speculative and built, as well as highlighting artistic works like Michelle Browder's »Mothers of Gynecology«[15] and how to perform an abortion's »Trigger Planting.«[16] It features an overview of the Reproductive Justice movement, highlighting key histories, figures, texts, material practices, and organizations in a large quilt-like wall graphic (fig. 6). As it did for the academic studios, the RJ framework serves as the theoretical foundation and knowledge base for the exhibition, emphasizing how the intersecting and compounding factors of race, class, and gender impact an individual's access to care.

Expanding from the academic studios, »*Spatializing Reproductive Justice*« aims to raise awareness within and beyond the architecture profession about the agency of spatial practices in the fight for reproductive justice. It endeavors to foster dialogue amongst design professionals, healthcare providers, scholars, activists, and the public about supporting reproductive justice in the US amid an increasingly volatile and evolving political land-scape. Together, the academic studio work and exhibition diverge from disciplinary neutrality vis-à-vis controversial political subject matter, not by articulating a particular position but in that the lived realities of those affected are revealed. The research displayed conveys objective data – histor-ical timelines of reproductive rights-related events, maps visualizing the state-by-state legality of abortion layered with relevant demographic data, and catalogs of forms of reproductive care. Running like a news ticker along the top of the wall displays is a continuous, repeating statement: »This is a Public Service Announcement.«

Designed by FLUFFF Studio[17] to travel to various institutions, the exhi-bition components are a kit of parts that can be reconfigured for subsequent venues, gathering local projects at each new location. The student projects are printed on fabric curtains hung from custom conduit frames, their arrange-ment pinching and folding the exhibition space, a spatial metaphor to the barriers and blockages encountered by those seeking reproductive care (fig. 7). Sheer curtains strung alongside the exhibition content evoke the curtained

---

15 https://www.anarchalucybetsey.org/, accessed October 20, 2024.

16 https://www.howtoperformanabortion.com/trigger-planting, accessed October 20, 2024.

17 https://www.fluffff.space/, accessed October 20, 2024.

5.
Experiential collage of reproductive care facility sited in a federally protected landscape. Student work by Valeska Abarca, Nathaly Castillo, Mauricio Guidos (CCNY).

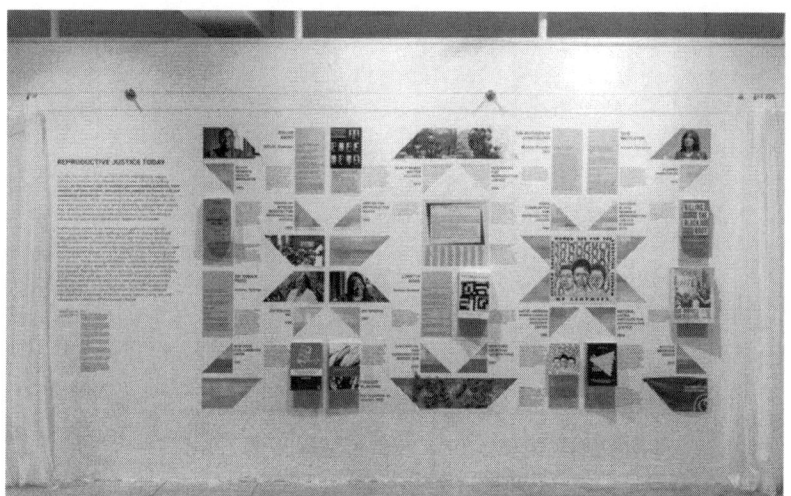

6.

Installation view, Reproductive Justice Today wall display, Spatializing Reproductive Justice, Center for Architecture, New York, 2024. Photograph by Asya Gorovits.

7.

Installation view, Spatializing Reproductive Justice, University of Wisconsin-Milwaukee, 2025. Photograph by Lucy Landre.

spaces of medical exam rooms and domestic environments. Punctuating the layout are handmade pink and green mop-head stalactites that dangle from frames and makeshift seating elements, softening edges and channeling domestic themes of care and maintenance.

From the research and design work of the students to the tactile details of the exhibition, *Spatializing Reproductive Justice* is a collective work about individual bodies in space and context. Human reproductive lives and freedoms are defined by their built environments – geographic location, access to transportation networks and infrastructures of care, and the look and feel of built spaces in which care is provided. They are also regulated, unequally and sometimes violently, according to aspects of their human identities and physical beings. Generic users and neutral design standards bear no relevance in these circumstances, where every aspect of embodied life is uniquely personal and situated. The real conditions in which these experiences occur reveal how much the discipline has yet to acknowledge about the politics of space.

For architecture, Reproductive Justice is a framework that designers could support and uphold through the design of built environments and learn from to better engage with individual experiences in relation to broader systems of power. Through education and design techniques that explore the interconnected scales of self, standpoint, and network, spatial practitioners could respond, meaningfully and non-neutrally, to political complexity. Autoethnography offers orientational methods to help navigate various contexts during the design process, at times drawing connections between the real lives of designers and end users in ways that foster more human-centric environmental outcomes. Networks are crucial for solidarity, support, and scalability in order for architecture to become political. Thus, a Reproductive Justice design philosophy is both deeply personal and universally transformative, intentionally nonstandard, and multi-situated in its pursuit of liberatory futures for every body.

References

Braine, Naomi (2023): *Abortion Beyond the Law*, New York: Verso Books.

Brown, Lori A./Dikhanov, Natalya/Harkema, Lindsay/Imae, Sadie/Roberts Bryony (2024): *Spatializing Reproductive Justice*, Center for Architecture New York, May 3–Sep 4, 2024.

Cooper, Brittney (2014): »*Feminism's ugly internal clash: Why its future is not up to white women*,« Salon. https://www.salon.com/2014/09/24/feminisms_ugly_internal_clash_why_its_future_is_not_up_to_white_women/., accessed November 30, 2024.

Crenshaw, Kimberle (1991): »Mapping the Margins: Intersectionality, Identity Politics, and Violence against Women of Color,« in: *Stanford Law Review*, 43/6, 1241–1299.

Ettore, Elizabeth (2017): *Autoethnography as Feminist Method*, London: Routledge.

Evans, Robin (1995): *The Projective Cast: Architecture and its Three Geometries*, Cambridge, MA: MIT Press.

Failed Architecture (2017): »*'Human, All Too Human': a Critique on the Modulor*,« https://failedarchitecture.com/human-all-too-human-a-critique-on-the-modulor/., accessed August 26, 2024.

Friedrich-Karnik, Amy/Stoskopf-Ehrlich, Emma/Jones, Rachel K. (2024): »Medication Abortion Within and Outside the Formal US Health Care System: What You Need to Know,« Guttmacher Institute, https://www.guttmacher.org/2024/02/medication-abortion-within-and-outside-formal-us-health-care-system-what-you-need-know, accessed April 28, 2025.

Haraway, Donna (1988): »Situated Knowledges: The Science Question in Feminism and the Privilege of Partial Perspective,« in: *Feminist Studies* 14/3, 575–599.

hooks, bell (1984): *Feminist Theory: from Margin to Center*, New York: London Routledge.

Lorde, Audre (1978): *Uses of the Erotic: The Erotic as Power*, Trumansburg: Out & Out Books.

Mathis, Dara (2023): »Three Days That Changed the Thinking About Black Women's Health,« The New York Times. https://www.nytimes.com/2023/11/11/headway/black-women-health.html., accessed November 30, 2024.

Ostwald, Michael J. (2001): »*The Modulor and Modulor 2 by Le Corbusier*,« Nexus Network Journal 3/1, 145–148.

Price, Kimala (2020): »*What Is Reproductive Justice?: How Women of Color Activists Are Redefining the Pro-Choice Paradigm*,« Meridians 19/S1, 340–362.

Roberts, Lynn (2017): »On Becoming and Being a Mother in Four Movements,« in: Loretta Ross/Erika Derkas/Whitney Peoples/Lynn Roberts/Pamela Bridgewater, *Radical reproductive justice: foundations, theory, practice, critique*, New York: Feminist Press At The City University Of New York, 111–133.

Ross, Loretta (2017a): »Conceptualizing Reproductive Justice Theory: A Manifesto for Activistm,« in: Loretta Ross/Erika Derkas/Whitney Peoples/Lynn Roberts/Pamela Bridgewater (eds.), *Radical reproductive justice: foundations, theory, practice, critique*. New York: Feminist Press At The City University Of New York, 170–232.

Ross, Loretta (2017b): »Trust Black Women: Reproductive Justice and Eugenics,« in: Loretta Ross/Erika Derkas/Whitney Peoples/Lynn Roberts/Pamela Bridgewater, *Radical reproductive justice: foundations, theory, practice, critique*. New York: Feminist Press At The City University Of New York, 58–85.

SisterSong (2025): »Reproductive Justice,« https://www.sistersong.net/reproductive-justice, accessed April 25, 2025.

Women of African Descent for Reproductive Justice (WADRJ) (1994): »*Black Women On Health Care Reform*,« The Washington Post. August 16, 1994.

Yanow, Susan (2024): »The Struggle for Bodily Autonomy: A Historical Perspective on Self-Managed Abortion in the United States,« South Atlantic Quarterly 123/3, 623–629.

Dimensions of Architectural Knowledge, 2024–08
https://doi.org/10.14361/dak-2024-0803

Becoming Architect-as-Ally:
A Conversation on Practice, Definitions, and
Privilege with Nature of Hope Participants

*Alina Paias, public works, Karin Reisinger, Lis-Mari Gurák Hjortfors,
Husos arquitecturas*

Abstract: In a polyvocal piece, one of the curators of the International Architecture Biennale Rotterdam (IABR) 2024 – *Nature of Hope* presents four exhibition participants: the design practice public works; collaborators Karin Reisinger (researcher) and Lis-Mari Gurák Hjortfors (Sámi ethnologist and researcher); and the architecture studio Husos arquitecturas – along with reflections and questions for them to consider. These questions concern their work in its situatedness and concreteness, and the complexity of transferring ideals into practice. What unfolds is a conversation on how working in alliance with the historical others of the discipline can reorient architecture toward a more ecological and just future. Reflecting on their own experiences, the curator and participants discuss the alliances they have forged, whether and how their practices are political, how their work and its definitions are changed by their alliances, and how they deal with vulnerabilities and privileges.

Keywords: Architecture; Alliances; International Architecture Biennale Rotterdam; Activism; More-Than-Human; Ecology; Extractivism; Soft Activism.

Corresponding authors: Alina Paias (Independent Scholar); public works (Andrew Belfield, Andreas Lang, Rhianon Morgan-Hatch); Karin Reisinger (University of Applied Arts Vienna, Austria); Lis-Mari Gurák Hjortfors (Umeå University, Sweden); Husos arquitecturas (Diego Barajas, Camilo García); info@alinapaias.com; https://orcid.org/0009-0009-5034-5318; info@publicworksgroup.net; https://orcid.org/0000-0003-4617-2142; https://orcid.org/0000-0002-5005-1645; https://orcid.org/0009-0005-6043-4059; karin.reisinger@uni-ak.ac.at; https://orcid.org/0000-0002-0955-438X; lis-mari.gurak@umu.se; plataforma@husos.info; https://orcid.org/0009-0007-5525-1316; estudio@husos.info; https://orcid.org/0009-0006-8663-2616

Introduction

Alina Paias | The 11th edition of the International Architecture Biennale Rotterdam (IABR), titled *Nature of Hope*, took place between June and October of 2024. I was invited to join the team of five curators along with Janna Bystrykh, Catherine Koekoek, Hani Salih, and Noortje Weenink. Our shared foundational desire was to amplify ecological sensibilities already transforming architectural practice from the margins to the center, addressing the problematics of a practice seeking to reorient itself, having historically relied on and undergirded ecological ruptures.

I am interested in architecture as a result of its conditions of production; that means I work with interpretive theoretical frameworks for architecture that encompass both its »social, economic, regulatory and industrial factors« and »the cultural, formal or aesthetic expression of materials,« as stated by Katie Lloyd Thomas (2022: 167). In the context of *Nature of Hope*, this was expressed in the curation of work that communicates how there is a continuous and co-constitutive process between what architecture can do and how architecture is done. This conversation, specifically, is focused on how the usual procedures of architecture are changed when architects forge alliances with the discipline's historical others.

My co-authors are four participants in the *Nature of Hope* exhibition: the architecture practice Husos Arquitecturas (2006), researchers and allies Karin Reisinger and Lis-Mari Gurák Hjortfors, and the not-for-profit design practice public works (2011). Their work is marked by a recognition of connected struggles, deep bonds of solidarity, and the sharing of resources in ways that are never exclusively commercial. The text picks up where these participants and I left off, providing an opportunity to diffractively re-make our own circumstances of coming together, now distant from the mediation between my responsibilities to the IABR and my attempts to extend the ethics of alliance (that is, an ethics founded on sharing a political project, and a vision for architecture) to the curator-participant relation.

This text is collectively and diffractively written (cf. Haraway 2018), with my reflections and prompts, in the form of questions, acting as jumping-off points for the other authors to establish their own perspectives. It grew and took shape during small pockets of time between our projects; ideas were changed and exchanged in emails and the furtive marginalia of word processor comments and suggestions. In it, the practices discuss the alliances they are part of, if and how their practices are political, how they are changed by their work with others, and how they find and appropriate different resources while dealing with the vulnerabilities specific to each of their situations.

Architects-as-allies | I first became aware of how architects relate to working through alliances at the start of my curatorial research, in conversation with different practitioners: The collective Cartografia Negra (2018), focused on reaffirming Black presences into the historical narratives of the formation of São Paulo, noted that they would often not benefit from one-off projects or events, when the approach to the valuable knowledge the group offered was often extractive. Lucas de Mello Reitz, an academic and architect, presented alliances as an intentional coming-together, focused on broader goals than just the production of architecture. Both mentioned preferring to work with people they already knew.

> I invited you to this conversation because your installations in the Nature of Hope exhibition foreground the forging of alliances in distinct ways. Could you describe your practice, especially in terms of which alliances you have forged?

public works | We are a not-for-profit critical design practice set up in 2004. We work across the terrain of art, architecture and performance to realize social and environmental change. Our roots are grounded in relational art practice (Bourriaud 1990), and we have always looked to nurture and amplify citizen voice in the production of the built environment. This is a matter of rights, and of our commitment to promote the rights of communities within which we work. More recently, our alliances have shifted from purely anthropocentric to more complex and messy entanglements involving the more-than-human (Haraway 2016).

Karin Reisinger | As a researcher I question how we know about architectures and the materials used in architecture (Reisinger 2020). Which areas and voices are excluded, and how can they become part of the knowledge of architectural practitioners and academics? I have been working with areas of extractivism, which provide raw materials for building, often at the cost of socio-environmental health. As a non-indigenous person based in Central Europe and educated by a Western architecture curriculum, I am part of the extractivist problem. No matter how critical I am, materially, I write this on a laptop which functions due to mineral resources, on a table with metal legs under a roof carried by metal pillars (cf. Reisinger). Under these conditions, I started relating to an area around a town which calls itself the »Mining Capital of Europe.« That is Gällivare, or as my friend and local practitioner Lis-Mari Gurák Hjortfors calls it, Váhtjer. I was mostly interested in the town's spatial practices caused by the disappearance of the entire neighboring town, Malmberget. During my relational research I learn from local cultural practitioners dealing with loss, living and coping with extractivism. I am grateful for the collaboration with Lis-Mari, which consists of writing, presenting, and organizing together, ongoing since 2016.

Lis-Mari Gurák Hjortfors | I am a Lule Sámi[1] ethnologist and researcher. I discuss the importance of the Sámi taking care of their own cultural heritage and their rights as indigenous people who have lived in this area long before the place became a mining community. The return to indigenous cultural heritage means for the Sámi identity to escape colonization. Taking back one's cultural heritage is part of the work of reconciliation, focusing on the importance of places to feel belonging. Váhtjer/Gällivare municipality is a mining community with a harsh climate for the Sámi.

My hometown is located between two very large mines, LKAB/Vitåfors and Boliden/Aitik. We are affected by mining, and as a Sámi people we fight for our rights. The ore mountain Málmmavárre/ Malmberget has disappeared bit by bit over many decades. Local residents have become accustomed to parts of the community being demolished or moved. Many say that there are a lot of emotions when houses are demolished or moved. »You don't have any roots left.« (fig. 1)

In my professional role, I teach the public about the Sámi culture by showing the presence of the Sámi in the area and work with educational methods in presentations, talks, articles, poetry, and exhibitions. The oral storytelling tradition has always played a central role in the Sámi culture. I bring the place to life and reconnect to the cultural and natural environment. The biggest threat to the Sámi is making Sámi culture invisible. This needs to be countered by conveying knowledge and providing counter-images through activism – soft activism (cf. Gurák Hjortfors/Reisinger 2024).

---

1 The *Lule Sámi* inhabit the central part of the indigenous Sámi area. It is called Sápmi and spans Norway, Sweden, Finland and Kola Peninsula in Russia.

Husos arquitecturas | In 2003, we began our collaborative practice in Madrid, between Colombia and Spain. We approach architecture as a tool for ecosocial transformation. For us, this transformation involves collectively opening multiple possibilities of existence for the vast diversity of sentient beings inhabiting the Earth, together with planetary care. From our perspective, these dimensions are inseparable.

Inspired by philosopher María Lugones' commitment to counter-hegemonic coalitions (Lugones 2005) and the broader framework of Abya Yala/Latin American and Caribbean decolonial feminisms (Curiel 2014), we explore the potential of interwoven architectures – simultaneously decolonial, interspecies, and post-heteronormative, approached through a lens of ecological interdependence.[2] These architectures are conceived in close dialogue with the territory and its communities, aiming to embrace their heterogeneity while simultaneously addressing structural asymmetries of gender, race, class, species, functional body capacities, and more.

Through this lens, we see transversal alliances as necessary to challenge normative, compartmentalized frameworks and imagine alternative collective possibilities.

Within this approach, each project we participate in functions as a shared micro-laboratory – imperfect and inevitably incomplete – yet offering a platform to test and refine ideas together with others toward tangible possibilities for ecosocial transformation through architecture (fig. 2).

Politics and the Design of the Coming-together

Alina Paias | The architects-as-allies featured in the exhibition are involved; their work makes them inextricably responsible to others. The involvement with the co-creators and users of architecture is sustained, tended to, never finished – although negotiations grounding collective work can be conflictual, the position of allyship is incompatible with an extractive practice.

The forging of alliances is grounded on a consciousness that the *how* of coming together is fundamental to a collective project; in many ways, it is

---

2 Abya Yala is the name used by the Guna indigenous people living in Panama and Colombia to refer to the territory now known as the Americas. Decolonial and other social movements around the region have reclaimed this term to remember and reimagine other ways of being and existing in this land.

1.
Lis-Mari Gurák Hjortfors (2013), Malmberget, the mining town, and the pit in the middle of the town. The pit in Malmberget is constantly growing due to the ongoing underground mining for iron ore. Photograph and copyright: Lis-Mari Gurák Hjortfors.

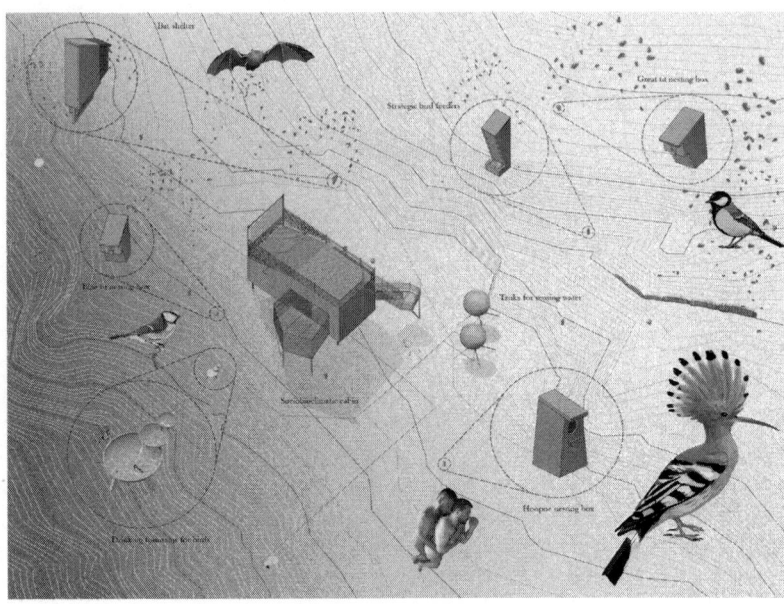

2.

Husos Arquitecturas (2020). (Synanthro)Love Shack. Spatial project: Husos arquitecturas (Diego Barajas and Camilo García with Aníbal Arenas, Almudena Tenorio, Giulia Poma). Gardening and animal architectures: with Daniel Prieto, Aristides Mettas, João Manfrinato. Construction: Nicasio Pato. Carpentry: Verticales Forme. Special Thanks to biologist Daniel-Martín Vega. Exhibited at the International Biennial of Architecture in Rotterdam, 2024. We list several entities whose previous related actions provided particularly valuable contributions to this work: human neighbors from Cadalso de los Vidrios (particularly Juan, Raul and Virginia), SECEMU (Spanish Society for the Conservation and Study of Bats), SEO/BirdLife, ASVEPA (Association of Neighbors, Property Owners, and Friends of San Bartolomé de Tormes), ASEORG (Association of Entrepreneurs of Northern Gredos), the Navarredonda Town Council, the MONAU Project promoted by the Valencian Society of Ornithology, the Valladolid Forestry Association, and the Ávila Forestry Association (associations of private forest owners), students and teachers from the Compensatory Education Classroom (ACE) of IES Marqués de Santillana, along with the rural warden of Dehesa de Navalvillar in Colmenar Viejo and the Sustainability Delegation of the Leganés Town Council + the Forest Health Service of the Balearic Islands. Image from the author's archives. © Husos arquitecturas.

the project. The architect-as-ally has to devise processes for coming together that include those who do not stand to gain anything from sticking to the standard Modus Operandi of architecture. Crucially, Isabelle Stengers' cosmopolitical proposal (2020), which involves an always emergent common political« procedure that depends on the »issue in its concrete environment« (ibid.: 237), presents the cosmopolitical negotiator as a designer (ibid.: 241). The hopeful horizon of architecture is certainly relational, but it is also political in the sense that it involves the »staging« (ibid.) of the coming together as a design task.

Do you experience your own practice as political?

public works | In simple terms, our practice is inherently political, if sometimes a little polite; our methods do not overtly protest, but set procedures and precedents. To take your curatorial term, »architects-as-allies,« we often find ourselves somewhere in the middle, mediating processes and interests. We're both comfortable advocating on behalf of grassroots communities, as we are working with institutional powers and gatekeepers to gain access. We see our role as a mediator or negotiator in this space, which can be a challenging space to occupy and hold, at times feeling conflicted when the power imbalance is too great, or the scope to extend and rethink the brief is too limited. Irit Rogoff describes this as embodied criticality, »producing criticality through inhabiting a problem« (2006: 1).

We regularly initiate our own projects, such as the R-Urban hub in Poplar, London (2023). This creates a different political arena from which to practice. Initiating projects directly allows for a more radical and critical approach, where citizen voice and other ecological values become the client. R-Urban Poplar is an attempt to build the future in the present by developing and testing new modes of governance, economies, and relational practices in the exploration of more resilient futures (fig. 3). In this case, we leveraged our practice track record or »capital« to negotiate free access to land with a housing association, something residents previously struggled with. Once secured via formal lease agreements, it has become possible to share access to this land with other grassroots groups, civic associations, and residents in the spirit of urban commoning.

3.
public works (2023). Civic and Climate Learning at R-Urban Poplar 2023.
R-Urban is a collaborative project between public works (London) and Atelier
d'Architecture Autogérée (Paris). The Poplar hub is a collective vision involving:
SunnyJar, MAD LEAP, Teviot People's Kitchen, London Wild Fruits, Bower Studio,
Women's Environmental Network, The University of Sheffield, Resident Food
Growers and the many citizens who take part. Image from the author's archives.
© public works.

Lis-Mari Gurák Hjortfors | My practices are political in the mining town, because in every presentation, poem, article, or exhibition, I make the Sámi culture visible through activism and soft activism.

Vuojŋŋanisán	In the spirit
Mijá ájttega ja mijá	*Our ancestors and our history are*
histåvrrå gávnnu juohkka sajen	*everywhere.*
várijn meran ja jávrijn	*In the mountains*
miehtsijn ja ednamijn	*in the seas and lakes*
Gejnudagájn	*in the forest and on the fields*
Vuojŋŋanisán	*On hiking trails*
	In the spirit

– Lis-Mari Gurák Hjortfors

Karin Reisinger | In an extractive field it is already political to raise questions about the environment. In my research, I ask why a diversity of local perspectives are invisible. Feminist Political Ecologies have taught me to stay exactly with the cracks and fissures (Harcourt/Nelson 2015; cf. Haraway 2016). Effects of the politics of extractivism and neo-colonialism connect profits to material, cultural, and environmental losses (cf. Truman 2019), such as a loss of ground, homes, etc. In a community where many people live from these material profits, this is a tricky connection with many cracks and fissures. The mined areas have, through time, become homes of diverse communities with different dependencies. An approach based on intersectional feminisms is helpful to work with a variety of knowledges and literacies that often go unheard in dominant research practices. The local practitioners from the videos in our installation have developed situated and complex practices of dealing with this loss (2024); the artist Miriam Vikman walks paths through woods to save them from clearcutting, the musical artist Pernilla Fagerlönn curated a farewell exhibition for the last remaining high-rise building of the mining town, while the artist and organizer Karina Jarrett embroidered houses before they were dismantled together with the women of the embroidery café (fig. 4). Like Lis-Mari Gurák Hjortfors, they live these ambivalences daily and elaborate and apply respective literacies (fig. 5). Opening up spaces for these contributions together is the politics of our collaborations.

4.
Karina Jarrett (2019). Embroidery, Insekterna flyttar in / The Insects Move in. Photograph and copyright: Karina Jarrett.

5.
Jacqueline Fuijkschot (2024). Listening Station on Practices of Hope amidst Extractive Violence – Karin Reisinger, Pernilla Fagerlönn, Lis-Mari Gurák Hjortfors, Karina Jarrett, with contributions by Miriam Vikman, Eeva Linder, Karina Engelmark and Lena Sjötoft. Exhibited at the International Architecture Biennale Rotterdam. © International Architecture Biennale Rotterdam (IABR).

Redefining the Practice

Alina Paias | Scholars Marisol De La Cadena and Mario Blaser (2018) have embraced the notion of cosmopolitics and developed it further into what they call a political ontology, with the crucial difference resting on the acknowledgement that negotiating between heterogeneous worlds is itself a world-making practice. By opening up political practice to the possibility of pluriversality – a term connected to the Zapatista demand for a world where many worlds fit (1996) –, political ontology both remakes the imaginary of politics and redefines its components.

The negotiation between worlds involved in forging alliances means that the architect-as-ally is open not only to new ways of coming and working together, but also to undoing their practice, its standard procedures and definitions, and their image and understanding of themselves. Ruinorama, a collective of Brazilian practitioners, presented an installation during *Nature of Hope* that was focused on this undoing: Through their work with traditional communities in Brazil and encounters with indigenous and Black thinkers in books and conversations, they have gathered a new lexicon, with entries for each letter of the alphabet, that unsettles the normative definitions of architecture (fig. 6) (2024).

> Do you also see your practice as changed by the alliances you have made?
> Can you let go of the conventional definitions of the practice?

public works | Our alliances and relational networks are crucial to how we function, working through long-sustained collaborations based on mutual trust and reciprocity. We don't subscribe to a uniform aesthetic or dictate specific outputs; instead, we value co-authorship with our allies, which defines the process and outcome of any commission. This is reflected in what we produce, from buildings to zines (and everything in between).

We try to avoid being gatekeepers to groups or knowledge, encouraging openness, care, and sharing with others in opposition to enclosure. Generosity is often repaid in kind (by allies) or somehow finds its way back into the practice in unexpected ways, allowing us to continue with certain lines of inquiry that weave through projects.

Karin Reisinger | My practice is determined by the inseparability of ethics, ontologies, and epistemologies (Barad 2007; Geerts 2016) and therefore

6.
Jacqueline Fuijkschot (2024). Ruinorama's work Lexicon at the IABR, at the center of the image. Around it, from left to right, are the installations of Alexandra Arènes & Studio SOC (Société d'Objets Cartographiques) with Atelier shaa (architecture urbanisme), MOULD, HouseEurope!, Extinction Rebellion UK, Théo Demans & Clemence Seilles, and CHRITH Architects & Emma Diehl Studio. © International Architecture Biennale Rotterdam (IABR).

needs to be accountable to the local inhabitants of the communities I work with and write with. This responds« to feminist practices and epistemologies of accountability (Butler 2005; Rendell 2016), which have demanded fore-grounding situated knowledges (Haraway 1988) and material environments generating (or suspending) agencies. Thus, my practices mess with who is the subject and who is the object, by changing roles and collaborating with prac-titioners from areas wrongly understood as »peripheries,« such as the ones occupied by traditional communities and extractive and mining settlements distant from large urban centers. I am not only dependent on local knowledge but also try to subordinate my work to local contributions and needs.

Husos arquitecturas | Alina, reflecting on your last two questions and exam-ples, we agree that building forms of togetherness through non-extractive practices is among the most pressing challenges for fostering genuinely transformative collective political projects today. For us, this commitment is rooted in personal experience.

Extractivism, especially epistemic extractivism (Grosfoguel 2016), is something we have endured firsthand as Norandean[3] migrant architects in Spain. This has occurred in specific relationships that initially seemed to be close friendships but ultimately proved extractivist, characterized by the recurring appropriation of intellectual work. Over time, we have sought to reinterpret these experiences not as isolated failures but as opportunities for learning and redefining our practice.

We've come to realize that, in Western-centric, racially hierarchical soci-eties, voices are valued differently, not solely for their content, but also based on the social perception of the body speaking. For a long time, we viewed these experiences in isolation, not infrequently blaming ourselves. However, through collective reflection, we began to recognize them as structural rather than personal issues. Discovering decolonial and anti-racist thinkers from Abya Yala/Latin America, and later meeting related activist communi-ties in Madrid, has been profoundly healing for us. We believe that the exis-tence of counter-hegemonic spaces for sharing such lived experiences are

---

3 We use the term »*Norandean migrants*« to refer to those of us who come from the northern Andes of South America – from countries such as Colombia, Ecuador, Peru, or Bolivia – shaped by a strong Indigenous heritage. In Spain, these migrations are often viewed through a particularly racialized and paternalistic lens, which associates them with manual and care work, and rarely with knowledge production.

7.
*Impresiones cotidianas/Juan Asolot (2022). Espacio Afro Cultural Center. Spatial
project: Conciencia Afro association (Yeison García, Esther Mayoko Ortega,
Moha Gerehou, Lucía Mbomío, Rubén H. Bermúdez), Husos arquitecturas (Diego
Barajas, Camilo García and Allyson Vila; with the collaboration of Almudena
Tenorio) and the association's expanded community. Gardening actions: Yania C.
Vicente, Husos, neighbors and expanded community. Construction: UZ studio.
Artistic works: Ken Province López and Larry Achiampong, among others.
Textiles: Candelas and expanded community. Image from the author's archives.
© Impresiones Cotidianas/Juan Asolot.*

crucial. Spaces that, while not always fully safe, foster trust and closeness, as described by Ecuadorian-Spanish architect and curator Camena Camacho of *La Parcería Cultural Center*. Only collective action can confront the structural asymmetries and extractivist logics that shape our society. In this context, resistance-based communities play a vital emancipatory role. This is why our participation together with the architect Allyson Vila in the design and construction of the community space Espacio Afro, developed by the activist-thinkers group Conciencia Afro in Madrid, has been so meaningful to us as urbanists and activists. This place centers Afro perspectives and anti-racism, while fostering alliances with other activist movements, which they view as essential (fig. 7).

In fact, we agree with the members of this group that while communities of shared subaltern experiences are necessary, they are not sufficient, regardless of how internally diverse they may be. We must broaden this »we« into the most heterogeneous communities possible, composed of widely varied experiences and perspectives. In our practice, a central question is how architecture can act as a caring ally to such communities while also helping to build a »broad and diverse we« through non-extractive practices in a structurally unequal society. In this respect, we find it especially interesting to explore some sort of »architectures of deep reciprocity,« having in mind Michi Saagiig Nishnaabeg scholar and artist Leanne Betasamosake Simpson's proposal of deep reciprocity as an alternative to extractivism (2017). Following Betasamosake Simpson's identification of deep reciprocity as a core of Nishnaabeg ethics, this architecture would be shaped by respect, relationship, and responsibility. Her reflections on interconnectedness, consent, empathy, caring, and sharing further echo the spirit of deep reciprocity.

We are continually learning in this direction: Long term collaboration with activists deeply aware of these issues has been very important. Many of our projects emphasize shared work across diverse spheres, though we often do so from a micro-community perspective – a dimension frequently undervalued. Authorship here expands without diminishing individual contributions and responsibilities. The participation in Espacio Afro (2022) with the Conciencia Afro Group and its expanded network is one example. For us, it is a shift towards »doing with« rather than »doing for.« It also means actively recognizing the contributions of other spatial agents – within or beyond our field – while paying particular attention to those whose voices are often pushed aside.

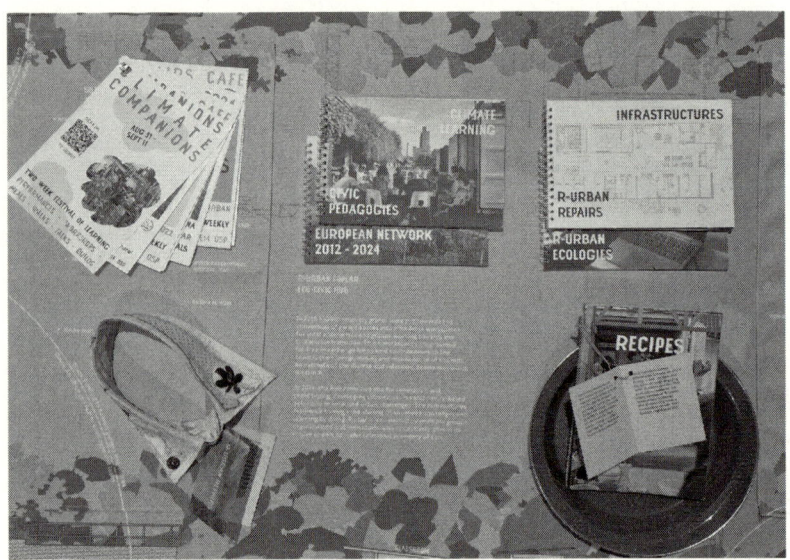

8.
public works (2024). »Give and Gain: Relational Economies of Care,« our contribution to IABR involved the restaging of the R-Urban dining space, telling the story of the more-than-monetary economy that has sustained the project in London from 2012-present. Image from the author's archives. © public works.

In these community-driven processes, extended time frames matter, as does keeping space open for doubt, to counterbalance overly confident positions. Since the *Host and Nectar Garden Building* (2005), within an interscalar territorial framework we refer to as »the expanded site,« we have pursued an exploration grounded in practices of material counter-extractivism, engaging with a broad interspecies »we,« as in the *(Synanthro)Love Shack* (2020), presented at *Nature of Hope* – often interwoven with post-heteronormative approaches. More broadly, it is about recognizing the overlapping systems of domination we work within, the resistances they generate, and understanding that, as architects, we are never outside these power dynamics.

Working through Systems and Institutions

Alina Paias | Much of the work conducted in alliance with cosmopolitical others happens at the margins of conventional and largely commercial practice, capturing resources from funds and grants and institutions such as museums and biennales, complementing those with academic activities, lectures, and residencies. A lack of material resources can be bypassed by adopting different means for their circulation, through the exchange of resources in-kind, through favors and gifts. Taking this position is, of course, not without its challenges: One of the installations in the *Nature of Hope* exhibition was the Practice Place, a soft assembly space for practitioners. Some of the discussions in this space revolved around strategies such as redistributing, misusing, and appropriating resources – while certainly valuable, they do not remove the practitioner from a fragile position in relation to those with economic and institutional power. And having to reconcile institutional expectations and demands with goals that serve the »undercommons« (Harney/Moten 2013), or the alliances forged outside these institutions, can be incredibly exhausting.

> How do you relate to the redistribution and appropriation of resources?
> Do you feel like you are in a fragile position?

public works | Our approach is characterized by flexibility and adaptability, in part born out of precarious work from the margins. Our strength is in the relational networks we have nurtured for over twenty years of practice, often turning to allies for help when resources are scarce.

Alliances and relational economies are a central theme of our exhibition contribution, which describes the relational economies of care sustaining the R-Urban hub (2023). Within this space, resources are shared and exchanged without commodification, through gifting, time banking, by sharing knowledge and swapping skills with members of the network. It is an example of another logic for how spatial urban resources can be designed and shared in cities, beyond modes of capitalist exchange, and to help (precariously) resist the enclosure and privatization of urban spaces. The project supports a network of allies and companions to tackle compounding climate and social injustices by creating a space for collective action at the neighborhood scale. Beyond this, it nourishes our practice and those of our close collaborators, providing a free space where we can experiment, prototype, and fail, whilst also being a space that gives us hope (fig. 8).

Lis-Mari Gurák Hjortfors | I expose myself and I feel vulnerable, but it is necessary for making the Sámi culture visible.

Karin Reisinger | Although my impacts on epistemologies of extractivism are very precarious and often get me in fragile positions because it is outside what is expected from architectural research, I have to acknowledge that I am privileged because I can leave the situation of extractivism. The house in which I live will not be torn down to extract more resources. However, there are moments when I can share a small part of the local fragilities with the people I work with, as I shared this invitation to join the article with Lis-Mari Gurák Hjortfors. Further ways of sharing fragilities are by asking uncomfortable questions to power, collating and empowering imaginaries of hopeful futures, and hosting local practices in moments of public attention (as in the exhibition); ideally, by doing things together.

Husos arquitecturas | Acknowledging our privileges helps us avoid self-centeredness and better understand the oppressions others face. As Afro-Brazilian feminist philosopher Djamila Ribeiro states »Privileges are not natural; they are constructed through the oppression of other social groups« (Ribeiro 2020, author's translation).[4] The hardest – and most transformative – task is finding imaginative ways to dismantle them. By examining our

---

4 From the original »Los privilegios no son naturales, se construyen sobre la opresión de otros grupos sociales [...].«

privileges, we believe we can build a stronger, broader, and more just »we.«
Engaging with a more just »we« from a situated perspective demands critical reflection on our practice. From our perspective, inclusion means little
without examining architecture's power dynamics. A truly diverse architecture must embrace difference from within, not merely reflect it outwardly.
Furthermore, we understand that there can be no collective »we« beyond
human nature without, as Black Brazilian historian Giovana Xavier puts it,
»restoring denied humanities« (Xavier 2017).

> Which bodies typically hold influence in shaping space – and which do not?
> How do we relate to that in our own practice?
> How do we share resources, recognition, and care?
> To which bodies are we willing to cede power – or even offer a little love?

These are questions that walk with us in these journeys.

Lis-Mari Gurák Hjortfors and Karin Reisinger | Reflecting privileges and
fragilities, we claim that long-term, collaborative and counter-extractive
work with sites and places shall be more valued in architecture and research
in general. In our collaborations, which concern specific extractivist areas in
Váhtjer/Gällivare municipality, we want to give our work back to the communities and the people, especially to indigenous communities and people with
strong roots to their environments, which often means struggle and pain in
extractive environments.

Karin Reisinger | Also, for these areas to allow for alliances with migrants
and refugees, as Lis-Mari Gurák Hjortfors has described in a previous work
of hers already in 1998, called *Vi har våra rötter både här och där (We Have our
Roots Here and There)* (Hjortfors 1998)[5].

Lis-Mari Gurák Hjortfors | Through our common working method and
research work, we build bridges and understanding when we work together.

---

5 At that time, Lis-Mari Gurák Hjortfors had not yet reclaimed her Sámi name.

Final reflection

Alina Paias | What emerges in this shared text is an explicit concern about power, how it is distributed and how it is expressed. This concern gives form to ways of acting that are openly political, against a pervasive depoliticization of the practice in the era of architectural commodification (Arantes 2019: 204). This commitment is connected to how much of the work detailed here already begins from a position that is marginal to conventional practice; as Husos aptly put it, the architect-as-ally is not so much the one who reaches out to the discipline's historical others from a position of unquestioned power as the one who attempts to connect to others through shared or familiar vulnerabilities. This is radically different from the paralyzing pessimism that so many architects can default to in the face of perceived powerlessness.

The work of Husos, Karin, Lis-Mari, and public works is contextualized by specific struggles such as the extreme inequality in the distribution of resources, often along racial lines, connected to the extension of the neoliberal turn in the United Kingdom and in the wake of Spain's colonial project; or the deeply entangled ecological collapse and existential threat to indigenous forms of life felt so directly in Sámi territory. In all of these contexts, architecture is confronted with its own reliance on material extraction and work exploitation; it seems impossible to work towards urgent change within the usual procedures of the practice, which have been so thoroughly captured towards the commodification of its objects. What the co-authors of this text have identified is that the only way to keep practicing is to change how we practice.

It is common to associate matters of location and distribution of power and of the vulnerability to this power with the matter of scale; for example, a traditional community is powerless against a nationally-backed mining enterprise because it is small and the enterprise is big. What can easily follow is the idea that a transformative practice in architecture would be as powerful as it is scalable. From early on in the making of *Nature of Hope*, we anticipated a critique of our work that would amount to how these situated practices could not be sublimated towards re-applicable models – especially when it came to transferring strategies from the Global South to the Netherlands – or towards national and international-level policy change. However, the work of my co-authors is changing architecture practice in how it replaces large-scale thinking with ecological thinking. At different points in this text, they have described their projects as prototypes, micro laboratories, and ways to envision and rehearse alternative collective futures. This approach resonates with architecture scholar Renata Tyszczuk and geographer Joe Smith's reframing of scenarios, especially in the context of the use and diffusion of climate change scenarios, as a »rehearsal space« for desired futures (2018: 58), and with my co-curator Catherine Koekoek's description of the prefiguration of desired ways of doing and living as preparation to »return to the city,« here understood as returning to the potential arena of institutional politics and large-scale industry change (2024: 28). Koekoek's argument that the inside-outside movement between alternative practices and institutional change is most successful when ways of doing otherwise also function as modes of awareness and advocacy is particularly relevant in the context of an exhibition (ibid.). Most crucially, their approach moves beyond and besides the issue of scale, acting on a form of planetary thinking which is framed by philosopher Yuk Hui as constitutively based on diversity and always engendering diversification, against the solutionism of systems that can be scaled up globally (2024). Working through and within alliances is transformative for architecture in how it allows for the construction and inhabitation of collectively designed and desired futures, while retaining and deriving strength from diversity in ways of understanding, technologies, and ways of being. Here might reside a fundamental response to the current crises of our discipline.

References

Arantes, Pedro Fiori (2012): *Arquitetura na era digital-financeira: desenho, canteiro e renda da forma.* – English translation: The Rent of Form: Architecture and Labor in the Digital Age, transl. from Portuguese edition by Adriana Kauffmann, Minneapolis: University of Minnesota Press, 2019.

Barad, Karen (2007): *Meeting the Universe Halfway: Quantum Physics and the Entanglement of Matter and Meaning,* Durham/London: Duke University Press.

Bourriaud, Nicolas (2002): *Relational Aesthetics,* Dijon: Les Presses du réel.

Butler, Judith (2005): *Giving Account of Oneself,* New York: Fordham University Press.

Cartografía Negra (2018): *Cartografía Negra.* https://www.cartografianegra.com.br, accessed July 19, 2025.

Curiel, Ochy (2014): »Hacia la construcción de un feminismo descolonizado,« in: Yuderkys Espinoza Miñoso/Diana Gómez Correal/Karina Ochoa Muñoz (eds.), *Tejiendo de otro modo: Feminismo, epistemología y apuestas descoloniales en Abya Yala,* Popayán: Editorial Universidad del Cauca, 325–334.

De la Cadena, Marisol/Blaser, Mario (2018): »Pluriverse: Proposals for a World of Many Worlds,« in: Marisol de la Cadena/Mario Blaser (eds.), *A World of Many Worlds,* Durham/London: Duke University Press, 1–22.

Ejército Zapatista de Liberación Nacional (1996): »Cuarta Declaración de la Selva Lacandona,« in: *Archivo Histórico, Enlace Zapatista*, January 1, 1996, https://enlacezapatista.ezln.org.mx/1996/01/01/cuarta-declaracion-de-la-selva-lacandona/, accessed July 19, 2025.

Fagerlönn, Pernilla/Reisinger, Karin (2024), »*Pernilla Fagerlönn on the Farväl Focus festival,*« online interview (Gällivare/Vienna). doi: 10.21937/ncws-yz26

Ferro, Sérgio (2006 [1976]): »*O canteiro e o desenho,*« in: Sérgio Ferro, Arquitetura e trabalho livre, São Paulo: Cosac Naify, 105–202.

Geerts, Evelien (2016): »Ethico-onto-epistem-ology,« in: *The Almanac of New Materialism – How Matter comes to Matter*, https://newmaterialism.eu/almanac/e/ethico-onto-epistem-ology.html, accessed November 23, 2024.

Grosfoguel, Ramón (2016): »Del ›extractivismo económico‹ al ›extractivismo epistémico‹ y al ›extractivismo ontológico‹: una forma destructiva de conocer, ser y estar en el mundo,« in: *Revista Tábula Rasa* 24, 123–143. doi: 10.25058/20112742.60

Gurák Hjortfors, Lis-Mari/Reisinger, Karin (2024), »*Spatial Practices of Decolonizing the Mining Landscape,*« workshop at the conference Learnings/Unlearnings: Environmental Pedagogies, Play, Policies, and Spatial Design. Stockholm, September 5-7. https://caravanize.nu/conference-2024/conference-learnings-unlearnings-the-call/, accessed May 23, 2025.

Gurák Hjortfors, Lis-Mari/Reisinger, Karin (2024), »*Lis-Mari Gurák Hjortfors on her work with Sámi heritage,*« online interview (Koskullskulle/Vienna). doi: 10.21937/9J42-T231

Haraway, Donna J. (1988), »Situated Knowledges: The Science Question in Feminism and the Privilege of Partial Perspective,« in: *Feminist Studies* 14/3, 575–599. doi: 10.2307/3178066

Haraway, Donna J. (2016): *Staying with the Trouble: Making Kin in the Chthulucene*, Durham/London: Duke University Press.

Haraway, Donna J. (2018 [1997]): *Modest_Witness@Second_Millennium. FemaleMan_Meets_OncoMouse: Feminism and Technoscience*, New York/Oxon: Routledge.

Harcourt, Wendy/Nelson, Ingrid, eds. (2015): *Practising Feminist Political Ecologies: Moving Beyond the »Green Economy,«* London: Zed Books.

Harney, Stefano/Moten, Fred (2013): *The Undercommons: Fugitive Planning & Black Study*, Wivenhoe/New York/Port Watson: Minor Compositions.

Hjortfors, Lis-Mari (1998): *Vi har våra rötter både här och där- Om människor och miljöer i Koskullskulle under 100 år (We Have our Roots Here and There)*, Gällivare: Gällivare kommuns folkbibliotek.

Hui, Yuk (2024): *Machine and Sovereignty: For a Planetary Thinking*, Minneapolis: University of Minnesota Press.

Husos arquitecturas (2006): *HOME*, https://husos.info/HOME, accessed July 19, 2025.

Jarrett, Karina/Reisinger, Karin (2021): »*Karina Jarrett on the Embroidery Café: In Conversation with Karin Reisinger,*« online interview (Gällivare/Vienna). doi: 10.21937/80BS-6W07

Koekoek, Catherine (2024): »Return to the City to Claim It: Temporalities and Locations of Feminist Refusal,« in: *Res Publica. Revista de Historia de las Ideas Politicas* 27/1, 23–29. doi: 10.5209/rpub.90727

Lugones, María (2005): »Multiculturalismo radical y feminismos de mujeres de color,« in: *Revista Internacional de Filosofía Política* 25, 61–76.

Public works (2011): *public works*. https://www.publicworksgroup.net/, accessed July 19, 2025.

R-Urban Poplar (2023): *R-Urban Poplar.*
https://r-urban-poplar.net/, accessed July
19, 2025.

Rendell, Jane (2016): »Giving an Account
of Oneself: Architecturally,« in: *Journal
of Visual Culture 15/3*, 334–348. doi:
10.1177/1470412916665143

Reisinger, Karin (2020): *Two Ore Mountains:
Feminist Ecologies of Spatial Practice.*
Research project. Austrian Science Fund
(FWF), Grant. doi: 10.55776/T1157, https://
www.mountains-of-ore.org/en/, accessed
July 19, 2025.

Reisinger, Karin (2024): »Doing Material
Positionality while Listening to the
Prolonged Coloniality of a Mining Town
on Indigenous Ground,« in: Christa
Kamleithner/Özge Sezer/Alexandra
Skedzuhn-Safir (eds.), *Architectures of
Colonialism: Constructed Histories, Conflicting
Memories*, Basel: Birkhäuser, 217–232.
https://www.degruyter.com/document/
doi/10.1515/9783035626704/html?lang=en,
accessed November 23, 2024.

Reisinger, Karin/ Fagerlönn, Pernilla/
Gurák Hjortfors, Lis-Mari/ Jarrett, Karina
(2024): *Listening Station on Practices of
Hope amidst Extractive Violence [multimedia
installation].* Rotterdam: International
Architecture Biennale Rotterdam 2024 –
Nature of Hope.

Ribeiro, Djamila (2020): Interview to Luna
Gámez: »El derecho a poder hablar como
mujer negra: el ›Lugar de enunciación‹ de
Djamila Ribeiro.« *Pikara Magazine*, December 09, 2020, https://www.pikaramaga
zine.com/2020/12/el-derecho-a-poder-
hablar-como-mujer-negra-el-lugar-de-
enunciacion-de-djamila-ribeiro/, accessed
November 21, 2024.

Rogoff, Irit (2006): »*Smuggling*« – *An
Embodied Criticality*, Vienna: European
Institute for Progressive Cultural Policies.

Ruinorama (2024): *Lexicon [installation].*
Rotterdam: International Architecture
Biennale Rotterdam 2024 – Nature of
Hope.

Simpson, Leanne Betasamosake (2017): *As
We Have Always Done: Indigenous Freedom
Through Radical Resistance*, Minneapolis/
London: University of Minnesota Press.

Stengers, Isabelle (2020 [2005]): »The
Cosmopolitical Proposal,« in: Andrés
Jaque/Marina Otero Verzier/Lucia
Pietroiusti, *More-than-Human*, Rotterdam:
Het Nieuwe Instituut, 233–242.

Thomas, Katie Lloyd (2022): *Building
Materials: Material Theory and the
Architectural Specification*, London:
Bloomsbury Visual Arts.

Truman, Sarah E. (2019): »Feminist New
Materialisms,« in: Paul Atkinson/Sara
Delamont/M.A. Hardy/M. Williams (eds.),
The SAGE Encyclopedia of Research Methods,
London: Sage.

Tyszczuk, Renata/Smith, Joe (2018):
»Culture and climate change scenarios:
the role and potential of the arts and
humanities in responding to the ›1.5
degrees target‹,« in: *Current Opinion in
Environmental Sustainability 31*, 56–64. doi:
10.1016/j.cosust.2017.12.007

Vikman, Miriam/Reisinger, Karin (2023)
»Miriam Vikman on her work in Kattån,«
online interview (Kattån/Vienna). doi:
10.21937/Q8SD-3Y25

Xavier, Giovana (2017): »Feminismo:
direitos autorais de uma prática linda
e preta,« *Folha de S. Paulo*, July 19, 2017,
https://agoraequesaoelas.blogfolha.
uol.com.br/2017/07/19/feminismo-
uma-pratica-linda-e-preta/, accessed
September 17, 2024.

Dimensions of Architectural Knowledge, 2024–08 ə
https://doi.org/10.14361/dak-2024-0804

Counter Architectures of Sex Work.
Collective Care Networks and their Spatial Productions along Potsdamer Straße in West Berlin in the 1980s

Beverly Engelbrecht

Abstract: This article explores the spatial strategies and practices of sex workers on Potsdamer Straße in West Berlin during the 1980s through the lens of Ewa Majewska's concept of »weak resistance«. It argues that sex workers, operating under conditions of legal marginalization and patriarchal violence, developed ephemeral, informal, and collective spatial practices that produced what I term »counter architectures of sex work.« These spatial productions – marked by improvisation, transience, and mutual care – challenged dominant distinctions between »public« and »private,« »intimate,« and »distanced« space. Based on architectural analysis, archival materials, interviews, photographs, and an artistic drawing, the study frames the street as both a site of exploitation and a terrain of feminist resistance. The article highlights how »collective care networks« emerged as vital forms of everyday, non-heroic resistance that enabled sex workers to survive, protect one another, and assert agency. It also reveals the limits of such self-organization in the face of pimp hierarchies. Ultimately, the text contributes to a feminist discourse on urban space by reclaiming the practices of marginalized actors as foundational to alternative modes of spatial production.

Keywords: Spatial Production of Sex Workers; Collective Care Networks; Weak Resistance of Marginalized Groups; Counter Architectures of Sex Work; West Berlin.

Corresponding author: Beverly Engelbrecht (Bauhaus-Universität Weimar, Germany); beverly.engelbrecht@uni-weimar.de; beverlyengelbrecht@posteo.de; https://orcid.org/0009-0007-5459-6208;

Introduction

With the concept of »weak resistance,« the cultural philosopher Ewa Majewska provided a concept that will serve as the basis for my investigations into the spatial strategies and practices of sex workers in the context of the street prostitution scene of Potsdamer Straße in West Berlin in the 1980s.[1,2] Majewska sees this form of disobedience, that I would like to apply to the spatial productions of sex workers, »as an alternative to the predominantly straight and masculine notions of heroic activism dominating our political imaginary (Majewska 2021: 5–6).« She thus understands »weak resistance« as »other« – i.e. as a contrast to the hegemonic practices of the white, Western, male, heterosexual, and privileged (cf. Majewska 2021: 146–147). »Weak resistance« manifests itself in ordinary, everyday, and communal actions, which in some cases would merely mean persistence and survival, but could often also cause subversion, rejection, and transformation of existing norms (cf. Majewska 2021: 5–6, 146–147) – »those publics or groups that form and organize through mutual recognition of wider public exclusions so as to overcome those exclusions (Majewska 2021: 1).«

In this article, I will examine the spatial strategies and practices of »collective care networks« among sex workers along Potsdamer Straße in West Berlin during the 1980s, to discuss how this marginalized group produced space. I argue that these strategies served as forms of resistance against hostile policies, exploitation, and both male and structural violence. Consequently, I understand the street prostitution of Potsdamer Straße and the spatial productions manifesting there as an example of a feminist building culture of the precarious group of sex workers, in which dynamics of socio-political exclusion and invisibilization in space overlap with practices of informal and fluid appropriation. In this context, I would like to introduce the concept of »counter architectures of sex work« as spatial strategies and practices of marginalized people in the urban field. I argue that these »counter architectures« question norms in architectural production

---

1 The term »sex work« was coined by sex worker and activist Carol Leigh and is intended to clarify that the exchange of a sexual service for resources (money, drugs, accommodation, etc.) is work.

2 I deal with sex work as criminalized, marginalized, and moralized, based on the close intertwining of economic necessity, affective work, and sexuality. As a result, sex workers in urban areas were and are often only (temporarily) tolerated and exposed to violence and exploitation.

of space and thus also classifications of modernity, such as »private« and »public« or »intimate« and »distanced« – and therefore, »move away from the status quo still centered around modernism, growth, resource consumption, tangible elements and technical solutions (Baxi et al. 2024: 1).« »Counter architectures« thus encompass deviant spaces allowing ambivalences and overlapping spatial categories. I also suppose that these architectures are characterized by a high degree of temporality and precariousness and that, in this respect, various constitutions and diverse transformations of these spaces can be revealed. Last, they represent segregated spaces, i.e. counter places amid socially legitimized places, whose delimitations and interferences with normalized architectures I will examine (cf. Foucault 2021: 9ff.). In this respect, I share the view of space as »reaching beyond the physical space, including social and action related spatial constellations, political spaces, ecological environments (Baxi et al. 2024: 1).«

So, how can spaces of sex work be described using the example of the Potsdamer Straße? In what way do the strategies and practices of sex workers materialize spatially, and to what extent do they intertwine with the concept of »weak resistance« as a strategy against violence and exploitation?

Methodological Reflection

This article is a deductive-inductive research project (theoretical-empirical) from the perspective of architecture, which also utilizes interdisciplinary positions (including sociology and philosophy). To obtain different perspectives on the spatial productions of sex workers on the Potsdamer Straße in the 1980s, which serves as a case study, I use a combination of different qualitative data methods (analyses of literature and archive documents), which I evaluate in a synthesis-forming process. I also make use of artistic forms of design as epistemic instruments for my descriptions – more precisely, a map with Potsdamer Straße at its center (fig. 1), photographs showing spatial productions on the street (figs. 2, 3, 4), and a drawing, showing spaces appropriated by the sex worker Roberta (fig. 5). I used these forms of design to draw conclusions about specific (precarious) forms of spatial production that a purely text-based work would not have made possible. As an architect, the medium of drawing is important to me in order to question norms in architectural production. In this way, the drawing combines different scales, textures, colors, and, at the same time, elaborates the essence of the spaces and spatial

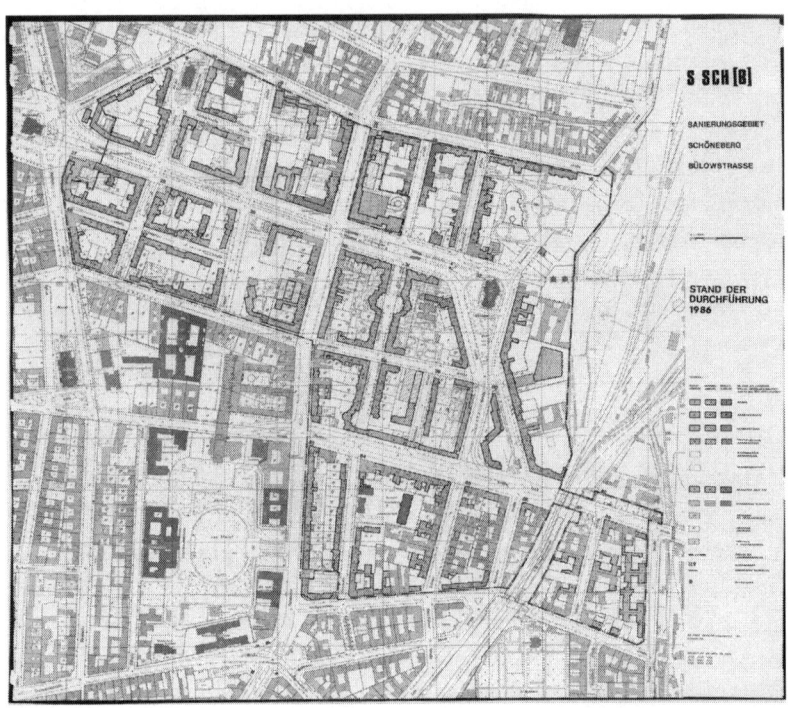

1.
Map with Potsdamer Straße in the center, 1986. Der Senator für Bau- und Wohnungswesen IV C. (ibid.) »S SCH (B) Sanierungsgebiet Schöneberg Bülowstrasse Stand der Durchführung.« Landesarchiv Berlin, Germany, B Rep. 016 (maps), Senatsverwaltung für Stadtentwicklung, serial no.: 279/Bl. 1.

2.
Street scene along Potsdamer Straße, 1983. Schneider, Günter (ibid.): »Handwerk und Gewerbe; Lotterie- und Wettwesen; Spielkasino ›Royal, Potsdamer Straße (Schöneberg)‹.« Landesarchiv Berlin, Germany, F Rep. 290-02-15, collection Günter Schneider, serial no.: 0254164.

3.
Interaction between a sex worker and a customer sitting in a car, 1980. Siegmann, Horst (ibid.): »Handwerk und Gewerbe; Prostitution; Straßenprostitution; Bülowstraße (Schöneberg),« Landesarchiv Berlin, Germany, F Rep. 290 (03) no. 0228865.

4.
Sex workers laboring in a group on Potsdamer Straße, 1983.Schneider, Günter
(ibid.): »Handwerk und Gewerbe; Lotterie- und Wettwesen; Spielcasino ›Hotel
Potsdam‹, Potsdamer Straße 156 (Schöneberg).« Landesarchiv Berlin, Germany, F
Rep. 290-02-15 no. 0254165.

5.
The spaces appropriated by the trans sex worker Roberta, 1980. Engelbrecht, Beverly 2025.

relationships. In this context, the format of drawing allows for ambivalence and not-knowing. It undermines linear thinking and creates visual counter-narratives to dominant, often patriarchal representations. In its openness, it can make marginalized perspectives visible and convey complex social realities in a sensual, immediate way. Drawings also have the ability to make the spatial productions of marginalized people visible and thus become part of their narratives. This highlights their potential not only as analytical tools, but as political and epistemic interventions within spatial discourse.

My contribution can be categorized as »interpretative interactionism«: »as an interpretative style of postmodernism that aims to make problematic life experiences accessible to readers in their cultural and social contextualization (Winter 2011: 10, author's translation).«[3] Following the basic principles, I situate the subjects (sex workers) historically and socially by examining the conditions that led to them having specific experiences (cf. ibid.: 9f.). In addition to the sex workers' personal stories, my research also focuses on analyses of planning and map material as well as photographs. To depict the perspectives of the sex workers, I analyze written interviews secondarily. For this, I utilize the magazines of the »Hydra Nachtexpress. Zeitung für Bar, Bordell und Bordstein,« which were published by representatives of the »whore movement« Hydra in (West) Berlin and depict the voices of sex workers from 1980 to 1995 (cf. Heying 2019: 75f.). I also found two publications with written interviews with sex workers in the archive of the »Schwules Museum« in Berlin – »Strichjungen-Gespräche«, which was conducted by the research team of Norbert Schmidt-Relenberg, Hartmut Kärner and Richard Pieper around 1975 in Hamburg in the context of queer sex work, and »An der Front des Patriachats«, which was carried out by Rose-Marie Giesen and Gunda Schumann in Berlin at the end of the 1970s (Schmidt-Relenberg et al. ibid.; Giesen/Schumann 1980). In addition, I use excerpts from the publication »Revolting Prostitutes« by sex workers and activists Juno Mac and Molly Smith (ibid. 2020), reports by sex workers in the context of the archive »Objects of Desire,«[4] observations and interviews from the publication »Licht- und Schattenseiten« by the authors Monika

---

3 »[A]ls einen interpretativen Stil der Postmoderne, der Lesenden problematische Lebenserfahrungen in ihrer kulturellen und sozialen Kontextualisierung zugänglich machen möchte (Winter 2011: 10).«

4 In 2019, the collective »Objects of Desire« interviewed over 40 sex workers in Berlin about objects that were significant to their work in order to reveal everyday, unspectacular stories beyond stereotypical representations (cf. OoD 2019a: n.p.).

Savier, Rita Eichelkraut, Andrea Simon, and Birgit Cramon-Daiber (ibid. 1987), as well as accounts by the city chronicler Willi Proeger in »Stätten der Berliner Prostitution« (ibid. 1930). To reconstruct the street spatially, I looked at plan material at the »Bauarchiv im Bezirksamt Tempelhof-Schöneberg« in Berlin. I also found maps and photographs in the »Landesarchiv Berlin« that showed the street. I contextualize the stories and analyses by placing other written texts and discourses in relation to them (cf. Winter 2011: 9f.). More specifically, I use newspaper articles that I found on Potsdamer Straße in the archive of »Museen Tempelhof-Schöneberg,« as well as brochures, correspondence, and newspaper articles collected by »Hydra« and kept in »das feministische Archiv FFBIZ.« Majweksa's »weak resistance« (ibid. 2021) also serves as a theoretical framework from which I examine spatial productions of resistance. I also use the concepts of »performativity« by philosopher and social scientist Judith Butler and »heteronormativity« (ibid. 2002) by cultural theorist Lauren Berlant and theorist and historian Michael Warner (ibid. 1998).

Potsdamer Straße as One of the Spatial Centers of the Sex Trade in West Berlin

Alongside Kurfürstendamm and Straße des 17. Juni, Potsdamer Straße was one of three central streets used for sex work in the western part of divided Berlin in the 1980s. Unlike other large West German cities, West Berlin was not spatially regulated by »restricted areas,« which meant that sex work was possible everywhere (cf. H N 1992/1993: 64). The three streets were centrally located on boulevards and easily accessible (cf. P H 1988: 210f.; cf. Künkel 2020: 230). While Kurfürstendamm was touristy and sex work mainly took place there at night, Straße des 17. Juni was used for sexual services in cars. Potsdamer Straße, on the contrary, was known for all-day street prostitution in front of hotels and guesthouses (cf. P H: 210f.).

During industrialization, the former elegant boulevard of the 19th century, where artists lived and frequented, was transformed into a commercial street with links to the sex trade. In the middle of the 19th century, the stately front houses of Potsdamer Straße were densified and new buildings – including more precarious forms of housing known as »Mietskasernen« – were erected, while at the same time the infrastructure changed with an elevated railroad. With the spatial transformation, the bourgeoisie moved further westward, while more and more actors in the sex trade established themselves in the area (cf. Jäkl 1987: title page, 14f., 49).

At the beginning of the 1970s, the section was characterized by its dense development; multistory buildings were built right up to the sidewalk, creating an urban atmosphere. The buildings themselves were heterogeneous. Some of the buildings date back to the Wilhelminian era, including several prestigious listed residential and commercial buildings (cf. Husse et al. 2018: 107–110, 132). Most of them were in a dilapidated condition after the bombings of Second World War, and some were derelict (cf. Jäkl 1987: 86). The (West) Berlin Senate at the time reacted to the situation by attempting to upgrade inner-city districts that were considered underdeveloped (»rückständig«), initially in the form of »area redevelopment« (»Flächensanierung«) and later, »object redevelopment« (»Objektsanierung«) – i.e. by demolishing existing buildings and building residential complexes that were considered »modern.« One of these areas was the »Sanierungsgebiet Schöneberg Bülowstraße,« the center of which was Potsdamer Straße (fig. 1). However, this urban renewal policy led to speculation, vacancies, and social resistance: from the mid-1970s, numerous tenants' and squatters' initiatives emerged to defend themselves against this urban planning, which was perceived as destructive. At the end of the 1970s, Potsdamer Straße became one of the focal points of the first wave of the (West) Berlin »Häuserkampf.« Squats took place almost daily, which were to be prevented by a massive police presence and the evacuation of houses. A conflict arose between squatters on the one hand and the Berlin Senate and (brutal) police intervention on the other. Eventually, the Senate began to negotiate with individual groups using the »Treuhandmodell,« splitting the movement. Ultimately, 105 of 165 squats were legalized by 1984; the rest were evicted (cf. Kuhn 2014: 69-84; cf. Savier et al. 1987: 44ff.). The renovations were thus enforced in the following years, so that existing buildings with dilapidated structures were increasingly demolished by »Neue Heimat,« a German non-profit construction and housing company commissioned by the Berlin Senate to carry out the renovations (cf. ARGE Sozialplanung 1994: 9; cf. Kuhn 2014: 71–79). With the changes in the street, authorities, banks, and stores successively settled in the southern part of Potsdamer Straße and a business center emerged (cf. Opprower 1957: n.p.; cf. Sontheimer 1991: n.p.).

Around 1980, the actors on Potsdamer Strasse were characterized by the coexistence of different groups and milieus. Alongside the various residents of the district, businesspeople, and employees were prostitutes and their customers, pimps, and operators of establishments associated with the sex trade. This coexistence can also be described in its spatial manifestations: In addition to residential buildings of various scales, banks, government offices, and bourgeois stores (jewelers, specialist bookshops, and fur stores), different restaurants and takeaways (from »Ellis Bratpfanne« to kebab stores) were lined up alongside various amusement businesses such as casinos and nightclubs, and numerous video stores. Sex department stores also opened next to the sex trade establishments (cf. Jäkl 1987: 86; cf. Markert/Nägele 2011: 205–206). As the image by photographer Günter Schneider shows, boards, signs, and lettering of various sizes – some of which protruded into the street space – drew attention to the many bars, clubs, and hotels (fig. 2). In this context, the lighting infrastructure played a key role: Unlike the adjacent side streets, Potsdamer Straße was also brightly lit at night (OS 1985: n.p.; cf. Savier et al. 1987: 41, 61). In addition to the boards, signs, and lettering, different colored light bulbs flashed, framing windows with (visible) references to the sex trade (cf. Savier et al. 1987: 52–53). Further down, on the first floor, shop windows that had formerly advertised the latest goods were covered with velvet – some of them hung with photographs of sex workers who worked in the establishment (cf. Härlin/Sontheimer 1983: 13). The actors in the sex trade thus appropriated buildings that were not built by architects for prostitution. To this end, managers of bars, clubs, and hotels, as well as pimps, marked their spatial claims by making the street space legible as belonging to the red-light district with advertising boards, flashing lights, and display cases. The sex workers themselves did not make any invasive spatial adaptations: In most cases, they were assigned spaces by managers and pimps. When sex workers transformed spaces, these adaptations were characterized by a greater degree of transience. They moved garbage cans in backyards or used the advantages of shop windows, as shown below.[5]

---

5 The implementation of the »Sanierungsgebiet Schöneberg Bülowstraße« led to gentrification processes: Higher-income residents displaced established milieus and organized themselves against sex work (e.g., in the »Anwohnerinitiative Lützowstraße«) (e.g. cf. BLZ 1998; cf. ARGE Sozialplanung 1994: 36f., 42, 55). The redevelopment company »Neue Heimat« also refused to rent to the sex industry, which exacerbated the conflicts (cf. TAZ 1988: n.p.). As a result, sex work shifted to Potsdamer Straße and side streets. Despite police orders to leave, sex workers returned again and again, defending their claims to space in the long term (e.g. cf. H N 1995: 26, e.g. cf. Künkel 2020: 108-149)

Spatial Productions of Sex Workers on Potsdamer Straße

The term street sex work initially refers to the place where contact is made: »The prostitutes stand on the side of the road and wait for clients, who usually drive past in a car, stop and choose a [sex worker] to get into the car with them (Feige 2003: 626, author's translation).«[6] Waiting and making contact was visible for bystanders, which made the prostitutes particularly vulnerable. More precisely, waiting meant for sex workers standing on the sidewalk or under canopies, leaning against (house) walls, sitting on chairs in entrances, or walking up and down the sidewalk (cf. Savier et al. 1987: 53–54; cf. Markert/Nägele 2011: 205–206). The trans sex worker Roberta, for example, as can be seen on the drawing (fig. 5) stood

> »[O]n the parking strip in front of Foto-Wegert, on the corner of Kurfürsten-straße; she uses the bright light of the display, in which matt black and silver SLR cameras, hi-fi towers and other marvels of home electronics gleam, to illuminate her charms (Härlin/Sontheimer 1983: 88, author's translation).«[7]

A picture taken by photographer Horst Siegmann (see fig. 3) shows the following contact between a sex worker and a customer on Bülowstraße: The photograph depicts a car stopped in the driver's lane; a sex worker leans over the open door on the passenger side and interacts with the customer. During the interaction between the sex worker and the client, agreements were made on the price, type, and location of the sexual act. If both agreed, they drove together to the place of service.[8] A plausible assumption is that they usually used one of the many hotels and guesthouses along Potsdamer Straße or the

---

6 »Die Prostituierten stehen am Straßenrand und warten auf Freier, die in der Regel im Auto vorbeigefahren kommen, anhalten und sich eine [Sexarbeiterin] aussuchen, die zu ihnen ins Auto steigt (Feige 2003: 626).«

7 »Auf dem Parkstreifen vor Foto-Wegert, Ecke Kurfürstenstraße; sie nutzt das helle Licht der Auslage, in dem matt schwarz und silbern Spiegelreflex-Kameras, Hifi-Türme und andere Wunderwerke der Heimelektronik glänzen, zur Beleuchtung ihrer Reize (Härlin/Sontheimer 1983: 88).«

8 When sex workers were approached by pedestrians, the process of making contact was quite similar: The pedestrian stopped and spoke to the sex worker or vice versa. A plausible assumption is that this was followed by agreements on the price, type, and location of the sexual service as well. Sex workers were not dependent on cars coming to a standstill, but addressed potential customers with phrases such as »Hello sweetie, mmh, shh, come here (plu 1981: n.p., author's translation).«

inside of the car after the sex worker and client had found a more secluded parking lot. The car could also be parked near where the contact was made and both left the location on foot: Roberta, for example, used an empty excavation pit behind the »Foto-Wegert« building. Later, the squatters living in the adjacent building set up a temporary space for her:

> »After lengthy debates, the housing assembly refused to give Roberta and [her circle] the first-floor apartment [of the occupied building] and preferred a daycare center. But at least we built her a small wooden hut in the pit, ›mein Käfisch,‹ as she proudly called it (ibid.: 85–86, author's translation).«[9,10]

She was unable to use the hut permanently, which is why she later appropriated a backyard around 100 meters away from her regular spot (cf. ibid.: 88) until she finally had to move to an underground car park (cf. Sontheimer 1991: n.p.). The city chronicler Willi Pröger also reported on areas in backyards partitioned off with garbage cans, which were used for sexual acts at the beginning of the century and certainly even later:

> »Around 11 o'clock in the evening [...] a woman approaches me. [...] To the obligatory question: ›Where?‹, the woman replies: 'A few houses away. We leave. The heavy woman unlocks a front building and leads me into a courtyard. Into a corner formed by piles of garbage cans. Sexual intercourse in the open, in the dark (ibid. 1930: 31f, author's translation).«[11]

This example illustrates the ambivalent character of the »counter-architectures«: Although the backyard appears spatially as »open,« it is at the same

---

9   »Roberta und den ihren die Parterrewohnung [des besetzten Hauses] zu überlassen lehnte die Hausversammlung zwar nach längeren Debatten ab und zog ihnen einen Kinderladen vor. Aber immerhin bauten wir ihr in der Grube eine kleine Bretterbude, ›meine Käfisch,‹ wie sie ihn voll Besitzerstolz nannte (Härlin/Sontheimer 1983: 85f.).«

10 As the example shows, there were brief alliances between sex workers and squatters that later dissipated. However, sex workers also acted as squatters themselves. Together with the self-help project »Hydra« and other women's groups, they renovated a building on Potsdamer Straße, which they left a few years later (cf. Engelbrecht 2025: 50–61).

11 »Gegen 11 Uhr abends spricht mich [...] eine Frau an. [...] Auf die obligate Frage: ›Wo‹, antwortet die Frau: ›N' paar Häuser weiter.‹ Wir gehen. Die dicke schließt ein Vorderhaus auf, führt mich in einen Hof. In eine Ecke, gebildet durch aufeinandergetürmte Mülleimer. Geschlechtsverkehr im Freien, im Dunkel' (Proeger 1930: 31f.).«

time partially shielded by informal, improvised boundaries – those of the garbage cans. The openness of the space is therefore not to be understood in the sense of public accessibility or complete visibility, but rather as a spatial transition zone in which »public« and »private« are blurred. The stacked garbage cans created a temporary, functional shelter. Sex workers also possessed keys to buildings adjacent to street prostitution areas to use the hallways for their services. In this context, Proeger described scenes that could have taken place on Potsdamer Straße using the example of another sex worker:

> »On ›good‹ days (Fridays, Saturdays and Sundays) [...] at least half a dozen courtyards and corridors are busy. And the prostitutes have keys to these houses, even though they don't live there! ›Money doesn't stink!‹ says the porter or some resident and sells a house key (ibid.: 72f, author's translation).« [12]

The »private« space that was originally attributed to the residents of a building only was thus overlaid by the uses of sex workers.

The examples show how, due to their historical criminalization and marginalization, sex workers appropriated and defended the spaces less actively, but rather passively, provisionally, and temporarily in the sense of »weak resistance.« They also fluidly changed the spaces they used for sexual intercourse and thus adapted to the frequently changing spatial conditions. At the same time, I read the sex workers' spatial productions, such as Roberta's, as persistent: she constantly seeks out new spaces. Displacement seems to be part of her everyday life. In addition, the sex workers' spatial awareness of the street space is remarkable. They used the advantages of the »public« street space, such as the brightly lit displays of department stores, to stage themselves. I see these places, which were used to buy and sell sex and deviated from social morals and heteronormative norms, as »counter architectures« because the sex workers added a new layer to the street space without changing it. After all, the space was not built by an architect for sex work, but rather appropriated and occupied by actors in the sex trade. Thus, the meanings of the buildings and the space in between, which were

---

12 »An ›guten‹ Tagen (Freitags, Sonnabends und Sonntags) ist [...] mindestens einem halben Dutzend Höfen und Hausfluren reger ›Absteige-Betrieb.‹ Und zwar besitzen die Prostituierten zu diesen Häusern Schlüssel, obwohl sie nicht im Hause wohnen! ›Geld stinkt nicht!‹ sagt auch der Portier oder irgendein Bewohner und verkauft einen Hausschlüssel (Proeger 1930: 72f.).«

intended as residential buildings, stores, offices, or restaurants, overlap with the uses by sex workers and their customers.

The sex workers used one place to contact clients and another for sexual acts, as well as a space connecting the two. While in the vocabulary of modern architectural production, the spaces for establishing contact could be described as »public« on the one hand and the spaces for sexual services as »private« on the other, a closer look reveals the ambivalences of such spatial attributions. This is because the contact between sex worker and client was »private«, but at the same time took place in a »public« place. The sexual services involved »distanced« acts between two strangers, which were nevertheless »intimate,« in spaces that were more »private« than the street space of Potsdamer Straße, but were often provisional, partially visible, and usually accessible at a low threshold. The transition to the site of the sexual act was usually marked by a spatial threshold, such as the garbage cans in the courtyard or the door to the »Bretterbude.«

The form and conditions of work were also social, political, and therefore of »public« relevance. As philosopher and social scientist Judith Butler argues:

> »The personal is thus implicitly political as much as it is conditioned by shared social structures, but the personal has also been immunized against political challenge to the extent that public/private distinctions endure. For feminist theory, then, the personal becomes an expansive category, one which accommodates, if only implicitly, political structures usually viewed as public. Indeed, the very meaning of the political expands as well (ibid. 1988: 522f.).«[13]

In addition, cultural theorist Lauren Berlant and theorist and historian Michael Warner discuss in their essay »Sex in Public« (1998) that sexuality is largely made invisible in heteronormative »public« life or contained in institutional forms such as marriage and family. Street prostitution, on the other hand, makes sexuality visible as an economic transaction, and is often perceived as a threat to this social order: »[H]eteronormativity is

---

13 »Somit ist das Persönliche implizit insoweit politisch, als es durch gemeinsame gesellschaftliche Strukturen bedingt ist, aber das Persönliche wurde auch so weitgehend gegen politische Herausforderungen immunisiert, daß Unterscheidungen von öffentlich und privat weiter fortbestehen. Für die feministische Theorie wird das Persönliche dann eine umfassende Kategorie, die, wenn auch nur implizit, politische Strukturen mit umschließt, die gewöhnlich als öffentlich betrachtet werden. In der Tat erweitert sich hier auch die Bedeutung des Politischen (Butler 2002: 307).«

a fundamental motor of social organization [...], a founding condition of unequal and exploitative relations throughout even straight society (ibid.: 564).« As a result, the »counter architectures« appropriated by sex workers are perceived as deviating from social norms. I also understand waiting, making contact, walking together to the location of the sexual acts and the sexual service itself as »performative acts« and thus as »public.« In this context, Butler writes:

> »Applying this conception of social performance to gender, it is clear that the ›action‹ is also directly public, although it is individual bodies that enact the meanings by stylizing themselves in gendered ways« (ibid.: 312f, author's translation).[14]

Butler also makes it clear that »gender performances [...] are governed by more clearly punitive and regulatory social conventions (ibid.: 527).«[15] This is particularly clear in the queer context, where the initiation of contact was less visible. The sex worker Andreas, for example, describes it as follows:

> »Yes, when a gay man walks past, he looks at him first. Not from up close, but from a bit further away. He always looks at him like he's looking in a shop window [...]. Then he looks at the boy first to see if he wants to earn some money. And when he has looked at him, he usually speaks to him (Schmidt-Relenberg et al. 1975: 182, author's translation).«[16]

The contacting of male sex workers, who addressed a male audience, thus differed fundamentally from the activities of female sex workers, who solicited male clients, as the criminal offence of homosexuality meant that clients

---

14 »Wendet man diese Konzeption der sozialen Performanz auf die Geschlechterzugehörigkeit an, so ist deutlich, daß die ›Aktion‹ auch unmittelbar öffentlich ist, obgleich einzelne Körper es sind, die die Bedeutungen inszenieren, indem sie sich geschlechtsspezifisch stilisieren (Butler 2002: 312f.).«

15 »Geschlechter-Inszenierungen [...] durch strafende und regulierende gesellschaftliche Konventionen beherrscht (Butler 2002: 313).«

16 »Ja, wenn da son Schwuler längsgeht, der guckt sich den erstmal an. Nicht so von der Nähe, sondern n bißchen weiter von so nem Abstand. Da guckt er immer so hin, als wenn er in n Schaufenster guckt[...]. Dann guckt er den Jungen erstmal an, ob der nich n bißchen Geld verdienen will. Und wenn er sich den angeguckt hat, dann spricht er ihn auch meistens an (Schmidt-Relenberg et al 1975: 182).«

and sex workers could not be recognized by outsiders (cf. Schmidt-Relenberg et al. 1975: 179f.). While sex work in West Berlin was legally regulated by the verdict of »immorality« and was spatially restricted in various laws, queer sex work was made almost invisible in the »public« space as a criminal offense.[17] Heterosexual intimacy is thus considered the norm, while queer sexuality has been criminalized as disruptive or inappropriate. In this context, the trans sex worker Roberta also had to be legible as »female« to be able to offer services in the »public« street space. And yet she was left with less popular and more vulnerable places than her cis female colleagues, who usually stood in front of the guesthouses and hotels that were considered popular.

The sex workers who worked on Potsdamer Straße changed shifts once a day. In this context, Carola explains the spatial organization:

> »The women who work there at night, I believe, have [no financial] [...] problems. They usually have pimps or are lucky enough to know someone from the clique. So, we, the women who work there during the day, have the biggest problems. We have to clear the street for the ›professionals‹ (as they call themselves) by 8 pm at the latest. We ›day women‹ are either drug addicts, foreigners, or simply women without certain connections (H C 1980: 11, author's translation).«[18]

The sex workers and third parties, such as pimps, thus organized the space through territorial and price agreements in which vulnerable groups were particularly marginalized. Carola's comment shows that solidarity behavior between sex workers runs along the lines of race, class, drug use, gender identity, and other (potential) exclusionary factors.

---

17 Section 175 of the Criminal Code (»§ 175 Strafgesetzbuch«) was defused in 1969, so that sex between men over the age of 21 was no longer punishable (cf. Arolsen n.d.: n.p.). However, homosexual prostitution remained punishable until the 4th Criminal Law Amendment Act (»4. Strafrechtsänderungsgesetz«) in 1973 (cf. LSVD n.d.: n.p.). With this amendment, the age of consent for male homosexuality was also set at 18 (cf. ibid.). The paragraph was not completely abolished until 1994 (cf. Arolsen n.d.: n.p.).

18 »Die Frauen, die dort nachts arbeiten, haben, so glaube ich, [keine finanziellen] [...] Probleme. Dafür haben sie meist Zuhälter oder das Glück, jemanden aus der Clique zu kennen. Wir, die Frauen die dort am Tag arbeiten, haben also die größten Schwierigkeiten. Um 20 Uhr müssen wir die Straße spätestens für die 'Profis' räumen (wie sie sich selbst bezeichnen). Wir ›Tagfrauen‹ sind entweder drogenabhängig, Ausländerinnen oder einfach Frauen ohne gewisse Beziehungen (H C 1980: 11).«

In addition, the descriptions of one of the authors of the publication »Licht- und Schattenseiten« (1987) show that the sex workers had fixed locations and formed alliances with other sex workers by working together in small groups: »Right on the corner are Turkish transvestites, a small heavy man and a huge thin man. They always seem to work together. At least I've always seen them together. This corner is their ›location‹ (Savier et al. ibid.: 32, author's translation).«19 And later on: »Fifty meters further along Potsdamer Straße are two German prostitutes. They belong to the professionals, the long-established, accepted women who have characterized the streetscape for years (ibid., author's translation).«20 The image by photographer Günter Schneider also shows several white sex workers waiting for customers in the entrance area of a hotel on Potsdamer Straße (fig. 4). They are certainly also working together. Such alliances were often only temporary due to the dynamic developments in the sex trade (cf. H N 1981: 7–10; cf. Savier et al. 1987: 43–44). The sex worker Kim described the spatial strategies and practices during the study period as follows:

> »But I usually kept my working hours, until 4 o'clock. I found it easiest when I had two new friends on the street, one next to me and one opposite. We got on really well. [...] The motivation to go to work was much better because each of us knew that the other would be there too (H N 1981: 7, author's translation).«21

Resident Ms. E. also confirmed Kim's statements: »Well, if one of them is provoked or something, the others are there straight away. They also talk to each other a lot (Savier et al. 1987: 43–44, author's translation).«22 From

---

19 »Gleich an der Ecke stehen türkische Transvestiten, ein kleiner dicker und ein riesiger dünner Mann. Sie arbeiten anscheinend immer zusammen. Ich habe sie jedenfalls immer zusammen gesehen. Diese Ecke ist ihr 'Standort' (Savier et al. ibid.: 32).«

20 »Fünfzig Meter weiter auf der Potsdamer Straße stehen zwei deutsche Prostituierte. Sie gehören zu den Profis, den alteingesessenen akzeptierten Frauen, die das Straßenbild seit Jahren prägen (ibid.).«

21 »Ich hielt aber meistens meine Arbeitszeit ein, bis 4 Uhr. Am leichtesten fiel mir das, als ich auf der Straße zwei neue Freundinnen hatte, eine neben mir und eine gegenüber. Wir verstanden uns ganz prima[.] [...] Der Antrieb zum Job hinzugehen war dadurch viel besser, weil jede von uns wußte, daß die andere ja auch da sein würde (H N 1981: 7).«

22 »Also, wenn da einmal eine provoziert wird oder so, dann sind sofort die anderen da. Die reden auch viel miteinander (Savier et al. 1987: 43f.).«

today's perspective, I would describe such forms of communal trade as »collective care networks« – i.e. alliances between prostitutes. By alliances, I mean loose, often informal associations of sex workers based on mutual support, protection, and solidarity within the »counter architectures.« These alliances aimed to create security and stability in a working environment characterized by competition, control, and social exclusion. They served to observe and warn each other, to intervene in conflict situations, and to provide emotional and practical support. Through this collaboration, sex workers actively appropriated the urban space and turned it – at least temporarily – into a place of mutual care and agency. These alliances are emblematic of the »weak resistance« and have always been common in sex work. Sex workers and activists Juno Mac and Molly Smith, who did not work on Potsdamer Straße, reported on other forms of solidarity and resistance among sex workers.[23] Examples they gave included sharing money, rooms, and clients, looking after children together, and supporting each other in times of need or illness:

> »For example, in nineteenth-century Great Britain and Ireland, prostitutes created communities of mutual aid, sharing income and childcare. Likewise, watembezi [street based] women in colonial-era Nairobi formed financial ties to one another, paying each other's fines or bequeathing assets to one another when they died. Although largely invisible to outsiders, this sharing of resources [...] persists as a significant form of sex worker activism today. Workers often collectively pitch in to prevent an eviction or to offer emergency housing. This kind of community resource-sharing is often the only safety net sex workers have if they're robbed at work or if an assault means they need time off to heal (Mac/Smith 2020: 6).«

Spatial characteristics of this solidarity-based resistance are therefore the »communal« and »intimate« appropriation and use of space beyond the boundaries of the traditional nuclear family – i.e. by groups that are considered more »distant.«

At the same time, relationships among sex workers were characterized by ambivalence. In addition to forms of mutual support, there was also competition, mistrust, and demarcation. Alliances were therefore often

---

23 The two women are currently working in the UK and are activists with the »Sex Worker Advocacy and Resistance Movement« (SWARM) (cf. Verso n.d.a, n.d.b).

situation-dependent and not always an expression of personal closeness. In this context, sex worker F. described her experiences:

> »I'm friends with one and maybe slightly friends with two, but I have to say ›friends‹ in quotation marks because I understand something completely different by ›private friends‹. I don't think there are any real friendships in prostitution[,] [...] because the competition between all the hookers is too intense. The friendship I have with a colleague is such that we meet up outside of work from time to time, and then she tells me her worries and I admire her clothes and, well, she gives me clients and doesn't take anything for it, well, she usually doesn't take anything for it, sometimes, that's something, you can call it being friends (Giesen/Schumann 1980: 175, author's translation).«[24]

In this respect, the sex workers' statements cover a broad spectrum from friendships and temporary alliances to disinterest. Sex workers, therefore, had very individual and contradictory experiences.

The street prostitution on Potsdamer Straße was also characterized by hegemonic power dynamics between actors in the sex trade (pimps and customers). In an internal letter from HWG e. V. Prostituiertenhilfe – a self-help project in Frankfurt am Main – to Hydra in 1997, they informed their colleagues: »Rape, assault, deprivation of liberty, and robbery are offenses that Frankfurt's prostitutes are constantly confronted with (HWG ibid., author's translation).«[25] The letter also described an internal security system among sex workers:

> »It is common practice on the streets that women usually work together with a colleague and look out for each other. The numbers of the client vehicles are

---

24 »Ich bin schon mit einer richtig befreundet und vielleicht mit zweien noch leicht befreundet, aber ich muß das ›befreundet‹ in Anführungsstriche sagen, weil ich also unter privat befreundet was ganz anderes verstehe. Ich glaube, daß es aufm Strich keine richtigen Freundschaften gibt [,,,], weil die Konkurrenz zu groß ist, die zwischen allen Nutten läuft. Die Freundschaft, die ich zu einer Kollegin hab, sieht so aus, daß wir uns außerhalb der Arbeit auch ab und zu treffen, und dann erzählt sie mir ihre Sorgen und ich bewundere dafür ihre Klamotten und, also, sie gibt mir dafür Freier ab und kassiert nix dafür, also, sie kassiert meistens nix dafür, manchmal auch, das ist schon was, kann man schon befreundet nennen (Giesen/Schumann 1980: 175).«

25 »Vergewaltigung, Körperverletzung, Freiheitsberaubung und Raub sind Vergehen, mit denen Frankfurts Stricherinnen permanent konfrontiert sind (HWG).«

written down. Various hand signals indicate which site the colleague is going to, people watch the clock, etc. [...] Car numbers are written down. [...] Car
numbers and the names of dangerous clients and their addresses are written
on billboards, trees, and walls. In some low-threshold drug facilities, there
are books in which the women write messages about clients (ibid., author's
translation).«[26]

I assume that not only in Frankfurt am Main, but also on Potsdamer Straße
in West Berlin, sex workers were exposed to potentially violent clients and
that they developed an internal security system in response. This assumption is also supported by sex workers Juno Mac and Molly Smith »All over the
world, sex workers use strategies to stay safe: working [...] in a small group
on the street; visibly noting down a client's car number plate or asking for his
ID, to show him that he is not anonymous (Mac/Smith 2020: 3).« Prostitutes
thus developed (spatial) strategies and practices to resist violence. I also
read these spatial productions as an everyday form of resistance that does
not express itself confrontationally, but through social proximity, persever-
ance, and mutual concern. Due to the criminalization of the sex trade, prostitutes protected each other instead of calling the police. In addition, there
were certainly also individual strategies for reacting to violent assaults. For
example, one sex worker reported that she carried a knife with her: »The
object that I most connect to sex work is a knife. I was attacked by a man I met
on the street. It turned out that he had killed sex workers before. He tried to
kill me with a knife. I fought him and escaped with my life (OoD 2019b).« This
quote makes it clear that sex workers were also capable of a heroic form of
resistance. While most of the examples were classified as »weak resistance,«
there were also exceptions here. Taken together, the examples show that sex
workers asserted themselves through various forms of resistance – mostly
through collective protection systems and spatial practices of mutual care,
but also through individual strategies of self-defense and acute resistance.
Resistance thus manifested itself in many ways: as every day and persistent

---

26 »Auf dem Straßenstrich ist es Usus, daß Frau meist mit einer Kollegin zusammenarbe-
    itet und die Frauen aufeinander aufpassen. Die Nummern der Freierfahrzeuge werden
    aufgeschrieben. Es gibt verschiedene Handzeichen, die erkennen lassen, auf welchen
    Stichplatz die Kollegin fährt, es wird auf die Uhr geachtet etc. [...] Autonummern und die
    Namen von gefährlichen Kunden und deren Adressen werden auf Plakatwände, Bäume
    und Mauern geschrieben. In manchen niedrigschwelligen Drogeneinrichtungen liegen
    Bücher aus, in die die Frauen Nachrichten über Freier schreiben (HWG 1997).«

resistance through solidarity and mindfulness, but occasionally also in the form of open confrontation.

Pimps also played a special role in controlling and distributing space. While the street space was initially hardly controlled by these actors, they later took on a more dominant role. Around 1980, it was possible to work without pimps – in contrast to the »tolerance zones« of other large West German cities – but this had consequences. If sex workers acted without them, they were left with far less popular locations, such as darker, more secluded, and less safe spaces (cf. Savier et al. 1987: 32–35; cf. H C 1980: 11). These contexts make it clear that sex workers did not position themselves arbitrarily on the street but were usually ordered to do so by higher-ranking actors in the sex trade. If prostitutes insisted on »placing« themselves, their striving for autonomy was punished with spatial marginalization. Thus, while sex workers organized themselves in the form of »collective care networks« against violent clients, they seemed to act more individually against pimps. In this context, sex worker H. reported:

> »[The prostitutes] unite when it comes to a client, the cohesion is incredibly strong. But when it comes to the pimps ... there are a few, but they get so many barriers ... All the Frankfurt pimps, they drove up here in huge buses and fought here because the Persians wanted to spread out [...] [in West Berlin]. The pimps marched in from all the cities and beat them up. They had an organization [...]. You can't fight them. No matter how many women join forces. [...] They always have a longer arm (Giesen/Schumann 1980: 178f., author's translation).«[27]

Collective self-organization was therefore not universally possible, but depended on the other side. While sex workers organized collectively against individually acting clients, this strategy hardly worked against structures such as pimp cartels. The descriptions also show the power imbalance in

---

27 »[Die Prostituierten] schließen sich zusammen, wenns um nen Freier geht, da ist der Zusammenhalt unwahrscheinlich stark. Aber in [B]ezug auf die Zuhälter ... da sind vereinzelte, aber die kriegen dann so viel Keile, nee. ... Die ganzen Frankfurter Zuhälter, mit Riesenbussen sind die hier aufgefahren und haben hier gekämpft, weil die Perser sich [...] [in West-Berlin] breitmachen wollten. Aus sämtlichen Städten sind da die Zuhälter aufmarschiert und haben die da fertiggemacht. Die haben ne Organisation [...]. Da kommst du nicht gegen an. Da können sich noch so viele Frauen zusammenschließen. [...] Die haben immer nen längeren Arm (Giesen/Schumann 1980: 178f.).«

the hierarchized sex industry: While sex workers actually sold sex, third parties such as pimps, those who managed street prostitution, and allocated sections of the street profited. The historically grown criminalization and marginalization, as well as sex workers' scepticism toward the police empowered pimps to use physical and psychological violence against sex workers seemingly without consequence to enforce their claims to space and power (cf. H N 1988: 6–26). The »weak resistance« of the sex workers here was more individualized, limited, passive, and invisible: It consisted of accepting locational disadvantages, paying off debts to free themselves from dependency (cf. Härlin / Sontheimer 1983: 89f.), persevering in the face of violence, and surviving.

Spatial Productions of Sex Workers as a Collective, and Resistant Practice

The analysis of the spatial productions of sex workers on Potsdamer Straße in West Berlin in the 1980s as an example of »counter architectures of sex work« shows how urban space was formed beyond official planning through everyday, barely visible actions. The street was shaped by the actions of those who were excluded from official spatial orders and was characterized by their routines – waiting, the targeted positioning of bodies, the persistent search for places for sexual acts, and the fleeting appropriation. Potsdamer Straße thus served not only as a transit space but also as a working environment for sex workers and was reinterpreted as a zone of collective care and a place of social negotiation. As hybrid spaces between »public« and »private,« »distanced« and »intimate,« they eluded clear spatial orders. This spatial ambiguity and ambivalence harbored a potential for resistance that permeated the spatial strategies and practices of sex workers and was articulated not through open confrontation, but through everyday presence, and ephemeral, fluid, as well as informal appropriation of space. Ewa Majewska's concept of »weak resistance« (cf. ibid. 2021) – a soft, non-heroic resistance that becomes effective in the vulnerable and is characterized precisely by concern – is a solution to this form of insistence.

Sex workers acted in a state of structural vulnerability: without state protection, socially stigmatized, and exposed to patriarchal violence and exploitation. However, it was precisely this vulnerability that gave rise to solidarity practices in which care became the central element of resistance:

In the absence of institutional securities, »collective care networks« formed – alliances based on shared experiences of exclusion, danger, and mutual dependence. Prices were agreed, territories divided up, and information about dangerous customers passed on. Colleagues stood by each other in the event of illness, emergencies, or violence. These networks of care were not merely survival strategies, but an expression of the resistant production of space by sex workers – based on trust, respect, and collective responsibility.

At the same time, they reveal the limits of collective self-organization. Within the hierarchized sex industry, marginalized sex workers – such as trans, queer, and racialized people – were once again excluded. Others deliberately refused to organize collectively, whether out of a sense of competition or a desire for independence. In addition, collective protection practices also reached their limits when it was no longer a question of organization vis-à-vis individual customers, but of organized power structures of pimps. These increasingly controlled the distribution of space on the street, allocated locations, and demanded debts if a sex worker wanted to free herself from dependency – often under the use of violence. Anyone who evaded their control was punished with spatial marginalization. Resistance to this form of structural violence often remained individualized and silent: it expressed itself in accepting inconvenient locations, in waiting, in survival.

Despite these ruptures, the spatial productions of sex workers on Potsdamer Straße in West Berlin in the 1980s reveal anti-hegemonic negotiation processes that can be read as part of a feminist building culture. This building culture undermined dominant planning and usage hierarchies, focused on marginalized perspectives on space, and made care work and collective organization visible as essential elements of spatial practice. Feminist building culture here does not mean architectural design, but rather resistant spatial production from below that challenges patriarchal orders by creating spaces beyond representation, control, and standardized publicity. These historical practices not only open up a new perspective on urban spatial production but also have relevance for current and future strategies of precariously living groups. In the presence of growing housing shortages, exclusionary migration regimes, and advancing precarization of work and state control, they show: Even under adverse conditions, collective infrastructures can be developed beyond institutional systems – through mutual care, shared knowledge, and strategic use of space. The »counter architectures of sex work« are therefore not only evidence of past self-organization, but also model forms of solidary space production for future urban struggles.

References

ARGE Sozialplanung [Arbeitsgemeinschaft für Sozialplanung und angewandte Stadtforschung AG SPAS e.V.] (1994): »Gutachten über den Verlauf und die Ergebnisse der Sozialplanung im Sanierungsgebiet Schöneberg-Bülowstraße,« in: *Landesarchiv Berlin*, Germany, B Rep. 009 Nr. 5973.

Arolsen [Arolsen Archive] (n.d.): »Paragraph 175: Die Geschichte der strafbaren Homosexualität in Deutschland,« in: *Arolsen Archive*, https://arolsen-archives.org/news/paragraph-175-strafbare-homosexualitaet/#:~:text=Paragraph%20175%3A%20Die%20Geschichte%20der%20strafbaren%20Homosexualität%20in%20Deutschland&text=123%20Jahre%20dauerte%20es%2C%20bis,BRD%20aus%20dem%20Gesetzbuch%20gestrichen, accessed October 29, 2024.

Baxi, Kadambari/ Glogar, Isabel/Heindl, Gabu/Krejs, Bernadette/Schneider, Tatjana (2024): »Changing Spatial Practice: Alliances, Activism and Networks. Call for Contributions,« in: *Dimensions. Journal of Architectural Knowledge*, https://dimensions-journal.eu/media/site/1e5a58af24-1726126862/dimensions_call-09-2025.pdf, accessed August 12, 2024.

Berlant, Lauren/Warner, Michael (1998): »Sex in Public,« in: *Critical Inquiry*, 24/2, 547–566.

BLZ (1998): »Rund um die Bülowstraße ist alles saniert,« in: *Berliner Zeitung*, https://www.berliner-zeitung.de/archiv/grundstueckseigentuemer-zahlen-fuer-wertsteigerung-rund-um-die-buelowstrasse-ist-alles-saniert-li.1179806, accessed April 14, 2023.

Butler, Judith (1988): »Performative Acts and Gender Constitution. An Essay in Phenomenology and Feminist Theory,« in: *Theatre Journal*, 40/4 (Dec. 1988), 519–531.

Butler, Judith (2002): »Performative Akte und Geschlechterkonstitution. Phänomenologie und feministische Theorie,« in: Uwe Wirth (ed.), *Performanz. Zwischen Sprachphilosophie und Kulturwissenschaften*, Frankfurt a. M.: Suhrkamp, 301–320.

Engelbrecht, Beverly (2025): »Sexarbeiterinnen und die Anfänge der Hurenbewegung ›Hydra‹. Widerständige Raumproduktionen am Beispiel der Instand(be)setzung eines Gebäudes in der Potsdamer Straße West-Berlins,« in: AG Denkmalschutzjahr 2025 des ICOMOS Suisse und dem Lehrstuhl für Konstruktionserbe und Denkmalpflege der ETH Zurich (eds.), *A future for whose past? Das Erbe von Minderheiten, Randgruppen und Menschen ohne Lobby*, Zürich: Hier und Jetzt, Verlag für Kultur und Geschichte GmbH, 50–61.

Feige, Marcel (2003): *Das Lexikon der Prostitution*, Berlin: Schwarzkopf und Schwarzkopf.

Foucault, Michel (2021 [2013]): *Die Heterotopien. Der utopische Körper*, 5th edition, Frankfurt am Main: Suhrkamp (Suhrkamp Taschenbuch Wissenschaft, 2071).

Giesen, Rose-Marie/Schumann, Gunda (1980): An der Front des Patriachats. Bericht vom langen Marsch durch das Prostitutionsmilieu, Bensheim: Päd.-Extra-Buchverlag, in: *archive of Schwules Museum*, Berlin, Germany.

Härlin, Benny/Sontheimer, Michael (1983): *Potsdamer Straße: Sittenbilder und Geschichten*, Berlin: Rotbuch-Verl.

Heying, Mareen (2019): *Huren in Bewegung. Kämpfe von Sexarbeiterinnen in Deutschland und Italien, 1980 bis 2001*, Essen: Klartext.

Husse, Katharina/Lemburg, Peter/Schulz, Gabriele (2018): *Denkmale in Berlin - Bezirk Tempelhof-Schöneberg: Ortsteil Schöneberg, Denkmaltopographie Bundesrepublik Deutschland*, Petersberg: Michael Imhof Verl.

HWG [prostitutes' self-help project] (1997), »Hotline,« [internal letter], in: *Das feministische Archiv FFBIZ*, Berlin,Germany, A Rep. 400 Berlin 20.2.15-75.

H C [Hydra Cafe] (eds.) (1980): Hydra's *Nacht-Express: Zeitung für Bar, Bordell und Bordstein* 1/1, Berlin. Hydra library, Berlin, Germany.

H N [Hydra-Nachtexpress für Bar, Bordell und Bordstein] (eds.) (1981): *Nachtexpress: Zeitung für Bar, Bordell und Bordstein*, 4, Berlin. Hydra library, Berlin, Germany.

H N [Hydra-Nachtexpress Zeitung für Bar, Bordell und Bordstein] (eds.) (1983): *Nacht-Express: Zeitung für Bar, Bordell und Bordstein* 4, Berlin. Hydra library, Berlin, Germany.

H N [Hydra-Nachtexpress Zeitung für Bar, Bordell und Bordstein] (eds.) (1984): *Nacht-Express: Zeitung für Bar, Bordell und Bordstein* 5, Berlin. Hydra library, Berlin, Germany.

H N [Hydra Nachtexpress Zeitung für Bar, Bordell und Bordstein] (eds.) (1988): *Nacht-Express: Zeitung für Bar, Bordell und Bordstein* 8, Berlin. Hydra library, Berlin, Germany.

H N [Hydra Nachtexpress Zeitung für Bar, Bordell und Bordstein] (eds.) (1992/1993): *Nacht-Express: Zeitung für Bar, Bordell und Bordstein* 11, Berlin. Hydra library, Berlin, Germany.

H N [Hydra Nachtexpress Zeitung für Bar, Bordell und Bordstein] (eds.). (1995): *Nacht-Express: Zeitung für Bar, Bordell und Bordstein* 12, Berlin. Hydra library, Berlin, Germany.

Jäkl, Reingard (1987): *Vergnügungsgewerbe rund um den Bülowbogen*, Berlin.

Kuhn, Armin (2014): *Vom Häuserkampf zur neoliberalen Stadt. Besetzungsbewegungen und Stadterneuerung in Berlin und Barcelona*, Münster: Westfälisches Dampfboot.

Künkel, Jenny (2020): *Sex, Drugs & Control. Das Regieren von Sexarbeit in der neoliberalen Stadt*, Münster: Westfälisches Dampfboot.

Löw, Martina/Ruhne, Renate (2011): *Prostitution. Herstellungsweisen einer anderen Welt*, Berlin: Suhrkamp.

LSVD Verband Queere Vielfalt (o.J.): »Paragraph 175 STGB: Verbot von Homosexualität in Deutschland,« in: *LSVD Verband Queere Vielfalt*, https://www.lsvd.de/de/ct/1022-Paragraph-175-StGB-Verbot-von-Homosexualitaet-in-Deutschland#:~:text=Mit%20dem%20 4.,Homosexualität%20auf%2018%20 Jahre%20festgesetzt, accessed June 23, 2025.

Mac, Juno/Smith, Molly (2020): *Revolting prostitutes. The fight for sex workers' rights*, London: Verso.

Majewska, Ewa (2021): *Feminist antifascism. Counterpublics of the common*, London: Verso.

Markert, Joy/Nägele, Sibylle (2011): *Die Potsdamer Straße. Geschichten, Mythen und Metamorphosen*, 2th edition, Berlin: Metropol.

OoD [Objects of Desire] (2019a): »Introduction,« in: *archive of Schwules Museum*, Berlin, Germany, Ka/400/Obj/1.

OoD [Objects of Desire] (2019b): »Knife,« in: *Objects of Desire*, https://www.projectofdesire.co.uk/knife-messer/, accessed July 17, 2024.

Opprower, Rolf (1957): »Die drei Gesichter der Potsdamer Straße,« in: *Archive of Museen Tempelhof-Schöneberg*, Berlin, Germany.

plu [Plarre, Plutonia] (1981): »Triebe und Untriebe auf der Potse,« [newspaper article in TAZ September 29, 1981], in: *Das feministische Archiv FFBIZ*, Berlin, Germany, A Rep. 400 Berlin 2.15.

Proeger, Willi (1930): *Stätten der Berliner Prostitution. Von den Elends-Absteigequartieren am Schlesischen Bahnhof und Alexanderplatz. Zur Luxus-Prostitution der Friedrichsstraße und des Kurfürstendamms*, Berlin: Auffenberg Verlagsgesellschaft, in Archive of Schwules Museum, Berlin, Germany.

P H [Prostituiertenprojekt Hydra] (1988): *Beruf. Hure*, Hamburg: Galgenberg.

Savier, Monika/Eichelkraut, Rita/Simon, Andrea/Cramon-Daiber, Birgit (1987): *Licht- und Schattenseiten: Forschungspraxis Mädchenarbeit*, München: Frauenoffensive.

Schmidt-Relenberg, Norbert/Kärner, Hartmut/Pieper, Richard (1975): *Strichjungen-Gespräche. Zur Soziologie jugendlicher Homosexuellen-Prostitution*, Darmstadt and Neuwied: Sammlung Leuchterhand, in Archive of Schwules Museum, Berlin, Germany.

Sontheimer, Michael (1991): »Die Domestizierung einer wilden Meile. Mythos Potsdamer Straße: Der ambivalente Charme ist dahin / Die wahre Potsdamer ist eine Straße der Erinnerung,« in: *Archive of Museen Tempelhof-Schöneberg*, Berlin, Germany.

Tagesspiegel (1985): »*Die Potsdamer Straße soll auch sozial saniert werden. Von Abrissen wird Verdrängung des kriminellen Milieus erwartet*,« [newspaper article October 6, 1985], in: Archive of Museen Tempelhof-Schöneberg, Berlin, Germany.

TAZ [newspaper] (1988): »Mit dem Bulldozer die Probleme verschoben. Die Sanierung der Potsdamer Straße nähert sich dem Ende – ein Fazit von Beteiligten,« in: *Archive of Museen Tempelhof-Schöneberg*, Berlin, Germany.

Verso (n.d.a.): »Juno Mac,« in: *Verso*, https://www.versobooks.com/blogs/authors/mac-juno, accessed July 18, 2025.

Verso (n.d.b.): »Molly Smith,« in: *Verso*, https://www.versobooks.com/blogs/authors/smith-molly, accessed July 18, 2025.

Winter, Rainer (2011): »Ein Plädoyer für kritische Perspektiven in der qualitativen Forschung,« in: *Forum Qualitative Sozialforschung*, 12, No. 1, Art. 7 Januar 2011. doi: 10.17169/fqs-12.1.1583

Dimensions of Architectural Knowledge, 2024–08 ꝺ
https://doi.org/10.14361/dak-2024-0805

Staying with the Trouble:
Feminist Spatial Practices and Hybrid Agency in Slovakia and the Czech Republic

Lýdia Grešáková

Abstract: This article presents the experience of organizations working in the field of feminist spatial practice in Slovakia and the Czech Republic. It thus gives attention to countries where such practice is not yet part of the formal planning context, understood as traditional top-down approaches led by state institutions, architectural studios, and planning education. The article aims to bring this practice into the local design discourse, and with it, contribute to changing the discourse toward better responsiveness and building capacity to generate positive change. In doing so, the article draws on the perspectives of *Feminism for the 99%* by Arruzza, Bhattacharya, and Fraser (2019), as well as those of hybridity and fluidity by Haraway (2008, 2016). It links these to situated examples from research of practitioners and alliances between architects, NGOs, educators, and community groups working with marginalized communities, such as Roma, long-term unemployed women, families facing homelessness, natural actors (e.g., pollinating insects), and others. I argue they can serve as an inspiration beyond the region for a unique spatial practice that addresses interconnected issues of social, gender, ethnic, and environmental justice.

Keywords: Spatial Practice; Spatial Sociology; Feminism for the 99%; More-Than-Human World; Feminist Planning; CEE Region; Slovakia; Czechia.

Corresponding author: Lýdia Grešáková (Spolka, Slovakia); lydia@spolka.cc; https://orcid.org/0009-0009-1941-264X

Introduction

Over the last 50 years, feminist approaches have gradually been integrated into planning practice. In Western countries like Germany and the USA, feminist planning has become institutionalized as a practice that critically examines how planning decisions are made, whose interests they serve, and whose voices are excluded (Angeles 2023). However, in Slovakia and the Czech Republic – historically interconnected countries – such institutionalization has not yet occurred. Due to their unique history, including a weak emancipation movement in the 1960s and the rejection of collectivity, which for many symbolizes pre-1989 politics and way of life, the region has reinforced a paradigm of individualization and privatization that dominates architecture and planning. This shift replaced the socialist-era ethos of collective provision with market-driven priorities and diminished public responsibility for the built environment (Lokšová 2023; Lokšová/Batista 2021; Moravčíková 2023; Moravčíková et al. 2023). Formal institutions often perpetuate top-down approaches, distancing themselves from care-oriented or intersectional practices, leaving spatial practitioners with limited avenues to challenge systemic inequalities, exacerbated by multidimensional crises.

Crises like environmental degradation, housing precarity, and the fallout of neoliberal capitalism demand a rethinking of architecture as a discipline. Naomi Klein (2007; 2023) describes neoliberalism as exploitative, deepening inequalities and neglecting care. The current political emphasis on capital accumulation overlooks socio-spatial aspects that do not align with neoliberal values of growth and efficiency, neglecting long-term planetary care, as well as human and non-human habitability (Fitz/Krasny 2019: 12). Since planning shapes our social environment, incorporating diverse perspectives, particularly from marginalized groups, is crucial to approach any crisis. While feminist spatial practices remain informal in Slovakia, the Czech Republic, and other Central and Eastern European (CEE) countries, many non-profit organizations and collectives incorporate feminist values into planning, advocating for care, equity, and inclusion in co-creating neighborhoods, cities, and regions. These initiatives exemplify hybrid approaches to systemic transformation that prioritize social and ecological justice.

In this article, I challenge the paradigm in two ways. First, I position feminist spatial practices within broader planning debates amidst crises, integrating them into the planning discourse of CEE countries. Drawing on *Feminism for the 99%* (Arruzza/Bhattacharya/Fraser 2019) and Haraway's concepts of fluidity and hybridity (Haraway 1988; 2008; 2016), I explore how Slovak and Czech feminist practitioners challenge global paradigms of growth and efficiency while addressing local nuances. Rooted in inter-sectionality and solidarity, these practices offer a framework for urban change that connects social, gender, ethnic, and environmental justice. This article reflects a long-term approach developed by the feminist spatial practice collective Spolka of which I am a member, which engages with the local history and complexities of the socialist past (Grešáková/Tabačková/Révészová 2020). Secondly, by highlighting relational, hybrid methodologies, I show how CEE approaches can enrich global frameworks, bridging local contexts with planetary care (Fitz/Krasny 2019: 12). Although CEE showcases intense neoliberalism, its rapid adoption makes it a crucial site for exploring how systemic shifts, including transitions toward care-driven frameworks, can be embraced and scaled.

Planning with Care and Beyond Gender

Before exploring methodologies and approaches, key terms must be defined. Feminist theorist bell hooks often argued that feminism, transcending gender, envisions rights for all bodies and identities (hooks in Schalk et al. 2017: 13). Feminism has evolved through waves including postcolonial, queer, ecofeminism and the fourth digital wave represented by move-ments against gender-based violence like #NiUnaMenos (Not One Less) or #MeToo. In Slovakia and the Czech Republic, contemporary feminism inte-grates intersectional perspectives, considering how gender, race, and class shape spatial experiences and inequalities. For this text, the *Feminism for the 99%* manifesto by Arruzza, Bhattacharya, and Fraser (2019) offers a rele-vant framework. It critiques mainstream feminism, often led by privileged white women, for overlooking economic and social inequalities affecting the majority. The manifesto calls for an anti-capitalist feminism rooted in solidarity, which recognizes how gender, race, and class oppressions are interconnected. In spatial practice, this translates to designing inclusive, accessible, and safe environments that reflect the diverse needs of people. In addition to human-centered considerations, integrating more-than-human perspectives – encompassing animals, plants, ecosystems, and non-living elements – into feminism is increasingly crucial. Haraway's (2008; 2016) work highlights the symbiotic relationships found in nature, such as those between fungi and algae in lichens, illustrating the resilience and mutual benefit of these interactions.

The link between feminism and planning, particularly in terms of power dynamics and structures, is well explored by Angeles (2023). Feminist planning ethics emphasize holistic approaches, care, empathy, rights, justice, and a balance between individual and collective responsibility, freedom, and duty. Angeles highlights intersectionality as a key analytical framework for spatial practice, helping to address inequality, injustice, and diversity by considering the intersecting identities through which different actors experience urban spaces and policies. This approach reveals how power relations reinforce marginalization. To return to Haraway's (2016) linked encounters, *staying with the trouble* and embedding it in narratives creates counter-narratives and can foster control over meanings and representations of marginalized experiences, contributing to broader social changes, such as their recognition in formal practice. This shows that applying the idea of a more-than-human world to spatial practice involves recognizing the entanglements between human and non-human actors and fostering environments that support this interdependence.

This article situates these frameworks in the context of crises, both as structural failures in built environments and as reflections of broader systemic injustices. Slovakia and the Czech Republic face pressing challenges including climate change, war-related migration, insufficient social protection, and housing affordability, where apartment prices reach nearly 13 times the average annual salary, alternately placing both countries among those with the highest housing inaccessibility (Linhart et al. 2024: 28 in Grešáková/ Mravčáková 2025: 7). Naomi Klein's (2007) critique of neoliberalism explains how crises like these are often exploited to deepen inequalities and reinforce market-driven development at the expense of collective well-being. Feminist spatial practice, by drawing on diverse methodologies, responds to them by proposing inclusive frameworks that address intersecting forms of marginalization (Roberts/Aiken 2023) and reimagine environments as sites of repair, care, and shared agency (Fitz/Krasny 2019). Examples include »experimental pedagogies, expanded histories, embodied theories, collaborative practices, spaces for non-conforming bodies and alternative materialities« (Roberts/ Aiken 2023), or »making differently« – that is, creating space through inclusive, justice-centered practices (Petrescu 2007; Schalk et. al. 2017: 15; Houston et al. 2018).

Peripheral Matters and Global Connections

Central and Eastern European cities have been explored by several theorists (e.g. Ferenčová/Gentile 2016; Chelcea/Druță 2016; Grubbauer 2012; Hirt 2012; 2013; Kalmar 2024; Krivý 2020; Kubeš 2013; Lokšová/Batista 2021; Tuvikene 2016; Wiest 2012), who have addressed the transformations of spatial practice and housing since the 1990s, often focusing on the socialist legacy and its rejection. The transition away from socialist planning reflected an orientation toward a market economy with minimal social aspects. This lack of social approaches influenced the spatial organization of post-socialist cities, marked by suburbanization, segregation, gentrification, and the commodification of architecture. The decline of public spaces and socially oriented planning continues to this day (Hirt 2012: 34-59, Krivý 2020), as illustrated by the under-maintained yet still-used urban space in Košice (fig. 1). Such spaces highlight the tension between institutional neglect and informal appropriation by marginalized groups.

The reorientation toward market values has been described as a process in which neoliberal policies exploit the »zombie socialism« – the lingering trauma of the previous regime – by using this narrative to justify the privatization of public assets and suppress social resistance (Chelcea/Druță 2016: 525). This includes selling state buildings, eroding public infrastructure, and undermining 20th-century architecture under the guise of modernization. But there is also poor support for education, health, social affairs, culture and the environment. These characteristics are encompassed under the term »post-socialist« city. However, as Ferenčuhová (2016) argues, the research on post-socialist cities and the term itself have limitations, including overlooking regional diversity and relying on knowledge from a few major cities (Kubeš 2013: 23). For this reason, it is challenging to rely on knowledge of the so-called post-socialist city to achieve a deep understanding of the context of »the periphery,« local (responsive) spatial practice, and its nuances.

In Slovakia and the Czech Republic, formal planning focuses on architecture and urbanism, separating them from social processes involving people, technology, animals, and plants. It is important to note here that, as observed in both contexts, the teaching of spatial practice as an interdisciplinary field of planning is virtually non-existent. There is also a lack of basic data, such as housing realities and conditions like the number of empty homes or rental practices (Grešáková/Mravčáková 2025). In response, informal and interdisciplinary practices have emerged to fill these gaps. Initiatives like Projekt

1.
An under-maintained space in one of Košice's housing estates, dating from the socialist era, photographed during field research. It remains in everyday use, particularly by those excluded from privatized leisure infrastructure.
Photograph by Lýdia Grešáková, 2021.

DOM.ov (10 years) and Nadácia DEDO (25 years) support families without adequate housing in Eastern Slovakia, collecting data and advocating for inclusive approaches that challenge neoliberal productivity logics (Gabauer et al. 2022; Jesenková 2016; Tronto 1993). These efforts resonate with feminist spatial practices abroad, as shown by the expanding online platform Feminist Spatial Practices[1] and *Arch+* issue on contemporary feminist spatial practices (Makele et al. 2023). Both highlight intersectional methodologies addressing systemic inequalities in urban and architectural paradigms, emphasizing the importance of linking local initiatives to global dialogues on care ethics, inclusion, and equitable development. Central and Eastern Europe's socio-political context offers distinct insights into these discussions, particularly through the lens of post-socialist transformation and its ongoing spatial challenges.

Research Methods and Approach

In the following section, the experiences of 21 organizations will illustrate what feminist spatial practice means in the Slovak and Czech context, how the term is used, and the type of experience it brings in terms of urban change for the region and beyond. This article is based on qualitative research methods inspired by Nedbálková (2015) and conducted with my colleague Tabačková (2022) in 2021 in Slovakia and the Czech Republic, including semi-structured interviews, ethnographic observations, photographs, videos, and textual analysis of materials from the organizations studied. These materials were analyzed through inductive qualitative coding in Atlas.ti, clustering recurring themes, comparing quotations across interviews, and creating interactive network citation maps to trace relationships between values, practices, and ideas. My reflections and experiences, documented in a field diary, were integral to shaping data interpretation, following feminist research principles (Jenkins/Narayanaswamy/Sweetman 2019: 424–425).

The organizations were identified using the snowball method, resulting in nearly 250 contacts before referrals began to repeat. These were sorted based on five main criteria. First, drawing on *Feminism for the 99%* (Arruzza/Bhattacharya/Fraser 2019), we focused on organizations that highlight marginalized perspectives and give voice to those often excluded from

---

1 https://feministspatialpractices.com/, accessed October 20, 2024.

formal spatial practice. Second, in the context of feminist spatial practice, we sought to translate individual efforts into broader, interdisciplinary collective action, emphasizing collectives that aim to shape the future of places. The third criterion was the frequency of referrals and their activity over the last five years, focusing on current practice and engagement with contemporary challenges. The fourth criterion was geography, ensuring a mix of collectives from both capitals and smaller cities, capturing urban, rural, and landscape experiences. Finally, we considered the scale of planning, including practices that range from local neighborhoods to national initiatives. In total, we contacted 7 practitioners in Slovakia, 13 in the Czech Republic, and one organization active in both countries. The 21 initiatives featured are introduced through their own narratives, with brief contextual details at first mention. A comparative table (fig. 4) further supports the overview, outlining their focus areas, modes of work, and scale. This format allows for a concise presentation while supporting the broader analysis developed in the text.

Most organizations were visited in person. While we sought a broad geographical context, more than half of the Czech organizations interviewed are based in Prague, though they collaborate regionally. In contrast, only three interviews took place in Slovakia's capital, with the majority based in regions outside it. Slovak organizations tend to be less interconnected but often collaborate with Czech counterparts, especially in fields like housing, for example, with Platforma pro sociální bydlení (Platform for Social Housing). This aligns with Ferenčuhová's (2016) observations on the unique contexts of Central and Eastern European countries. The infrastructure for feminist spatial practice is closely tied to location and networks. For this study, I grouped the organizations by the marginalized perspectives they aim to include in formal planning. This reflects my own analytical framework and acknowledges significant overlaps: people cycling and walking; people in housing need; public space for the 99 percent; post-coal and post-industrial landscapes; and more-than-human actors. These categories reflect responses to interconnected crises in both countries – including, among others, car-centric infrastructure, housing shortages, the privatization of public spaces, the erosion of environmental and architectural heritage, post-industrial employment loss, and the ecological impacts of the climate crisis.

Narratives of Communication Partners

>It's simply a question of what feminism means to whom. To me, feminism actually means equality for everybody, which means like non-egoistic planning, which means planning where you can just walk down the street, where other species can live, where you actually feel safe. [...] It's not just for women's equality, it's for everyone's equality.« (COLridor, design collective focused on more-than-human actors such as pollinators and bats, through community events)

In the narratives of the communication partners, a common observation emerged at the end of the interviews. Those who address the needs of vulnerable or excluded groups, whose voices are often overlooked in planning, automatically find themselves aligned with some form of feminist planning, even if they had not explicitly identified as feminist before, »because that is a concept that I think is closer to that theme of vulnerability and inclusion than, like, the standard traditional attitude that we have here« (Nadácia DEDO, focused on people in housing need). What is meant here by the standard or traditional approach is top-down planning, carried out by formal architectural studios or city departments, without the involvement of other disciplines or actors in a given space. If there is a conscious overlap with anti-capitalist planning that addresses the needs of more than just female users (aligned with feminist spatial practice for the 99 percent) this typically only becomes apparent after deeper discussion of individual values in collectives. Our questioning allowed the communication partners to indicate whether they perceived themselves as a feminist spatial practitioner and, if so, what kind of feminist thinking they reflected, according to the political, ideological, but also religious or cultural influences and preferences of individual members.

In defining feminist spatial practice, two-thirds of communication partners linked it primarily to women's equal rights in design, focusing on issues like space accessibility for women with strollers and gender representation in organizations. Values such as solidarity, justice, transparency, diversity, and care were seen as personal approaches rather than team-wide strategies. Practices that view feminist spatial practice as part of the broader struggle against patriarchy often emphasize supporting vulnerable groups but do not necessarily align with global feminist spatial approaches (such as in Schalk et. al. 2017 or Makele et al. 2023). There is often confusion between inclusion and equality in the field, which several of them were themselves clarifying for the first time only during the interview:

> »What is important, apart from this sort of interdependence and equality, is some form of plurality, that at the same time it is very important for us that the world is not as if it is universal, but that it is, that it is actually very diverse, and to continue to encourage that diversity. Because then it is, the world becomes more resilient as well, I think, through that plurality.« (Spolka, non-profit architecture and sociology studio focused on public space for the 99 percent, through education and participatory design).

As Coleman (1996: XII) argues, simply changing the surface-level rules of inclusion does not bring about meaningful shifts in architectural culture. Through my analysis, I observe a similar pattern: the appearance of inclusion or representation often fails to challenge the deeper, underlying power dynamics in patriarchal structures. This highlights the importance of addressing multiple layers of inequality, such as class differences, ethnicity, economic status, and even post-anthropocentric concerns. The feminist spatial practices I explore align with the notion of serving the 99 percent. However, delving into the complexities of their practice reveals the multifaceted challenges of the region, offering a new dimension to their work.

Qualities of Local Spatial Practice

Some collectives face challenges like privatization, market-driven priorities, and weak support systems, which hinder their ability to fully develop practices for the 99 percent. However, I suggest that their engagement in a distinct context, different from typical examples of good practice, serves as a powerful aspect of their feminist spatial work, offering inspiration beyond regional borders. A core feature of their practice, aligned with Arruzza, Bhattacharya, and Fraser's manifesto (2019), is amplifying marginalized voices by collecting and sharing data to make these perspectives visible within power structures. This approach mirrors global feminist spatial practices, such as those outlined in *Contemporary Feminist Spatial Practices* (Makele et al. 2023), where similar strategies challenge dominant structures. These activities include contributing to city strategies, monitoring development plans, providing early feedback, and engaging in personal

2.
Coburg Manor House, Jelšava. A late-18th-century Baroque and French classicist residence on Renaissance foundations, gradually restored since 2015. Čierne diery made parts of the decaying site accessible to the public through minimal interventions; the 2021 tourist-cells project won the CE ZA AR Architecture Award, and in 2024 the group received the Patron of Architecture Award for their heritage work. Photograph by Lýdia Grešáková, 2021.

activism – practices often undertaken by the interviewed collectives. For example, organizations focusing on public space for the 99 percent emphasize mapping, gathering input for planning documents, and analyzing data to support regeneration and care through positive narratives.

Several collectives also adopt the principle of hybridity. One such group, Čierne Diery (Black Holes), focuses on the care of abandoned technical and modernist buildings through graphic design and storytelling. Another, Včelí kraj (Bee County), promotes pollinators and green diversity through education and social entrepreneurship. Both create adaptive frameworks for power dynamics: rather than negotiating between the dominant and the marginalized, they inhabit both positions simultaneously. In doing so, they embody the hybridity and fluidity Haraway (2008) describes, working within systems to transform them from the inside. This approach is reflected in their emphasis on accessibility and ethical engagement in everyday practice.

»The graphics we do are fixed price so that everyone can afford it. And we could sell it for a lot more, and only the rich could afford it, but we don't really want to. You know, that, and then that spills over into other areas actually, that what we do is that we (invest) our own money in projects that we don't want to generate profit. […] Like in a sense, we are some kind of a mover in that today we can already buy some objects in the regions and bring some new function there. And then something else will be packed onto them like a magnet. I mean, first of all, they will be that center where people will go and explore the surroundings and so on, and they will also be an inspiration for various other projects and so on. So that's where it's like so moving.« (Čierne Diery, focused on post-coal and post-industrial landscape).

While on the one hand, Čierne Diery popularizes abandoned regions, their success in selling stories and graphics about buildings in such regions funds their other, less publicized projects with a social dimension, such as supporting a local non-profit organization engaged in the restoration of the Coburg manor house in Jelšava (fig. 2) or the purchase and a reconstruction of a house for social housing. Their approach is built on storytelling and positivity, avoiding the direct enumeration of positive examples and ideological narratives that may not resonate effectively, but instead opting for a nuanced presentation aimed at communicating knowledge within local legislative frameworks, narratives and networks of relationships.

3.
A photograph of the Kokava nad Rimavicou area, home to the Včelí kRaj (Bee County) initiative, capturing the atmosphere of the part of Slovakia often referred to as a »forgotten region.« Photograph by Lýdia Grešáková, 2021.

Another attribute of this hybridity is the promotion of diversity, alongside Haraway's (2016) idea of staying with the trouble and spending time in place. Similar to Čierne Diery, several communication partners working in post-industrial areas often describe their regions as »forgotten« and refer to them as »hungry valleys« with great potential for transformation (fig. 3). These regions are home to three of the four organizations presented above, all of which engage with more-than-human actors – modernist monuments, pollinating insects, birds, and natural landscapes. Their motivation lies in pursuing a just transformation of local life, with a nuanced understanding of complex issues. These areas face high unemployment and significant socio-economic disparities, particularly in education and the number of excluded localities. A fair transformation would reduce inequalities, but current funding often benefits large coal companies, continuing exploitation. Despite this, these organizations narrate their local society in their own terms.

»Last year, for example, we did a climate ride, which we're going to do again this year, which is about getting to know people from the coal regions and actually having some space for them to talk about their ideas about the future of those regions and what they can want from the climate movement and how we can work with them. So that it's not just some paternalistic stuff that we export to some so-called regions, but rather that we have that relationship mutually and it's based on trust and that we want to do things together. So we're going to repeat that this year to foster those bonds and friendships.« (Limity jsme my, focused on post-coal and post-industrial landscape, through direct action and community engagement).

By staying in the places they work for long periods, these organizations foster active dialogue across different frameworks, creating space for care. I argue that this strengthens and connects communities, making their engagement in spatial practice and aftercare more qualitative and sustainable. This process takes different forms: for some, it's through touring and storytelling; for others, it's about creating activities that encourage slowing down and doing nothing, in contrast to performative actions.

Evolving Dialogue in Local Feminist Spatial Practice

However, not all actors identified their organizations as part of feminist spatial practice. This applies to MAK / Mobilní architektonická kancelář and Punkt, both of which focus on public space for the 99 percent through temporary interventions and participatory workshops, as well as Projekt DOM.ov, which addresses housing needs. The MAK interviewee expressed limited engagement with feminist values, which may relate to the perspective of the male individual interviewed. Projekt DOM.ov and Punkt reject feminism due to its negative associations – specifically, in Projekt DOM.ov's case, which is linked to Christian beliefs and conservative debates around so-called »gender ideology.« Punkt, meanwhile, hesitates toward feminism partly because they perceive it as a controversial or divisive term, sometimes even as a »f-word,« which they feel may create barriers to engagement. These positions resonate with Coleman's (1996: X) observation that feminism can be misunderstood or even feared, including among women themselves. Despite this, these organizations are significant for their community-focused work. Other collectives either identify as feminist spatial practitioners or aspire to be, with many newly recognizing feminist principles and evolving beyond traditional gender roles. The limits of research are temporal, feminist spatial practice is growing, and since then, new initiatives such as Kafkárna (Center for Arts and Ecology UMPRUM) and Sady Vihorlatu (Vihorlat orchards) have emerged. Activist groups such as Limity jsme my (Limits are us) may face challenges in a political climate hostile to marginalized perspectives, underscoring the need for further exploration of these organizations' values and dynamics.

As Terezie Lokšová (2023) and the Office of the Plenipotentiary for the Development of Civil Society (Úrad splnomocnenca 2020) observe, the growing emphasis on participation in Slovakia and the Czech Republic has been shaped by successive waves of participatory governance, strongly influenced by the processes and conditional requirements linked to EU accession in 2004. This shift altered institutional rules and the rhetoric around partnership. While city planning institutions like IPR (Institute of Planning and Development Prague) and MIB (Metropolitan Institute Bratislava) have started incorporating participatory spatial practices, both Slovakia and the Czech Republic face challenges in adopting successful foreign examples. This difficulty stems from a lack of education and employment opportunities in the field, as well as policy differences on marginalized issues such as environmental needs. These gaps highlight a fundamental challenge in the region. Although local efforts aim to integrate the architectural profession into socially and politically active, multidisciplinary roles, these attempts are often stifled by post-socialist attitudes and a deep-rooted respect for private property over the public interest (Moravčíková 2023: 219). Furthermore, NGOs – who often have a longer history of reflecting diverse, localized solutions – remain excluded from formal planning processes and continue to work independently. I argue that this independent approach should be more formally recognized and supported. Forming broader alliances could help overcome local challenges, aligning with recent insights on knowledge production and the transformation of spatial practice (Tabačková 2022).

Lastly, for those working in hybrid feminist spatial practice, it presents both opportunities and challenges. While hybridity can foster care and adaptability, I note that it may also reinforce dominant systems if collectives fail to challenge existing structures. In Slovakia, the current political climate poses significant obstacles, with government actions suppressing marginalized perspectives, including attacks on migrants, LGBTQ+ rights, and cultural and climate measures. The non-profit sector faces threats from funding cuts and restrictive policies. Despite these challenges, hybridity holds potential for resilience if it prioritizes forward-looking strategies.

While this research has provided valuable insights into feminist spatial practice, it is limited by its inability to fully explore the internal dynamics of organizations and their alignment with stated values.

Conclusion

This article explores spatial practices from Slovakia and the Czech Republic that engage with intersecting crises of care, housing, and the environment, responding not through abstract utopias, but through situated, collective agency. Emerging from a context shaped by decades of privatization, dismantled infrastructures, and regional inequalities, these practices exemplify Haraway's (2016) concept of *staying with the trouble*: working within the constraints of local contexts to envision more just and livable futures. Although not always explicitly feminist, these practices align with feminist spatial values such as solidarity, inclusion, intersectionality, anti-capitalism, and care for both human and non-human life (Angeles 2023; Arruzza/Bhattacharya/Fraser 2019). I argue that their key contribution lies in a hybrid approach that integrates professional, activist, and lived knowledge, navigating the contradictions between state neglect and civic responsibility. Unlike some Western practices, which often take resistance or counter-hegemonic positions, these practices work within and across dominant political structures, creating space for alternatives to emerge from within the system itself. This hybrid positioning is particularly relevant in the Slovak and Czech context, where neoliberal frameworks are deeply embedded in local realities, shaping engagement with existing political and economic structures. The feminist spatial imaginaries offered by these practices are both grounded and generative, fostering diverse ways of knowing and acting. Such feminist hybridities, while locally rooted, transcend national borders, creating points of resonance without generalizing. To address today's intersecting crises, architecture must learn from these practices, not as exceptions, but as part of a broader shift toward collective, care-based, and politically situated spatial work. Such an approach not only responds to the challenges of resource-depleting capitalism with greater nuance but also fosters transnational feminist solidarity and inspires collective, care-based futures – highlighting the role of collaboration and alliances, including with marginalized groups, as key to gradual transformations within entrenched systems.

Name	Marginalized perspective	Marginalized perspective (grouped)
Auto*Mat	sustainable mobility (walking, cycling, public transport) and the people who use it	People cycling and walking
Cyklokoalícia	sustainable mobility (cycling) and the people who use it	People cycling and walking
Pešky městem (before as Pražské matky – Prague mothers)	sustainable mobility, children and youth, safe routes to school	People cycling and walking
»Bedřiška (pře)žije!«	housing of mostly Roma families in housing crisis	People in housing need
Nadácia DEDO	housing of homeless people, vulnerable families, children and youth	People in housing need
Projekt DOM.ov	housing of Roma families	People in housing need
Realistická utópia Veľký Krtíš (RUVK)	post-coal country transformation, mostly Roma families in housing crisis	People in housing need
Architekti bez Hranic	segregated people and localities/objects	Public space for the 99 %
MAK / mobilní architektonická kancelář	space and life quality in suburbs	Public space for the 99 %
Pěstuj prostor	space and life quality in Plzeň, participation of all local actors	Public space for the 99 %
Punkt	space and life quality, participation of all local actors	Public space for the 99 %
RESET: Platforma pro sociálně-ekologickou transformaci	just transformation for the 99% (natural world, public spaces, housing)	Public space for the 99 %
Spolka	space and life quality, participation of all local actors	Public space for the 99 %
Ateliér • Tečka	space and life quality in post-coal region	Post-coal and post-industrial landsca
Čierne Diery	stagnating technical and modernist buildings	Post-coal and post-industrial landsca
Galerie Hraničář	space and life quality in post-coal region	Post-coal and post-industrial landsca
Limity jsme my	space and life quality in post-coal region	Post-coal and post-industrial landsca
Arnika	space and life quality in relation to the natural world	More-than-human actors
COLridor /COLL COLL	insect pollinators, birds – bats	More-than-human actors
LES - společenství pro pěstování, teorii a umění	more-than-humans in the forest	More-than-human actors
Včelí kRaj	insect pollinators, butterflies, heterogeneity of vegetation	More-than-human actors

4.

Table of collectives and companies with situated-spatial practices based in the Czech Republic and Slovakia. Table by Lýdia Grešáková.

terdisciplinarity of the collective (active in last 5 yrs)	Location	Office	Scale
ban planning, sociology, social anthropology, urbanism, odesy, transportation engineering,...	CZ, all	CZ, Praha	neighborhood, city, country
ban planning, geography, beekeeping	SK, Bratislava	SK, Bratislava	city
chitecture, sociology, social anthropology, transportation gineering,...	CZ, Praha	CZ, Praha	neighborhood, city, country
chitecture, sociology, social work,...	CZ, Ostrava	CZ, Praha	neighborhood
cial work, law, international relations, mass media commu- ation,...	SK, Košice	SK, Košice	city
chitecture, social work, education,...	SK, Prešov, Rankovce	SK, Prešov, Rankovce	neighborhood
chitecture, social anthropology, social geography, graphic de- n, law, information studies and librarianship, social work, art	SK, Veľký Krtíš –CZ, Brno	SK, Veľký Krtíš –CZ, Brno	neighborhood
chitecture, graphic design, social work	CZ, Praha	CZ, Praha	object
hitecture	CZ, suburbs of big cities	CZ, Praha	neighborhood
hitecture, landscape architecture, sociology, art,...	CZ, Plzeň	CZ, Plzeň	city
hitecture, cultural studies, photography, art, sociology	SK, Bratislava	SK, Bratislava	neighborhood
iology, social anthropology, environmental science,...	CZ, all	CZ, Brno	region, country
hitecture, sociology	SK, Košice	SK, Košice	neighborhood, city, region
architecture – but collaborating widely outside of their anization	CZ, north-west /post-coal area	CZ, Praha	city, region
hitecture, journalism, graphic design	SK, Gemer area	SK, Bratislava	object
hitecture, environmental science, art and design, curator- ,...	CZ, Ústí nad Labem	CZ, Ústí nad Labem	city
ironmental science, sociology, social anthropology, art,...	CZ, north-west /post-coal area	CZ, all	region, country
hitecture, sociology, environmental science, economy,...	CZ, all	CZ, Praha	country
hitecture, biology	CZ, Praha	CZ, Praha	object
education, permaculture design and gardening,...	CZ, Hnátnice	CZ, Hnátnice	region
scape architecture, beekeeping	SK, Kokava nad Rimavicou	SK, Kokava nad Rimavicou	neighborhood, city, region

Acknowledgment

The members of Spolka laid the foundation for this work through their own collective efforts. I am especially thankful to Zuzana Tabačková, with whom I developed the idea and methodology, and conducted 21 interviews with spatial practice collectives in Slovakia and the Czech Republic, which are presented in this paper. Thanks to the research supervisors: Maria Beňačková Rišková, Adriana Jesenkova, Zuzana Tabačková, and Angela Million. This work was supported using by funding by the Slovak Arts Council.

References

Angeles, Leonora C. (2023): »Feminist planning in the face of power: from interests and ideologies to institutions and intersections,« in: Michael Gunder/ Kristina Grange/ Tanja Winkler (eds.), *Handbook on Planning and Power*, Cheltenham, UK: Edward Elgar Publishing, 289–304.

Arruzza, Cinzia/Bhattacharya, Tithi/Fraser, Nancy (2019): *Feminism for the 99 percent: a manifesto*, London; Brooklyn, NY: Verso.

Chelcea, Liviu/Druţă, Oana (2016): »Zombie socialism and the rise of neoliberalism in post-socialist Central and Eastern Europe,« in: *Eurasian Geography and Economics* 57(4-5): 521–544. doi: 10.1080/15387216.2016.1266273

Coleman, Debra (1996): »Introduction,« in: Carol Henderson/Debra Coleman/ Elizabeth Danze (eds.), *Architecture and Feminism*, New York: Princeton University Press.

Ferenčuhová, Slavomíra/Gentile, Michael (2016): »Introduction: Post-socialist Cities and Urban Theory,« in: *Eurasian Geography and Economics* 57/4–5: 483–496.

Ferenčuhová, Slavomíra (2016): »Explicit Definitions and Implicit Assumptions about Post-Socialist Cities in Academic Writings: Explicit Definitions and Implicit Assumptions,« in: *Geography Compass* 10: 514–524. doi: 10.1111/gec3.12282

Fitz, Angelika/Krasny, Elke (2019): »Introduction. Critical Care. Architecture and Urbanism for a Broken Planet,« in: Angelika Fitz/Elke Krasny (eds.), *Critical Care: Architecture and Urbanism for a Broken Planet*, Cambridge, Massachusetts: Architekturzentrum Wien and The MIT Press, 10–25.

Gabauer, Angelika/Knierbein, Sabine/ Cohen, Nir/Lebuhn, Henrik/Trogal, Kim/ Viderman, Tihomir/Haas, Tigran (eds.) (2022): *Care and the City: Encounters With Urban Studies*, New York and London: Routledge.

Grešáková, Lýdia/Mravčáková Viktória eds. (2025): *Bývanie v čase kríz. Housing in Times of Crisis*, Košice: Spolka/Bratislava: Kapitál.

Grešáková, Lýdia/Tabačková, Zuzana/ Révészová, Zuzana (2020), »Mapping with care as an outline for post neoliberal architecture methodologies – tools of the Never-never school,« in: *Architektúra & urbanizmus* 54/1–2: 6–19.

Grubbauer, Monika (2012), »Towards a more comprehensive notion of urban change: linking post-socialist urbanism and urban theory,« in: Joanna Kusiak/ Monika Grubbauer (eds), *Warsaw: Socio-Material. Socio-Material Dynamics of Urban Change since 1990*, Frankfurt, New York: Campus Verlag, 35–60.

Haraway, Donna (1988):»Situated knowledges: The science question in feminism and the privilege of partial perspective,« in: *Feminist Studies 14/3*: 575–599.

Haraway, Donna (2008): *When Species Meet*, Minneapolis, MN: University of Minnesota Press.

Haraway, Donna (2016): *Staying with the Trouble: Making Kin in the Chthulucene*, Durham: Duke University Press.

Hirt, Sonia A. (2012): *Iron Curtains: Gates, Suburbs and Privatization of Space in the Post-socialist City*, Oxford, Malden: Wiley-Blackwell.

Hirt, Sonia (2013), »Whatever happened to the (post)socialist city?,« in: *Cities 32/1*, S529–S538.

Houston, Donna/Hillier, Jean/MacCallum, Diana/Steele, Wendy/Byrne, Jason Antony (2018):»Make kin, not cities! Multispecies entanglements and ›becoming-world‹ in planning theory,« in: *Planning Theory*, 17/2: 190–212. doi: 10.1177/1473095216688042

Jenkins, Katy/Narayanaswamy, Lata/ Sweetman, Caroline (2019):»Introduction: Feminist values in research,« in: *Gender & Development 27/3*: 415–425. doi: 10.1080/13552074.2019.1682311

Jesenková, Adriana (2016): *Etika starostlivosti*, Košice: Univerzita Pavla Jozefa Šafárika v Košiciach.

Kalmar, Ivan (2024): *Bílí, ale ne tak docela Iliberální vzpoura ve střední Evropě*, Praha: Utopia Libri.

Klein, Naomi (2007): *The Shock Doctrine: The Rise of Disaster Capitalism*, New York: Henry Holt.

Krivý, Maroš (2020): »Faceless Concrete Monsters, ca. 1990,« in: Kenny Cupers/ Catharina Gabrielsson/Helena Mattsson (eds.), *Neoliberalism on the Ground: Architecture and Transformation from the 1960s to the Present*, Pittsburgh: University of Pittsburgh Press, 89–109.

Kubeš, Jan (2013):»European post-socialist cities and their near hinterland in intra-urban geography literature,« in: *Bulletin of Geography 19(2013)*: 19–43.

Lokšová, Terezie (2023): *Participace jako nástroj změny: historické trajektorie a současná uspořádání odborných rolí*. [Doctoral dissertation, Katedra sociologie, Fakulta sociálních studií Masarykovy univerzity v Brně].

Lokšová, Terezie/Batista, Lucie G. (2021), »Postsocialist suburban governmentality: A shift from reactive to proactive discourse in the case of Brno, Czech Republic,« in: *Cities 110*. doi: 10.1016/j. cities.2020.103074

Makele, Melissa/Ngo, Anh-Linh/ Lange, Torsten/Malterre-Barthes, Charlotte/Ortiz dos Santos, Daniela/Schaad, Gabrielle eds. (2023),»Contemporary Feminist Spatial Practices,« in: *ARCH+ 246*, https://archplus. net/en/archiv/english-publication/ Contemporary-Feminist-Spatial-Practices/, accessed October 18, 2024.

Moravčáková, Henrieta (2023), »Je verejné ozaj verejné? Alebo ako postsocialistická transformácia ovplyvnila chápanie verejného záujmu, verejného priestoru aj verejných budov,« in: Gabriela Smetanová/Henrieta Moravčíková/ Katarína Haberlandová/ Laura Krišteková/ Monika Bočková/Peter Szalay (eds.), *Správa o slovenskej architektúre*, Bratislava: Oddelenia architektúry Historického ústavu SAV, 203–232.

Moravčíková, Henrieta/Haberlandová, Katarína/Krišteková, Laura/Szalay, Peter/ Bočková, Monika/Smetanová, Gabriela (2023): *Správa o slovenskej architektúre*, Bratislava: Oddelenia architektúry Historického ústavu SAV.

Nedbálková, Kateřina (2015): »Ethnography, Fieldnotes, and Interviews,« in: Kateřina Nedbálková/ Kateřina Sidiropulu Janků (eds.), *Doing Research, Making Science: the Memory of Roma Workers*, Brno: CDK, 75–98.

Petrescu, Doina, (ed.) (2007): *Altering Practices: Politics and Poetics of Space*, London: Routledge.

Roberts, Bryony/Aiken, Abriannah (2023): »Feminist Spatial Practices, Part 1,« in: *Jencks Foundation*, https://www. jencksfoundation.org/explore/text/ feminist-spatial-practices-part-1, accessed October 20, 2024.

Schalk, Meike/Kristiansson, Thérèse/ Mazé, Ramia, eds. (2017): *Feminist Futures of Spatial Practice: Materialisms, Activisms, Dialogues, Pedagogies, Projections*, Baunach: AADR and Spurbuchverlag.

Tabačková, Zuzana (2022): »Transforming Spatial Practices Through Knowledges on the Margins,« in: *Urban Planning* 7/3: 219–229. doi: 10.17645/up.v7i3.5415

Tronto, Joan (1993): *Moral Boundaries: A Political Argument for an Ethic of Care*, New York: Routledge.

Tuvikene, Tauri (2016): »Strategies for comparative urbanism: post-socialism as a De-territorialized concept,« in: *International Journal of Urban and Regional Research* 40/1: 132–146.

Úrad splnomocnenca vlády SR pre rozvoj občianskej spoločnosti (2020): »Analýza socioekonomického prínosu neziskového sektora a stavu a trendov rozvoja občianskej spoločnosti,« in: *Ministerstvo vnútra SR*, https://www.minv. sk/swift_data/source/rozvoj_obcianskej_ spolocnosti/vyskum_neziskoveho_ sektora_a_obcianskej_spolocnosti/2020/ ANALYZA_NP%20VYSKUM_17.12.2020_ FINAL.pdf, accessed August 20, 2023.

Wiest, Karin (2012), »Comparative debates in post-socialist urban studies,« in: *Urban Geography* 33/6: 829–849.

ACTIVISM

Dimensions of Architectural Knowledge, 2024-08 ∂
https://doi.org/10.14361/dak-2024-0806

Architects as Climate-Activists

Armelle Breuil

Abstract: The intertwined crises of climate breakdown, socio-economic inequities, and ecological degradation demand urgent rethinking of architecture's role. How can we use our voices as architects in the climate crisis? How can we use our skills for the climate movement? How does the climate movement influence our practices?

The climate movement surge in 2018-2019 has given a boost to architects to involve themselves with activism and change their practice. Some have taken the decision to engage in civil disobedience, engaging their bodies and their time in the struggle. Following the path of three architect-activists, we will see how architects, primarily seen as designers of physical spaces, are increasingly called upon to address systemic challenges.

This paper explores the work of architect-activists Nick Newman, Tom Bennett, and Léa Hobson, examining their alliances, activism, and networks, redefining the scope of architecture. By analyzing their actions, this research identifies pathways for architects and researchers to respond effectively to crises, fostering collective action, and planetary care.

Keywords: Architect-activists; Climate Crisis; Civil Disobedience; Spatial Justice; Spatial Activism; Systemic Change.

Corresponding author: Armelle Breuil (independent Scholar); armelle@actstudio.eu; https://orcid.
org/0009-0001-7445-9506 ∂ Open Access. © 2025 Armelle Breuil published by transcript Verlag. This
work is licensed under the Creative Commons Attribution 4.0 (BY) license.
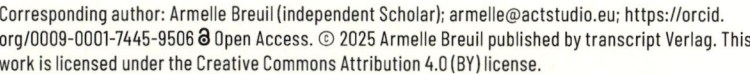

Architects as Spatial Activists

Historically, architecture has engaged with social and spatial justice. Projects like *Spatial Agency: Other Ways of Doing Architecture* (Awan/Schneider/ Till, 2011) document architectural practices since the 1960s that challenge the normativity of the architecture field, while *Radical Pedagogies* (Colomina et al. 2022) archives radical practices in architectural education since post-World War II. Starting in the 1970s, architect and writer Hannah Sloan Wood's analysis (Sloan Wood 2017) began observing a growing number of politically engaged architects following the 2008 financial crisis. Yet, as an architect drawn to architecture as a changemaker possibility, I wonder: is it possible for architects to use their position in climate activism, when their role is intrinsically linked to crossing the planet boundaries, such as pollution, extractivism, and CO_2 emissions?

In August 2018, the young Swedish activist Greta Thunberg bartered school time for strikes on Fridays in the three weeks leading up to the national elections. Alone, she sat outside her school to demand international political action towards the climate crisis. Soon enough, many other students joined her around the globe, starting the movement Fridays for Future.

Thunberg's strike happened ten years after the Conference of the Parties (COP) in Copenhagen and two years after the COP in Paris and the Paris Agreement, which has been recently breached (Cannon 2025). A few weeks later, she joined the official launch of the campaign Extinction Rebellion (XR) by RiseUp! in London with their call for mass civil disobedience during their declaration of Rebellion on the 31st of October 2018. On November 17th, after a week of actions, 6000 XR »rebels« blocked simultaneously five central bridges of London for the first time in history, shedding light on a potential extinction of humanity (Gayle 2018). For many people, including myself, an architect-activist engaged with social issues and, recently, climate issues at the time, the autumn of 2018 was a turning point: Physical civil disobedience seemed the only way to push for political change. In a few months, millions of people joined the movement in the streets, used artistic actions to raise awareness and were willing to be arrested in an attempt to overflow the jails. Following the theory of change of XR: to achieve systemic change, 3,5% (Chenoweth 2020) of the population should engage in mass civil disobedience to force the government to act. (Extinction Rebellion 2019)

A large part of civil society across the globe engaged with civil disobedience the following year, from Paris to Kinshasa. Among them, we also found architects. The built environment is, after all, a major catalyst of the climate crisis: its reliance on urban expansion, resource extraction, and exploitative labour practices perpetuates socio-economic inequalities and ecological harm. This article emerges from a need to understand other peers who, despite knowing the harms our industry causes, like me, choose to pursue this in the field. It investigates the role architects had to play in the climate movement between 2018 and 2024, following the path of three of them through a series of interviews conducted in 2024 in London and online. These architect-activists are Nick Newman (Studio Bark / XR / ACAN), Tom Bennett (Studio Bark / XR, ACAN), and Léa Hobson (Léa Hobson Architecte / XR / Les Soulèvements de la Terre/Earth Uprising).

They were selected because of their acts of civil disobedience in Extinction Rebellion, as well as the impact their practices have had on the climate movement and vice versa. They come from movements I have engaged with, as I have been both very active in XR France and Norway and a co-founder of the Architects Climate Action Network (ACAN) Norwegian Chapters, as well as the international coordinator for the movement for two years. By blending grassroots activism with architectural practice, they propose pathways for reimagining architecture in an era defined by crisis.

From Climate Movement to Architecture Movements

The 2018-2024 climate movement also saw the rise of built environment movements of individuals focusing on climate and environment, like Architects for Future (Germany), the Architects Climate Action Network (UK), Architectes pour le Climat (Switzerland), Frugalité Heureuse et Créative (FR). These organizations are still active today and aim to transform the profession through systemic change.

Understanding what harms our industry causes and how little power we have can lead architects, like those in Denmark (Thon 2025), to quit their professions to become full-time activists, or the building industry at large. In the article, we will focus on another group, which the interviewees belong to, that chooses to continue working as architects but engages in change. I will call them »architect-activists« and define them by the fact that they keep practicing architecture at the same time as engaging in advocacy, public protest, and direct action. It is their way of confronting the cognitive dissonance between creating and harming. By blending activism with

B.Y.O.B
BUILD YOUR
OWN BOX
PROTOTYPE 1

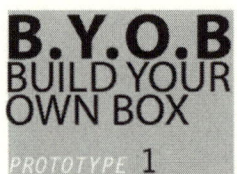

Person: 3
Time: 8 mins
Boxes:17
Nuts & Bolts: 42

1

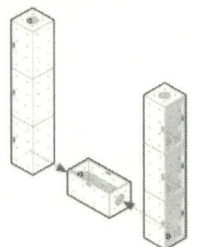

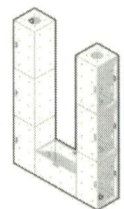

Build a
U-shaped
structure as
shown.

2

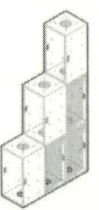

Build a
step struc-
ture and a
platform as
shown.

3

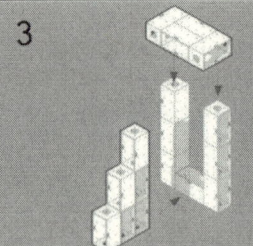

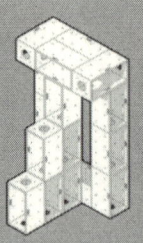

Combine the
step and
platform
with the
U-structure
and voila!

Disclaimer: All struc-
tures are for hypothetical
project, build it at your
own risk!

1.
U-Build module explained, courtesy of StudioBark.

architectural practice, they exemplify how architecture can transcend its conventional boundaries to foster resilience, equity and environmental care.

Designing Protest

The first interview I conducted was with Nick Newman, a co-founder of the engaged practice Studio Bark, while I was in London for the fifth anniversary of ACAN, on the 10th of October 2024.

Studio Bark, founded in 2014 by Wilf Meynell, has a mission to merge environmental design with architecture and hands-on methods, and voice this:

>»When Wilf came up with the name it was because of two meanings. It was bark, like the lifeblood of a tree, but also like bark as in speaking loudly about the environment. It has always been in our DNA.«

Meynell gained attention for a house design shown on a TV show and used the influx of new work to gather a team of friends to start the studio, including Nick Newman. The studio has since then won multiple awards, including the »Archiboo Activism Award.«

Newman's transition from architect to activist came with the 2018 (The Intergovernmental Panel on Climate Change) IPCC special report on 1.5, Greta Thunberg's influence and XR's emergence, and an understanding of the limitations of incremental change, »just specify timber buildings instead of concrete and expect that is going to fix everything is not enough.« Looking for systemic action, he joined XR with his colleague Tom Bennett. In April 2019, their firm contributed to the success of the blockades in London after a massive crackdown on the XR warehouse and the confiscation of its material by the police. For two to three years, they had developed a modular system, the U-Build, a sort of wooden box produced by CNC milling that can easily be assembled to give shape to anything from furniture to house extension. They originally created it to enable community self-builds, and had created a non-profit firm developing it as they wanted it to be a social enterprise. Luckily, these modules were stored in another location and were not confiscated by the police. It became a cornerstone for the protest after being adapted for using as modular roadblocks.

During the Trafalgar Square occupation in October 2019, Newman was arrested in what he describes a life-changing event:

2.
U-Build at Trafalgar Square in 2019. Photography by Natasa Leoni.

»It was quite a big moment. In my life in general, standing on top of a tower and have the whole of Trafalgar Square looking at you, and being arrested in an elaborate manner with this huge cherry picker and police. (...) It was quite transformational for me, also because it was captured with a beautiful photograph. There was enough for it to become a story; Dezeen contacted us, and others like RIBA asked if we could write about it. And, suddenly, from what had been an action to contribute with some boxes to try and block the road became a whole personal thing. Such as ›an architect is arrested.‹ There was two ways of reacting. Either, shy away from, cover it up. Or own it.

I felt I could use this as a platform to communicate change in the industry, like a bit of notoriety (...). It helped me feel more comfortable using the term activist because if you're not a climate activist when you're arrested like at XR, when are you?«

The U-Build tower (fig. 2) was not »just a roadblock,« rather »a symbol.« It was an element working as a meeting point and was key in making the occupation last, as it was difficult for the police to remove it with Newman atop the structure. It was visually interesting. Extinction Rebellion has been reviving the idea of designing protests in an era of social media, where images carry the power of change through communication. Building on the term *artivism* (art+activism, a new term with a long history), XR activists transformed the cities with their actions, »imagining the present and future city« (Arnold, 2022). It was the case of the Waterloo Bridge occupation, during which Newman understood that »people, plus architecture, plus activism could change things.« The bridge was transformed with a skate ramp, trees, and pedestrianization, achieving with no budget what many proposals intended to with large budgets. On that same action and same bridge, the idea of ACAN was born – the idea to induce systemic change in our industry. Newman was part of some of the first ACAN meetings and is still a member today.

Newman has shown in his book Protest *Architecture: Structures of Civil Resistance* that architecture has the power to elevate a protest, to »improve the safety, visibility and effectiveness of protests« (Newman, 2024). His documentation of the history and typologies of protest design shows how it changed the built environment and how architects and designers have been contributing to the field. With his book, Newman aims to inspire practitioners and activists. One of the cases documented is the Beacon (fig. 3), designed by the artist Julian Maynard Smith and developed with the newly

3.

The Beacon reproduced in the Extinction Rebellion occupation of Paris in April 2022. Photography by Armelle Breuil.

4.
The Beacon exposed at VA in London in October 2024. Photography by Armelle Breuil.

appointed Studio Bark engineer, Morgan Trowland. Designing structures that are both impossible to move once activists are occupying them and aesthetics has contributed to the success of occupations.

Newman's activism impregnates his practice. His dual role as firm principal and activist highlights a critical pathway for architects seeking to align their practices with systemic change. Activism transformed Studio Bark's daily action as they use radical listening, check in on meetings, and work on diversity and flat hierarchy. Their working mode is an alternative to the current mainstream scheme of the architecture offices: they introduced a free day every other week – Newman said he used a lot of them to write his most recent book- and on climate strikes, closed the office, to encourage their employees to join the strike. To have a different office for the non-profit for the U-Build module allowed them »to explore some of these alternative things that Studio Bark couldn't do.« Activism influenced them even in their projects, instead of covering mistakes the firm might have done, they would rather speak about it, show their process and learn from others to change, saying »as long as you're aware of those and again, you're willing to own the mistakes as well as owning the successes, then hopefully other people can see your process.« StudioBark is a great example of how one can learn from activism and implement its learning in the office while helping shape the protests.

Creating a Network of Collective Action and Climate Justice within the Building Industry

I conducted the interview with the activist-architect Tom Bennett online on the 18th of October 2024. We had been in contact over the years through ACAN. His first encounter with activism sparked at university: »Like a lot of people, I encountered activism at university. I became very politicized by the Iraq War era, realizing the government had lied to us. It pushed me into anti-war and anti-capitalist movements, and later, environmental activism.« Even if you could imagine that students of architecture would be engaged in these topics he often felt alienated, remarking I was always frustrated during my time at university that architecture students seemed so ›head in the sand,‹ focusing on their tiny bit of the world without worrying about anything beyond it. His climate activism was built on his peace activism, as it had a »*holistic view*,« and the activists in the peace movement saw »climate breakdown as a peace issue.« At the time, the UK had several climate camps, which later on inspired the way Extinction Rebellion (XR) was organized.

Bennett's involvement in XR marked a turning point in his activism. XR's bold emphasis on mass civil disobedience, aesthetic spectacle, and systemic advocacy deeply resonated with his belief in architecture's potential as a tool for change. He recalls: »When XR came along, it tapped into this deep frustration – this sense of hopelessness that no one was doing anything about climate change.« It reignited a movement that had been dormant in the UK for nearly a decade, and the new energy made him feel there was a momentum and, as he told me, »Demands could be met.«

Emerging during XR's 2019 Waterloo Bridge protest (BBC 2019), ACAN became a central hub for mobilizing architects toward systemic reform. Bennett played a significant role in building up the movement and advancing its mission of rapid decarbonization, ecological regeneration, and cultural transformation within the profession. As he explains:

> »The big work is to bring system change. It should be a priority. A lot of groups have sprung up, like ACAN, and can play a role. There is a new sense of an eco-system of collective groups within the sector that was really needed.«

Despite engaging with design for direct action during the XR protests, ACAN differs in its methods, focusing on campaigning, lobbying, and public engagement rather than direct action. It is a

> »network of individuals and organizations within architecture and related built environment professions taking action to address the twin crises of climate and ecological breakdown. ACAN operates as a network, bringing together governments, businesses, civil society organizations, and individuals, united by a shared commitment to building a sustainable and resilient future« (ACAN 2025).

The group got the public's attention after their paper plane action. In 2020, ACAN sent an open letter to Foster + Partners and Zaha Hadid Architects, asking them to pause their involvement in aviation expansion, using their signature of the Architects Declare's manifesto as a leverage point. After no answer was received from the offices, they sent paper planes made of their letter to the offices, urging architects working there to »take meaningful action outside of their employment« (Dezeen 2020). Both targeted offices

5.
ARB meets ACAN. Photography by Architects Climate Action Network Limited.

6.
ACAN in front of the ARB. Photography by Keith Van Loen.

withdrew from the network, pursuing their airport projects; proof that tackling the climate crisis was not their priority. This dilemma tactic, well known in XR, places authorities in a position where they must answer. Activists win in both cases: either by revealing the true intention, the violence or the ideas of the authorities, or by imposing change on the authorities.

In a similar way, Bennett used his arrest during the Waterloo Bridge protest to challenge the regulatory frame of the profession. Convicted under the Public Order Act of the UK, he used his required notification to the Architects Registration Board (ARB) as a platform for advocacy, making an ACAN event to hand out his letter to the ARB (fig. 5, fig. 6). The ARB responded and issued not long after a guidance affirming that peaceful activism aligns with professional responsibilities (ARB 2019). His publicized case drew attention to the role of architects in activism and contributed to a broader cultural shift, allowing other architects like Newman to feel secure to engage in civil disobedience, knowing it wouldn't necessarily put their position at risk. While the profession prioritizes compliance with regulatory frameworks over ethical advocacy, Bennett's case demonstrates how architects can challenge these norms and use their positions to advocate for change.

Today, the self-organised and open movement ACAN has become a strong environmental voice in the UK and is regularly contacted to give its position on climate-related matters, contributing to a shift in collective conscience. The movement organizes its efforts around nine working groups, such as Circular Economy, Embodied Carbon, Professional Standards and Natural Materials. It tackles specific issues within the building industry, fostering interdisciplinary collaboration and empowering architects to act collectively. ACAN is about advocacy and building alliances, which happens naturally in the working groups as well as around events ACAN organizes, such as their stand at FutureBuild, an international fair about ecological construction happening every year in London; or public debates such as the one Bennett organized in November 2023 in London: »Should There be a Moratorium on New Build Construction?«

ACAN illustrates the transformative potential of collective networks in challenging industry norms. The international reach of ACAN, with branches into twelve countries, demonstrates how architects can amplify their impact with collaboration across the globe. The first international campaign targets demolition and rallies the Nordic countries with the UK, Netherlands, and Australia, giving it more power. Once the awareness is raised around the crisis and challenges our field poses, building industry actors have a more legitimate position to initiate change, and might join the movement if they did not before. Conscious building industry actors who feel the industry needs to be transformed often feel powerless and wonder how to initiate change. And in fact, there are many different ways. ACAN's goal is to gather, »to empower [individuals] to unite and speak up, take action and share knowledge between practices« (AJ 2020). ACAN is the proof that climate activism can be brought to our profession as spatial practitioners with networks contributing to cultural change; lobbying and campaigns pushing for change of regulations, and knowledge exchange as the only way out. By getting to know inspiring practices, in person through the network or through the webinars, practitioners can be inspired and see that change is possible and have the possibility to ask questions about their project in the WhatsApp chat. It is interesting to notice that several ACAN's members switched their architects' hats to engage fully in systemic change: the co-founders Joe Giddings is now European Networks Lead at Built by Nature, Lauren Shevills is now Lead Retrofit Innovation and Delivery Officer at Westminster City Council, and Joe Penn is Sustainability Officer at the City of London. The editors' note of Everything Needs to Change explains as such:

> »To be part of systemic change, we can no longer entertain the traditional view of the architects that designs and builds alone. We must build on each other's ideas, encouragement, knowledge and most important, expertise. We have neither the time nor the resources to waste or to get it wrong.« (Pelsmakers/Newman 2021)

To conclude, activism such as that of Tom Bennett, centered around developing a network of engaged architects and has contributed to the empowerment of spatial practitioners – as a group it is easier to find the energy, confidence, and resources to challenge the conservative construction field. It contributed to creating a platform for change, where architects could, with less individual risk, take actions or reflect on how they approach their career entirely. In his article »Movement Building: Activism in an Age of Crisis« (Pelsmakers/Newman 2021), Bennett introduces the concept of »architectural activists« that he defines »as a third group [that] believes that architects do have agency [...] while recognising that this necessitates some kind of re-engagement with wider questions of sociopolitical change.« His article is an analysis of architects and movements that identify with this term.

Stopping the Concrete Industry – Embracing a Diversity of Tactics

The third interview I conducted was with Léa Hobson, which took place online on the 25th of October 2024. Her journey as an architect-activist is defined by her uncompromising dedication to confronting unsustainable practices with a focus on concrete and advocating for climate justice. Hobson's activism is deeply rooted in her upbringing. Raised by an English family passionate about wildlife conservation and a French agricultural lineage that rejected industrial practices, her early environmental awareness shaped her worldview: »When I was a kid, I dreamed of being in Greenpeace, boarding boats to protect wildlife« she reflects, adding »[...] that desire to fight for something bigger was always there, it just shifted to architecture and the built environment later.«

Since joining XR France in 2019, where we met, and since then, Hobson has relentlessly addressed the construction industry's immense ecological footprint and its social impacts. While being an employee in the studio Encore Heureux, a progressive French architectural firm, she started to shape actions targeting the concrete industry. Unlike Newman and Bennett, whose leadership roles within their firms afford them autonomy, Hobson faced the challenge of being an employee in a system resistant to change. Reflecting on this period, Hobson described a »*double life*« emerging, where her professional obligations and activist commitments existed in separated spheres.

In February 2020, Hobson initiated and co-organized the XR direct action with others including myself at Lafarge's cement factory in Paris »*Fin de Chantier,*« where hundreds of activists occupied the site and paralyzed the production for a day. Concrete mixers were painted with slogans such as »*Cement = 8% of World CO_2,*« and Lafarge's illegal pollution of the Seine was exposed. This investigative approach garnered significant public attention and resulted in legal action against Lafarge. Direct action can highlight blind spots within the construction industry and catalyze systemic change. As Hobson explains: »The fight against concrete isn't just about the material; it's about the extractivist systems it represents.«

»Fin de Chantiers« was not only a direct action, it also created a temporary experimental place showcasing the alternatives of the industry. Speakers at the action included Alain Bornarel, engineer co-founder of *Frugalité Heureuse (Happy Frugality)*, an architect from Archipel Zero, and LESA an association

7.
Red Rebels at Fin de Chantiers in 2020. Image credit: Yanis Langeraert.

8.

Concrete = 8% of world's CO₂ emissions. Image credit: MarieAnne58 / Extinction Rebellion France.

9.

Video showing the action »Fin de Chantiers,« Credit: Extinction Rebellion France, https://www.dropbox.com/scl/fi/z364g00tq5nx0kj463gtm/FDC-filmactionh264. mov?rlkey=urap4cj701qkax1sbybu0u379&dl=0, accessed October 5, 2025.

promoting earth construction, which built 1:1 elements with natural materials (Guitton-Boussion 2020).

Hobson encouraged colleagues to join her civil disobedience actions; however, she was disappointed when she witnessed the lack of mobilization within the firm. While she told colleagues about agriculture fields being covered in concrete in Saclay near Paris, they told her it was »unfortunate« and she was thinking »it's not unfortunate, you just move yourself, come with me and sit to avoid that [from happening].«

Out of frustration, she left the office and embraced a nomadic lifestyle. Hobson's activism extended beyond XR to *Les Soulèvements de la Terre (Earth Uprising)*, a radical grassroots-based environmental movement dedicated to uniting the climate movement in France to resist industrial local projects that harm ecosystems and communities; founded in 2021 by activists of the ZAD de NNDL and local collective of farmers (Les Soulèvements de la Terre, 2024). The movement, inspired among others by Ende Gelände, employs direct action tactics such as sabotage and large-scale interventions to challenge local struggles against destructive practices like quarries and mega-basins.

With concrete as a central focus of Hobson's activism, she critiques it also as a symbol of extractivism, prioritizing profit over planetary health. Hobson highlights the material's broader impacts, including deforestation, habitat destruction and water depletion caused by raw material extraction, as well as exploitative labor conditions and community displacement in quarrying regions. Within Earth Uprising, Hobson co-founded *Les Bâtisseur. euse.s des Terres (The Builders of the Earth)*, a branch focused on mobilizing architects, builders, and activists to collectively address ecological and social justice challenges. This idea came from her observation that »the struggles of the agricultural world were carried by farmers (paysans);« while all the actions against concrete had been carried by citizens or activists, not by workers in the building industry. She noticed that there was »very little talk of work conditions, health at work, living conditions and exploitation of workers.« Her initiative fosters interdisciplinary collaboration and echoes ACAN strategy of network, as she explains:

»We understood that for now we are connecting struggles. If every member is connected to different dynamics that makes the movement grow very quickly. Beyond growing, the notion of a large network is important: it is much more about connecting than about actions. If you manage to unblock

10.
»We are the weed disarming the concrete.« Image credit: Yanis Langeraert /
Extinction Rebellion France.

situations because you've connected two people who weren't connected be-fore, that's great.«

As *Earth Uprising* gained in visibility, the heavy repression of the state did too. During the »Battle of Sainte Soline« 5000 protesters were confronted with 3000 police officers, which left two protesters in a coma, leading the UN experts to »urge France to review its policing practices« (Chrisafis 2023). Hobson has herself suffered from political repression, being arrested and held in custody and having her belongings confiscated for her potential engagement in organizing an protest against Lafarge in Marseille.

This led to a pause in her activism to focus on independent practice, which became a platform for addressing systemic challenges, working on a book Désarmer le béton Ré-habiter la terre (Hobson 2025) about concrete scenog-raphy and often working on underfunded, community-oriented projects. Her book aims to demystify the construction industry and make its complex-ities accessible to activists and professionals alike. Her architectural work has had a large focus on helping the association of refugees get building permits.

Despite her passion and commitment to aligning her architectural prac-tice with activism, Hobson faces significant economic challenges that illus-trate the systemic barriers encountered by architect-activists. Projects rooted in activism, such as for the Refuge Solidaire, often operate with minimal funding. Hobson undertook extensive feasibility studies for these organiza-tions, with financial compensation barely covering her efforts. Reflecting on these difficulties, she shared: »It's hard to dedicate so much time and energy to projects that you know are meaningful but aren't supported financially.«

Hobson acknowledges the broader systemic issues at play, pointing to the architectural profession's focus on profit-driven work and the limited support for initiatives rooted in social and ecological justice. As she explains: »The industry isn't set up to reward or even recognize this kind of work. You're constantly trying to justify why it's important, but that doesn't pay the bills,« highlighting a critical need for structural reforms to support archi-tect-activists to continue their transformative work.

Another important aspect of Hobson's climate activism is the incorpo-ration of a feminist perspective, emphasizing the often overlooked human dimensions of construction, such as labor conditions and health impacts. She critiques the architectural profession for its detachment from these realities, arguing for a holistic rethinking of architectural ethics that centers on both environmental and social considerations. Hobson envisions a future where architects, activists, and other professionals work together to disrupt exploitative paradigms and foster equitable systems. Her work exemplifies how architecture can transcend conventional boundaries to enable resistance and drive systemic change.

Architect-Activists Can Show the Way

In the face of intersecting global crises, architecture stands at a transformative crossroads. Awareness has been raised globally through movements like XR, pushing architects to organize their profession as a catalyst for systemic change. Architecture must embrace its inherently political nature, embedding environmental justice, social equity, and ecological responsibility into its core. Architects must move beyond designing for private clients to address broader systemic crises while reimagining the profession's role as one of care, advocacy, and resilience.

Newman's protest architecture demonstrates how design can amplify movements and reframe the role of the architect as a change-maker. Bennett's work showcases the power of collective action to transform industry norms. Hobson's local engagement and focus on interspecies struggle highlight how the building industry can get support from other groups and species. Collectively, these practitioners exemplify how the built environment can be redefined to serve as a platform for resistance and systemic reform. Indeed, not only did they transform as individuals, but their practices were deeply influenced by the climate movement of the last years and influenced it back: from new methodologies in their projects to different working modes in their offices, they dare to create the change they want to see. The way they create awareness among their clients, develop their businesses to take part in non-commercial projects or fight for what they believe in, such as preservation rather than demolition, is inspirational. StudioBark shares their critical thinking through their website and social media, as well as books, and so does Hobson. As they are willing to share their critical thinking and how it led them to successes and misfortunes, they inspire spatial practitioners.

Across Europe, new movements carried by architects have emerged in recent months. HouseEurope! is creating a movement around a petition to transform the industry and abolish demolition in favor of rehabilitation, using bold esthetics and powerful movies such as Demolition Drama. Byggestopbevægelsen in Denmark is calling for a moratorium on new constructions, echoing the moratorium on new construction carried by Charlotte Malterre-Barthes and B+ (Charlotte Malterre-Barthes 2025).

The future of architecture lies in a subtle mix of being able to voice out against the struggles of the industry, broaden our understanding of architecture, such as including rehabilitation, as well as adopting regenerative approaches and new working modes. This transformation demands a new economy and legal framework. Grassroots initiatives like *Earth Uprising* illustrate how localized actions can spark systemic change, while educational reform is vital to prepare future architects for the complexities of today's crises. Ultimately, the reimagining of architecture as a force for social and ecological justice is needed, and the narrative from profit-driven and aesthetically focused outputs to one of equity, care, and resilience. To meet the urgent demands of our era, architects must adapt, act boldly, and work beyond disciplinary boundaries. By doing so, they can turn the built environment into a keystone for a just and regenerative world.

References

Arnold, Emma (2022): »Extinction Rebellion and the Future City,« in: Håvard Haarstad/Jakob Grandin/Kristin Kjærås/Eleanor Johnson (eds.), *Haste: The Slow Politics of Climate Urgency*, London: University College London Press.

Architects Registration Board (n.d): »Taking part in protests,« in: *ARB*, https://www.arb.org.uk/architect-information/guidance-notes/taking-part-in-protests/, accessed September 5, 2025

Architects Declare (n.d.): »*Architects Declare*,« https://uk.architectsdeclare.com/, accessed August 4, 2025.

Architects Climate Action Network (n.d.): »*Architects Can*,« https://architectscan.org/, accessed August 4, 2025.

Architects' Journal (n.d.): »*Architects Climate Action Network: ›We've Yet to See Change on the Scale We Know Is Necessary,‹*.« https://www.architectsjournal.co.uk/practice/architects-climate-action-network-weve-yet-to-see-change-on-the-scale-we-know-is-necessary, accessed August 4, 2025.

Awan, Nishat/Schneider, Tatjana/Till, Jeremy (2011): *Spatial Agency: Other Ways of Doing Architecture*, London: Routledge.

BBC News (2019): »London Climate Change Protest: Extinction Rebellion Ends,« in: *the BBC*, https://www.bbc.com/news/uk-england-48051776, accessed August 4, 2025.

Byggestopbevægelsen (n.d.): »*Byggestopbevægelsen*,« https://www. byggestopbevaegelsen.dk/, accessed August 4, 2025.

Cannon, Alex J. (2025): »Twelve months at 1.5 °C signals earlier than expected breach of Paris Agreement threshold,« in: Nature Climate Change 15, 266–269. doi: 10.1038/s41558-025-02247-8

Chenoweth, Erica (2020): *Questions, answers, and some cautionary updates regarding the 3.5% rule* [Carr Center Discussion Paper 2020-005], Cambridge, Ma: Harvard Kennedy School. https://www.hks.harvard.edu/centers/carr/publications/questions-answers-and-some-cautionary-updates-regarding-35-rule, accessed June 10, 2025.

Chrisafis, Angelique (2023): »France to shut down climate protest group citing public safety risks.« *The Guardian*, June 20, 2023, https://www.theguardian.com/world/2023/jun/20/france-to-shut-down-climate-protest-group-citing-public-safety-risks, accessed June 10, 2025.

Colomina, Beatriz/Galán, Ignacio/Kotsioris, Evangelos/Meister, Anna-Maria (eds.), (2022): *Radical Pedagogies*, Cambridge (MA): MIT Press.

Ende Gelände (n.d.): »*Ende Gelände*,« https://www.ende-gelaende.org/en/, accessed August 4, 2025.

Extinction Rebellion (2019): *This is not a drill: An Extinction Rebellion handbook*, London: Penguin.

Extinction Rebellion (2018): »*Over 1000 People Block Parliament Square to Launch Mass Civil Disobedience Campaign Demanding Action on Climate Emergency*,« https://extinctionrebellion.uk/2018/10/31/over-1000-people-block-parliament-sq-to-launch-mass-civil-disobedience-campaign-demanding-action-on-climate-emergency/, accessed August 4, 2025.

Fairs, Marcus (2020): »*UK architects feud over airport projects.*« Dezeen, https://www.dezeen.com/2020/12/04/uk-architects-feud-airport-projects-architects-climate-action-network/, accessed June 10, 2025.

Gayle, Damien/Taylor, Matthew (2018): »Thousands gather to block London bridges in climate rebellion.« *The Guardian*, https://www.theguardian.com/environment/2018/nov/17/thousands-gather-to-block-london-bridges-in-climate-rebellion, accessed June 10, 2025.

Guitton-Boussion, Justin (2024): »Extinction Rebellion dénonce le BTP ›climaticide‹ en bloquant une cimenterie,« *Reporterre*, February 18, 2020. https://reporterre.net/Extinction-Rebellion-denonce-le-BTP-climaticide-en-bloquant-une-cimenterie, accessed November 30, 2024.

Hobson, Léa (2025): *Désarmer le béton Réhabiter la terre*, Paris: Zones.

House Europe! (n.d.): »House Europe!,« https://www.houseeurope.eu/, accessed August 4, 2025.

IPCC (n.d.): »*IPCC*,« https://www.ipcc.ch/, accessed August 4, 2025.

Les Soulèvements de la Terre (2024): *Premières secousses*, Paris: La Fabrique Éditions.

Malterre-Barthes, Charlotte (2025): *A Moratorium on New Construction*, Berlin: Sternberg Press.

Newman, Nick/Pelsmakers, Sophie (2022): *Everything Needs to Change: Architecture and the Climate Emergency*, London: RIBA Publishing.

Newman, Nick (2024): *Protest Architecture: Structures of Civil Resistance*, London: RIBA Publishing.

Refuges Solidaires (n.d.): »Association Refuges Solidaires,« https://refugessolidaires.com/, accessed August 4, 2025.

RIBA – Royal Institute of British Architects (n.d.): »*RIBA*,« https://www.architecture.com/, accessed August 4, 2025.

Rise Up Network (2018): »*About Rising Up - An Overview*,« Google Document, https://docs.google.com/document/d/1l3h6R4kWJGYGxJd3sLbQdG8zjV4sj5bmIM4Z-9Tk5X8/edit?tab=t.0#heading=h.ldkwcr94fux2, accessed August 4, 2025.

RFI (2020): »Paris Probes Cement Giant Lafarge over Seine Pollution Allegations, Claims Sabotage,« https://www.rfi.fr/en/france/20200902-paris-probes-cement-giant-lafarge-over-seine-pollution-allegations-claims-sabotage, accessed August 4, 2025.

Sloan Wood, Hannah (2017): »Spatial Activism: Profiling a New Wave of European Architecture Collectives and Their Spatial Manifestos,« in: *Archinect*, https://archinect.com/features/article/149989510/spatial-activism-profiling-a-new-wave-of-european-architecture-collectives-and-their-spatial-manifestos, accessed October 24, 2025.

Spatial Agency (n.d.): »*Spatial Agency*,« https://www.spatialagency.net/, accessed August 4, 2025.

The Ecologist (2024): »*Lessons from Extinction Rebellion: The Origins*,« https://theecologist.org/2024/jul/26/lessons-extinction-rebellion-origins, accessed August 4, 2025.

Thon Holjen, Thon (2025): »Danmark er på vei inn i ukjent farvann.« In: *Arkitektur*, https://www.arkitektur.no/aktuelt/tema/danmark-er-paa-vei-inn-i-ukjent-farvann/, accessed November 30, 2024.

U-Build (n.d.): »*U-Build*,« https://u-build.org/, accessed August 4, 2025.

UNFCCC (n.d.): »*Conference of the Parties (COP)*,« https://unfccc.int/process/bodies/supreme-bodies/conference-of-the-parties-cop, accessed August 4, 2025.

Dimensions of Architectural Knowledge, 2024–08 ♱
https://doi.org/10.14361/dak-2024-0807

Transing Space(s)

Vio:la Wagner, Alvie Augustin

Abstract: In *cis*normative societies, space is defined through a binary categorization of gender rooted in essentialist ideals. These frameworks inscribe gender stereotypes and social norms into space – archiving, reproducing, and consolidating structures that contribute to a non-binary erasure. Identities and bodies beyond essentialist classifications are marginalized and often rendered invisible in spatial definitions and practices. This dynamic becomes visible through binary patterns of thought, power relations, *cis*normative perspectives, and the influence of *cis*normative feminisms on space. In order to uncover and deconstruct *cis*sexist structures, we ask ourselves how they are inscribed in space and our understanding of space. Starting the research from a *trans*-activist perspective, the following text gives directions on our way to trans understandings and practices of space. A literature review was conducted within fields of architecture theory, *trans* studies, disability studies, as well as urban studies, and complemented by qualitative interviews with *trans* activists, overall aiming to foster an interdisciplinary and intersectional lens.

Keywords: Non-binary; *Transing*; Embodied Space; Spatial Practices; Digital Space.

Corresponding authors: Vio:la Wagner (independent scholar), Alvie Augustin (independent scholar);
wagner.viola111@gmail.com; https://orcid.org/0009-0006-8022-9973; alvie.augustin@gmx.at; https://
orcid.org/0009-0007-6622-679X ♱ Open Access.

This work wouldn't be possible without community.

Introduction

This transdisciplinary approach to spatial practices explores links between space and gender beyond (*cis*[1])normativity, exposing harmful normativities in spatial practices. Throughout the whole work, we follow the aim of »transing« our spatial practice, inspired by Tim Gough's (2017) notion of »transing« as a way to challenge binary structures and categories in architecture. We seek to apply this lens to our research by identifying the normativities that stand in the way of such an approach and deriving possible methodological pathways from it.

A systematic literature review centering *trans* scholars is complemented by qualitative interviews with *trans* activists, as well as supplemented with non-academic sources, creating a blend of knowledge forms. We interviewed two activists, who are situated within the wide area of *trans* research. We (the authors) are *white, trans,* have an academic background, and were born in the Austrian countryside, and now live and study in Vienna. With this paper, we contribute to an Euro-centered academic form of knowledge production. However, we find it important to remember that what appears to be *trans* studies and disability studies have their origins in activism, struggles of everyday life, and in the respective minorities. We are writing this text not with the aim of providing an integration of *trans* studies and spatial or architectural theory, but rather to collect possible paths of thought inspired by *trans* activist and *trans* scholar practice that can be pursued in further research and discussion.

Exposing Normativities / The Binary Machine

According to architect, artist and theorist Tim Gough, what architecture »is« or is assumed to be is determined through a performative way. In other words, architecture is not just about objects or spaces, but about how we understand and experience them. Architecture is made to fit into a »binary machine,« a term Gough borrows from theorist Gilles Deleuze (2006), meaning that it

---

1   cis: someone whose gender is aligned with the gender assigned by others at birth

gets divided into rigid categories. Gough introduces »transing« to challenge or queer a binary system (Gough 2017: 4). In Gough's words: »The transing task, then, is to queer this binary machine, to make architecture not something sieved through the categories, but mixed across them« (ibid.: 7). Importantly, Gough notes that transing (like queering) does not just add a trans perspective to something non-*trans*, but instead highlights the ways materiality is already *trans*. In doing so, the normative processes that make gendered transing seem exceptional or diagnosable become revealed (ibid.).

For us, transing space offers an urgent and necessary approach to spatial practices, thinking, and collaborations: It helps us uncover the binaries and fixed categories that shape how we design, plan, use, and think gender and space and their relations with bodies. This urgency stems from the continued dominance of binary gender norms in architectural and spatial practices, which marginalize non-fitting bodies and experiences. A *transing* of space means a *transing* of our everyday practice, which seeks to uncover and disrupt normativities in order to resist growing anti-trans sentiments worldwide.

Wrong Embodiment

A common *trans*normative narrative is to be stuck in the wrong body. It assumes that the trans subject is in the wrong skin, or – as depicted in *Silence of the Lambs* (Harris 1991) – wants to have a different skin. This narrative of being in the wrong body is often framed through the experiences of *trans* individuals like Christine Jorgenson, the first American to undergo gender confirmation surgery, whose public transition in the 1950s made her a well-known figure and symbol of medical transition (Prosser 1998). The narrative is also reinforced by public discourse, which has historically been shaped by medical perspectives. Early on, sexologists were at the forefront of engaging with *trans* issues, laying the groundwork for the medicalization of gender identity. The umbrella term »trans« is historically grown out of sexology and has its roots in 1910, when the sexologist Hirschfeld introduced the term »Transvesititismus« (Dobler 2004). The image of the *wrong* body can also refer to a body that does not conform to societal norms and is therefore considered not right. This idea resonates with how other movements, such as Disability Studies, discuss the ways in which bodies are pathologized and marginalized when they do not conform to dominant norms (Junge and Schmincke 2007). We want to build on these insights and explore how these social mechanisms affect the body through feelings, rather than just through physical alteration, and subsequently how the body influences space and vice versa. As Prosser explains, »To be oneself is first of all to have a skin of one's own and, secondly, to use it as a space in which one can experience sensations« (Prosser 1998: 73).

> »I personally had and also mostly have right now a difficult relation with bodies and especially with my own. Not because there was a development needed or brought forward through the term trans. But rather how the terms the majority of our societies nowadays describe the terms of what is normal and what is a particularity. My own experience of my body was never fitting with those understandings, but also not with the term trans for the most time of my life because it was understood outside the community mostly as being on the transit from one fixed gender towards the other and that was never how I felt myself.« – Interview[2] with *trans* activist

Spatial Maladjustment

> Who has access to spaces? And whose bodies are excluded or delegitimized by these spaces?

The conceptual history of the term *trans* is being continued by theorist, historian and activist Susan Stryker, among others. Stryker does not define being *trans* as something that has a destination (for example, *a sex change*, or *the other sex*), but as a movement away from an unchosen starting point (Stryker 2008). This movement carries a strong spatial dimension, which is also reflected in spatial metaphors such as »coming out of the closet« or »being at home in the own body« (Crawford 2020). However, spaces as well as movement are not neutral, rather shaped by power relations determining who can move freely and who cannot (Ahmed 2006). Within this, the understanding of movement is narrowed to normative understandings, while it can be discussed in various forms, e.g. over orientations, which may not be only physical, but also social or cultural (ibid. 2006). There can be racial and ableist effects to the universalization of trans as movement, as this »movement away from something« is primarily narrated through *white*, Eurocentric *trans* experience. It tends to associate movement with corporal freedom and space, often leaving racialized and disabled bodies portrayed

---

2 The interviews were conducted by Alvie Augustin and Vio:la Wagner in September 2024 with trans activists.

as fixed, immobile, or excluded (Awkward-Rich 2022). Or as poet and theorist Awkward-Rich (2022: 8) writes:

>»Despite the literal and metaphorical association of transition and transness itself with travel, mobility, and movement, trans life under racial capitalism is at least as much about stuckness, waiting, ›lag time‹, and recurrence – about living in definitely.«

Awkward-Rich interprets this movement as a departure from forms of maladjustment. For this, Awkward-Rich borrows Garland-Thomson's (2011) understanding, which is widely discussed in disability studies, whereas maladjustment occurs when »an environment does not sustain the shape and function of the body; that enters it« and has the consequences of rendering misfitting bodies as social misfits (Awkward-Rich 2022: 7). The use of maladjustment, again, carries a strong spatial dimension; however, one that holds space accountable (in its physical and social and societal form) rather than the movement of the *trans* subject. Here, space does not remain metaphorical but can be interpreted as the very environment that produces the misfitting body.

How and where do spatial environments fail to sustain *trans* bodies? Or do they sustain some of them and fail others? What does this mean for spatial practices? It must be affectively and structurally accessible and designed in such a way that it does not mark different bodies and identities as maladjusted. Spaces are not neutral; the creation of separate spaces, »integration,« only shifts exclusion to other places, but does not eliminate it. Inclusion does not mean including bodies, but changing the environment that excludes these bodies. This also means that space must be able to contain non-normative temporal and spatial realities. Instead of asking what a space has to look like to be *trans*-inclusive, we should first question where norms are embodied in spaces and how we can break down these norms.

A concrete example of the problems that arise when marginalized groups are merely integrated but not considered inclusively is the OG5 project, which was a temporary accommodation for queer homeless people in Vienna. The project intended to create a safe space for homeless *trans* and queer people who experience discrimination and violence in regular facilities that rely on a binary gender system. However, as in the beginning, *trans* people were hesitant to use the new facilities, while at the same time, there was an overall acute shortage of homeless shelters in Vienna. Due to their free beds, the OG5 opened their doors also to cis men. As a result, trans people and trans women in particular no longer felt safe and experienced violence by their roommates. The care staff were not sufficiently trained to react appropriately to these situations. In the end, one *trans* woman was even expelled from the center (Habringer et al. 2023). This example underscores the urgent need for a shift from merely integrating marginalized groups into existing spaces, to rethinking and transforming the very structures and norms that govern these spaces.

Passing

In 1994, Susan Stryker wrote the text »My Words to Victor Frankenstein Above the Village of Chamounix: Performing Transgender Rage.« In it, Stryker compares the »*trans*(sexual)« body with its modifications and uses the monster metaphor for the experiences of trans bodies, in particular for the feeling of being rejected by society and regarded as »unnatural« or in the wrong body. In order not to confront people with visible *transness*, *trans* people sometimes speak of adopting a strategy of »passing.« To *pass* is to be perceived as normative (for example, cis-passing: to be perceived as cis). »Passing means to live successfully in the gender of choice, to be accepted as a ›natural‹ member of that gender« (Stone 1991: 12).

However, passing also means erasing a part of one's own experience, leaving it behind, with forgetfulness as integral to becoming. Passing has long been a tool to be invisible and safe(r), not to be perceived as alien, but it also adheres to binary images. Passing is thus only a coping strategy in a binary *cis*sexist social order, but not a way out of binarity. »The Master's Tools Will Never Dismantle the Master's House« (Lorde, 1984: 110). If a body exists within the social order, then it must subordinate itself to it. If it does not or cannot subordinate itself, then it is a foreign body within this order and has the potential to disrupt this order. Non-passing bodies not only claim space, they expose and destabilize the very systems that seek to render them invisible. Yet not everyone can afford non-passing, as the privileges tied to passing are often shaped by *whiteness*, able-bodiedness, and other intersecting forms of social advantage. According to scholar and theorist Judith Butler, subjectivation refers to the process by which individuals are shaped as subjects through social norms and power structures, simultaneously constrained by and enabled through these norms (Butler 1990). If the built environment has been shaped by norms of gender, race and sex over and over again throughout past centuries, cisnormativity becomes deeply embedded in space.

Whose spaces?

In the 1980s, gender planning emerged as an independent planning discipline to answer this question. Historically, gender planning has primarily focused on addressing the distinct roles, needs, and inequalities experienced by »women« and »men,« rooted in binary gender perspectives (Moser 2014). It ignores the body itself as a fully legitimate source of knowledge (embodied knowledge) and manifests socially constructed binary gender roles by defending them rather than breaking out of them. Something similar happens with the conception of so-called »*FLINTA*-spaces*« (German acronym for woman, lesbian, inter*, trans*, agender). In an aim to create a truly inclusive space for people with diverse gender identities, reference is made to existing categories. In this way, these spaces often fail to maintain the bodies for which the space is intended, as normative understandings of how those categories should look like, as well as social hierarchies between the categories, remain. Bodies that have already adapted to the expectations of another system (e.g., are *cis*-passing *trans* men) or didn't have the possibility to adapt (e.g., non-*cis*-passing *trans* femmes), become invisible or have no space at all. In order to do *trans*-inclusive gender planning, gender planning would have to break out of the existing categories and stop forcing trans bodies into the need to pass within these categories.

An example from my (Vio:la) own activism: the conception of a body-positive space for Sapphic individuals is concerned with who is actually allowed into this space. There was also a desire not to allow men into this space. We avoided the term FLINTA* here by introducing the term *sapphic*, with the intention of being trans-inclusive. However, this led to friction and a feeling of insecurity, especially among trans masc[3] people, making them hesitant to enter the space. In an attempt to give those people the opportunity to decide for themselves if they want to enter this space, one person said, »There is simply no more space for me. Neither in gay spaces, nor in lesbian/sapphic spaces. I am *trans*, and yet invisible within the community that I need.« As long as spaces that want to be *trans*-inclusive are using existing labels, it will be difficult to create a truly *trans*-inclusive place.

Affective Archives

The Institute for Sexology in Berlin was ransacked on May 6, 1933, by fascist students from the Hochschule für Leibesübungen and members of the Sturmabteilung (SA). On May 10, 1933, large parts of the institute's archive were burned at Opernplatz, now Bebelplatz. It is a historic event most people have heard of, but hardly anyone learns that it is a part of *trans* history. The collective memory was destroyed and disappeared with the burned books. Stories such as that of Dora Richter (the first known trans person to undergo gender reassignment surgery) was forgotten for a long time (Staatsbibliothek Berlin 2023). These repressions also affect knowledge about *trans* bodies and *trans* bodies themselves. The embodied knowledge of repression became archived.

The term archive is taken up by *trans* theorist Lucas Crawford (2020) in the text »Transgender Architectonics« and discusses the *trans* body as an archive. Crawford argues that, in order to consider the *transgender* body as an archive, two modes of analysis are required: »first, self-critical remembrance and, secondly, a forward-looking bodily forgetfulness« (Crawford 2020: 5). If we see the body as an archive, power structures are inscribed in it, carrying them within space and reproducing these normativities. Or, as philosopher Jacques Derrida says in *Archive Fever*: »There is no political power without control of the archive« (Derrida 1995: 4). According to Derrida, »The archive is not a place of originary truth. It is always partial, deferred, constructed« (ibid.). The suppression of trans bodies is therefore also a means of maintaining power, and space that does not include trans bodies is therefore an eraser of embodied knowledge (ibid.). Could Crawford's view on the Body-as-an-archive give us a tool to confront harmful normativities? Could it give us forms of freedom to discard them? Or would it mean we would carry them around with us indefinitely?

In addition to the body itself as a spatialized form of knowledge, urban and global geographies are archives, shaped by colonial and patriarchal histories marked by erasure and violence. Spatial territories such as public space have long been used to control and exclude bodies marked by race, gender, disability, and class (Sears 2015). The international spread of cross-dressing laws from the 1850s to the 1970s exemplifies this: gender non-conformity in public was criminalized, turning space itself into a tool of exclusion (Eskridge 1999). A current example of this is the LGBT[4]-free zones in Poland, where the last LGBT-free zone was only dissolved in April 2025 (Notes From

Poland 2025). The mentioned laws did not ban identities per se, but their visibility in the public and therefore, archiving their absence in spaces.

A very recent example is the introduction of the so-called »bathroom bans« in the USA, which ban trans people from public bathrooms or facilities according to their gender identity (Movement Advancement Project 2025). This is not the first time that toilets have been misused as a tool for maintaining power. Decades ago, segregation laws made by mostly non-racialized people separated racialized bodies. »African American women and *white* women were prohibited from using the restroom together because of what it would represent: ›their integration starkly symbolized social equality‹ and policy could not permit that to exist« (Spence-Mitchell 2020: 16). This legislation makes it clear once again that spaces are not neutral places – in this case the bathroom becomes a tool of control and invisibilization of non-normative bodies. »*Trans* women, even *white trans* women, are unable to use the assigned restroom for women because they have historically been deemed a danger to *white* women« (ibid.).

Transing: Methodological Urgency

Transing as a methodological aim means an urgent need to reshape binary modes of gendered planning, spatial thinking, and collaboration. Or as architectural theorist Tim Gough (2017: 53) writes: »[...] to queer this binary machine, to make architecture not something sieved through the categories, but mixed across them.« Intersectionality must be at the center of this effort, foregrounding marginalized communities in their activist practice and embodied experiences.

Practicing Relationality, Demanding Collaboration

Transing does not mean adding *trans*-ness to something previously non-*trans*. Instead, it reveals that change, movement is inherent to materiality, body, and space (Gough 2017). One way to read this through a trans activist lens is to look at theorist Lucas Crawford's answer to what *transgender* space is: those spaces we visit and navigate on a daily basis. Through *trans* bodies moving and navigating in spatial environments, a transing of space itself occurs within cisnormative constraints (Crawford 2020).

»I think the easiest way to describe it is by thinking at moments in which one tries to enter a space or open a door. The reactions of others in this particular moment are everything one needs to see the power relations and with them the structures which are shaping the room. Even if nobody is actually hostile in an open or aggressive way, the mood of the room reveals itself throughout the smallest cracks of neutrality. Every moment that is not as easy going for the people that do not fit in the *cis*normativity as for the people who do shows how deeply rooted the structures of *cis*normativity are within the spaces.« – Interview[3] with *trans* activist

By understanding space as something lived through social practice, action, affect, interaction, and being in relation with space and others (Lefebvre 1991 [1974]), we can broaden our imagination and open up for transing ways of spatial practice. A relational and affective lens onto space further requires embracing the complexity and fluidity of *trans* lives, resisting simplified spatial understandings, and fostering a practice that welcomes the messiness of multiple voices, conflicting perspectives, and the inherent tensions between collaboration and difference.

When centering everyday practices and spatial complexity, modes of collaboration beyond what we define as disciplines become essential. This means forms of collaboration with, e.g. social workers, activists, community organizers, artists, storytellers, and writers enable a deepened methodology that prioritizes the lived experiences and challenges power dynamics in social relations. By centering *trans* activist practices, research, and storytelling in all their heterogeneity and everyday defiance, we open up radical grounds for experimentation. In other words, we begin to open up collaborative spaces where we can begin to smash the architectural binary machine.

Cyber Transing – Reimagining of Digital Space

Where offline spaces fail, digital spaces often step in. Activists, scholars, and various marginalized communities repeatedly describe digital spaces as counterspaces to offline everyday life, with the potential to establish new concepts of self and subjectivity (Rottmann et al. 2023). Numerous studies show that especially *trans* youth experience aspects of their gender

---

3 The interviews were conducted by Alvie Augustin and Vio:la Wagner in September 2024 with trans activists.

identity online that they cannot and do not experience offline. This ranges from feeling safe, experiencing care, hope, a sense of belonging, and finding community. They sometimes even open up life-saving pathways for navigating everyday life in *cis*normative spatial environments (Austin et al. 2020). Digital spaces hold the potential for creating environments where bodies are neither immediately visible nor subjected to the normative gaze of *cis*normative expectations. Or as trans novelist Imogen Binnie writes in *Nevada* (2013: 61), her debut novel which is seen as important landmark in *trans* fiction literature (Rosenberg 2022): »In this weird way, Internet message boards, livejournal, all these things feel like they're a safe way to talk about being *trans* – to exist without this problematic body you're stuck with, when you're offline in meatspace, [...] Which rules.«

> »Digital spaces often allow us to move, dwell, and be without the limitations of trans bodies being necessarily perceived and interpreted by others – they circumvent the issue of (cis)passing. Digital spaces also are essential to counteract the invisibility or hiddenness of queer/trans spaces as well as community events. They thereby help to build alternatives. The usage of digital spaces is also grounded in the lack of offline spaces, nevertheless, the ones that do exist can be found via online searches. As a result, digital spaces are key for connecting trans people with each other.« – Interview[4] with *trans* activist

It is evident that digital spaces are not exempt from the violence and power hierarchies that exist in offline contexts and even create new forms of exclusion. The radical potential of digital counterspaces, however, lies neither in romanticizing them nor in escaping the material world, but in reshaping how we inhabit both, while raising the question of what role human-centered technologies can play in this. An illustrative example of this can be video gameplay and its ways of empowering *trans* people through forms of gender euphoria. Video gameplay holds the potential to offer intense spatial and embodied experiences involving identities, bodies, social interaction, and movement through diverse spatial worlds (Liang et al. 2025). Liang et al. (2025) took this as a starting point and asked themselves in their research how video gameplay that facilitates gender euphoria can be designed. Important parameters for this were the possibility to build trust, create safe spaces, and enable

---

4 The interviews were conducted by Alvie Augustin and Vio:la Wagner in September 2024 with trans activists.

self-expression within the game. The creation of such games offers a transing potential for spatial practice by providing valuable cues to reimagine physical spaces as sites of comfort, belonging, and change. At the same time, they turn virtual worlds into spatial experimental zones where normative assumptions about bodies, relations, and environments are reassembled.

Another example of this is architect and designer Xavi Aguirre's work with Stock-a-Studio, where augmented reality, 3D scans, and immersive media merge to create spatial experiences that blur the line between the physical and digital. Aguirre's use of digital and material components challenges conventional architectural perceptions and encourages us to rethink the very texture and materiality of space itself (Aguirre 2022a, 2022b). This artistic practice resonates with critical spatial theories that argue that digital tools do not merely supplement physical spaces. Rather, they transform access, participation, and inclusion. *Trans* activist practices illustrate this shift, creating what scholars from the disciplines of social work call »vireal appropriations of space.« The word »vireal« is a combination of the words »virtual« and »real,« and, therefore, happens where virtual and physical practices converge in the act of claiming space (Ketter 2014: 299; Röll 2014: 259).

Digital counter practices not only challenge the gender binary but also blur the spatial boundaries between online and offline, digital and analogue, real and unreal, space and non-space, materiality and immateriality. By interweaving online and offline practices, we open up the potential to transing spaces – transforming them into zones of survival, joy, hope, and resistance that challenge and disrupt normative social orders.

Process and Possibilities

When we are asked, »What does a *trans* inclusive spatial practice look like?,« people often expect norms and suggestions like a »*trans* Neufert,« a »*trans* modulor« or »*trans* gender planning« with a 10-step plan to a »transgender-just« city. However, this paper should make it clear that *trans* spatialities and spatial practices are processes, just as the understanding of *trans* and being *trans* is a process. Spatial environments typically sustain only certain bodies, while non-normative bodies do not necessarily adhere to any singular norm. The real challenge is not how to establish a norm for non-normative bodies but how to rethink spatial practices in a way that allows the space to adapt to the body, rather than the body adapting to the space.

As mentioned, this paper is about possibilities and questions rather than answers and solutions. Here we ask you to think about queering or transing your own spatial practices:

- What does it look like for spaces to adapt to bodies, instead of expecting people to change to fit the space?
- How can we think about the emotional and sensory experiences of people when designing spaces?
- Where are spaces of joy, comfort, and belonging, and how can they inspire us to rethink physical spaces as places of community?
- How can planners integrate social practice into their work, recognizing that planning itself must be a form of community organizing, rooted in collaboration and active engagement with the people it serves?
- What else can become imaginable if spatial disciplines did not rely on normative understandings of time and everyday life, normative understandings of social interaction, or movement, as well as the physical-material as the only and primary foundation of space?

Answers and Solution

The understanding of *trans* has evolved from medicalized frameworks to more fluid, self-determined meanings by moving through time and space. Similarly, we observed how spaces are not static but created, transformed, and challenged through the interplay of (non-normative) bodies, social practices, and power structures. *Trans*(ing) our view on space reveals that meaning and identity are relational and shaped by movements, interactions, and everyday life within space. Navigating *trans* bodies through (*cis-*, hetero-, *dya*[5]-)normative environments is not merely reactive; rather, it can be transformative. Recognizing space as inherently dynamic and shaped through movement, social encounter, and time reveals its political dimension.

A transing of spatial disciplines means paying attention to the complexities of everyday life and bodily experience through an intersectional lens. It calls for an active inclusion of non-academic forms of knowledge production, especially those rooted in activism and lived experience. Future research must seriously engage with how such methodologies can take shape. The aim requires not only recognition but a power-shifting commitment to integrate everyday ways of knowing into spatial thinking and practice. Anything less risks reproducing the very exclusions we seek to challenge.

References

Aguirre, Xavi (2022a): »Taking Stock with Architectural Designer Xavi Aguirre,« in: *PIN–UP Magazine*, https://archive.pinupmagazine.org/articles/taking-stock-with-architectural-designer-laida-aguirre, accessed May 09, 2025.

Aguirre, Xavi (2022b): »Someparts x Berghain x HIVE RISE,« in: *Stock-a-Studio*, https://stockastudio.com/following/stockastudio.com/someparts-x-berghain-x-HIVE-RISE, accessed May 09, 2025.

Ahmed, Sara (2006): *Queer Phenomenology: Orientations, Objects, Others*, Durham: Duke University Press.

Austin, Ashley/Craig, Shelley/Navega, Nicole/McInroy, Lauren (2020): »It's my safe space: The life-saving role of the internet in the lives of transgender and gender diverse youth,« in: *International Journal of Transgender Health* 21, 33–44. doi: 10.1080/15532739.2019.1700202

Awkward-Rich, Cameron (2022): *The Terrible We: Thinking with Trans Maladjustment*, Durham: Duke University Press.

Binnie, Imogen (2013): *Nevada*, New York: Topside Press.

Crawford, Lucas (2020): *Transgender Architectonics: The Shape of Change in Modernist Space*, London/New York: Routledge.

Deleuze, Gilles/ Parnet, Claire (2007): *Dialogues II*, New York: Columbia University Press.

Derrida, Jacques (1995): *Mal d'Archive: Une Impression Freudienne.* – English translation: Archive Fever: A Freudian Impression, transl. by Eric Prenowitz, Chicago/London: The University of Chicago Press.

Dobler, Jens (ed.) (2004): *Prolegomena zu Magnus Hirschfelds Jahrbuch für sexuelle Zwischenstufen (1899-1923): Register, Editionsgeschichte, Inhaltsbeschreibungen, Schriftenreihe der Magnus-Hirschfeld-Gesellschaft*, Hamburg: von Bockel.

Eskridge, William (1999): *Gaylaw: Challenging the Apartheid of the Closet*, Cambridge: Harvard University Press.

Garland-Thomson, Rosemarie (2011): *Extraordinary Bodies: Figuring Physical Disability in American Culture and Literature*, New York: Columbia University Press.

Gough, Tim (2017): *Trans-Architecture*, Delft: FOOTPRINT.

Harris, Thomas (1988): *The Silence of the Lambs*, New York: St. Martin's Press.

Habringer, Magdalena/Wild, Gabriele/Bischeltsrieder, Anja/Scharf, Verena (2023): *LGBTIQ+ in der (niederschwelligen) Wiener Wohnungslosenhilfe. Erfahrungswerte und Bedarfslagen aus Sicht von Fachkräften und Nutzer*innen: Forschungsbericht im Auftrag des Fonds Soziales Wien*, Wien: FH Campus Wien. doi: 10.34895/fhcw.0010

Junge, Torsten/Schmincke, Imke, eds. (2007): *Marginalisierte Körper: zur Soziologie und Geschichte des anderen Körpers*, Münster: Unrast.

Ketter, Verena(2014): »Das Konzept ›vireale Sozialraumaneignung‹ als konstitutive Methode der Jugendarbeit,« in: Ulrich Deinet/ Christian Reutlinger (eds.), *Tätigkeit – Aneignung – Bildung*, Wiesbaden: Springer Fachmedien, 299–310.

Lefebvre, Henri (1991): *The Production of Space*, Cambridge: Blackwell Oxford UK & Cambridge USA.

Liang, Shano/Cormier, Michelle/Bohrer, Rose/Toups Dugas, Phoebe (2025): »Designed & Discovered Euphoria: Insights from Trans-Femme Players' Experiences of Gender Euphoria in Video Games,« in: *Proceedings of the 2025 CHI Conference on Human Factors in Computing Systems*, 1–21. doi: 10.1145/3706598.3714081

Lorde, Audre (1984): *Sister Outsider: Essays and Speeches*, Trumansburg New York: Crossing press.

Moser, Caroline (2014): *Gender Planning and Development: Revisiting, Deconstructing and Reflecting*, London: DPU Working Paper Series.

Movement Advancement Project (n.d.): »*Equality Maps: Bathroom Ban Laws,*« https://www.lgbtmap.org/equality-maps/nondiscrimination/bathroom_bans, accessed May 09, 2025.

Notes from Poland (2025): »*Poland's Last 'Anti-LGBT' Resolution Repealed,*« https://notesfrompoland.com/2025/04/27/polands-last-anti-lgbt-resolution-repealed/, accessed May 09, 2025.

Prosser, Jay (1998): *Second Skins: the Body Narratives of Transsexuality, Gender and Culture Series*, New York: Columbia University Press.

Röll, Franz Josef(2014): »Die Macht der Inneren Bilder. Zum Spannungsverhältnis von Virtueller und Realer Aneignung von Wirklichkeit,« in: Ulrich Deinet/ Christian Reutlinger (eds.), *Tätigkeit – Aneignung – Bildung*, Wiesbaden: Springer Fachmedien, 259–272.

Rosenberg, Jordy (2022): »*The Invention of the Trans Novel,*« https://www.newyorker.com/magazine/2022/06/27/the-invention-of-the-trans-novel-imogen-binnie-nevada, accessed July 23, 2025.

Rottmann, Andrea/Gammerl, Benno/ Lücke, Martin, eds. (2023): *Handbuch Queere Zeitgeschichten I: Räume*, Bielefeld: transcript Verlag.

Sears, Clare (2015): *Arresting Dress: Cross-Dressing, Law, and Fascination in Nineteenth-Century San Francisco, Perverse Modernities*, Durham: Duke University Press.

Spence-Mitchell, Tynslei (2021): »Restroom Restrictions,« in: *Gender, Work & Organization* 28/S1, 14–20. doi: 10.1111/gwao.12545

Staatbibliothek zu Berlin (n.d.): »*Das Institut für Sexualwissenschaft und seine Bibliothek (1919 – 1933),*« https://blog.sbb.berlin/institut-fuer-sexualwissenschaft/#:~:text=Das%20gr%C3%B6%C3%9Fte%20Konvolut%20oder%20am,jemals%20wieder%20nach%20Deutschland%20zur%C3%BCckzukehren., accessed November 2, 2024.

Stone, Sandy (1991): »The Posttranssexual Manifesto,« in: Julia Epstein/ Kristina Straub (eds.), *Body Guards: The Cultural Politics of Gender Ambiguity*. New York: Routledge, 280–304.

Stryker, Susan (1994): My Words to Victor Frankenstein Above the Village of Chamounix: Performing Transgender Rage, in: *GLQ* 1/3, 237–254. doi: 10.1215/10642684-1-3-237

Stryker, Susan (2008): *Transgender history, Seal studies*, Berkeley: Seal Press.

Dimensions of Architectural Knowledge, 2024–08 ∂
https://doi.org/10.14361/dak-2024-0808

Reimagining Architectural Practice through Relation:
Notes from the In-Between

Ana Bisbicus, Sarah Hachem – [habi practice]

Abstract: Architecture is never neutral. It enforces racialized brutality, ecological extraction, patriarchal domination, and capitalist accumulation. *habi practice* traces these entanglements across maps, cities, forests, seas, classrooms, and skies, revealing the structures that govern what is legible, livable, and imaginable. We write from disorientation, from the in-between, refusing singular stories, fixed identities, or universal truths. Through relation, we see how life, histories, and knowledge intertwine. Through reimagination, we call forth new forms of being and inhabiting the world. To dwell in what is broken is to confront power and to insist on futures that were and could be otherwise.

Keywords: Reimagination; Coloniality; Architecture Education; Relation; In-Between/Third Space.

Corresponding authors: Ana Bisbicus (University of Kassel, Germany), Sarah Hachem (independent Scholar); ana.bisbicus@uni-kassel.de; https://orcid.org/0009-0004-3559-837X; info.habi.practice@gmail.com; https://orcid.org/0009-0005-9694-2688 ∂ Open Access.

Every building is a planet

he map
he dictionary
he classroom
he building
he forest
he european city
he sea
he third space
the sky

1.
Drawing: »Our [thoughts] are geographies of selves made up of diverse, bordering, and overlapping [territories]. [They're] each composed of information, billions of bits of cultural knowledge superimposing many different categories of experience. Like a map with colored web lines of rivers, highways, lakes, towns, and other landscape features en donde pasan y cruzan las cosas, we are marked. [...] As our bodies interact with internal and external, real and virtual, past and present environments, people, and objects around us, we weave (tejemos).« (Anzaldua 2015:69) © Ana Bisbicus, Sarah Hachem – [habi practice]

Introduction

We write from entangled and diasporic positions – dispersed, liminal and emerging from the unsettled cracks.[1] Our perspectives are informed by institutional training in European architectural thought, yet they are carried by memories and silences that exceed the frames of Western academia and its architectural canon. Our lives unfold across and within the geographies this tradition has mapped, theorized and built upon. These are geographies we have moved through, been shaped by and at times implicated in. We do not fully belong to them (anymore), and yet we are not entirely outside them either. We write from grounds that drift, resisting fixed identities and inherited certainties. We do not speak from neutrality. To us, there is no such ground. To claim it is to erase, to order, to dominate.

Our knowledges have been formed both within and in tension with architectural education, a field always entangled with the regulation and organization of land, movement, and life, folded into the long histories of possession, displacement and control. Between ancestral attachments, anti-colonial urgencies, activist insurgencies and the languages of academia, we dwell in the in-between: a site of friction and refusal. But the in-between is also where we make sense, make kin, make home, and transform.

The following notes on terms and propositions emerge from that space. Alongside, outside, and against the institution. They are fragments: incomplete and uncertain, reflecting our current thoughts yet bound to shift as circumstances, urgencies, and relations change. What appears here is not definitive. These notes are mutable; they invite revision, refinement, and critique. Where language falters, we remain open to engaging it together. We do not seek to fix meaning or impose determined forms; rather, we attend to indetermination, embrace »ongoingness,« and practice refusal, choosing to dwell in the broken rather than the fixed. In this sense, the following is also a way for us to literally come to terms.[2]

---

1 By cracks we mean sites of in-betweenness and collective subversion, informed by Chicana/Latinx feminist thought (Anzaldúa, *Borderlands/La Frontera*, 1987), postcolonial theory on cultural interstices (Bhabha, *The Location of Culture*, 1994), and the Black radical tradition (Moten & Harney, *The Undercommons*, 2013).

2 We draw on thinkers whose work attends to incompleteness, relationality, and collective knowing, providing frameworks for engaging with the unfinished, emergent, and non-linear. These include, among others, Collins (1990), Halberstam (2011, 2018), Haraway (2016), hooks (1994), and Moten & Harney (2013).

We understand architecture not as a set of isolated forms or objects, but as a web of relations between life forms, knowledge systems, and power structures. Our practice seeks to render visible and work against the mechanisms that are normalized or taken for granted, through which architecture participates in shaping social, spatial, and ecological conditions, producing structural forms of violence and brutality.[3] At the same time, we attend to what remains in shadow: the movements and relations that refuse capture, that insist on opacity, and that sustain emergent, collective, and other ways of inhabiting the world.[4]

In doing so, we challenge ourselves and our learning environment to ask:

What does it mean to design in relation?

We do not seek to reinvent from scratch. We reimagine as Éduard Glissant teaches us and Frantz Fanon asks of us. Through relation. Through refusal of the universal. Toward an architecture of entanglement.

The Drift

Nothing exists untouched. Nothing begins in isolation. We join threads that precede us: the web, the mesh, the rhizome, the woven cosmos, the *Feral Atlas* (Tsing/Deger/Keleman Saxena/Zhou 2020).[5] Ingold (2000) and Haraway (2007), Deleuze/Guattari (1980) and Jongerius (2021), amongst others, remind us that every act, every thing and every thought is entangled.

---

3 We use *brutality*, following Harney and Moten, to name the structural and logistical operations of domination explored in violence (Harney & Moten, 2021, 2022).

4 cf. Michel Foucault (*Discipline and Punish*, 1977) on how power operates through regimes of visibility and ordinariness; and Édouard Glissant (Poetics of Relation, 1997) on opacity as a refusal of imposed legibility and the colonial gaze.

5 cf. Feral Atlas (Tsing/Deger/Keleman Saxena/Zhou 2020) offers an interactive platform of feral landscapes, tracing entanglements of human and nonhuman processes that interact in complex, often unpredictable ways. For example, the introduction of the Chinese mitten crab (Eriocheir sinensis) from the Yangtze River Delta to European waterways exemplifies such entanglements. Initially transported via ballast water, this species has since established itself in various European rivers, including the Rhine, where it has become an invasive species. Its spread underscores how human activities, such as global trade and infrastructure development, facilitate the movement of species across ecosystems, leading to unforeseen ecological consequences.

Relation, like mycelium, sometimes is hidden, sometimes breaks through, is ever evolving, and weaves connections as conditions shift (Tsing 2015).

We move, think, and imagine in relation. Thought itself emerges from entanglement, where ideas, spaces, and histories intertwine. Colonial frameworks seek to fix, categorize, compartmentalize, contain, and hierarchize. But relation drifts. It resists enclosure. Édouard Glissant (1990) calls this the »Poetics of Relation«: identities and knowledges formed across movement, encounter, and exchange. Difference meets difference without demanding sameness.

Moten and Harney (2013) warn that the individual is a form of enclosure, produced when entanglement is cut off. Individuation is therefore an illusion of separation: the very idea of the individual depends on denying entanglement. We are never simply individuals, but always entangled in systems of suffering, histories of dispossession and survival, and in the webs of cultural and ecological interdependencies, which make visible the falsely constructed boundaries between self and other, past and present, human and more-than-human. It is neither enough nor possible to act ethically alone; what matters is how we organize together, cultivate collectivity, modes of gathering, because no single act can dissolve systemic and intertwined forces (Shotwell 2016).

Reimagining emerges in these spaces. It emerges through our entanglements with others, with histories, and with the worlds we inhabit. Fanon (1961) teaches that imagination is the condition of struggle: to envision the new human, new ways of knowing, new spaces where life together unfolds beyond colonial categories. »New« here is not to be understood as something unprecedented in time, but as transformed through struggle, reimagined ways of being, and renewed relations. For Glissant (1990), imagination, too, refuses to be determined by the past and unfolds improvisationally through encounter and relation, where connections across difference shape what might yet emerge.

>   »What is to be done is to found a new society [...] by cultivating the spaces and places that by dint of their existence instantiate the impossibility of the normative bastion that surrounds us. We might call this justice. We might call it a non-utopic utopia, a sanctuary. We might call it the undercommons.« (Bey 2019: 8:55 min)

For Bey, liberation is not only about dismantling oppressive structures. It is also about creating and inhabiting practices that make other ways of living tangible; here and now. It is about sustaining the shared life that already insists in us. We do not only react to brutality. We live otherwise in the midst of it, protecting and reimagining what we inherit and what we do not yet know.

»The future already was,« affirms Llanquiray Painemal at the panel *The Unity of Our Struggle, the Diversity of Our Tactics II* (Brick by Brick Collective 2025), invoking a proverb also cited by Miriam Pixtun of the Maya Kaqchikel from Nacahuil, Guatemala (cf. Espinosa Miñoso 2015). The world we fight for, a world without borders, prisons, patriarchal violence, or imperial domination, is not an impossible horizon. It has already existed. Before colonization, before the carving of land into private property and nation-states, before the creation of police, prisons, and capitalist extraction, there were societies rooted in reciprocity and responsibility to land and to each other. Abolition is not an invention but an ongoing practice. Anti-colonial struggle is not nostalgia but the work of sustaining what colonialism could not fully extinguish. The future already was, and it moves with us still, in the ongoing drift and in entanglements that resist containment.

Moten and Harney (2013) caution against determination, against representation, against fixity. We remain in the broken – not the fixed, the completed, the normalized. We live otherwise, in and with others, pursuing the unimaginable even as it pursues us. Liberation is a collective endeavor, a continual drift: inhabiting what persists in the cracks, sustaining other forms of life and love, and imagining worlds that emerge from entanglement.

We hold together disorientation. That is the relational.

»All that you touch
You Change.
All that you Change
Changes you.
The only lasting truth
Is Change.«
—Octavia Butler, *Parable of the Sower* (1993:3)

The Map

Our work interrogates the colonial and imperial logics embedded in architectural tools – maps, plans, and diagrams – that have long served as instruments of authority and domination. These tools were not simply techniques of representation but of occupation: of knowledge, land and life. They rendered space knowable in order to render it governable. Maps were integral to the creation and enforcement of borders and territories that defined colonial control. Produced by colonial powers, these maps were and still are used to justify the division of land, the imposition of artificial borders, and the displacement of Indigenous peoples, marking a brutal reorganization of space under colonial rule.

In our teaching and research, we therefore turn to the map not as a fixed object, but as a site of contestation. We ask:

Who gets to plan? Who gets mapped, and on whose terms?

In order to be heard by systems of colonial governance, many Indigenous communities have been coerced into translating their spatial knowledge into colonial cartographic forms. Not due to a lack of their own systems, but because settler states have systematically denied the legitimacy of Indigenous territorial understandings. This forced translation is not benign: It reflects the ongoing imposition of epistemic hierarchies where recognition is contingent upon assimilation to the colonizer's terms. Long before colonial borders and cadastral grids, Indigenous peoples articulated spatial relations through systems deeply embedded in cosmology, kinship, and ecological stewardship. From *Micronesian stick charts of the Marshall Islands* (cf. Ascher 1995) and *Inuit carved maps* (cf. Decolonial Atlas 2016) to *Aboriginal Australian songlines* (cf. Micalizo 2016; cf. National Film and Sound Archive 2016). These were not merely »alternative« maps, but ontologically distinct ways of being in and with space, brutally disrupted by the mapping regimes of the empire.

We learn from indigenous practices and insurgent cartographies that use mapping not to reproduce colonial order, but to reclaim territory, history, and relation. Indigenous communities have long resisted spatial brutality by developing counter-mapping strategies as tools of sovereignty and memory. For example, the *Gitxsan* and *Wet'suwet'en First Nations in British Columbia* produced detailed maps of their traditional territories in the 1990s to assert land rights in court, mapping not just geography but stories, songs, trails, fishing sites, and spiritual places. (cf. Spike 1998: 88) Similarly, the *Zapatistas* in Chiapas, Mexico, began creating maps in 1994 that ignored official political boundaries and instead illustrated community spaces, resistance sites, and self-governed zones (cf. Waldseemüller/School of Chiapas). In the Philippines, the *Pulangi River Basin people* initiated participatory mapping in the 1990s to resist hydropower projects, combining oral histories with GPS data to assert ancestral land claims (cf. Southeast Asia Sustainable Forest Management Network 1993; cf. Environmental Science for Social Change 2023).

In a similar vein, Forensic Architecture collaborates with Indigenous communities to create maps that document and assert land rights. For example, they have worked with the Nama and Ovaherero communities in Namibia to reconstruct the town of Swakopmund as it existed during the 1904–1908 genocide, locating the concentration camp, sites of forced labor, and unmarked graves, which persisted in community memory but were erased from official narratives, using oral histories, testimonies, and forensic archaeology (cf. forensic architecture 2024). This mapping was carried out to support the communities' calls for preservation of burial grounds, to counter genocide denial, and to promote education about historical injustices. This approach reflects a mapping methodology that parallels Indigenous strategies of reclaiming territory and memory from colonial narratives.

As Audre Lorde reminds us, »Even when they are dangerous, examine the heart of those machines which you hate before you discard them. But do not mourn their lack of power, lest you be condemned to relive them« (Lorde 1997 [1973]: 59). Here, the »machines« can be read as the map, the plan, the diagram – the very instruments of surveillance and extraction. Lorde's words urge us not to abandon these tools naively, but to interrogate their logic, understand their mechanisms, and subvert them without reproducing them. She warns us, »the master's tools will never dismantle the master's house« (Lorde 1984). The map can be temporarily repurposed for survival, advocacy, or counter-mapping, but it will always tend back toward the structures it was designed to serve. The risk of cooptation is ever-present: If left unchallenged, the map's grammar of borders, property, and legibility will simply redraw the master's house. What is required, then, is not only repurposing but also the difficult work of unmaking – dismantling the map's colonial order in order to imagine spatial practices otherwise.

The Dictionary

A dictionary is to language what a map is to space: A structured representation that claims to define boundaries and meanings, yet often reveals the biases and power dynamics of those who produce it. As a tool of authority, the dictionary has long served to codify language, standardize thought, and marginalize expressions deemed outside the norm as deviant or illegitimate, enforcing dominant ideologies while silencing other forms of speaking, knowing and being.

In the German language, the *Wörterbuch* (dictionary, literally »book of words«) is perceived as a container of definitions, objectivity, and truth, while the *Bilderbuch* (literally »book of pictures«) is associated with children, play and imagination. This contrast exposes a deeper hierarchy embedded in Western knowledge systems: The privileging of the written word as rational and serious over the image, which is rendered imaginative and unserious. What is considered knowledge and who is considered knowledgeable, is thus already prefigured in the very structure of language. The dictionary reveals who is granted societal participation and whose voices are excluded in the production of »truth« and knowledge. As Gayatri Chakravorty Spivak argues in *Can the Subaltern Speak?* (1988), those who are marginalized in society, particularly in colonial contexts, are often denied the authority to speak, and by extension, the power to define. This exclusion is again mirrored in the hierarchy of knowledge production, where written and published forms are valued above oral and embodied traditions, erasing or disregarding knowledge systems that do not conform to Western modes of understanding.

Building on this, Homi K. Bhabha writes in *The Location of Culture* (1994), language is not a neutral medium but a site of negotiation, ambivalence, and hybridity where meanings are constantly reshaped through cultural encounters and power struggles. The dictionary, therefore, is a tool with which dominant ideologies attempt to stabilize language, to make it behave. But meaning is never fixed. The very act of definition reveals its instability. It does so by suppressing the fluidity inherent to language. Definitions within a dictionary reflect not universal truths but the contested terrain of cultural authority and legitimacy. Bhabha's notion of *cultural translation* offers a way to think about the dictionary as a living site of negotiation rather than a static record. In this view, the act of defining is inherently ambivalent: It seeks to establish boundaries but also reveals the instability and contestation of those boundaries.

In our experience, when entering newly formed classrooms, we lack language, especially when addressing colonialism and racism, due to their systemic underrepresentation in curricula. To confront this gap and to find common ground, we create an evolving, participatory dictionary where meanings are not fixed but continuously shaped by context, interaction, and reinterpretation. This shared vocabulary becomes a space where terms are negotiated and reimagined to reflect the perspectives of all contributors. In doing so, the dictionary becomes not just a tool for understanding but a site of transformation. It resists the imposition of rigid structures and invites contributors to inhabit the *third space*[6] where new meanings and possibilities are forged. To envision new approaches to design, or even unsettle what it means to design, we must reimagine the language of design itself as a fluid, collaborative, and transformative process.

Because we »reject the supposed voice we have inherited from whiteness [...] We resonate. Rhythms. Collectively because there is no single one. Against the privatization of the world and of words.« (Guerra Arjona, Asamblea Opaca, 2024:14, author's translation)

The Classroom

In the territories that are today known by their colonizers' name *Latin America*, but were called *Abya Yala* by the Kuna people before colonization, the 1960s saw the emergence of a new pedagogical movement shaped by the Brazilian educator Paulo Freire. In *Educação como prática da liberdade* (Education as the Practice of Freedom) (Freire 1967) and *Pedagogia do Oprimido* (Pedagogy of the Oppressed) (Freire 1968), the oppressed are understood as active creators and producers of knowledge for their own liberation. *Educación popular* emerges in the streets, in neighborhoods, in the forest, and on the field. These spaces become classrooms where knowledge is generated in everyday life, through relationships and coming together. Today, many of these approaches can be found in self-organized groups, toy libraries (*ludotecas*), community spaces and gardens in the neighborhoods on the outskirts of *Abya Yala*, as well as in rural areas with self-organized universities of Indigenous people the *Intercultural Autonomous Indigenous University* (UAIIN) in Cauca by the Consejo Regional Indígena del Cauca (CRIC) in southwest

---

6   The term »third space« was introduced by Homi K. Bhabha in *The Location of Culture* (1994) to describe an in-between space where cultural identities and meanings are not fixed but continuously negotiated. It is a site where differences interact and new forms of identity and understanding can emerge beyond established binaries. Although Gloria Anzaldúa does not use the term »third space« explicitly, her concepts of »*Nepantla*,« »*Borderlands*,« and »*mestiza consciousness*« similarly describe spaces of cultural and personal in-betweenness, where overlapping identities coexist and transform, highlighting the complexity of living between multiple worlds.

of Colombia. *Epistemological disobedience* (2018), as Silvia Rivera Cusicanqui writes in her book *Un mundo ch'ixi es posible*, refers to the practice of rejecting the Eurocentric canon that continues to marginalize or appropriate knowledge. The classroom can be understood here as a space of negotiation that transforms not only materially and spatially but also conceptually: from different scales, from ideas in people's minds to larger grassroots organizations or movements.

Moten and Harney offer a complementary perspective by distinguishing study from education. Education seeks order, hierarchy, and the transmission of knowledge from teacher to student. Study, by contrast, unfolds in its own rhythms: dissonant, emergent, and often collective (Moten and Harney 2013: 125ff). Study is not defined by the official start of a class or the teacher's direction. It does not need the »call to order« (Moten 2013: 126). It is present in the anticipations, murmurs, interactions, and conversations that exceed any lesson. It defies neat distinctions between teacher and student, »noise and music, chatter and knowledge, pain and truth« (Halberstam 2013:9).

Study holds the power to reimagine the world, to challenge entrenched systems of injustice, and to cultivate spaces of gathering where creativity and critical thought can flourish. Architecture, we argue, has the potential to transform not only the built environment but also the structures of power that shape our lives. The classroom, as bell hooks reminds us, can be »the most radical space of possibility« (hooks 1994:12), where participants collectively envision new ways of being and moving beyond conventional boundaries. Knowledge in this space is not transferred one-way; everyone is an expert in the lived experience of space. Each participant, regardless of background or formal training, contributes insight into how space functions, feels, and shapes life. For us, the classroom extends beyond academia: it is where theory emerges from practice and ultimately must return to it.

The Building

On November 18, 2024, the Palestinian Youth Movement shared a haunting image of a drone, captured an instant before it struck a housing building in Lebanon, dropped by Israel. The accompanying text read: »Every building is a planet.«

To destroy a building is not only to erase a physical structure; it is to annihilate worlds – the intimacies, livelihoods, histories, and stories connected to its walls. It is an attempt to extinguish the very possibility of its people's future. Such destruction severs relationships – with others and with oneself – displaces communities and makes visible the stakes of architecture as both shelter and instrument of control. It is also a moment in long histories of dispossession, state neglect, and militarized governance, where spatial power shapes who lives and who is made vulnerable.

While some view buildings as isolated objects or enclosed systems like containers or machines, we understand them as worlds in themselves. They do not merely house existence; they shape it, scar it, and are scarred in turn. They are embedded in geographies of power, inequalities written into land and stone, reflecting decisions about whose lives are protected and whose are exposed. They carry the rhythms of life, the laughter, whispers, and daring dreams of those within, insisting quietly on futures yet imagined. These acts of living – of inhabiting, creating, and dreaming – are themselves forms of resistance to the structures that would annihilate them. Their walls testify to those who built, dwelled, or were barred from entering. Every building is a manifestation of power: Some reveal it brutally and overtly, as in prisons, border checkpoints, or military outposts; others encode it more quietly, in the spaces of the everyday.

Architecture is never only about material form. It organizes environments, governs behavior, influences atmospheres and inscribes hierarchies, even as it can also nurture relations, provide refuge, and hold the daring possibilities of imagination and dreaming. Buildings both reflect and enforce the uneven distribution of life, yet they are also grounds where persistence, improvisation, and collective care emerge. Buildings both embody and reproduce the social and political orders that bring them into being. It is both the scene of devastation and the ground on which life insists. Our work begins from this entanglement: To trace how power is inscribed in space, to dwell with its ruins, and to imagine how worlds might still be made otherwise.

The Forest

Forests, as such, hardly exist anymore. What we are shown are often tree plantations, monocultures designed to serve industrial timelines rather than life's cycles. Declared nature reserves, forests are regulated in ways that rarely consider who else lives there: Indigenous peoples, animals, fungi, or spirits. Displacement and extraction go hand in hand, furnishing our furniture, building materials, metals for construction, and the critical minerals used in batteries and electronics here in Europe, all while severing deep-rooted connections to land. The forest embodies a site of both refuge and resistance, as well as colonial extraction and environmental brutality. It is a scarred archive of loss, but also a dense and layered network of entanglement, aliveness, and endurance.

What does it mean for us as spatial planners to view the forest not merely as a resource and dead material, but as a living, »vibrant matter« (Bennett 2020). Bennett asks how political responses to public issues might change if we were to take the vitality of non-human species seriously. How can a forest, a tree, be considered not only as a resource, but also as an equal actor? How do we protect the forest as a system of relations and stories, rather than just a resource? The precedent-setting case of *Los Cedros* in Ecuador, in which a cloud forest was recognized as a legal subject by the Constitutional Court as a means of protection against a mining project, could set the tone.

The European City

The word »city« originates from the Latin civitas, which means citizenship or state. But who can have citizenship in the city? Who defines what citizenship is? According to the Merriam-Webster Dictionary, a citizen is defined as »a member of a state« and a citizenship is the »status of being a citizen« or »a membership in a community.« But how does one become a »member,« especially when that membership is constantly denied or even revoked, and when officially granted, it can be entirely stripped away? This exclusion »has been enduring throughout the history of citizenship: [Enslaved people], women, colonial subjects, guest workers, legal aliens, [illegalized] immigrants, refugees – all have been identified as noncitizens at one point in the past, and some continue to be so in the present.« (Akcan 2020:337)

Thus, people are categorized into citizens and non-citizens, restricting or denying their access to spaces in the city. Akcan highlights how race intersects with citizenship, noting that even when racialized people in European cities have formal citizenship, they are marked as non-citizens through racism and racialized assumptions (cf. Akcan 2020). This is echoed in the words of the activist Biplab Basu (1951–2024) from KOP (Campaign Against Racist Police Violence) during a conversation on police violence in November 2023. He roughly stated, »It doesn't matter if you possess citizenship as a racialized person. The police ultimately determine which passport you end up with.« (Basu 2023, author's translation)

Being part of the »state/city« is not only about having this »membership,« but also about how this »member« looks and is being read. European cities become spaces where border-like controls are integrated into everyday life. At the airport, in deportation centers, through pushbacks in the mountains, in temporary shelters for permanent use, in immigration offices, in Heimantministerien, in sublease agreements, in return flight tickets as advertising posters for election campaigns, at the turnstile of public swimming pools, or at Hermannplatz during an »aleatory« police check. All these spaces serve as an everyday reminder that »no, you don't belong here.« These structures create *hostile environments* (Pezzani 2020) for those who fall outside the created norm. Does only the citizen have the right to the city?

We often shift coloniality to the former or still-colonized territories. City and Migration Researcher Noa K. Ha argues that, instead of attributing the problems of inequality within European cities to migration and a supposedly failed integration, the coloniality within Europe's borders should be more acknowledged (cf. Ha 2017).

Whether here or there, it is still clear that, imposed as a blueprint for the establishment of cities in contested and colonized territories, the European city serves as a model that many aspire to emulate in some way. However, following Fanon's words in *The Wretched of the Earth* (1965), particularly in chapter 6, the model of Europe – and here, the European city – is one that should be overturned.

> »So, my [spatial planners], how is it that we do not understand that we have better things to do than to follow that same Europe[an city]?
>
> Come, then, comrades [fellow planners] the European [city] game has finally ended; we must find something different. We today can do everything, so long as we do not imitate Europe, so long as we are not obsessed by the desire to catch up with Europe.
>
> Europe now lives at such a mad, reckless pace that [it] has shaken off all guidance and all reason, and [it] is running headlong into the abyss; we would do well to avoid it with all possible speed.« (Fanon 1963 [1961]: 312)

The Sea

The souls swimming in the sea have been witnesses to centuries of violence. Brutality inflicted on bodies that were once forcibly taken on ships to build the wealth of *white* nations. Nations that are now sought by others, on boats that sink into the sea. With 10,659 tons of weight, 93.44 meters long, and 27.43 meters wide, *Bibby Stockholm* was built in 1976 by a Dutch company and converted in 1992 into an accommodation barge (cf. Bibby Maritime 2020). A boat that has been contracted by the UK Government to house people seeking asylum at Portland Port. According to the UK Refugee Council (2023), its owner, the company Bibby Marine, has historic ties to the slave trade (cf. UK Refugee Council 2023; cf. Andrews/White/Kerins 2024). The sea bears witness to the brutal cramming of people, once vessels for enslavement, now prisons on water for refugees seeking to enter Fortress Europe. As Hartman (2008) reminds us, the afterlives of slavery are not confined to the past. They persist in the spatial, social, and structural forms that continue to constrain Black and marginalized bodies. Architectures on water, like Bibby Stockholm, extend the logic of containment and control across centuries.

It is said that all water is connected. The water in our bodies that we exhale and that becomes one with the environment around us, the clouds which then, in the form of rain, drip down and flow into the rivers, and the water that flows into the rivers, and the seas. The sea, the ocean, the Atlantic Ocean, and the *Black Atlantic*, as described by Paul Gilroy, have been shaped by the violence stemming from the enslavement of Black bodies and the transatlantic slave trade. Yet, it can also be understood as a transnational and transcultural space, functioning not only as a border but also as a space of connection for the Black Diaspora (Gilroy 1993). We could consider the sea as a space that was and is not only a witness to coloniality but also a space that has been, and continues to be, subjected to colonial negotiations. Renisa Mawani describes in her Book *Across Oceans of Law: The Komagata Maru and Jurisdiction in the Time of Empire* (2018) how international law did not emerge in European cities or along colonial borders, but rather on ships during imperial struggles at sea.

> »All the dead who sail our waters, we will not forget them.« (The Truth in Exile
> – Road to Peace 2025, author's translation).[7]

---

7 Sentence extracted from a textile in the exhibition *The Truth in Exile – Road to Peace* (Berlin 2025). The exhibition was created through various workshops with people from the

The Third Space

We build on the ideas of those who came before us and wrote extensively about how spatial understanding can be conceived. Not as something closed or fixed, but as something fluid that can extend beyond geographical boundaries, spanning across dreams, memories, and experiences. Space, as something constantly in flux, emerges through the friction and encounters of diverse experiences and perspectives, opening up new spaces, spaces of possibility. These are spaces that, as Homi Bhabha taught us, allow processes to unfold precisely where difference exists (Bhabha 1994:1). Spaces that are produced in the in-between and provide a »terrain for elaborating strategies of selfhood – singular or communal – that initiate new signs of identity, and innovative sites of collaboration and contestation, in the act of defining the idea of society itself« (Bhabha 1994:2). These are spaces that challenge binary constructions, which structure the way our world is built.

Borderspace, as author Gloria E. Anzaldúa has taught us, is thought from the border, from the in-between. By studying and learning from the US/Mexican border, as well as from the intersection of being a lesbian, Chicana, and woman of color, she lands on the concept of *Nepantla*, a word from Nahuatl meaning »to stand in the middle.« For her, it is both a psychological and emotional space, a creative space that, from the painful border experience, can give birth to new things. Liminal beings, or *Nepantleras*, the people that inhabit Nepantla are people who, from their perspective, develop practices that allow them to navigate this border space (Anzaldúa 2015). They develop practices of creativity and care, resistance and resilience. Translated into the city, this border space – or third space – becomes a space of possibility that can respond to issues of spatial justice (Soja 2010).

»What if we start from the space of difference rather than add difference?« (Boys 2020)

Building on Boys' provocation to start from the space of difference, we can extend the idea of third space into the realm of imagination. Speculative fiction becomes one such space, where the boundaries of identity, power, and possibility are not only observed but actively reconfigured. Speculative

---

Colombian exile community in Germany, addressing the war and enforced disappearances. In the rivers, the bodies of murdered individuals are often found in Colombia.

fiction, as theorists like Donna Haraway (2016) and Kodwo Eshun (1998) suggest, can also be understood as a third space. By imagining worlds beyond the constraints of the present, it becomes a site of in-betweenness where established norms, hierarchies, and material realities can be questioned and reconfigured. In these imagined spaces, identities, relations, and power structures are not fixed but open to experimentation, offering a laboratory for thinking and practicing alternative futures. Authors like Octavia Butler (1993) demonstrate how speculative fiction can cultivate new ways of understanding difference, power, and community, transforming the narrative of the possible and creating imaginative terrains for marginalized perspectives. Reading or writing speculative fiction is, therefore, an act of inhabiting a border space.

The Sky

For millennia, the sky has been a site of wonder, connection, and guidance. The stars illuminated the paths of peoples across deserts and seas, while the moon, in her phases, taught of cycles, renewal, and time. In the creation story of the *Haudenosaunee*, Skywoman descends from Skyworld, carrying seeds of life in her hands, a gift she offers to the earth below. Her story teaches that the cosmos is not an empty expanse but a living, relational web where reciprocity and care bind all beings together, reminding us of the responsibilities that come with receiving such gifts. Yet, the sky is also inscribed with histories of domination. The language of »decolonizing Mars,« so casually repeated in media, echoes the same extractive logics that continue to scar earthly territories during colonial expansions, extending ambitions of possession and exploitation into the celestial realm. What does it mean to claim the heavens while the violent legacies of colonial conquest remain unresolved here on Earth?

Airspace, far from being a passive or neutral expanse, is shaped by histories of control and exclusion. Borders drawn through aviation treaties, satellite paths, and militarized drone operations mirror the colonial partitioning of land, turning the sky into another contested domain. Airports, often mislabeled as »non-places,« are deeply politicized spaces, entangled with histories of surveillance, migration, and global inequality. As Sinthujan Varatharajah, in an interview with Deutschlandfunk in 2022 observed, colonial histories persist in aviation routes: Lufthansa's flights to Namibia,

Spanish airlines' links to Latin America, and the militarization of airspace through drones and satellites. (Varatharajah 2022). These infrastructures do not simply organize movement. They assert control, dictate who can traverse the skies, and render others surveilled, excluded, or constrained. Where once people looked up and dreamed of the stars, many now hear drones overhead – an unrelenting sound that seeps into the body, producing constant fear and exhaustion. The sky becomes a reminder that it is not free, that we are not free. Yet in our longing, we reach toward a sky that can once again inspire wonder.

References

Akcan, Esra (2020): »Open Architecture, Rightlessness, and Citizens-to-Come.« in: Irene Cheng/Charles L. Davis II/Mabel O. Wilson (eds.), *Race and Modern Architecture: A Critical History from the Enlightenment to the Present*, Pittsburgh: University of Pittsburgh Press, 324–338.

Andrews, Charlotte/White, Marcus/Kerins, Dan (2024): »What is the Bibby Stockholm and why is it controversial?« in: *BBC News*, https://www.bbc.com/news/articles/c3e83k8z85vo, accessed August 25, 2025.

Anzaldúa, Gloria E. (1987): *Borderlands/La Frontera: The New Mestiza*, San Francisco: Aunt Lute Books.

Anzaldúa, Gloria E./Keating, AnaLouise, eds. (2015): *Light in the Dark/Luz en lo Oscuro: Rewriting Identity, Spirituality, Reality*, Durham/London: Duke University Press.

Ascher, Marcia (1995): »Models and Maps from the Marshall Islands. A Case in Ethnomathematics,« in: *Historia Mathematica 22*, 347–370.

Asamblea Opaca/Guerra Arjona, Felipe (2024): *Coreografías del Habitar*, Madrid: OnA Ediciones.

Basu, Biplab (2023): »Campaign Against Racist Police Violence.« *Talk on police violence*, Oyoun, Berlin.

Bennett, Jane (2010): *Vibrant Matter: A Political Ecology of Things*, Durham/London: Duke University Press.

Bey, Marquise (2019): »10/13 | The Undercommons I.« in: *Panel part of Critique and Praxis, Columbia Center for Contemporary Critical Thought, Columbia Law School*, New York, https://blogs.law.columbia.edu/praxis1313/10-13/?cn-reloaded=1, accessed August 18, 2025.

Bhabha, Homi K. (1994): *The Location of Culture*, London/New York: Routledge.

Bibby Marine Limited (2020): » Bibby Stockholm Factsheet,« in: *Bibby Maritime*, https://web.archive.org/web/20230404201335/https://n01.od2.myftpupload.com/wp-content/uploads/2020/09/Stockholm-Factsheet.pdf, accessed May 05, 2025.

Bourriaud, Nicolas (2002): *Relational Aesthetics*, Dijon: Les Presses du réel.

Boys, Jos (2020): »Starting from Difference with Zoe Partington and Jos Boys. From the DisOrdinary Architecture Project,« in: *F_PODCAST*, https://f-podcast.podigee.io/4-starting-from-difference, accessed September 15, 2025.

Butler, Octavia E. (1993): *Parable of the Sower*, New York: Four Walls Eight Windows.

Collins, Patricia Hill (1990): *Black Feminist Thought: Knowledge, Consciousness, and the Politics of Empowerment*, Boston: Unwin Hyman.

Decolonial Atlas (2016): »Inuit Cartography,« https://decolonialatlas. wordpress.com/2016/04/12/inuit-cartography/, accessed August 04, 2025.

Environmental Science for Social Change (2023): »*Social vulnerability profiling: Contributing to the effective management of forest ecosystems in the Agus and Pulangi watersheds (Part 2)*,« https://essc. org.ph/content/social-vulnerability-profiling-contributing-to-the-effective-management-of-forest-ecosystems-in-the-agus-and-pulangi-watersheds-part-2/, accessed August 20, 2025.

Eshun, Kodwo (1998): *More Brilliant than the Sun: Adventures in Sonic Fiction*, London: Quartet Books.

Fanon, Frantz (1952): *Black Skin, White Masks*, Paris: Éditions du Seuil. – English translation: *Black Skin, White Masks*, transl. by Charles Lam Markmann, New York: Grove Press, 1967.

Fanon, Frantz (1961): *Les Damnés de la Terre*. – English translation: *The Wretched of the Earth*, transl. by Constance Farrington, New York: Grove Press, 1963.

Forensic Architecture (2024): »German Colonial Genocide in Namibia: Swakopmund,« in: *forensic architecture*, https://forensic-architecture.org/ investigation/swakopmund, accessed August, 21, 2025.

Gilroy, Paul (1993): *The Black Atlantic: Modernity and Double Consciousness*, Cambridge, MA: Harvard University Press.

Glissant, Édouard (1990): *Poétique de la Relation*. – English translation: *Poetics of Relation*, transl. by Betsy Wing, Ann Arbor: University of Michigan Press, 2010.

Ha, Noa K. (2017): »Coloniality within Europe's Borders: Rethinking Migration and Integration,« in: *European Urban and Regional Studies 18/2*, 112–128.

Halberstam, Jack (2011): *The Queer Art of Failure*, Durham/London: Duke University Press.

Halberstam, Jack (2013): »The Wild Beyond: With and for the Undercommons,« in: Stefano Harney/Fred Moten, *The Undercommons: Fugitive Planning and Black Study*, Wivenhoe/New York/Port Watson: Minor Compositions, 9.

Halberstam, Jack (2018): *Trans: A Quick and Quirky Account of Gender Variability*, Boston: MIT Press.

Haraway, Donna (1988): »Situated Knowledges: The Science Question in Feminism and the Privilege of Partial Perspective,« in: *Feminist Studies 14/3*, 575–599.

Haraway, Donna (2007): *When Species Meet*, Minneapolis: University of Minnesota Press.

Haraway, Donna (2016): *Staying with the Trouble: Making Kin in the Chthulucene*, Durham/London: Duke University Press.

Hartman, Saidiya (2008): *Lose Your Mother: A Journey Along the Atlantic Slave Route*, New York: Farrar, Straus and Giroux.

hooks, bell (1994): *Teaching to Transgress: Education as the Practice of Freedom*, New York/London: Routledge.

Ingold, Tim (2000): *The Perception of the Environment: Essays on Livelihood, Dwelling and Skill*, London/New York: Routledge.

Jongerius, Hella (2021): *Woven Cosmos. Solo exhibition at Gropius Bau*, Berlin, Germany.

Lefebvre, Henri (1974): *La production de l'espace*. – English translation: *The Production of Space*, transl. by Donald Nicholson-Smith, Oxford: Blackwell, 1991.

Lorde, Audre (1973): *From a Land Where Other People Live*, Detroit: Broadside Lotus Press.

Lorde, Audre (1984): »The Master's Tools Will Never Dismantle the Master's House,« in: Cherríe Moraga/Gloria Anzaldúa (eds.), *This Bridge Called My Back: Writings by Radical Women of Color*, New York: Kitchen Table: Women of Color Press.

Lorde, Audre (1997): *The Collected Poems of Audre Lorde*, New York/London: W.W. Norton.

Mawani, Renisa (2018): *Across Oceans of Law: The Komagata Maru and Jurisdiction in the Time of Empire*, Durham: Duke University Press.

Mawani, Renisa (2021): »Ocean as Method: Ocean, Law and Climate Catastrophe,« in: *The Funambulist 39*, https://thefunambulist. net/magazine/the-ocean, accessed May 04, 2025.

Mbembe, Achille (2019): *Necropolitics*, transl. by Steven Corcoran, Durham/ London: Duke University Press.

Micalizio, Caryl-Sue (2016): »Aboriginal Songlines Helped Draw the Map in Australia,« in: *National Geographic*, https:// blog.education.nationalgeographic. org/2016/04/08/aboriginal-songlines-helped-draw-the-map-in-australia/, accessed August 03, 2025.

Moten, Fred/Harney, Stefano (2013): *The Undercommons: Fugitive Planning and Black Study*, New York: Minor Compositions.

Moten, Fred/Harney, Stefano (2021): *All Incomplete*, London: Minor Compositions.

Moten, Fred/Harney, Stefano (2022): »On Violence #2« Online lecture as part of the Decolonial Studies Program, Akademie der Künste der Welt (ADKDW) and HAU Hebbel am Ufer,« in: *Akademie der Künste*, https://www.adkdw.org/en/article/3522_ on_violence_2, accessed August 20, 2025.

Musharbash, Yasmine/Tsing, Anna et al. (2015): *Mushroom at the End of the World: On the Possibility of Life in Capitalist Ruins*, Princeton: Princeton University Press.

National Film and Sound Archive (2016): »*The Songlines – Indigenous Studies, Culture*,« https://dl.nfsa.gov.au/module/1539/, accessed August 03, 2025.

Painemal, Llanquiray (2025): »*The Unity of Our Struggle, the Diversity of Our Tactics II*.« Panel by Brick by Brick collective, Spore Initiative Berlin.

Pezzani, Lorenzo (2020): »Hostile Environments: The Politics of Border Control in European Cities,« in: *Migration and Society 6/1*, 25–42.

Rivera Cusicanqui, Silvia (2018): *Un mundo ch'ixi es posible: Ensayos desde un presente en crisis*, Buenos Aires: Tinta Limón.

Robertson, Roland (1995): »Globalization: Time-Space and Homogeneity-Heterogeneity,« in: Mike Featherstone/ Scott Lash/Roland Robertson (eds.), *Global Modernities*, London/Thousand Oaks: Sage Publications, 25–44.

Roy, Ananya (2005): »Urban Informality: Toward an Epistemology of Planning,« in: *Journal of the American Planning Association 71/2*, 147–158.

Southeast Asia Sustainable Forest Management Network (1993): »Pulangi: Securing the upper catchment,« in: *Upland Philipine Communities, Guardians of the final forest frontiers*, https://www. communityforestryinternational.org/ publications/research_reports/upland_ philippine_communities/PART5/, accessed August 20, 2025.

Shotwell, Alexis (2016): *Against Purity: Living Ethically in Compromised Times*, Minneapolis: University of Minnesota Press.

Soja, Edward W. (2010): *Seeking Spatial Justice*, Minneapolis: University of Minnesota Press.

Spike, Matthew (1998): »A Map that Roared and an Original Atlas: Canada, Cartography, and the Narration of Nation,« in: *Annals of the Association of American Geographers 88*, 48–66.

The Truth in Exile – Road to Peace Exhibition (2025): *Text in embroidered exhibition piece*, Berlin.

Tsing, Anna / Deger, Jennifer / Keleman Saxena, Alder / Zhou, N., eds. (2020): *Feral Atlas: The More-than-Human Anthropocene*, https://feralatlas.supdigital.org, accessed August 15, 2025.

UK Refugee Council (2023): »An Open Letter to Bibby Marine,« in: *Refugee Council*, https://www.refugeecouncil.org.uk/press-office/media-centre/an-open-letter-to-bibby-marine/, accessed August 25, 2025.

Varatharajah, Sinthujan (2022): »Wie sich Kolonialgeschichten in den Himmel schreibt,« in: *Deutschlandfunk, Interview with Ramona Westhof*, https://www.deutschlandfunkkultur.de/fliegen-und-kolonialgeschichte-100.html, accessed September 15, 2025.

Waldseemüller: »Three Zapatista-related maps of Chiapas,« in: *School of Chiapas*, https://schoolsforchiapas.org/library/maps/, accessed August 25, 2025.

Wynter, Sylvia (2003): »Unsettling the Coloniality of Being/Power/Truth/Freedom,« in: *The New Centennial Review 3/3*, 257–337.

Dimensions of Architectural Knowledge, 2024-08 ⓐ
https://doi.org/10.14361/dak-2024-0809

Counterproposals in Zurich: Constructive Criticism of Destructive Practices by ZAS, ZAS*, and their Accomplices

*Milena Buchwalder, Ella Eßlinger, Sonja Flury, Jens Knöpfel, Blanka Major, Meghan Rolvien as part of ZAS**

Abstract: In 1959, a group of architects in Zurich began to organize themselves into an association called ZAS (Zürcher Arbeitsgruppe für Städtebau [Zurich Working Group for Urban Planning]). The group, which stayed active until the late 1980s consisted of figures such as Fritz Schwarz, Beate Schnitter, Manuel Pauli and Eduard Neuenschwander. ZAS always acted with a clear political stance – never just by opposing, but by making constructive counterproposals. In 2021, ZAS* was formed as a reactivation of ZAS. In the last four years, ZAS* developed different strategies to enter the processes of political decision-making on urban transformation, e.g. through counterproposals. The counterproposals from ZAS, ZAS* and their accomplices presented in this article show that when architects combine their professional and civic agency, they can directly shape the material and political conditions of democratic practice in the built environment. In the Swiss context of direct democracy, such interventions have the potential to transform both spatial planning and urban life. Through collaborative design, speculative practice, and civic engagement, we aim to reposition architectural work as a means of resistance and transformation. In times of ecological urgency and social fragmentation, the counterproposal is not merely an act of opposition; it is an essential instrument for reimagining and reclaiming the future of our cities.

Keywords: Civic Engagement; Collective Knowledge; Complicity; Counterproposal; Demolition; Democratization of Planning Procedures; Re-use; Speculative Practice.

Corresponding authors: ZAS* (ETH Zurich, Department of Architecture); m.buchwalder@arge.co; ellaesslinger@gmail.com; mail@jensknopfel.com; blanka.d.major@gmail.com; mail@meghanrolvien. com; flury@arch.ethz.ch; info@zas.life; https://orcid.org/0009-0000-2609-236X ⓐ Open Access. ©

As members of ZAS*, we seek to understand how architects might move beyond applying their expertise in design, construction, and architectural history solely in response to competition briefs or commissions. This leads us to question how, as active citizens, architects might proactively put to use their professional knowledge, so that they may advocate for communal interests, explore alternative visions for preserving a city's unique qualities, and contribute to a more democratic and ecologically responsible approach to urban development.

In 2021, the City of Zurich experienced an unprecedented wave of housing demolition. Approximately 1770 flats were torn down that year alone – (Stadt Zürich 2022). Most of the apartments lost were »low-rent units in good condition, which [were] then substituted by larger dwellings unaffordable to the previous tenants« (Malterre-Barthes 2025: 42). These drastic actions, typical of Zurich's current approach to spatial development, must be understood in the context of a 2014 revision to the *Raumplanungsgesetz* [Swiss Spatial Planning Act] (Bundesamt für Raumentwicklung, ARE). This updated piece of legislation requires that urban growth direct itself inwards. Instead of expanding into undeveloped land, cities must increase density within their existing built-up areas. In cities like Zurich, where available land is already scarce, this policy of densification has significantly increased pressure on the existing building stock (DeVylder et al. 2024: 37f). To achieve densification, cities too often turn to *Ersatzneubau* [replacement construction], or in other words, tearing down old buildings and replacing them with new structures. In fact, Zurich's Municipal Structure Plan[1] explicitly endorses *Ersatzneubau* as both »desired« and »necessary.« (Kommunaler Richtplan, Zürich 2021). However, in practice, replacement construction does little to achieve its goal of easing the existing housing shortage.[2] The demolition affects not only residential buildings; the prevailing *tabula rasa* approach by real estate developers has brought sweeping changes to the general urban fabric, with significant political, economic, and social implications (DeVylder et al. 2024: 35).

While the current trend of demolition in Zurich is rightfully concerning, the city's contentious erasure of urban fabric is not a new phenomenon.

---

1   The municipal structure plan [Kommunaler Richtplan] is a strategic planning instrument that defines and coordinates the long-term spatial development of a municipality.

2   According to the Federal Office for Housing [Bundesamt für Wohnungswesen BWO], a housing shortage is said to exist when the vacancy rate falls below 1 percent. In Zurich, the current vacancy rate is just 0.7%.

Attempts by the city to remove buildings and neighborhoods that foster social diversity and affordability have historically provoked resistance, not only from tenants but also from political actors. Local protest movements such as »Globuskrawall«[3] in the late 1960s and the »Opernhauskrawalle«[4] in the 1980s were pivotal moments. They gave the younger generation a voice, as well as bringing about broader institutional awareness of civic participation in urban planning processes. Such events spawned a range of alternative forms of citizen engagement with urban planning, including a specific form of practice of particular interest to us: the counterproposal.

Counterproposals, typically emerging from activist and grassroots networks, not only challenge demolition practices but also proactively propose alternative spatial practices. They generate interventions which envision different urban futures, such as adaptive reuse instead of demolition in the face of planning, housing, and equity crises. Unlike official proposals put forward by institutions, political bodies, or private developers, counterproposals arise from informal, often ad hoc collectives operating without official authority. To gain a greater influence, these groups often include those directly affected by redevelopment, as well as individuals with deep local knowledge or professional expertise. (fig. 1)

With case studies from the 1960s, the 1970s, and the present, respectively, this article examines three significant examples of counterproposal movements in Zurich. Despite differences in scope and context, they share methods, actors, and forms of engagement with planning authorities. Moving gradually from the city center to the outskirts, all three cases unfold within Switzerland's system of direct democracy, which allows citizens to propose constitutional changes or challenge legislation through popular

---

3 On the night of June 29, 1968, young demonstrators and police clashed for hours in the streets of Zurich. The trigger for the confrontation was a demand to establish an autonomous youth center in the temporary structure of the former department store of *Globus*. (Schweizerisches Sozialarchiv, 2018)

4 In May 1980, young people protested the allocation of 60 million CHF for the renovation of the Zurich Opera House, while demands for an autonomous youth center remained unmet. This marked the beginning of a wave of protests that would continue for the next two years.

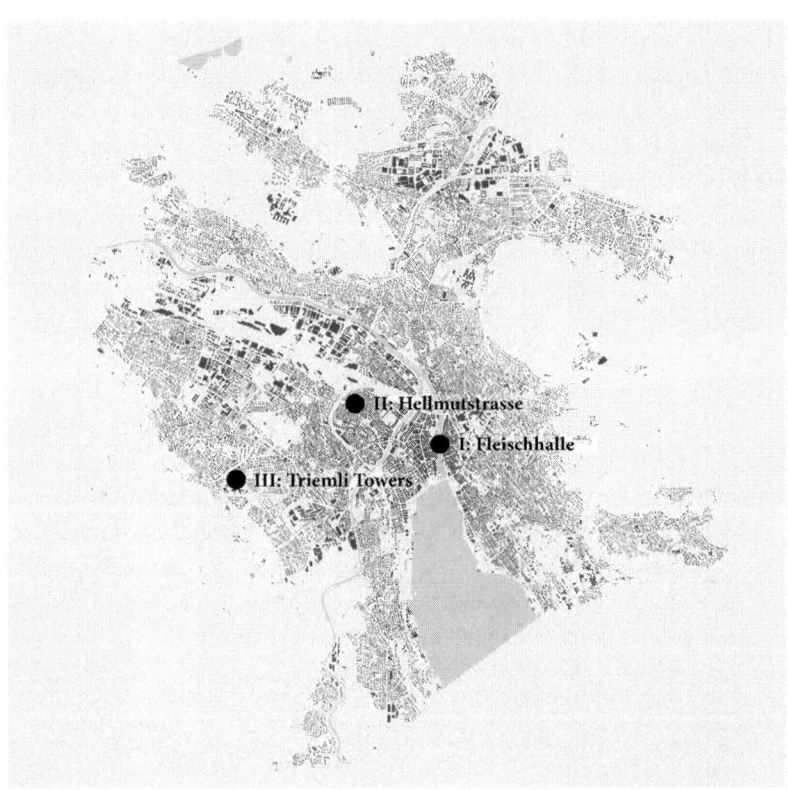

1.
Map of Zurich with three Case Studies, ZAS*.

initiatives[5] and referenda[6] (Die Bundesversammlung – Das Schweizer Parlament: Parlamentsporträt n.d.). These policy instruments are deeply embedded in Swiss civic culture. In fact, Swiss constitutional law includes the *Gegenentwurf* [counterproposal] as an official instrument of parliament for putting forward alternatives to popular initiatives submitted by citizens (Die Bundesversammlung – Das Schweizer Parlament: Parlamentswörterbuch n.d.). Importantly, while the Swiss political system allows citizens to vote on proposals for major public development, it currently offers no such mechanism for contesting demolition. When a new development is proposed, the existing building on the site and its demolition are usually omitted from the proposal description or presented as a necessary, non-negotiable step to meet the brief. In this context, a principled vote for more housing can become an inadvertent mandate for demolition. Architects' political engagement with urban development is generally limited to either their role as commissioned designers of projects (where their influence is limited), or their civic right to vote. Proposing an actual alternative to demolition requires inserting one's agenda much earlier in the decision-making process. The three examples examined below demonstrate how architects, alongside their fellow citizens, have used counterproposals to put forward ideas at an early stage to avert unnecessary demolition.

In the section titled »Reprogramming,« we explore how the Zürcher Arbeitsgruppe für Städtebau (ZAS) [Zurich Working Group for Urban Planning], an association of recently graduated architects active between 1959-1989, occupied the city's historic butchers' market building, the *Fleischhalle*, in the 1960s to protest its planned demolition and spark public dialogue. »Anticipating« looks at the 1970s struggle over a collection of historic residential and commercial buildings at *Hellmutstrasse* (»Hellmi«), where inhabitants, activists, and architects collaborated to halt the buildings' destruction. Their work shows how strategic, long-term action can reshape a building or neighborhood's fate, and contribute to conserving resources. Finally, in the section »Speculating,« we reflect on our own recent actions as architects and citizens to challenge the planned demolition of

---

5 In Switzerland, citizens can propose changes to the Federal Constitution through a Federal Popular Initiative.

6 In Switzerland, referendums allow the public to approve or reject decisions made by parliament. Citizens vote directly on a proposed law or policy.

Zurich's Triemli Towers[7], where we initiated a »speculative idea competition« to gather multiple counterproposals to the towers' destruction.

Each counterproposal case study is examined through the following questions:

- What were the urgencies in city planning of the time?
- What was the official planning strategy?
- What were the reasons to oppose the initial planning strategy?
- What did the counterproposal suggest?
- What media and methods were used to develop and present the counterproposal?
- And, lastly, what results were achieved through these counter-strategies, and what were their effects?

Our interest in the three counterproposals presented – from a spontaneous reuse project to a political initiative – did not begin as an academic pursuit. Instead, we encountered these projects through our own activist engagement – discovering them in archives, through media reports, or by word-of-mouth among peers. Researching them proved challenging: Sorting mechanisms of architectural archives often omit the political documents needed to understand the broader planning context, while political records lack visual or spatial material. In some cases, such as the »Hellmi« project, direct conversations with those involved were crucial to reconstructing their narratives. By analyzing the organizational strategies, media, and outcomes of these counterproposal movements, we aim to better understand and document their political and architectural significance and speculate on how such initiatives might continue to shape urban futures today.

---

7 Three concrete high-rise buildings constructed by the city in 1971 as accommodation for the Triemli Hospital, with a total of 750 rooms.

Reprogramming

Case I Limmat-Galerie: Toward Public Space instead of Traffic Infrastructure (fig. 2)

In 1962, the number of Zurich's inhabitants reached an all-time peak that has only been surpassed recently in 2023 (Stadt Zürich/Bevölkerungsentwicklung 2025). At this time, much like other major European cities built around medieval centers, Zurich was struggling to deal with its rapidly growing population. The resulting densification and expansion of the urban fabric led in turn to increased traffic congestion and air pollution. The widespread belief was that Zurich needed to be modernised, and that this was best achieved by expanding and segregating automobile infrastructure (Schwyn 1960: 827). However, the historical center of Zurich, with its narrow streets and its many protected historic buildings, posed a big challenge to this aim.

   In October 1958, the political party *Landesrings der Unabhängigen* handed in the *Motion »Freie Limmat«*[8] demanding that Zurich's disused historic butchers' market building, the *Fleischhalle*, that stood on the river Limmat right next to the *Ratshaus*[9], *Hauptwache*[10] and the spacious *Rathausbrücke*[11], should be demolished to unblock the view to the Alps from the historical city center. The *Fleischhalle*, built in the Byzantine style in 1866 by the then-city architect Ludwig Hanhart, was not considered worthy of heritage protection by the standards of the time and was only used by a small number of vendors by the 1950s[12]. The *Motion »Freie Limmat«* included a second demand, which was to use the newly won space to widen the street, thereby connecting two

---

8 »Freie Limmat« translates to »Free Limmat.« The Limmat is the main river flowing out of Lake Zurich and through the historical city center.

9 Zurich's city hall, where the municipal and cantonal council meet to this day.

10 Zurich's historical main guardhouse.

11 Rathausbrücke »city hall bridge« is a wide, square-like bridge at the narrowest part of the river Limmat, that connects both parts of the historical old town. It hosts markets to this day and is also called *Gemüsebrücke* colloquially. Furthermore, it is also an important site for protests such as the recent »Wohndemo« – the demonstration for the right to affordable living space on the April 5, 2025. https://wohndemo.ch/, accessed October 8, 2025.

12 Since the late Middle Ages, meat was only allowed to be sold in the city's butchery. In the same year the Fleischhalle was completed; however, the right to sell meat was liberalized, and the number of vendors using the space fell rapidly. By the 1950s, only six of the former forty stalls remained (Marquard 2010).

2.

(top) The old Fleischhalle before demolition, 1895. Photograph: Hana Gebrüder Gerrit Anton & Willem Elias, Baugeschichtliches Archiv der Stadt Zürich (center) Limmat-Galerie: a counterproposal by ZAS, 1960. Drawing by: Rolf Keller, gta Archiv / ETH Zurich (Lorenz Moser). (bottom) After the demolition: Postcard showing the newly built staircases leading to the river Limmat, 1968. Photograph: Photoglob, Baugeschichtliches Archiv der Stadt Zürich.

congested traffic nodes: *Central* to the south of the historical center, and *Bellevue* to the north.

The proposed demolition of the *Fleischhalle* sparked a movement of resistance by artists and architects alike, that – as a side effect – led to the founding of the working group ZAS, Zürcher Arbeitsgruppe für Städtebau, in 1959. ZAS's reasons for protest were manifold: They criticized that official city planning and the initiators of the Motion »Freie Limmat« were one-sidedly focused on providing short-term solutions for traffic infrastructure and were all too ready to forsake a »characteristic situation in which even buildings that are insignificant in themselves can play an indispensable role« (Peter Meyer 1959). They were worried that the old town of Zurich would become faceless and devoid of liveliness, and therefore unattractive for residents and visitors, especially from the perspective of a pedestrian. In the words of Rolf Keller, founding member of ZAS, the river Limmat was to be understood as the most distinctive element of Zurich and the *Fleischhalle* was situated at its »navel« (Rolf Keller 1960: 692, authors' translation). ZAS also argued that the city's inhabitants would lose the resource of 1000 square metre of public, city-owned land at the heart of Zurich; that the river Limmat would be degraded into an »industrial channel« (ZAS 1959; Aktionskomitee zur Erhaltung des historischen Limmatraumes 196, authors' translation); and that the cost of demolition not only exceeded that of refurbishment, but also took much longer to implement (ibid.). Finally, they also believed demolishing the *Fleischhalle* would set a dangerous precedent: If it was demolished by public vote, which other characteristic spaces might be threatened as well? (ibid.)

Importantly, the members of ZAS and their fellow campaigners did not base their reasons for opposing the demolition of the *Fleischhalle* on ecological considerations, the quality of the *Fleischhalle's* architecture, or its historical importance. Rather, their opposition was founded on the building's contribution to the »character of uniqueness and unmistakability« of Zurich (Peter Meyer 1959); that it was simply existing public space; and its potential to transform into a more contemporary public space. Rolf Keller writes:

>»But back to the example of the dilapidated and unsightly *Fleischhalle* [...]: Here, as in every unique situation: do not demolish, do not end something, but renew, transform – let the ugly duckling in the Limmat be transformed into a proud, white swan!« (Rolf Keller 1960: 702, authors' translation).

Rolf Keller and Lorenz Moser, politically supported by Adrian Willi, opposed the demolition of the *Fleischhalle* with a self-initiated, alternative architectural vision. The counterproposal, titled *Limmat-Galerie*, saw the *Fleischhalle* refurbished into a »hall for flaneurs with a café« that redirected pedestrians through an »open, sunny gallery in direct relation to the flowing water and the riverbank of the *Schipfe* on the other side of the river« (Rolf Keller 1960: 689, authors' translation). This proposal eliminated the need for a pavement along the street, and even provided enough space to widen the street to meet the demands of traffic as well. The designers also believed that every intervention at the riverside must be set within the context of the Limmat area; therefore, the plans and visualizations of the *Limmat-Galerie* were supplemented with a second, wider-ranging study for the waterfront area downstream. Both studies were handed into the city authorities, published in architectural magazines, and presented in self-initiated press conferences (Zürcher Arbeitsgruppe für Städtebau 1959: 9f). In order to persuade the public of their proposal, ZAS members also wrote newspaper articles, organised demonstrations, and handed out leaflets. A unique aspect of the counterproposal was the reprogramming of the *Fleischhalle* into a café and theatre during the time of its vacancy, a concept that would today be called a »pop-up« or *Zwischennutzung*[13].

In November 1960, the proposal for the demolition of the *Fleischhalle*, along with the counterproposal by the *Aktionskomitee zur Erhaltung des historischen Limmatraumes* was submitted to be voted upon by the citizens of Zurich. In 1962, the *Fleischhalle* was ultimately demolished. However, seven years later, another vote proved how short-lived the decision in terms of city planning was: The people voted for a reversal of the Open Limmat Decision, stating that a new building should be built where the old *Fleischhalle* used to stand (Bauen + Wohnen 1979: 324–325). The *Fleischhalle* became a kind of emblematic battlefield representing a larger dispute between supporters of the existing, layered urban fabric and the *tabula rasa* demands of the car-friendly city.

---

13 »Zwischennutzung« can be translated as »interim use« and means the rental and use of a space for a contractually settled, limited amount of time. They have become a recurring side-effect of the wide-spread demolitions in Zurich and now Zwischennutzungen are even embedded in the municipality's innovation strategy (Toepfer 2025). https://www.stadt-zuerich.ch/artikel/de/stadt-der-zukunft/zwischen-den-nutzungen-entsteht-raum-fuer-neues-.html, accessed October 5, 2025.

As architects, members of ZAS used their skills (including designing, drawing and planning; communicating with multiple actors; and understanding urban planning procedures) to intervene in political processes affecting Zurich's cityscape. Their intervention resulted in convincing both city officials as well as the public to transform the *Fleischhalle* instead of tearing it down. They sought an architectural solution that could meet the demands of traffic, but also retain the unique character of the *Fleischhalle* and even develop it further to contribute to a vision of Zurich's old town as a lively place to stroll and live (Rolf Keller 1962). Along the way, the ZAS members also stepped into roles not usually occupied by architects, such as running a pop-up café, writing articles, or organizing demonstrations. Finally, the expansion of the occupational profile of the architect that resulted from these forms of activism was a contribution to the architectural field that we, as ZAS*, value greatly.

Anticipating

Case II Hellmutstrasse: Toward the Democratization of Housing Development (fig. 3)

About a decade later, in the early 1970s, the Swiss Post, Telephone and Telegraph Company (PTT) launched a project to construct a telecommunications center in the Aussersihl district located west of Zurich's historical center. Back in 1963, a plot of land comprising some of the neighborhood's oldest houses from the late 19th century, were acquired by the Zurich entrepreneur Sven Hotz, who intended to undertake a large-scale redevelopment. It was at this point that the residential buildings on Hellmutstrasse were designated for demolition. A few years later, Hotz sold the site to PTT, which planned to realize the telecommunications center in collaboration with Hotz's older brother – the renowned architect Theo Hotz. The project entailed the demolition of approximately 200 flats and several workshop buildings (Lindenmeyer 2021: 92).

Upon learning about the project, the tenants of the residential buildings on Hellmutstrasse began organizing demonstrations and holding public meetings to protest the planned demolition, arguing that the massive telecommunications center did not require such a centrally located site. Ultimately, the project failed due to strong tenant resistance, which local

3.

(top) Houses along Hellmutstrasse surrounded by building profiles, indicating ongoing planning activities, 1972. Photograph: Baugeschichtliches Archiv der Stadt Zürich. (center left) A counterproposal for the refurbishment and extension of the existing residential buildings, 1983. Model by: Bryan Thurston, Peter Gygax and Christian Frey, gta Archiv / ETH Zurich (Bryan Cyril Thurston). (center right) Project for a new telecommunications center by the Swiss Post, Telephone and Telegraph Company (PTT), 1972. Model by: Theo Hotz, gta Archiv / ETH Zurich (Theo Hotz). (bottom) Hellmi-neu, the new housing development forms an ensemble with the older buildings, 1991. A.D.P. Walter Ramseier.

politicians, including town councilor Bruno Kammerer supported. In 1972, the national newspaper *Tages-Anzeiger* published an interview with Kammerer in which he stated: »The giant building planned by the PTT [...] was therefore nonsense not only given the rampant housing shortage but also for urban planning reasons« (Tages-Anzeiger 1972, authors' translation). That same year, the Federal Council compelled the City of Zurich to negotiate a land exchange with the property owner. The telecommunication center was eventually built by Theo Hotz on the city's periphery, in Zurich Herdern, thereby preserving the residential buildings on Hellmutstrasse – marking a first success for the tenants.

After the municipality's initial reluctant agreement to the land swap the decision was made by the new owner, the municipality, to demolish the buildings seven years later. Fearing illegal occupation, the municipality temporarily rented out the flats, and later made them unusable for squatters by dismantling or smashing the toilets and cookers with sledgehammers. Since squatting was illegal and could not last more than two days, a group of young people within Zurich's leftist squatting scene considered alternative strategies to secure the old buildings as living spaces for the city's residents.

In 1979, after more than ten apartments had become uninhabitable, the non-residents did not »occupy« the apartments, but rather »took control« of them. They did not allow anyone to spend the night there, but they changed the look of the doors, and anyone interested was welcome to view the empty apartments (Lindenmeyer, 2018: 113, authors' translation). They set up a »control office« (ibid.) in one of the empty flats to monitor any occurrences within the vicinity and opened the doors to the media during the day to document the abuses. In the evenings, they guarded the houses »to prevent further destruction by city officials« (ibid.). This attracted the attention of the media and other activists, including ZAS, and raised critical questions about the municipality's destruction of flats within the context of a housing crisis. The engagement of the press and activists pressured the municipality into introducing the practice of the »Gebrauchsleihvertrag« – loan-for-use-agreements[14], which originated in Geneva and was used in the case of Hellmutstrasse for the first time in Zurich, effectively legalizing and temporarily tolerating the occupation (Lindenmeyer 2021: 105–114). The municipal administration understood this situation as a provisional arrangement,

---

14 An agreement whereby one party lends an item to another for use, free of charge.

limited to the duration of the loan-for-use agreement. The Hellmut buildings remained designated for demolition.

After serving as a central meeting place for the youth movement in the early 1980s, the future of the site became uncertain following the termination of the loan-for-use agreement. For the residents, after years of caretaking the buildings, both social rehabilitation and structural renovation had become persistent topics of concern. They actively sought engagement with the municipal administration, urging it to undertake necessary renovations of the existing structures. With political support from Municipal Council Rudolf Steiger, a motion in 1981 prompted the authorities to commission a design strategy for Hellmutstrasse. The subsequent study, conducted by the municipal building department, concluded that the buildings had been in a state of disrepair for some time and that a final inspection by the city's building commission would be necessary to confirm the decision to proceed with demolition.

Aware that this would be their last chance to save the buildings on Hellmutstrasse, the activist residents sought the help of prominent professionals in the architectural field. In 1983, a reception was held for members of the city council to present the counterproposal for the site: an architectural project for the renovation and extension of the residential buildings, drawn up by architect Bryan Thurston with colleagues Peter Gygax and Christian Frey. Following negotiations with the council, the self-organized project of the collective to redevelop the site was able to move forward, with the council agreeing to make the site available with planning permission in the future (Lindenmeyer 2018: 153–164). The land was to be granted under a *Baurechtsvertrag*[15] [a building rights agreement] to the newly founded *cooperative Wogeno*, allowing the residents to jointly develop the site in collaboration with the cooperative.

Hannes Lindenmeyer, who was a participant in the activist movement at the time and still lives on Hellmutstrasse, describes the process that followed[16]: Over the following four years, the evolving group of residents collectively outlined various principles for the architectural project in

---

15 A building rights agreement (*Baurechtsvertrag*) is a legal contract in which the owner of a piece of land grants another party the right to construct and use buildings on that land for a specified period of time – usually several decades – without transferring ownership of the land itself. This type of agreement is common in Switzerland, and often used by public authorities to retain control over land while enabling private or cooperative development.

16 During a conversation with one of the authors on November 19, 2024.

extensive discussions with roughly 10 teams of architects. This included the provision of a public outdoor space, semi-public external staircases, and a semi-public internal corridor for the apartments. The central principles of the project were the diversity of the residents and the flexibility of the flats, which could be changed at a later date. As Lindenmeyer explained, this collaboration culminated in a public jury process including interested residents (some of whom were ZAS members), the city architect, and the *Wogeno* cooperative, which was to develop the site as the owner of the building rights. The jury finally met outside among the dilapidated old buildings, where all the teams' plans were displayed, and decided to select the project developed by A.D.P architects.

By anticipating the actions and motives of the respective owners of the site, the group of activists (including residents, politically motivated youth movements, and allied architects) succeeded in writing a significant chapter in Zurich's urban history, ultimately preventing the demolition of an entire neighborhood. This case illustrates how counterproposals, such as the one by the architects Bryan Thurston and his colleagues, can emerge not only as planned reactions to political decisions but also as a form of alliance, driven by grassroots momentum. Even though the direct negotiation with the city council by the activist group representing Hellmutstrasse drew criticism from the more radical factions of the left, it could be counted as a big success for the right-to-housing: A squat was legalized using a utility loan agreement for the first time, and subsequently collectivized into the cooperative *Wogeno*, whose aim was to provide affordable housing. This model for a socially sustainable development of a neighborhood provided a replicable framework and was adapted in other areas of Zurich throughout the 1990s. The process galvanized spatial and social aspiration towards more democratic planning processes by demonstrating how activism could shape the built environment, rather than merely respond to it. Here, political engagement was not just reactive but generative, giving rise to architectural forms rooted in communal values and self-determination.

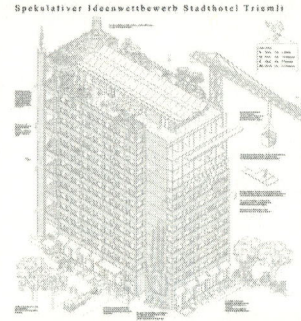

4.

(top) Construction site of the three towers at Triemli, 1963. Photography: Koehli Ernst, Baugeschichtliches Archiv der Stadt Zürich. (center left to right) Stadthotel Triemli - Wie weiter?, An exhibition organized by ZAS* showing all contributions to the open idea competition, ZAZ Bellerive, 2022. Poster: ZAS*; Proposal to convert the brutalist towers into collective housing, competition entry, 2022. Drawing by: OAEU Laura Stock, Johannes Walterbusch; Strategies to maintain and transform the buildings in relation to different time horizons, competition entry, 2022. Rendering by: KOSMOS Architects. (bottom) Today the Triemli towers are still standing and will be used mainly for asylum accommodation at least until 2040. Photograph by Anne Morgenstern, 2023.

Speculating

Case III Triemli Towers: Toward the Collective Reimagination of Built Resources (fig. 4)

In 2021, ZAS* was formed by reactivating the activist collective ZAS, which had been active until the late 1980s. Its new members discussed current architectural practices and working modes, and introduced new forms of work and time sharing. As Fritz Schwarz, founding member of ZAS shared with ZAS*: One of their guiding principles was that each expert should devote five percent of their working hours voluntarily to the service of society (ZAS* 2023: 37). While this may be more of a reference point for the roughly twenty members ZAS*, it led them to understand themselves not only as architects but also as citizens, and critically reflect on current urban planning processes; and, to propose productive opposition to official proposals. Around the end of 2021, ZAS* learned about the upcoming destruction of three concrete towers in the Triemli district at the western edge of the city that were formerly used as staff housing for the Triemli City Hospital. Scheduled for 2023, the demolition had completely bypassed the public discourse, as the decision for the development of the city's hospital had already been made years prior. But since the Ukrainian-Russian war had started in 2022, and subsequently the arrival of refugees in Zurich, the towers suddenly provided temporary housing, proving their potential in times of crisis.

The hospital towers originated in the 1950s when there was a severe shortage of hospital beds and hospital staff in Zurich. The project for the Triemli City Hospital envisioned a central hospital tower with low-rise buildings, along with three 15-story towers offering 750 rooms for nurses and nursing students. Although the project was publicly criticized for its brutalist architectural appearance and height, the city's population approved the construction of the new hospital in a vote in 1960 (Stadtspital Zürich 2024). Designed by a team of architects comprising Ernst Schindler, Rudolf Joss, Helmut Rauber, Roland Rohn, Rolf Hässig, and Erwin Müller, the project was finally built between 1963 and 1969 (Schindler et al. 1974). Already in the 1990s, 25 years after the hospital had opened, the three towers originally built to house nursing staff no longer met contemporary living requirements and gradually became vacant. In 2003, as part of its reworked long-term strategy paper, the city decided to demolish the three towers once the ongoing hospital renovation was complete and establish a park in their stead, as there was no foreseeable future use for them (Weisung 203, GR Nr. 1996/370; Baumann/Frey 1994). At the time, the city argued that renovating the towers at »80 percent of the cost of new construction would not be worthwhile« (Weisung 203, GR Nr. 1996/370, authors' translation; cf. Stadt Zürich/Amt für Hochbauten 2017). Due to their pending destruction, minimal maintenance was provided in the following years. Rooms were converted into offices or rented out to students, and in 2012, a temporary retirement home was set up on the top floors of Tower C (Stadt Zürich/Amt für Hochbauten 2005).

When ZAS* started to investigate the case, they realized how vague the arguments surrounding the imminent demolition were. They directed public attention to the three Triemli towers by publishing the article »Die Betonreserven am Triemli« (ZAS* 2021) on the online news platform *Tsüri*[17], framing the structures as »concrete reserves in the form of buildings that could offer a potential for sustainable urban development due to their massive structures and accordingly their very long service life« (ZAS* 2021). Demolishing such material-intensive structures in favor of a park appeared questionable in light of the climate crisis and housing shortage. By then, concrete elements from the three towers had already been reserved for reuse in the Recyclingzentrum Juchhof project after the planned demolition. For this project, a resource assessment report, including a catalog of building parts, had already been prepared by the office *Zirkular*[18] and the Polytechnic University EPFL (Devènes/Bastien-Masse/Küpfer/Fivet 2022). The report found that 96 percent of all structural components of the building were in good or acceptable condition and formed the basis for further investigation by ZAS* (Devènes/Bastien-Masse/Küpfer/Fivet 2022: 29–68). ZAS*'s follow-up study, »Triemli Papers,« examined the towers' structural adaptability, habitability, fire protection and high-rise shadow regulation[19] – directly challenging the rationale for demolition.

To oppose the discreet demolition, ZAS* decided to organize a speculative ideas competition (*Spekulativer Ideenwettbewerb Stadthotel Triemli*) for

---

17 *Tsüri* is a phonetic play on »Züri,« which is Swiss German for Zurich. It is an online news portal that was founded in 2015 with the aim of promoting independent journalism focusing on the city of Zurich.

18 *Zirkluar* is a specialist planning office for circular material use in construction based in Basel.

19 Building regulations in Zurich stipulating that high-rise buildings must not significantly affect their neighborhood by casting shadows. For example, inhabited buildings must not be shaded for more than three hours on average winter days.

architects to propose architectural projects demonstrating how the existing built structures of the Triemli towers could continue to be used in the future (ZAS* 2022). Rather than proposing a singular alternative vision for the future, ZAS* chose to draw on the collective knowledge of the architectural community to oppose the municipal plans for demolition with a multitude of counterproposals. As the buildings had already served as a kind of surplus living space, taking up everyone from Ukrainian refugees to the elderly, the competition proposed the program of the *Stadthotel* for Zurich's inhabitants (city hotel), stemming from the Latin *hospitalis*, a place where people can stay for short or long periods of time. Launched in September 2022, the open competition[20] attracted 45 submissions, each exploring alternatives to demolition. Five projects were awarded by the jury, which comprised architects such as Elli Mosayebi and Jolene Lee, as well as the ETH professor of heritage protection Silke Langenberg, researcher on urban politics and processes Philipp Koch, and expert for sustainable urban development Sarah Schalles. The spatial proposals of each contribution were reframed as arguments for transformation and adaptation and collected in a document, named *Argumentarium*, put together by ZAS* that advocates for the towers' future potential.

The group's ambition was to reintroduce the Triemli towers into the public and architectural discourse and create awareness of demolition practices. The initial article on *Tsüri* was taken up by other media outlets such as the national newspaper *NZZ*, which prompted a back-and-forth between newspapers, the city administration, the architecture community, parliament and government, Zurich's citizens, and ZAS* (Kälin 2021: 15). ZAS* introduced the concept of the speculative ideas competition, to propose an alternative vision as citizens of Zurich – and therefore to a certain extent as owners of the towers.

The counterproposal strategy of ZAS* is to appropriate and repurpose existing formats and tools of city planning and, in doing so, shift their own professional role. The competition was based on established formats, such as the rules for architectural and engineering competitions set by The Swiss Society of Engineers and Architects (SIA) and was published on official competition websites (Konkurado 2022). To enable a wider public discourse, the jury of the competition was held publicly at *Zentrum Architektur Zürich*

---

20 The open call for the competition can be found here: https://www.zas.life/triemli/wett-bewerbsprogramm_triemli.pdf, accessed October 8, 2025.

Bellerive[21] in December 2022. The discussion of the five-member jury was well attended and simultaneously streamed live on YouTube. To allow for even greater accessibility, the results of the competition were exhibited for a week, and workshops with the architects that contributed to the competition, politicians, and the city administration were held to discuss the topics addressed in the contributions.

In response to the counterproposal competition, the feasibility of the competition entry projects was further investigated in a study by the members of ZAS*. The study compared projects with different depths of intervention and calculated after which prolonged lifespan they would become ecologically and economically feasible (Oswald 2023: 80f). It was followed by an urgent written request to the municipal council, *Dringende Schriftliche Anfrage* (a tool used by politicians), on the issue of extending the interim use of the towers (Beschluss des Stadtrats 2023). In response, the municipality carried out its own feasibility study, which came to similar conclusions as the study carried out by ZAS*: none of the projects were economically or ecologically feasible if one extended the lifetime of the Triemli towers for less than 10 years, but from 20 years onwards projects of all depths of intervention were ecologically feasible, and after 30 years even large investments would become economically feasible (Stadt Zürich/Amt für Hochbauten 2023; GR Nr. 2022/105). As a result of the wider public discourse, the current interim use of the towers as living quarters for refugees and the elderly will now be extended until 2040 (Stadt Zürich/Gesundheits- und Umweltdepartement 2024). In November 2024, it was confirmed that two of the three towers will be renovated by the municipality. The city council has allocated approximately 80 million francs for the refurbishment of two of the towers. The remaining one – excluded from the renovations due to its anticipated reuse by the city hospital – will temporarily continue to accommodate refugees, while pending an extended operating license (Turin 2024). Importantly, the decision to refurbish rather than demolish the towers reflects a growing awareness of the climate crisis, emphasizing the urgency of resource conservation and the environmental benefits of reusing existing structures.

The high public interest of Zurich's citizens in the continuing use of the Triemli Towers showed that the time had come to question outdated plans and propose alternative approaches. For the architects involved, as well as

---

21 The ZAZ Bellerive is an exhibition space with a focus on architecture and planning that exists since 2018.

the inhabitants, the actions taken to preserve the towers demonstrated a practical blueprint for channeling democratic opposition against top-down decision-making. Since then, the methods and formats developed during the speculative idea competition have been adopted by other groups with similar goals, such as the group *Abbrechen Abbrechen*[22] in Munich. Whether a building in Zurich is demolished or not is still largely determined by its owners and hardly ever by its inhabitants, since they are usually only informed when the decision has already been made.[23] We see the formulation of a design brief, even where none exists, as a strategy for architects and citizens to gain more influence on the built environment by intervening earlier in the decision-making process.

Conclusion

The series of case studies presented in this article demonstrate that the harmful ecological and social impact of demolition in Zurich is not just a contemporary issue, but rather a persistent challenge faced by the city since the post-war period. While differing in historical context, scale and strategy, the actors behind the Fleischhalle, Hellmutstrasse, and Triemli Towers movements all employed a common method, the counterproposal, to challenge the demolition of important features of Zurich's urban fabric. Rooted in civic engagement and architectural expertise, these counterproposal initiatives critically responded to top-down planning, preserved affordable and socially diverse spaces, and introduced spatial, organizational, and programmatic alternatives.

Instead of waiting for official commissions, architects and their fellow campaigners asserted their civil rights through proactive design. By intervening early in the planning process, they were able to pre-emptively shape urban development, rather than belatedly react to a closed brief. Their counterproposals aimed not only to contest dominant narratives, but also to promote more democratic, ecologically mindful, and socially inclusive

---

22 An initiative to preserve the Munich Justice Centre, which is threatened by demolition. https://abbrechenabbrechen.de, accessed October 5, 2025.

23 In Switzerland, construction projects that are waiting for approval from the building permit office must mark the planned outlines of their project on site for the public using rods that delineate the corners of the volume. Neighbours or established national ecological associations have the right to object to the project during a certain period of time.

visions of the city. They questioned what makes urban life vibrant and resilient, and how spatial development can reflect collective rather than purely economic interests.

While not all projects prevented demolition, each left a lasting impact on the cityscape, architectural practice, and public discourse. Hellmutstrasse became a model for self-organized cooperative housing. The Triemli Towers signified a growing institutional commitment to reuse over demolition and provided a blueprint for building the case for the adaptive reuse of existing structures. And, while initially approved by public vote, the reversal of the decision to demolish the *Fleischhalle* just a few years later showed the impact the counterproposal had left on public opinion.

Each example emerged from a particular moment of spatial urgency, be it car-centric redevelopment in the 1960s, corporate urban renewal in the 1970s, or unsustainable demolition practices amid today's climate crisis. In all instances, demolition was presented as inevitable, yet was met with resistance that evolved into proactive and at times realized alternatives: ZAS's *Limmat-Galerie* emphasized pedestrian urbanism and adaptive reuse; *Hellmutstrasse* activists prevented demolition through direct action and collaborative planning; and ZAS* reintroduced the idea of long-term reuse through its speculative competition for the Triemli Towers.

The trajectory from protest, to proposal, to tangible influence illustrates a methodological continuum which brings architects together with civic actors. It signals a shift toward a mode of practice rooted not in market-driven logic, but in community-based, socially engaged, and ecologically conscious values. The counterproposals discussed were not merely reactive: They articulated alternative futures towards resource-consciousness, collective ownership, and care for the built environment.

The reformation of the group ZAS* in 2021 enabled us to highlight and engage with pressing urban topics across both professional and civic spheres. Writing this article is part of that effort. It is a vehicle for us to deepen our archival research as well as a means of activating discourse, sharing methods, and expanding the reach of the counterproposal as a critical design practice. By contributing to the democratization of the planning process, the reformation of ZAS* marks the emergence of a new working mode that is open, process-based, and collaborative, and which creates alliances between architects, residents, activists, researchers, and municipal administrators. Our approach values situated knowledge and long-term engagement over quick solutions, and creates space for imagination, experimentation, and structural transformation.

The counterproposals presented in this article show that when architects combine their professional and civic agency, they can directly shape the material and political conditions of democratic practice in the built environment. In the Swiss context of direct democracy, such interventions have the potential to transform both spatial planning and urban life. Through collaborative design, speculative practice, and civic engagement, we aim to reposition architectural work as a means of resistance and transformation. In times of ecological urgency and social fragmentation, the counterproposal is not merely an act of opposition; it is an essential instrument for reimagining and reclaiming the future of our cities.

ZAS[24], ZAS*[25], and their Accomplices[26]

24 ZAS: Zürcher Arbeitsgruppe für Städtebau [Zurich Working Group for Urban Planning], a collective active between 1959–1980s.

25 ZAS* is the reactivation of ZAS, a collective active since 2021.

26 In this context, »accomplices« refers to collaborators, and co-practitioners who act alongside ZAS and ZAS* – not merely in support, but in shared authorship and complicity.

References

Aktionskomitee zur Erhaltung des historischen Limmatraumes (1961) »Halt den Abreissfanatikern in unserer Altstadt!« political leaflet, gta Archiv / ETH Zurich, (Nachlässe ZAS).

Bauen + Wohnen (1979): »Überbauung Fleischhallenareal, Zürich = Ensemble de la halle aux viandes, Zürich = Building project on the Butchers' Market site, Zurich.« in: Bauen + Wohnen = Construction + habitation = Building + home: internationale Zeitschrift 33/9, 324–325. doi: 10.5169/seals-336344

Baumann, Max/Frey, Georges J. (1994): Gesamtplanung Stadtspital Triemli Zürich, 1989–2003, https://gjfrey.allyou.net/855115 9/gesamtplanung-stadtspital-triemli-zuric h-1989-2003, accessed November 25, 2024.

Beschluss des Stadtrats, GR Nr. 2023/97.

Burch, Oliver/Junghanss, Jakob/Ryffel, Lukas (2024): »Prologue. Zurich is now bigger than ever before,« in: De Vylder, Jan/Burch, Oliver/Junghanss, Jakob/Ryffel, Lukas (eds.): Towards Transformation. The 33.3% Attitude / Zurich. Zurich: Triest Verlag, 35–42.

Devènes, Julie/Bastien-Masse, Maléna/Küpfer, Célia/Fivet, Corentin (2022): Zürich – Stadtspital Triemli Personalhochhäuser – Resource assessment of structural elements, Fribourg: Ecole Polytechnique Fédérale de Lausanne (EPFL). doi: 10.5281/zenodo.6020923

Die Bundesversammlung –
Das Schweizer Parlament:
Parlamentswörterbuch (n.d.):
»Counterproposal to a popular
initiative.« https://www.parlament.
ch/en/%C3%BCber-das-parlament/
parlamentsw%C3%B6rterbuch/
parlamentsw%C3%B6rterbuch-
detail?WordId=268, accessed
November 29, 2024.

Die Bundesversammlung –
Das Schweizer Parlament:
Parlamentsporträt (n.d.): »Referenden.«
https://www.parlament.ch/
de/%C3%BCber-das-parlament/
parlamentsportraet/stellung-der-
bundesversammlung/das-volk-und-
die-bundesversammlung/referenden,
accessed July 21, 2025.

Grünefelder, Anja (2012), »Die
Kalbshaxenmoschee.« in: NZZ, October
8, 2012, https://www.nzz.ch/zuerich/
archivbilder/die-kalbshaxenmoschee-
ld.815695, accessed January 25, 2025.

Kälin, Adi (2021): »Der Widerstand
gegen Totalabbrüche wächst. Maag-
Hallen, Triemli-Hochhäuser, städtische
Siedlungen – die Debatte um deren
Erhaltung ist entbrannt.« in: NZZ,
December 31, 2021, 15.

Keller, Rolf (1960): »Zürich - als ein
lebendiges Ganzes am Beispiel der
Limmatgalerie,« in: Schweizerische
Bauzeitung, 7/43, 691–704. doi: 10.5169/
seals-64975

Konkurado (2022): Stadthotel Triemli.
Ideenwettbewerb, September 2, 2022,
https://konkurado.ch/de/stadthotel_
triemli, accessed November 25, 2024.

Lindenmeyer, Hannes (2021): Aussersihl
bewegt: der Zürcher Kreis 4. 1st edition,
Zürich: Rotpunktverlag.

Lindenmeyer, Hannes (2018): Hellmut:
Die lange Geschichte einer kurzen Strasse,
1st edition, Zürich: Rotpunktverlag.

Marquard, Denise (2010): »Die
Kalbshaxenmoschee,« in: Tages
Anzeiger August 13, 2010, https://
www.tagesanzeiger.ch/die-
kalbshaxenmoschee-754148955474,
accessed July 20, 2025

Merriam-Webster (2024):
»Counterproposal,« in: Merriam-Webster.
com Dictionary, https://www.merriam-
webster.com/dictionary/counterproposal,
accessed November 29,2024.

Meyer, Peter (1959): »Erhaltung der
Fleischhalle« in: Zürcher Lokalchronik, Blatt
12 (8.7.1959), gta Archiv.

NZZ (2009): »Auch Hochhäuser haben
ein Verfallsdatum,« in: Neue Zürcher
Zeitung, March 28, 2009, https://www.
nzz.ch/auch_hochhaeuser_haben_
ein_verfalldatum-ld.556011, accessed
November 25, 2024.

Oswald, Sebastian (2023): Personalhochhäuser Triemli. Abschlussarbeit CAS
»Strategische Gebäudeerneuerung,« HSLU,
2022–23, January 31, 2023, 80–81.

Schärer, Caspar (2023): »Comeback der
Architektur,« Hochparterre, March 30, 2023,
https://www.hochparterre.ch/nach
richten/wettbewerbe/comeback-der-arch
itektur, accessed November 25, 2024.

Schindler, Ernst/Joss, Rudolf/Rauber,
Helmunt/Rohn, Roland/Hässig, Rolf/
Müller, Erwin (1974): »Stadtspital Triemli,
Zürich: Architektengemeinschaft Ernst
Schindler, Rudolf Joss, Helmunt Rauber,
Roland Rohn, Rolf Hässig, Erwin Müller
= Hôpital municipal Triemli, Zurich,« in:
Das Werk: Architektur und Kunst = L'oeuvre:
Architecture et Art, 61/2, 111–123. doi:
10.5169/seals-87691

Schweizerische Nationalbibliothek (n.d.):
Recherche »Schlachten und Schlachthöfe im
Wandel der Zeit in Zürich.« https://www.
nb.admin.ch/snl/de/home/recherche/r-
monat/schlachthoefe.html, accessed
November 29, 2024.

Schwyn, Erich (1960): »Der Zürcher in seiner Stadt: (Und warum die Fleischhalle abgebrochen werden darf),« in: *Schweizerische Bauzeitung, Verlags-AG der akademischen technischen Vereine Band 78/51*, 826–828. doi: 10.5169/seals-65008

Stadt Zürich (1996): Stadt Zürich Gemeinderat, Weisung 203, GR Nr. 1996/370.

Stadt Zürich (2022): Stadt Zürich Gemeinderat, *Postulat, GR Nr. 2022/105*, April 6, 2022, https://www.gemeinderat -zuerich.ch/geschaefte/detail.php?gid= 094843434b154c95bcbaa898310d5db1, accessed September 19, 2025.

Stadtspital Zürich (2024): »*Meilensteine.*« https://www.stadt-zuerich.ch/triemli/de/ index/ueber_uns/das-triemli/geschichte-spital/meilensteine.html, accessed November 25, 2024.

Stadt Zürich (2007): »*Abstimmungszeitung 25. November 2007,*« Zürich stimmt ab, https://www.stadt-zuerich.ch/portal/de/ index/politik_u_recht/abstimmungen_u_ wahlen/archiv_abstimmungen/verga ngene_termine/071125/abstimmung szeitung25november2007.html, accessed November 25, 2024.

Stadt Zürich/Amt für Hochbauten (2005): *Temporäres Altersheim im Stadtspital Triemli*, November 2005.

Stadt Zürich/Amt für Hochbauten (2017): »*Bauliche Strategieplanung STZ 2020–2050,*« Bauliche Entwicklungsstrategie Areal STZ 2020–2050, Arealstudie 8063 Zürich-Wiedikon, November 3, 2017.

Stadt Zürich/Amt für Hochbauten (2023): *Zwischennutzung Personalhäuser Triemli. Zürich-Wiedikon*, Machbarkeitsstudie, June 21, 2023, https://www.stadt-zuerich. ch/gud/de/index/departement/medien/ medienmitteilungen/2023/juli/230705c. html, accessed November 25, 2024.

Stadt Zürich, Gesundheits- und Umweltdepartement (2024): »*Medienmitteilung. Wohnraum für Geflüchtete auf dem Triemli-Areal,*« March 21, 2024, https://www.stadt-zuerich.ch/ gud/de/index/departement/medien/ medienmitteilungen/2024/03/wohnraum-fuer-gefluechtete-auf-dem-triemli-areal. html, accessed November 25, 2024.

Stadt Zürich/Bevölkerungsentwicklung (2025): »*Mittlere Wohnbevölkerung.*« https:// www.stadt-zuerich.ch/de/politik-und-verwaltung/statistik-und-daten/daten/ bevoelkerung/bestand-und-entwicklung/ aktuelle-bevoelkerung-und-entwicklung. html, accessed July 20, 2025.

Stadt Zürich/Präsidialdepartmenent (2024): »*Bisherige Bevölkerungsentwicklung.*« https://www.stadt-zuerich.ch/prd/de/ index/statistik/themen/bevoelkerung/ bevoelkerungsentwicklung/bisherige-bevoelkerungsentwicklung.html, accessed November 29, 2024.

Stadt Zürich/Präsidialdepartement (2024): »*Begriffe zu Bauen und Wohnen.*« https:// www.stadt-zuerich.ch/prd/de/index/stati stik/FAQ/wichtige-begriffe/begriffe-zu-bauen-und-wohnen.html#:~:text=Der%2 0Ersatzneubau%20umfasst%20untersch iedliche%20Formen,einem%20r%C3%A4 umlichen%20und%20zeitlichen%20Zusa mmenhang, accessed November 26, 2024.

Toepfer, Nina (2025): »Zwischen den Nutzungen entsteht Raum für Neuesl,« in: *Stadt Zürich*, https://www.stadt-zuerich. ch/artikel/de/stadt-der-zukunft/zwischen-den-nutzungen-entsteht-raum-fuer-neues-.html, accessed July 19, 2025.

ZAS* (2021): »Die Betonreserven am Triemli,« in: *tsüri*, December 11, 2021, https://tsri.ch/a/die-betonreserven-am-triemli-hochhaeuser-stadt-zuerich-betonreserven-architekturkolumne, accessed November 25, 2024.

ZAS* (2022): *Wettbewerbsprogramm. Stadthotel Triemli. Spekulativer Ideenwettbewerb*, September 1, 2022, https://zas.life/triemli/ wettbewerbsprogramm_triemli.pdf, accessed November 25, 2024.

ZAS* (2023): »Triemli Files.« in: *ARCH+ The Great Repair*, 253, 162–165.

ZAS* (2023): »Fünf Prozent unserer Zeit.« in: *werk, bauen + wohnen*, 12, 37.

ZAS* (2024a): *Stadthotel Triemli Ideenwettbewerb*, https://zas.life/triemli/ wettbewerbsprogramm_triemli.pdf, accessed November 25, 2024.

Zürcher Arbeitsgruppe für Städtebau (1959): »Umgestaltung der Fleischhalle in eine Limmat-Galerie?,« in: *Bauen, Wohnen, Leben*, 37 (1959), 9f. doi: 10.5169/ seals-651220

Dimensions of Architectural Knowledge, 2024–08 &
https://doi.org/10.14361/dak-2024-0810

Toward Poetopolitics:
Attempts at Landing as a Collective in Portugal

Rui Ferreira dos Santos

Abstract: This article returns to an intentional collective in Alentejo (2011–2013) that later coalesced into Minga. Through a feminist, post-qualitative, diffractive method, I track how a patient wager on regeneration encountered hard limits: Absent shared livelihoods, low legal literacy, and a technophobic localism blind to planetary urbanization, and infrastructural entanglements. From this failure-that-taught, I propose poetopolitics – a grammar for acting under constraint that holds care with legality and presence with property. Coupled to pericapitalism, a deliberately disenchanted agenda, the emphasis falls on subsistence before symbolism, legal legibility, infrastructural sobriety, and structured horizontality. Rather than a model, the contribution is a practical lexicon and prompts for composing reciprocity between citizens, cooperatives, municipalities, and universities, pointing toward pluriversities as living platforms for durable transformation.

Keywords: Integral Cooperatives; Intentional Communities; Pericapitalism; Pluriversity; Regenerative Culture.

Corresponding author: Rui Ferreira dos Santos (TU Braunschweig, Germany/Fundação para a Ciência e a Tecnologia – FCT, Portugal); r.ferreira-dos-santos@tu-braunschweig.de &

Introduction

A line in the sand

Between 2011 and 2013, I was part of an intentional collective[1] of around 100 people of all ages and backgrounds aiming to imagine and realize an integral cooperative[2] in the deserted areas of rural Portugal. Arising in a context of deep economic, financial, and social crisis (following the subprime global meltdown), the idea was to escape the »urbanized world« in order to imagine, research, and experiment with post-growth, postcapitalist ways of living loosely aligned with the ideals of the 1974 Carnation Revolution[3]. Even though there was no local or state public policy to support cooperativism, the project mobilized many Portuguese and European foreigners living either in Portugal's urban areas or in the diaspora (many of whom, like me, were living in and fed up with Berlin). We called it the Research Center for Culture and Sustainability (Centro de Investigação Cultura e Sustentabilidade) – CICS – with the intention to establish interdisciplinary partnerships with multiple research institutions in a wide range of issues: co-housing, regenerative farming, transformative learning, socioecological economies, eco-tech, participatory decision-making, etc.

To this end, we created a substantial, participatory document that we affectedly named »Integrated Regional Development Plan« (Plano de Desenvolvimento Regional Integrado); it contained a long list of projects, from LETS to agroecology, eco-construction to solidarity economy, and transformative pedagogy to the recovery of local knowledges. The title was carefully engineered to appeal to city councilors, though the »plan« was not

---

1   I take »intentional collective« as a critical iteration of the term and idea of »intentional community.« This iteration aims, simultaneously, to highlight both the need for modes of communing/communalization typical of intentional communities while refusing the identitarian traits that often and deliberatively bind them.

2   An integral cooperative is a type of multisectoral cooperative that aims to be comprehensive, encompassing various aspects of social and economic life within a community - such as housing, work/production, consumption, education, health, culture, etc. The first self-named experience was »Cooperativa Integral Catalana,« begun in 2010 in Barcelona, Catalonia, Spain.

3   *The Carnation Revolution* (April 25, 1974) was a military movement in Portugal that ended almost five decades of dictatorship and established democracy in the country. The name comes from the fact that the demonstrators wore carnations as a symbol of peaceful resistance.

particularly integrated, nor regional, nor much of a development strategy. For several months, some of us toured the deserted and impoverished municipalities of Portugal's deep hinterland – north to south, away from the urbanized coastline – with this plan in hand, hoping to get a piece of rural land upon which we could implement the project.

The local response, however, oscillated between curiosity and mistrust. Montemor-o-Novo (fig. 1), located about 20 kilometers from Évora and 90 kilometers east of Lisbon, was the only one to offer us, through a potential long-term concession contract, 33 ha of land within its urban industrial perimeter (figs. 2 and 3). It was not the rural idyll we were looking for, because, according to the Portuguese land-use law, it is not possible to build privately on rural land, with the exception of agricultural, forestry, or touristic purposes, but we accepted the terms imposed and, over the course of a year, dedicated ourselves to collective work, meeting frequently in Montemor.

We wanted to root ourselves in the long term in a local context, and to escape and oppose the logic of the event (that much-abused word!). We did not want to activate a place, but to try to regenerate it, as well as ourselves in the long term. From the outset, we started to relationally cartograph and establish equal partnerships with local organizations and entities to avoid duplication and, where ethos and pace aligned, to hand over coordination to local entities. In parallel, we cultivated translocal networks (Greiner & Sakdapolrak 2013) – ties with research centers and civic organizations capable of deepening the practice on the ground without turning Montemor into an academic outpost. Collaboration, not objectification, was the rule (fig. 4).

Unlike many intentional communities of the 1970s, we were neither governed by dogma, single discourses, nor obedience to any diktat. We cultivated an ethic of adventure (Debaise and Stengers 2017; Ingold 2015; Savransky 2016), in which contradictions, ignorance, and dissonance could fit. Conflict was seen as an engine for collective maturation, not as a threat to cohesion. The spectrum of political positions on the left spanned from the most radical to centrist moderation (anarcho-communism, communism, libertarian socialism, and social democracy), and some of the people involved had non-negligible financial, social, or cultural capital. Even so, the group responded to the paradoxes with frank discussion, without ostracism or purism. We were there to learn from each other, to reflect on differences, and not to establish armored identities (Agier 2016), while trying together to transform contradictions into questions of politics and structure, rather than of individual conduct (Ahmed 2012).

1.
Montemor-o-Novo in 2019. Photograph by União de Freguesia de Nossa Senhora da Vila, Nossa Senhora do Bispo e Silveiras.

2.
CICS, Location Plan and Preliminary Site Proposal. Plan by author, adapted from Tânia Teixeira, 2012.

3.
*Crossroads leading to the proposed CICS plot of land in 2013. Photograph by the
author, 2013.*

4.
A sense of (un)commoning. A celebratory dinner. And a piano concert by Ulf
Ding from the 2013 festival, »Shadows Are Offered,« curated by Vera Mantero,
a choreographer and member of CICS in Montemor-o-Novo. Adapted by author,
credit: Inês Ivangelista, 2013.

Gradually, however, the collective imagination was confronted with material realities.

- How would we finance a common house?
- How could we self-build when paid work was a hundred kilometers away and childcare was scarce?
- How to live on intermittent research contracts under one thousand euros?
- How to share unequal project incomes without reproducing privilege? How many local jobs would we actually create?
- How to justify a public grant of land amid long social-housing lists?

These were practical and political questions: of legitimacy, distribution, and fair access to property, voice, and decision-making.

After painful moments of unbearable dissension, approximately a dozen people remained who managed to settle in Montemor-o-Novo. The project later gave rise to the integral cooperative named »Minga« – a nod to South American indigenous practices of local mutualism, cooperation and solidarity – the genesis of which preserved many of the premises of the collective. Today, twelve years later, Minga is well known in the Portuguese cooperative milieu as a kind of a benchmark in second-generation (non-agricultural) cooperativism in Portugal. It continues to bloom, however slowly, into a fully developed multi-sectoral cooperative that may come to integrate dimensions of production, consumption, co-housing and, perhaps, education.

However, that part of the story will not be explained here. Instead, I am interested in understanding what went wrong, where things went awry and how we ended up contributing to the crushing statistics of failure. Around ninety per cent of all »intentional communities« collapse in their early stages (Stevens-Wood et al. 2021). Most seriously of all, I want to understand how we ended up reproducing a logic of urgency that disproportionately overburdened the most precarious and vulnerable people, thereby reversing the very ethics of care that we had set out to defend. The intention is not to humiliate or disqualify, but rather to provide a heuristic platform from which I can craft tentative proposals; proposals that, from my insider perspective and as a student of socio-spatial practices, could have prevented the collapse of the project, or at least avoided many of the (inter-)personal costs involved in its dissolution.

Factors of Implosion

One of the major blind spots was the means of subsistence. In CICS, the directive was neoliberal: Everyone was to generate their own income through individual research gigs. That »ethos« not only prevented the collective from stabilizing, it actually reproduced precarity by design. The housing component of the project added contrast to the already evident fault line. Construction or renovation required a financial equity, owned, borrowed or donated capital, which most of us, despite our relative privilege, were unable to access. Unlike the Uruguayan model of housing through mutual aid (FUCVAM 2012) or the Danish co-housing communities, both sustained by long-term policies (Larsen 2019), public policies on cooperative (co-)housing in Portugal were limited to some post-revolutionary years after 1974.

From the outset, CICS would have needed a common economy, however partial and minimal, with the capacity to mutualize risk, infrastructure, and property; An income-generation ecosystem anchored in social ecological economies (Spash 2024) and ecological technologies (Bihouix et al. 2022), paradoxically recognizing that cooperatives compete at a structural disadvantage against capitalist firms which are trained for marginal-cost competition (Das et al. 2023). The charts show it clearly: Most proposals clustered around arts/education with mainly public or non-profit partners, while initiatives capable of generating a sustained independent revenue were almost non-existent (fig. 5).

Another challenging issue, which is by no means unique to CICS, concerned the paradox of the rural bias. Like so many other intentional collectives and communities, CICS cultivated a diffuse distrust of technoscience – a kind of new-generation luddism, associated with the celebration of »appropriate technologies« and DIY aesthetics (Schumacher 1974; Wahl 2016). Instead of forcing necropolitical industries and extractive landscapes to transform, that nostalgia made projects like CICS dependent on technologies with as little energy yield or scalability and as labor-intensive as micro wind turbines, solar ovens, or home chemistry. And while doing so, it also escaped the reality that, in order to build all of these, there must still be mining, metalworking, magnet production (Michaux and Butcher 2022), as well as rail networks, public investment and global logistics (Crary 2022). In other words, while CICS never rejected the relevance of the »urban« as node of encounters, negotiation, and supra-local governance, it also lacked – perhaps feared – to gaze non-innocently, and responsibly, at the monstrous translocal entanglements of planetary urbanization and industrialization with radical honesty (Brenner 2014; Ghosh 2016).

Finally, there was also a glaring lack of legal literacy, including an almost ignorance of the land-use planning tools in force: Municipal Development Plans, land use restrictions, health and building regulations, e.g., legal restrictions imposed on self-building due to seismicity or documented dangers to public health, or even the instruments of the Alentejo's Regional Development Coordination Commission[4]. Most of the projects designed for the »Integrated Regional Development Document« ignored previous local diagnoses, as if the state were just an intrusive presence and not an arena for legitimate dispute (Mouffe 2005; Tormey 2005).

This rejection of anything that smacked of »institutionality« was also manifested in the internal domains of the CICS: governance, organization, and planning. As in so many community experiences – such as the eco-village of Findhorn, Scotland, or the eco-city of Auroville, India – horizontality was confused with the absence of structure. Information circulated unevenly; decision-making channels were sometimes opaque; meeting agendas could be changed at the last minute or iterated by figures with greater symbolic capital; charismatic authority – the one that fares worst in participatory arenas (Gaventa 2006; Caser et al. 2017) – emerged alongside the tacit exclusion of less confident voices (Freeman, 1972; Polletta 2002). Figure 6 tries to capture the atmosphere with stark economy: »freedom is indeed an endless meeting.«

Under these pressures, time and care were the first to yield. Relocating to Montemor required a support system able to absorb different speeds, child-care needs, and uncertain incomes. Those who remained were, tellingly, people already living locally, able to work remotely, or hosted by local organizations; single parents and the most precarious rarely had a way in. Our optimism bowed to familiar lines of privilege, as we lost sight of the necessarily relational limits of our agency against the brutal agency of (power) institutions to constrain through discipline or submission. »All that is solid melts into air, all that is holy is profaned, and man is at last compelled to face with sober senses, his real conditions of life, and his relations with his kind.« (Marx and Engels 1848)

---

4 The Regional Development Coordination Commissions are peripheral services of the Portuguese State's direct administration, endowed with administrative and financial autonomy, which have powers in the areas of coordination and articulation of various regional sectoral policies: https://www.ccdr-a.gov.pt/, accessed October 5, 2025.

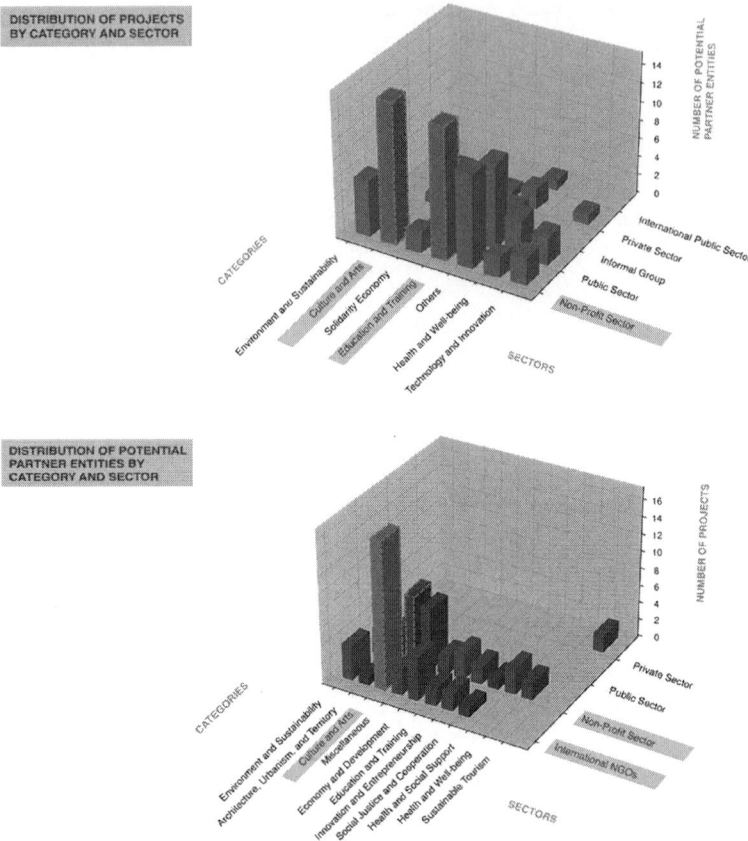

5.

3D graphs provide detailed insight into the socioeconomic categories and sectors of activity of the projects listed in the »Integrated Regional Development Plan,« as well as their potential partner entities. A substantial number of projects is evident in the arts and culture sectors, whilst there is an almost total absence of projects aimed at creating financial autonomy through the generation of an independent income. A similar trend is evident when the planned partner entities are analyzed. These entities are predominantly from the cultural and educational fields, with the vast majority falling within the non-profit or public sector – (though) many of these entities are research, experimentation, or artistic creation centers. This fundamental cultural and intellectual vibrancy stands in stark juxtaposition with the inability to conceive of subsistence strategies that would facilitate a »partial/selective de-linking« (Friedmann 1987). Graphs by author.

6.
Credit: Inês Evangelista, 2013.

Pericapitalism

In retrospect, and from my perspective alone, establishing a praxis like CICS meant, and still means, squaring the circle: Sustaining the gesture of radical openness while ensuring the pragmatic conditions of survival through caution, protection, and infrastructural grounding. On the one hand, the proposal of (in)communalizing everyday life requires an ethos of radical openness and adventure (Debaise and Stengers 2017; Ingold 2015; Savransky 2016). On the other hand, the toxicity inscribed and reproduced in most of our current institutions (Stengers 2009) – from market to courts, from tax codes to state forms – has a formidable force that must be recognized and never underestimated (Foucault 1977). It's not a question of choice, having to deal with legal systems that often suppress possibilities of social experimentation or the crushing forces of capitalist competitive markets.

From here, I adopt a deliberately disenchanted agenda: *Pericapitalism* as the craft of composing at the edge of capitalist circuits without letting them script the ends (Tsing 2015). More specifically, my view is that the survival or collapse of projects like CICS or Minga depends largely on their capacity to operate within, and not outside, the constraints imposed by state and market. To keep experimentation possible, one must first secure subsistence, (a)legality, and time – otherwise it will not work. Projects like CICS must be able to compose with the frictions at hand while crafting provisional infrastructures of habitability, to respond to the tensions between care and legality, presence and property, desire and constraint.

Following this harsh proposal, I would like to summarize, briefly, seven points in this deliberately exploratory agenda. First, livelihoods must be secured up front so that precarity does not besiege every promise: Design the subsistence layer early, favoring modest revenue engines with predictable flow sized to local purchasing power. Second, treat bureaucracy like geology: slow, shaping, and non-optional. Legibility is not capitulation; it is a condition for staying. Third, practice infrastructural sobriety: Compose with what exists, however monstrous, rather than fantasizing off-grid autonomies that externalize dependencies. Fourth, root-structured horizontalities: Participation needs form, that is, clear mandates, decision rights, time boxes, and conflict protocols that protect slower life rhythms. Horizontal does not mean amorphous – structure prevents charisma from ossifying into power. Fifth, address property and access. If land and tools are the backbone, their governance cannot slide into uncertainty; explore forms of common property, such as community land trusts, and design entry/ exit rules that do not punish precarity. Less heroic generosity, more boring justice embedded in instruments. Sixth, budget for time and care. Arrival requires a support ramp; housing transitions, childcare, retraining, and local learning are financed by small funds and shared-care networks; otherwise, urgency will again fall along predictable lines of class, gender, and even citizenship. Seventh, cultivate reciprocity with institutions: Work with municipalities, cooperatives, unions, and universities as sites of co-production, not audiences, that is, mutualize revenues, risks, and responsibilities.

Poetopolitics = Poiesis + Ethos + Topos + Politicus

Adding to its »cruel optimism« (Berlant 2011), I also think that CICS lacked a dense post-disciplinary ecology of practices: A set of integrated, situated and grounded methods/processes, (social) technologies, knowledges, competencies and skills capable of grounding ambitious visions of infrastructural, affective and institutional conditions of survival (fig. 7). A post-disciplinary platform (Lykke 2012; Wodak 2005) capable of generating integrated, symbiotic, thick alliances between different kinds of necessary knowledges from multiple cosmos/worlds: a tool of and for *transknowledging(s)* (King 2012).

Take the example of certain practices of landing – in the literal and in the *Latourian* sense: Not seizing control and exploiting the land to fulfill a civilizational telos indissociable from infinite growth, like the Moderns did and do, but rather becoming with the land/earth, as terrestrials bounded by finite resources (Latour 2017). Specifically, and to name just a few, Permaculture (Watkins 1993), Sustainable Urban Livelihoods Framework (Rakodi and Lloyd-Jones 2014), and the eco-swaraj experimentation of Vikalp Sangam (Kothari et al. 2019). Each of these, in their own way, reflects an attempt to assemble infrastructures of life that intertwine everyday life, knowledge production, spatial composition and institutional experimentation through entangled *transknowledgings* and ways of working. Permaculture reminds us of the domains that must be braided together – care of the earth, tools, education, culture, and finance. Vikalp Sangam's »Flower of Transformation« maps interconnected arenas – ecology, justice, democracy, economy, and culture – as sites for rooted transitions and transformations (fig. 8). The Sustainable Livelihoods Framework insists on the basics: Assets (human, social, natural, physical, financial), then structures, then processes; and only then decide who cares, and how (fig. 9).

Read together, these three practices converge on a double recognition: First, that everyday life is woven through socioterritorial meshworks rather than arborescent logics; second, that institutions powerfully regulate access to resources, services, and even capabilities. It is along this double recognition that I conceive poetopolitics – a tentative and post-disciplinary toolkit and grammar that can be self-described as design, ethics, spacing, and politics. Because of this fourfold nature, I call it *poetopolitics*, a name that I hope can put the four vectors on an equal footing and simultaneously signal, not a model, but a practice of compostable co-composition across lands, institutions and people's everyday life. In my difficulty to decide on the centrality of politics in the production of space to the detriment of design and vice versa, or to take a definitive position on the primacy of *praxis* over *poiesis*, I aggregate them through juxtaposition. *Poiesis* refers to the act of world-making through situated creation, fabulation, and design-with: Not as projection, but as tentative crafting with what is already present. *Ethos* names the affective and relational disposition to stay-with, to remain present, to care, to become involved even in brokenness and risk. *Topos* designates not a neutral geography, but a terrain charged with memory, infrastructure and friction: A ground never innocent, but never uninhabitable either. *Politicus* invokes the field of shared conflict, where coexistence is not given but must

7.

Permaculture Flower. Adapted from David Holmgren, 2002.

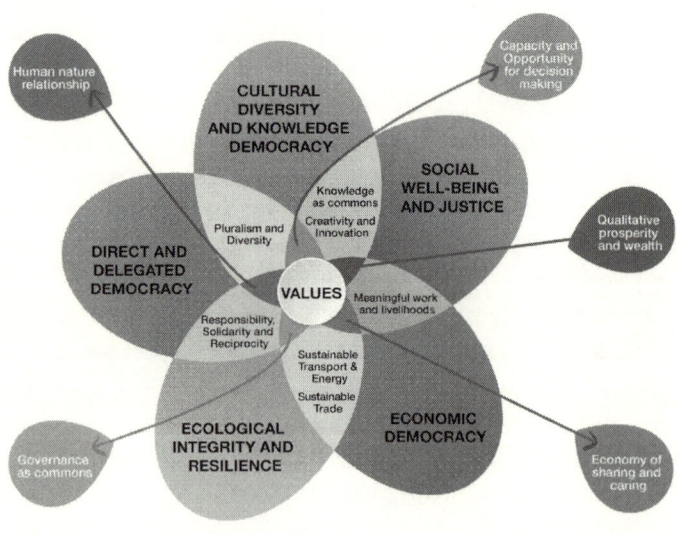

8.

Vikalp Sangam's guiding framework, the Flower of Transformation. Adapted from Vikalp Sangam, 2014.

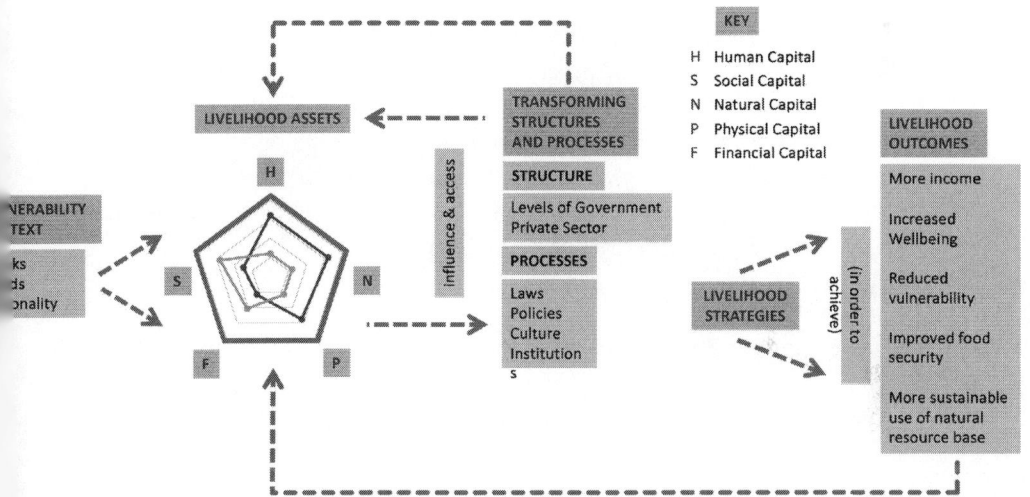

9.

Sustainable Livelihoods Framework was a conceptual tool used by the UK Department for International Development developed in the late 1990s to analyze how people make a living in complex and changing environments. It highlights the crucial importance of available goods and resources as capital(s). Although it was designed to understand and eradicate poverty, and despite the comprehensible criticisms of those who would rather have political revolution over capacity building, it remains a valuable tool for identifying and mapping the minimum material conditions critical for survival and flourishing. Adapted from DFID, Sustainable Livelihoods Framework, 2002.

be composed, negotiated, and held without guarantee. Together, these vectors do not form a system, nor their articulation a concept, but a kind of »compostable dispositive« that tries to address and articulate technical, socio-economic, ecological, political, and cultural matters-of-concern.

Poetopolitics may, or may not, have an obvious spatial/territorial expression and bear an observable mark in the built environment. As Latour (2017), Stengers (2009) and Haraway (2016) rightly point out, all entities, living or not, untouched or manufactured, as well as all actions, have their subsistence territories which mobilize, in one way or another, a translocal set of materials and energy, many of which are limited, either absolutely or through manufactured scarcity. Keeping this in mind, the word topos in poetopolitics means precisely that, a Gaia-graphic, terrestrial translocatily without which the exercise of politics or poiesis may become dangerous or even deadly. We should never forget the terrible consequences that both the »u-topos,« e.g., terra nullius, and the contrasting blood/land nexus have imposed on humans and non-humans in recent centuries. Poetopolitics, therefore, is deeply and deliberately partial by design, situated by necessity, and mesopolitical by temperament – not a bird's-eye concept, a »view from nowhere,« or a »God-trick« device (Haraway 1988).

Epilogue: Pluriversities

Because space/territory can be rethought as translocalities of subsistence – rather than as nowhere/everywhere or as a singular locus with its *genius loci* – poetopolitics emerges as a fitting lens for imagining, and perhaps implementing, platforms like CICS where change can learn to persist. Indeed, had CICS pursued a more pericapitalist, poetopolitical trajectory, one might imagine it evolving not as a conventional research center but as an incipient pluriversity – a living platform holding learning, doing, and governance together long enough for habits to ripen in the body. Platforms always in the making, yet to be fully defined, stitching cross-cutting alliances among knowledges, organizations, and territories without claiming a single center; platforms which are honest about power and infrastructure. The point would not be not to collect flags, but to assemble procedures, scopes, and tools that make reciprocity legible and durable.

This connects with the notion of *pluriversity* (Escobar 2018; Tinel et al. 2018): Though post-colonial Portugal may not be the most obvious site to invoke the practices and institutions of *pluriversity*, they might be pivotal as critical *non-occidentalist Western* (Santos 2009) living laboratories for situated transition and transformation. At this juncture, where political, human, and more-than-human histories converge under climate collapse (Chakrabarty 2014), the question is no longer whether institutions will change by decree but what sort of restorative practices we might be able to conjure together. A *pluriversity* is, therefore, a call: A potential choreography where citizens, cooperatives, municipalities, and research bodies can share resources, knowledges, revenue, power, responsibilities and risks for joint invention and careful adventures towards a horizon of possibilities beyond pericapitalism.

In these arrangements, universities could act as compostable, not central, institutions. Concentrating forms of capital that mediate access to rights and obligations under law–and to essential goods, services, knowledges, and capabilities–their role is not epistemic sovereignty but contribution: Co-producing situated experiments, lending legal legibility, and offering labs and budgets that can braid with civic infrastructures. Municipalities, in turn, could provide places to live and robust, long-term, cross-sectoral support so that such projects could flourish safely, durably and in an integrated manner. Finally, projects like CICS or Minga should sustain durable pacts between citizens and local government, not to fine-tune a sector here or there, but to recompose everyday *modi vivendi* under planetary urgency.

The challenge is immense, the path uncertain, and error likely. Even so, we are called before future generations and as non-innocent heirs of modernity's monstrous project to answer their appeals and to learn from one another on the platforms of the possible. As in Haraway's (2016: 6) words, »either we become with each other, or not at all.«

References

Acosta, Alberto (2013): *El Buen Vivir: Sumak Kawsay, Una Oportunidad Para Imaginar Otros Mundos*, Barcelona: Icaria Editorial.

Agier, Michel (2016): *Borderlands: Towards an Anthropology of the Cosmopolitan Condition*, Cambridge: Polity Press.

Ahmed, Sara (2014): *The Cultural Politics of Emotion*, 2nd ed., Edinburgh: Edinburgh University Press.

Bihouix, Philippe/Jeantet, Sophie/Selva, C. de (2022): *La Ville Stationnaire : Comment Mettre Fin à l'Étalement Urbain ?* Arles: Actes Sud.

Bourdieu, Pierre (1980) : »Le Capital Social,« in : *Actes de la Recherche en Sciences Sociales 31*, 2–3.

Brenner, Neil, ed. (2014): *Implosions/ Explosions: Towards a Study of Planetary Urbanization*, Berlin: Jovis Verlag.

Caser, Ursula/Cebola, Cátia M./ Vasconcelos, Lia/Ferro, Filipa (2017): »Environmental Mediation: An Instrument for Collaborative Decision Making in Territorial Planning,« in: *Finisterra 52/109*, 109–120. doi: 10.18055/Finis6969

Chakrabarty, Dipesh (2014). »Climate and capital: On conjoined histories,« *Critical Inquiry 41/1*, 1–23. doi: 10.1086/678154

Crary, Jonathan (2013): *24/7: Late Capitalism and the Ends of Sleep*, London: Verso.

Das, Raju J./Gough, Jamie/Eisenschitz, Aram (2023): *The Challenges of the New Social Democracy: Social Capital and Civic Association or Class Struggle?* Leiden: Brill. doi: 10.1163/9789004546882

Debaise, Didier/Stengers, Isabelle (2017): »The Insistence of Possibles: Towards a Speculative Pragmatism,« in: *Parse 3/7*, 13–19.

Escobar, Arturo (2018): *Designs for the Pluriverse: Radical Interdependence, Autonomy, and the Making of Worlds*, Durham: Duke University Press. doi: 10.1215/9780822371816

Foucault, Michel (1977): *Discipline and Punish: The Birth of the Prison*, New York: Pantheon Books.

Freeman, Jo (1972): »The Tyranny of Structurelessness,« in: *Berkeley Journal of Sociology 17*, 151–165.

Friedmann, John (1987): *Planning in the Public Domain: From Knowledge to Action*, Princeton: Princeton University Press.

Ghosh, Amitav (2016): *The Great Derangement: Climate Change and the Unthinkable*, Chicago: University of Chicago Press. doi: 10.7208/ chicago/9780226323176.001.0001

Greiner, Clemens/Sakdapolrak, Patrick (2013): »Translocality: Concepts, Applications and Emerging Research Perspectives,« in: *Geographical Compass 7/5*, 373–384. doi: 10.1111/gec3.12048

Haraway, Donna (1988). »Situated Knowledges: The Science Question in Feminism and the Privilege of Partial Perspective,« in: *Feminist Studie 14/3*, 575–699. doi: 10.2307/3178066

Haraway, Donna (2016): *Staying with the Trouble: Making Kin in the Chthulucene*, Durham: Duke University Press. doi: 10.1215/9780822373780

Ingold, Tim (2015): *The Life of Lines*, London: Routledge. doi: 10.4324/9781315727240

King, Katherine (2012): *Networked Reenactments: Stories Transdisciplinary Knowledges Tell*, Durham: Duke University Press.

Larsen, Henning (2019): *Co-Housing in Denmark: A Model for Sustainable Living*, Copenhagen: Danish Architecture Press.

Latour, Bruno (2017 [2015]): *Facing Gaia: Eight Lectures on the New Climatic Regime*, Cambridge: Polity Press.

Marx, Karl/Engels, Friedrich (2015 [1848]): *The Communist manifesto*, London: Penguin Books, 2015.

Michaux, Simon P./Butcher, Andrew R. (2022): »Some Observations on the Current Circular Economy Model: In Particular, the Mineral-Metal-Material Stream Blind Spots,« in: Sabine Barles et al. (eds.), *The Impossibilities of the Circular Economy*, Abingdon: Routledge, 153–179.

Mouffe, Chantal (2005): *On the Political*, London: Routledge.

Polletta, Francesca (2002). *Freedom is an Endless Meeting: Democracy in American Social Movements*. University of Chicago Press.

Rakodi, Carole/Lloyd-Jones, Tony (2014): *Urban Livelihoods: A People-Centred Approach to Reducing Poverty*, London: Routledge. doi: 10.4324/9781849773805

Santos, B. Sousa (2009): »A Non-Occidentalist West? Learned Ignorance and Ecology of Knowledge, Theory, Culture & Society,« in: *SAGE* 26/7–8: 103–125. doi: 10.1177/0263276409348079

Savransky, Martin (2016): *The Adventure of Relevance: An Ethics of Social Inquiry*, London: Palgrave Macmillan. doi: 10.1057/978-1-137-57146-5

Schumacher, Ernst F. (1973): *Small Is Beautiful: A Study of Economics as If People Mattered*, London: Blond & Briggs.

Spash, Clive L. (2024): *Foundations of Social Ecological Economics*, Manchester: Manchester University Press. doi: 10.7765/9781526171498

Stengers, Isabelle (2009) : *Au Temps des Catastrophes : Résister à la Barbarie Qui Vient*, Paris: La Découverte.

Stevens-Wood, Kirsten/Coates, Chris/Dennis, James/How, Jonathan (2021): *Diggers & Dreamers: Intentional Community in Britain*, 12th ed., London: Diggers and Dreamers Publications.

Tinel, François-Xavier/Herrera Monsalve, Diana/Hernandez Umaña, Brayan A./ Moreno Pérez/Eliana Y. (2018): »De la Universidad a la Pluriversidad: Alternativas Educativas en América Latina para Otros »Desarrollos,«« in: *Social Review: International Social Sciences Review 7*, 6.

Wahl, Daniel Christian (2016): Designing Regenerative Cultures, Axminster: Triarchy Press.

Watkins, David (1993): *Urban Permaculture*, East Meon: Permanent Publications.

Wodak, Ruth (2005): »Editorial: Inter/ trans/post-disciplinarity and the Study of Language and/in Politics,« in: *Journal of Language and Politics 4/2*, 169–171. doi: 10.1075/JLP.4.2.02wod

NETWORKS

Dimensions of Architectural Knowledge, 2024–08 ∂
https://doi.org/10.14361/dak-2024-0811

Entangled Thresholds:
Building Multispecies Envelopes Beyond Human Comfort in the Philippines and Japan

Natalya Dikhanov-Juswigg, Sadie Imae

Abstract: Answers to some of the greatest ecological problems can be addressed by recognizing human's part in nature. In the architectural spaces we create, it is through recognition of our interdependencies with the natural world that designers can begin to tackle issues, such as alienation from nature, extractivism, unrestrained growth, and consumption. We reject these harmful approaches and look to collaborative models for designing and living. We need to incorporate »becoming by living together,« as urged by biologist Lynn Margulis (Aanen/Eggleton 2017: 99). »Life did not take over the world by combat, but by networking« (Margulis/Sagan 1997: 29). How do we, as designers and other specialists, collaborate for a more symbiotic future?
In this essay, we study the building envelope – the threshold between inside and outside – to reveal human and nonhuman collaborations in the built environment, along with opportunities for repair. By allowing nature to spill through our walls, new multispecies and community alliances emerge. What are the environmental potentials while expanding the human comfort zone? In dismantling the envelope, what relationships arrive, and how does the role of the architect change?

Keywords: Multispecies Entanglements; Porosity; Abject Spaces; Incremental Building; Dissolving Envelopes; Multisensorial Aesthetics; Adaptive Reuse; Symbiogenesis.

Corresponding authors: Natalya Dikhanov-Juswigg (FLUFFFF studio, USA); Sadie Imae (FLUFFFF studio, USA); ndikhanov@gmail.com; https://orcid.org/0009-0004-8764-055X; sadie@fluffff.space; https://orcid.org/0009-0006-4502-0971 ∂ Open Access. © 2025 Natalya Dikhanov-Juswigg, Sadie Imae published by transcript Verlag. This work is licensed under the Creative Commons Attribution 4.0 (BY) license.

»Never to tire of [...] opening holes for the world to fall, slip, or seep into oneself.« (Coccia 2017: 99)

Introduction

Humans are part of and inseparable from nature. Due to the destructive impacts of our exploitatively built environment, spatial practitioners must acknowledge interdependency and the benefits of multispecies entanglement. As designers, we reject alienation from »nature« and our communities. We oppose extractivism, unrestrained growth and consumption. Biologist Lynn Margulis urged »becoming by living together«[1] (Aanen/ Eggleton 2017: 99). But how do we evolve spatial practices for a more symbiotic future for humans and nonhumans alike?

In architectural discourse on multispecies entanglement, there is a push to connect interior to exterior space (cf. Ingraham 2006; Frichot 2018; Amir 2021) but limited analysis of its potentials (cf. Mertins 1996; Hwang 2013; Frichot 2019). Through case studies, our paper shows that porosity cultivates environmental attunement and human–nonhuman kinship. The »messiness« of wildlife entering buildings mandates a psychological shift to broaden our sense of community and care for the natural world, fostering more resilient communities. Despite the architectural impulse to separate from nature, the intelligence, and ways of working and living together in animals,[2] plants, fungi, and even bacteria, suggest models for mutual survival (cf. de Waal 2016; Haraway 2016; Tsing 2015; Margulis/Sagan 1997). Architects must learn from nonhuman symbiotic relationships to build collaborative communities – for abundance, wellness, and safety in ecological uncertainty.

This paper's case studies embrace interdependency. The architects design with reverence for nature and a reliance on community, as reflected in the openness of their envelopes. As spatial practitioners, their homes instruct us, disrupting typical learning hierarchies. They viscerally engage with the building

---

1 In reference to »symbiogenesis,« a concept explored by Lynn Margulis, which comes from the Greek roots *sym* (together), *bio* (life), and *genesis* (origin or creation), and can be understood as »becoming by living together.« It describes the evolutionary process by which new organisms emerge through long-term symbiotic relationships.

2 Cf. primatologist Frans de Waal, *Are We Smart Enough to Know How Smart Animals Are?* (2016), which challenges human-centered definitions of intelligence and highlights the cognitive capacities of nonhuman animals.

process by inhabiting the home and welcoming nonhumans and humans from conception to completion, enriching both the design and daily life.

Architectural knowledge today needs empathic design – looking at the world with soft eyes: We abandon the illusion of dominion over nature, recognizing our mutual roles for survival. Philosopher Emanuele Coccia states: »Cities are from the beginning projects of coexistence with other species« (Coccia 2025a). But how do we balance the traditional desire for comfort and safety in airtight homes, while allowing other species into the design process? We examine this in two case studies, an analysis of their building envelopes, and a speculative section reimagining the standard architectural paradigm.

Theoretical Framework for Expanding the Building Envelope

During the Covid-19 pandemic, people experienced »species loneliness«[3] – the worsened emotional state of those »not encircled by plants and animals« (Gruber 2021). Many felt adrift without human support networks. The imposed separation led many to challenge the nature–culture divide with plants and pets combatting lockdown's loneliness (Ruppert 2022; Ratschen 2020; Cordero Jr. 2021). We suggest the human urge for connection should inform spatial practice: dissolving thresholds between humans–nature, inside–outside, and individual–community.

Tracing the origins of the nature–culture divide, Catherine Ingraham, in *Architecture, Animal, Human: The Asymmetrical Condition*, marks »post-animal life« – the severing of humans from animals – as starting during the Renaissance. Humans separated from nature as they sought to tame it. Animals were removed from both the home and the interior life of the human, the former a metaphor for the latter (Ingraham 2006: 85).

In his 1753 *Primitive Hut* treatise, architectural philosopher Marc-Antoine Laugier wrote about the human relationship to nature and the walls separating them. He argued that architecture was a naturally occurring mediator between man and nature (Laugier 1753) (fig. 1). For centuries, architects worked to keep the outside world *out*. The building envelope shelters, but also reveals our paranoia of the »other,« of dangers perceived – objects of abjection. Psychoanalyst Julia Kristeva describes »abjection« as elements like

---

3 In *Like Hearts of Birds: Ottoman Avian Microarchitecture in the Eighteenth Century*, Christiane Gruber discusses the concept of »species loneliness,« as popularized by novelist Richard Powers.

1.
Engraving by Charles Eisen for Marc-Antoine Laugier's Primitive Hut, 1755.

decay, dirt, and waste, deemed disturbing because they are outside societal norms (Kristeva 1982). Architecture became a sterilization tool, to exclude the world's messiness, including insects, plant and animal life.

The architect's desire to master nature with impenetrable walls disconnects from surroundings and people, a devolution of communities. Architect Andrea Kahn quotes philosopher Luce Irigaray: »Everywhere you shut me in. Always you assign a place for me... You set limits even to events that could happen with others... You mark out boundaries, draw lines, surround, enclose...« (Kahn 1996: 176). The architecture of division reflects anxiety about loss of control – one that forecloses the possibility of mutual flourishing of humans and others. Architect Sarah Wigglesworth urges us to »debate what is meant by ›tidy‹, ›humane‹, ›safe‹, ›clean‹: concepts that architects [...] accept unquestioningly« (Wigglesworth 1996: 278). These values uphold a fantasy of »mastery,« suppressing complexity, diversity, and opportunity for messy collaboration across species, scales, and disciplines – the latter promoted by multispecies feminist theorist Donna Haraway (Haraway 2016).

To accept the messiness of collaboration, we look to architecture theorist Hélène Frichot's *Dirty Theory*. Using anthropologist Mary Douglas' definition of dirt as just »matter out of place« (Frichot 2019: 9), Frichot calls on architects to evolve »an ethics of care and maintenance« for our precarious world by accepting the »dirt« that nature and other species bring in (Frichot 2019: back cover). Some designers now rally with nature: Joyce Hwang's Bat Tower offers roosting space for bats[4]; CookFOX's terracotta facade shelters bees, birds, and plants[5]; and Emilio Ambasz's Prefectural International Hall features green terraces hosting birds, insects, and people[6]. The challenge, as Hwang writes in Living Among Pests, is to also fundamentally »rethink the spatial and visible dimensions of animals and urban organisms [...] to envision the possibilities of living among ›pests‹« – shifting architecture to embrace new priorities and entangled ways of living-together (Hwang 2013).

Fortified by the theories and projects above, we, the authors, »stay with the trouble,« as Haraway urges, or rather, *let's run with it* (Haraway

---

4 Hwang, Joyce/Ants of the Prairie (2010): »Bat Tower,« https://www.antsoftheprairie. com/?page_id=203, accessed May 15, 2025.

5 COOKFOX Architects (2022): »COOKFOX and Buro Happold Design Bird and Bee Friendly Façade for Architectural Ceramics Assemblies Workshop,« https://cookfox.com/news/ cookfox-and-buro-happold-acaw/, accessed May 15, 2025.

6 Emilio Ambasz & Associates (1990): »Fukuoka Prefectural International Hall,« https:// www.ambasz.com/fukuoka-prefectural-international, accessed May 15, 2025.

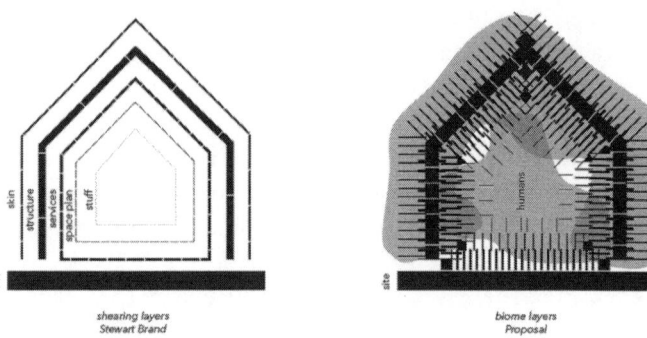

2.
Recreation of Stewart Brand's »shearing layers« diagram (left), and the authors' proposed diagram for »biome layers« of permeable walls (right). Drawings by FLUFFFF studio, 2024.

3.
Bird palace at the Ayazma mosque complex, Üsküdar, Istanbul, constructed 1758–1761. Photograph by Dosseman, 2023.

2016). Not fearing nature, we embrace it to thrive amid planetary crises. Haraway's Chthulucene (in revolt against the Anthropocene/Capitalocene/ Plantationocene) offers worlds of interspecies collaborations for hopeful futures. The building envelope can be a zone for alliances and a renewed sense of community.

Rejecting modernist isolationism, environmentalist Stewart Brand, in *How Buildings Learn* (1994), reevaluates buildings as living organisms that change, influenced by materials, inhabitants and climate. Based on architect Frank Duffy's »shearing layers,« Brand identifies distinct, interacting strata, evolving on different timescales: Site, Structure, Skin, Services, Space Plan & Stuff (fig. 2). Traditional building, he notes, allows for adaptability to shifting needs, unlike modernist designs professing purity of form. This adaptability is facilitated by »slippage« of layers: Layers with longer times-cales (Structure) do not hinder those with shorter timescales (Services). Thus, spatial practitioners can work with the slippage – welcoming time, life, and decay into our walls.

Throughout history, we've seen slippage *and spillage* in built form, approx-imating the multispecies walls of the Chthulucene. In 18th century Ottoman avian microarchitecture, we find stone walls made not for agricultural or extractive purposes but as safe haven for birds, based on human-nature custodianship and harmony (fig. 3). Building envelopes amplified their phys-ical and sonic presence – the rush of wings and echoing of song – within the bustling city, contrasting with Euro-American values of utility and control (Gruber 2021). Bird dwellings also brought bird excrement – the discom-fort of living together – versus the modern cleanliness fetish exemplified by bird-deterrent spikes. The Ottoman walls articulated »an ethics of engage-ment with nonhuman others [...] embracing a multisensorial aesthetics of delight« (Gruber 2021), proving there is »no sanctuary from the inclusiveness of nature«, as environmental aesthetics philosopher Arnold Berleant states (Berleant 1992: 8).

Designing with intentional openings, we become attuned to the envi-ronment, shifting how we think about buildings, cities, and ourselves. Challenging monolithic walls, we should design with porosity: permeable thresholds that »[breathe] with openness, connection, and light« (Holl n.d.). Urbanist Sophie Wolfrum traces the term »porosity« to Walter Benjamin and Asja Lacis's reflections on Naples, where the boundaries between spaces are fluid, creating a stage for improvisation. Wolfrum notes the term's evolution into an urban and architectural paradigm that describes the »layering and mélange of spaces,« structures, and urban textures (Wolfrum 2018: 9).

Porosity can be understood as not only physical – allowing in air, moisture, and light, flora, and fauna – but an expanded ethics for social and ecological intertwining. By giving our walls flexibility and life, new alliances emerge. Pleasurable spaces (cf. Lacaton/Vassal 2024) nurture a sense of place for humans and nonhumans. Porous skins reveal surprising symbioses, guiding spatial practitioners in repair and new ways of building and living together, as in the case studies below.

Here we focus on two paradigm-shifting homes – in the Philippines and Japan – that radically rethink the building envelope, challenging conventional boundaries between inside and outside, human and nonhuman. They embrace porosity and allow nature to co-shape space. Our methodology included a remote interview with Filipino architect Justin Guiab, and an email exchange with his wife, Sarah Strugar, who offered a vivid glimpse into the home's multispecies life. For the Japanese case study, we draw from a firsthand site visit in 2019 and publications and lectures by Mio Tsuneyama and Fuminoru Nousaku.

These architects seek to disintegrate walls and extend thresholds, creating space for the environment and nonhumans to enter. When nature came knocking, the designers grabbed a sledgehammer and made openings.

Case Studies

Happy Valley House by Justin Guiab, El Nido, Palawan, the Philippines, 2021-present

> »We live here, but the insects, animals lived here before me. And as they build their homes in our home, I feel happy to share it with them. This is really their space and we're just trying to coexist with them.« (Guiab 2024)

In our engaging interview with architect Justin Guiab, we discovered that the porosity of his home was less a formal plan than a lifestyle extension involving both community and environment. When Guiab and his wife, Sarah Strugar, acquired land in the El Nido, Palawan Forest, they cleared only a small portion, thereby preserving trees. For a year, they lived in a hut, observing their environment (fig. 4). Guiab noted, »I tried to get to know the trees, the birds, the animals, and insects that lived here« (Guiab 2024). He studied the sun, wind, and topography. »I kept asking the house what it wanted to be. Later, it told me where to build, and what it could become« (Guiab 2024). The result is a project that dissolves the envelope, allowing nature – trees, animals and insects – inside.

Constructed with almost no walls, using »humble materials« like clay, wood, rammed earth, and concrete, and with no clear entrance, the house can be approached from any angle. With only the bedroom, study, and pantry enclosed, the envelope is just a floor slab and roof that gesture to its thresholds (fig. 5). The steep incline of the roof preserves the traditional method of cogon grass secured to purlins with rattan. Gaps in the roof allow natural light and ventilation, while artificial lighting mimics natural lighting. The open-air bathroom houses a bathtub hand-carved from river rock, where the family bathes using spring water (fig. 6). Greywater flows to an adjacent pocket garden with swamp taro plants filtering and absorbing runoff.

Guiab utilized locally sourced materials like *ipil* wood to support animal and insect life within their home. The use of on-site materials with a minimal envelope allowed for a scaled layering of homes and the species associated with them. The cellular logic of a mud wasp nest is built upon the timber frame logic of the house (fig. 7). Brand's theory of shearing layers is expanded to include a layer for ecological integration, that of multispecies slippage and *spillage*. A collage of aesthetics results, generating community in a barely present envelope:

> »From the wasps who build their little clay homes on the walls, to the sun-birds that hang their nests from the passionfruit vines in the bathroom to our dogs, our cats, our chickens... everything feels alive. Even the house feels alive. Even the concrete feels alive because of all the life around it.« (Strugar 2025) (fig. 8)

Driven by an empathic heart, Guiab initially refused to use the local *ipil* tree (*Intsia bijuga*, also merbau), which is threatened by illegal timber activity. However, alternate wood sources proved unsuitable for the climate and cross-species cohabitation. *Ipil* thrives in harsh conditions and is termite-resistant, carbon-negative, long-lasting, and beautiful. Only two trees would be needed to build a home to last 100 years. Guiab's deep consideration of material and sourcing reflects his activist approach.

4.
The hut Justin Guiab and Sarah Strugar lived in for a year before constructing their home. Photograph by Justin Guiab, 2021.

5.
An open envelope allows for other critters to freely wander in and through the home. Still from video by Design Anthology, 2024.

6.
It took three months to carve a bathtub into this rock (bottom), collected from a nearby river (top). Stills from video by Design Anthology, 2024.

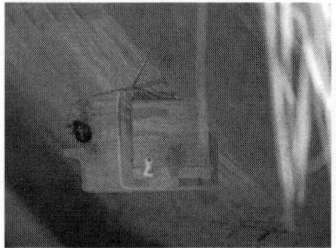 

7.

A human-constructed insect home (7a) and a mud dauber wasp nest (7b). Stills from video by Design Anthology, 2024.

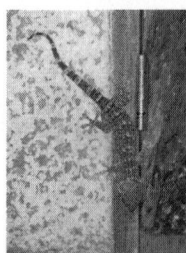  

8.

Some nonhuman species sharing the home: a tuko gecko visiting the open-air bathroom (left), sunbirds nesting in passionfruit vines in the bathroom (center), and one of many cats cared for by the family (right). Photographs by Sarah Strugar, 2025.

The original state in March 2017.   After the demolition in April 2017.   The state after fixing new windows
                                       Lived in open air for a year.   in April 2018.

9.

Exterior changes over time of Holes in the House. Photographs by Studio mnm/ Fuminori Nousaku Architects and Ryogo Utatsu, 2017–2018.

In a radical reversal, Guiab hired workers who were usually engaged in illegal logging to construct his home and plant trees. In addition, his profits are reinvested into purchasing surrounding land – otherwise destined for resorts – to reforest with indigenous trees, creating a feedback loop of care and restoration. To date, he's planted over 4,000 *ipil* trees. By his calculations, planting 25,000 trees over eight years on 30 hectares of land (just 0.027% of El Nido's land area) could construct homes for El Nido's entire population, help restore the water table, and provide habitat for nonhuman species (Guiab 2025).

Guiab's patient approach to spatial practice challenges industry norms. Fortunately, his family and clients are open to a slow approach, despite others' skepticism. Patience allowed for design-responsive moments, like shifting the envelope to preserve bird flight paths or moving the building site far from a termite mound instead of poisoning the soil. Rather than letting ego dictate, Guiab's designs respond to the site and remain adaptable, during and after construction. Wilderness and wildlife morph the design for unique visual outcomes of a home embedded in the forest (fig. 8), with visibly irregular lengths of harvested lumber – beyond the usual controlled architectural approach.

By reintroducing traditional and ecologically entangled building techniques, Guiab's wildly unorthodox approaches challenged the local construction industry. But the workers' initial skepticism gave way to pride and a transformed understanding, influencing the building of their own homes and on other job sites. *Happy Valley House* remains adaptable after construction, allowing for expansions and multi-generational living, echoing Brand's incremental growth concept.

Holes in the House by Fuminori Nousaku and Mio Tsuneyama, Tokyo, Japan, 2017–present

»We want people to rediscover their own sense of wilderness and what it means to be human in the city.« (Tsuneyama, in Alihodžić 2024)

Another example of porosity in building envelopes is uniquely set in an urban environment: Architects Mio Tsuneyama and Fuminori Nousaku purchased an »unappealing« house in a former industrial neighborhood in Tokyo. Reflecting the raze-repeat-rebuild mindset prevalent due to earthquakes and post-World War II demand, their building was designed to last only 20 to 30 years (Berg 2017). After a local plant and workers left in the 1990s, the building stood in limbo, unworthy of a real estate listing (Alihodžić 2024). Committing to the property was itself a radical act by the architects.

Named both *Holes in the House and Urban Wild Ecology*, the house was immediately inhabited and reimagined, starting with the envelope (fig. 9). They cut holes in the facade and roof and opened the interior with a continuous stairway from street to roof (fig. 10), reconnecting the occupant with the exterior, inviting the breeze in, and passively cooling the home. Cutting holes in the floor slabs and foundation also introduced the earthy smell of soil. After a large portion of the front elevation was removed, covered only by a blue tarpaulin, all four seasons seeped into the home – dissolving inside and outside (fig. 11). The home's peculiar perforations embody Coccia's statement of »opening holes for the world to fall, slip, or seep into oneself« (Coccia 2017: 99). Tsuneyama explains:

> »As homes are organically connected to our lives and we are inseparable [from] and intertwined with them, I thought: ›What if we could create a kind of wild connection between our lives, evolving needs for space, and our house? Could we discover a new way of living? [...] of being at home? [...] of being in architecture? [...]‹« (Alihodžić 2024)

The architects' commitment to bring nature – a »wild connection« – into an urban context began with assessing the site's resources: the house's orientation; sun exposure in a corner location; a small side-alley; and large ground floor connecting the house to the neighborhood. The »bones« of the building were also part of »tapping into what is already in abundance.« Natural elements were brought in, e.g., rainwater via a pipe from the roof to a showerhead on the ground floor (fig. 12). The architects incorporated a traditional semi-external dirt floor (doma) entrance corridor, extending the outdoors into the home. Though urban, the house evokes traditional Japanese countryside homes.

The couple's approach reflects the movement to reevaluate construction, extraction and material supply chains. A notable example is *A Global Moratorium on New Construction*, issued in 2021 by architect and scholar Charlotte Malterre-Barthes. This provocative moratorium calls to halt new building, take stock of existing resources (e.g., vacant housing), and challenge predatory real estate practices. It urges us to focus on »repairing and prolonging« instead of ever-building (Malterre-Barthes 2021).

Malterre-Barthes' call to action and the example of *Holes in the House* provide a guide for the architectural crises we face.

With the birth of Tsuneyama and Nousaku's child, making holes extended to the surroundings (fig. 13). They ripped out the side-alley asphalt to create a garden and play area, restoring nature and microorganisms to the alley, »unpaving paradise«[7] in an area suffering from the heat island effect. They reclaimed the street gutter, enabling water to reach the soil for tree growth. Neighbors contributed plants and earthworms as gifts.

Tsuneyama explained, »Tinkering with ready-made tools and doing small agriculture in the city [...], tapping into leftover resources and repurposing what others discard: That is what we understand as ecology« and what has been separated from our profession« (Alihodžić 2024). With this approach, they softened thresholds delineating inside–outside, underground–above ground, and wet–dry areas. The building became more resilient and porous – a sponge integrated into local ecology and community. The envelope became a link, not a divider, between humans and the environment.

The architects describe *Urban Wild Ecology* as existing at the intersection of both political and deep ecology. They »seek to bring out the wilderness that every one of us instinctively has,« even if forgotten in the comforts of urban consumerism (Alihodžić 2024). Tsuneyama states:

> »[...] comfort should come from understanding and supporting life in a way that respects other species. This approach [...] acknowledges multiple species, fosters connections, and envisions an architecture that is not exclusively human.« (Fletcher 2025)

For them, like for Brand, architecture is in a constant state of becoming, »led by the needs, budgetary possibilities, available resources and lifestyles of its inhabitants.« (Alihodžić 2024)

Intentional or not, opening up their home (with the conspicuous blue tarp and other manipulations) allowed more than »nature« to enter. The home became an architecture laboratory within a greater urban laboratory, where guests are welcomed to learn the lessons of *Holes in House* firsthand.

---

7 In reference to Joni Mitchell's famous 1970 song »Big Yellow Taxi,« the architects took back the alley/parking lot, reversing her lyrics and concept: »They paved paradise and put up a parking lot.«

10.

Holes in the House is inhabited in a constant state of de- and re-construction. Photograph by Ryogo Utatsu, 2018.

11.

The architects lived an entire year with large parts of the front facade cut out, covering this opening with only a blue tarpaulin, the air and breeze of all four seasons permeating and flowing through their home. Photograph by Studio mnm/ Fuminori Nousaku Architects, 2017.

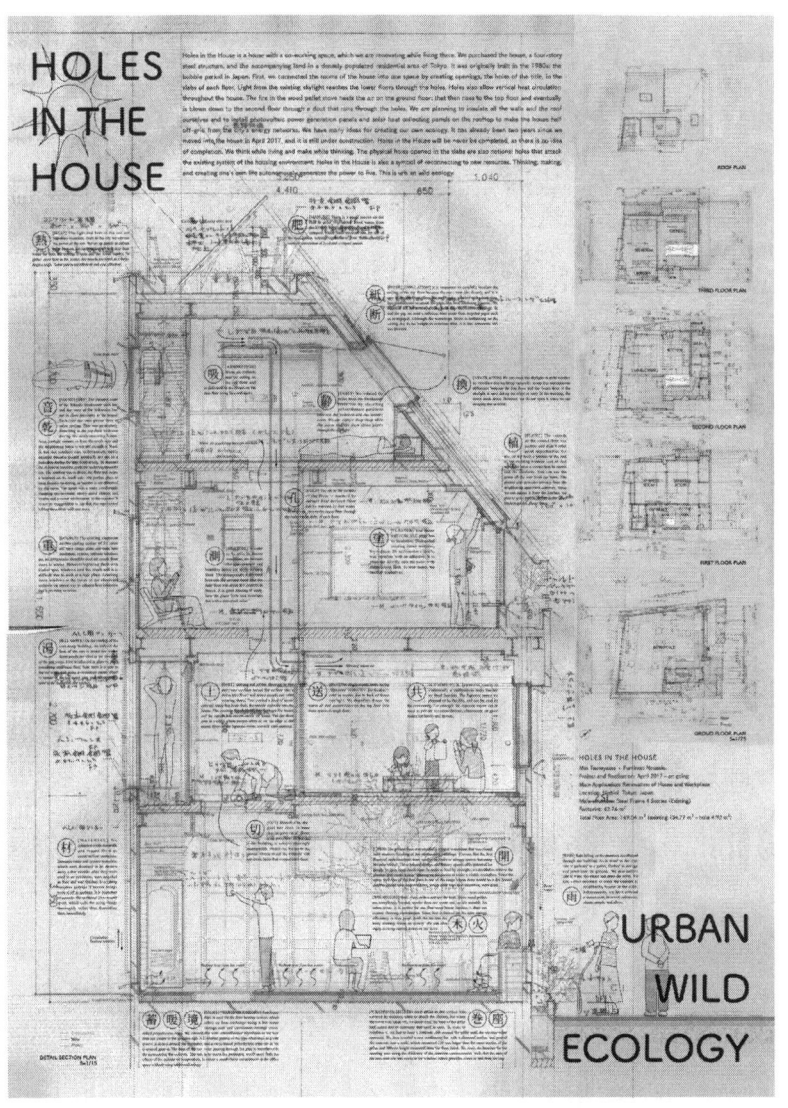

12.
Section drawing by Studio mnm/Fuminori Nousaku Architects, 2021.

13.
*With the help of bamboo charcoal, humus, earthworms, an oak tree, and support
from the local community, signs of life – including white mycelium – appeared
after two months. The popular food, bitter melon, grows on vines along the
main street facade. Photographs by Studio mnm/Fuminori Nousaku Architects,
2019–2020.*

This work reflects an acceptance of process, just as none of the life cycles are rushed in nature. Camping in the home allowed time to attune to the »nature« of the site. Building within an existing structure motivates an ethics of care. Slowing down and accepting natural elements contradicts capitalist standards in homebuilding. Creating *Holes in the House* became an act of care and activism.

Porous Practice and the Expanded Envelope

Both case studies – one urban and one in the wilderness – serve as models for future spatial practices. Many sustainable and biophilic homes invite comparison, but these projects stand out in how they challenge dominant developer-driven practice through porosity and patient building, resisting extractive paradigms. Their approaches are inherently anti-capitalist, against binary divisions of nature–culture, public–private, interior–exterior, and human–nonhuman. They echo feminist architectural critique, folding theory into practice to create thresholds teaming with life (cf. Rendell 2010).

Architectural discourse has favored buildings of large investment, judged by market value over ecological or social aspects. The case studies herein counter this with, as Brand states, value in slow growth and incremental building (Brand 1994: 202). The envelope becomes a temporal as well as spatial threshold – inviting a more situated and thoughtful design process.

Fast construction gained prevalence post-World War II to address the rebuilding, population growth, and rapid urbanization crises (Berg 2017). This persists: Housing crises are met with ever-new construction, ignoring vacant building stock and materials. In our haste, we neglect human, nonhuman, and environmental health. »Fast gets all our attention, slow has all the power« (Brand 2018). The Palawan and Tokyo projects exemplify slow power: Incremental building allows for better integration of nature and nonhumans. Reimagining the architect as a mediator working across multiple timescales allows genuine interspecies negotiation and coincidences to incorporate resources, energy, construction waste materials, and community input.

The case studies emphasize how the architect's role can expand to bring nature, human and nonhuman together as collaborators, with building occupants mingling, bumping elbows with plants, sharing pathways with critters, even breaking bread with bugs. The envelope no longer excludes nature, but is rather an armature of intermingling of natural elements. From

Coccia's elegant defiance of urban alienation: »The solution to climate change lies not in replacing cities with the countryside, but in designing cities more radically, extending the culture of urban congestion to a culture of congestion of species density, biodiversity« (Coccia 2025b).

Coincidentally, both couples in our cases welcomed their first child in their homes, not altering their fundamental designs. In Palawan, Justin and Sarah completed construction just days before giving birth in their stone bathtub. In Tokyo, the coming child was an impetus to cover exposed insulation, tuck away wires, and install nets over floor openings. Rather than baby-proofing with gates, a porous envelope became a learning tool for the children to develop bodily and spatial awareness and kinship with the world around them.

These homes also became laboratories for ecological innovation in their communities. *Happy Valley House* shifted local builders' mindsets to appreciate a new building process. *Holes in the House* welcomed students and educators to witness construction and ecological interventions firsthand. In both projects, to open the home to »nature« was to open it to nonhuman and human communities.

There is inherent risk in porosity, allowing the community, insects, animals, and weather to enter one's home. However, both families saw value in creating homes as spaces of encounter, not retreat. They dared to carve holes or forgo envelopes altogether, demonstrating how to feel at home in unusual conditions. A unique aesthetic quality arises as we embrace the dust, dirt, and ambiguity of letting the outside in, echoing Wigglesworth's question to modern architects about what is safe and clean (Wigglesworth 1996). The architects transform the abject and uncomfortable into something rich with meaning, yielding environmental, aesthetic, and economic benefits. Old exploitative building mindsets are disassembled by gently subversive architecture.

Kindness, Crisis, and the Comfort Zone

As women in spatial practice, we authors admire these case studies for wrestling with discomfort to allow interspecies entanglement and messiness. In Guiab's project, comforts like central air-conditioning were given up to preserve an open envelope with passive cooling strategies. He demonstrated an ethics of care and kindness: What is not good for one is not good for all. Such altruism invites physical patinas of other life, like the mud homes of wasps on Guiab's walls. »To live means to leave traces,« as philosopher Walter Benjamin said (Benjamin 1940).

By engaging discomfort, we wonder how to extend the human comfort zone through adjacency to other species. The modern »comfort crisis« (cf. Easter 2021) must be addressed by architecture: Constant human comfort consumes energy. Beyond energy-intensive mechanical systems, building envelopes are the primary site to mediate thermal comfort. The »comfort zone« and its relationship to architecture is analyzed through psychrometric graphs, charting temperature and humidity. Expanding this graph to the nonhuman, the threshold becomes a zone of human–nonhuman negotiation. Regions of overlap, symbiotic intersections, can help develop building strategies from interior – through building envelope – to exterior (fig. 14). Do they enhance our comfort zone? Can we see beyond our discomfort into the entangled envelope zone and expand physical and psychological comfort for all?

Care and kindness in the design process allow for expansion of the comfort zone. In *Humankind: Solidarity with Nonhuman People*, philosopher Timothy Morton, drawing from geographer Peter Kropotkin, calls for mutual aid that sees nonhumans not as »companion species‹ or as beings under stewardship,« but as *neighbors* in a shared world, »a concept far more intense« (Morton 2017:173). Similarly, architects Sareh Saeidi and Matthew Anderson's manifesto for *kind architecture* »re-thinks, re-situates, and re-makes architecture [to] prioritise other-than-capital values [...] porous in its spatial attitude.« This architecture »celebrates lifeworld, coexistence, beauty, and time« and »heightens the perception of human-nonhuman entanglements in built environments« (Saedi/Anderson 2021).

Beyond Entanglement to Speculative Photosynthesizing Futures

Given accelerating ecological crises, the role of spatial practice must evolve to support entanglement among species and to imagine and facilitate new forms of living and building together. We look to biological findings on species interdependence in the call for kindness towards our planetary co-dwellers. A more radical concept is explored in *A Symbiotic View of Life: We Have Never Been Individuals* by biologist Scott F. Gilbert et al. Building on Lynn Margulis' symbiogenesis theories, the self-contained body myth is dismantled – we are mosaics of intermingling microbial, viral, and fungal life (Gilbert/Sapp/Tauber 2012). We are 90–99% bacteria, and over 8% of

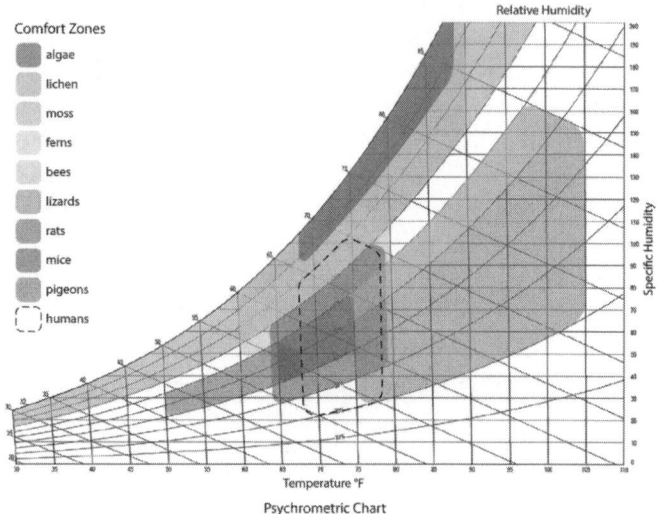

14.
Overlaying the comfort zones of other species (lichen, moss, bees, mice, pigeons, etc.) onto the human comfort zone. Drawing by FLUFFFF studio, 2024.

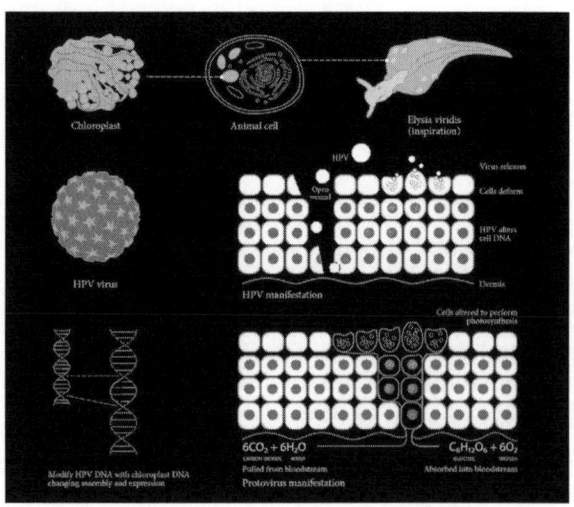

15.
The speculative co-opting of a virus with chloroplasts to create photosynthesizing tissue. Drawing by FLUFFFF studio, 2023.

our DNA is viral fragments (Bassler 2013; Zimmer 2012). What may seem monstrous is the fact of interdependence and life.

In our research-design practice, FLUFFFF studio, we explore the blurred boundaries between self–other and inside–outside, to reorient spatial practice. Biological facts can be conceptual provocations for design. Architecture can respond not only with technical solutions for building envelopes, but also through speculative imaginaries that offer models for symbiotic futures. Our short film *Elysia*[8] was born from this impulse (FLUFFFF 2020). Inspired by Jeff VanderMeer's »New Weird« novel *Annihilation*, in which the protagonist resists viewing a nonhuman force as destructive – »It's not killing everything. It's changing everything« (Garland 2018) – *Elysia* envisions transformation as a survival tactic. Drawing from the photosynthesizing sea slug *Elysia viridis*, which retains in its skin functional plastids from the algae it eats (Griffiths 2015), we speculated:

What if our bodies and our buildings could photosynthesize, absorbing sunlight to clean air like a plant, instead of merely enclosing space?

In our imagined symbiotic future, a virus inserts photosynthetic chloroplast DNA into human skin, allowing us to generate energy from the sun to adapt to new climates (fig. 15). Our building envelopes co-evolve: Facades become chloroplast landscapes of folding, light-responsive surfaces; living walls hum with energy – the envelope goes beyond entanglements to unify with nature (fig. 16). Not a utopian escape, this speculation is a provocation for spatial practices grounded in care and planetary attunement. Community and energy production are woven into the facades here, offering optimistic futures in post-capitalist worlds. The building envelope – once only a protective barrier for human comfort – becomes a site of exchange, transformation, and shared survival (fig. 17). We tackle these ideas to reframe architecture as a caretaker and collaborator in ecological restoration. Through speculative practice, we rehearse alternate futures where the world is no longer built for humans alone.

---

8 Watch on YouTube at https://www.youtube.com/watch?v=IChC9KXDQoU, accessed October 8, 2025, selected winner of the AA Visiting School's »Visions for Human/Animal Cohabitation« competition, 2021. The short film was screened as part of the *ARCH+* exhibition »Cohabitation: A Manifesto for the Solidarity of Non-Humans and Humans in Urban Space« at silent green, Berlin, June 4–July 4, 2021, https://archplus.net/de/cohabitation-EN/#article-30039, accessed October 8, 2025.

16.
Stills from the short film Elysia, by FLUFFFF studio, 2021.

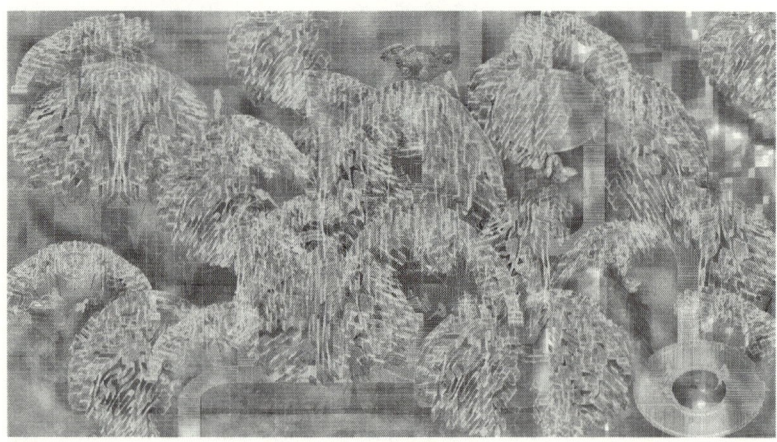

17.
Speculative visions of interspecies, photosynthesizing envelopes. Drawing by FLUFFFF studio, 2025.

Conclusion

The projects examined in this paper – both speculative and built – present new roles for the building envelope. The case studies' diverse approaches to the construction process and envelope reflect shifting priorities in spatial practice to incorporate care, biological interdependence, and survival in the face of ecological crises. New perceptions »exhibit more than ways of building; they provide ways of being« (Berleant 2005: 33). An empathic approach centers community involvement and species entanglement in the design process. As Haraway reminds, »individual animals, human and nonhuman, are […] entangled assemblages of relatings knotted at many scales and times« (Haraway 2008: 88).

By designing with intentional openings, spatial practitioners can attune to the environment and change how we live in our buildings and cities. Envelopes become less a boundary and more a site of exchange, adaptable to flux. Porosity, then, is not a failure of the wall, but an opportunity for ecological and community connection. We propose easing architecture from its habitual anchors – comfort, enclosure, control – toward collaborative practices with an incremental approach embracing change and the unknown. Thus, we can design not just for human needs, but for shared planetary futures. *Let the outside seep in.*

References

Aanen, Duur K./Eggleton, Paul (2017): »Symbiogenesis: Beyond the endosymbiosis theory?,« in: *Journal of Theoretical Biology* 434, 99–103. doi: 10.1016/j.jtbi.2017.08.001

Alihodžić, Selma (2024): »Radically Unfinished.« in: *Disegno Journal_36*, https://disegnojournal.com/newsfeed/radically-unfinished-holes-in-the-house, accessed November 12, 2024.

Amir, Fahim (2021): »Solidarity Is the Tenderness of the Species: Cohabitation Its Lived Exploration,« in: *ARCH+, Cohabitation: A Manifesto for the Solidarity of Non–Humans and Humans in Urban Space,* https://archplus.net/de/cohabitation-EN/#article-29894, accessed May 3, 2025.

Bassler, Bonnie (2009): »*How Bacteria ›Talk‹,*« on: Youtube, TED2009, https://www.youtube.com/watch?v=KXWurAmtf78, accessed September 18, 2024.

Berg, Nate (2017): »Raze, Rebuild, Repeat: Why Japan Knocks Down Its Houses After 30 Years,« *The Guardian,* https://www.theguardian.com/cities/2017/nov/16/japan-reusable-housing-revolution, accessed November 23, 2024.

Benjamin, Walter (1940): *Über den Begriff der Geschichte.* – English translation: Illuminations: Essays and Reflections, transl. by Harry Zohn, Arendt, Hannah, ed., New York: Schocken Books, 1968.

Berleant, Arnold (1992): *The Aesthetics of Environment*, Philadelphia: Temple University Press.

Berleant, Arnold (2005): *Aesthetics and Environment: Theme and Variations on Art and Culture*, Aldershot: Ashgate.

Brand, Stewart (1994): *How Buildings Learn: What Happens After They're Built*, New York: Viking Press.

Brand, Stewart (2018): »Pace Layering: How Complex Systems Learn and Keep Learning,« in: *Journal of Design and Science*, doi: 10.21428/7f2e5f08

Coccia, Emanuele (2017): *La vie des plantes: Une métaphysique du mélange.*— English translation: The Life Of Plants: A Metaphysics Of Mixture, transl. by Dylan J. Montanari, Cambridge, UK; Medford, MA: Polity Press, 2019.

Coccia, Emanuele (2025a): »The Museum for Contemporary Nature,« *lecture presented at: La Maison Française*, New York University, https://as.nyu.edu/research-centers/maisonfrancaise/events/spring-2025/the-museum-for-contemporary-nature.html, accessed May 3, 2025.

Coccia, Emanuele (2025b): »*Life Terrains Lecture #3: The Museum For Contemporary Nature*,« on: YouTube, Aarhus School of Architecture, https://www.youtube.com/watch?v=Zro8UkMMAHs, accessed May 15, 2025.

Cordero Jr., Dalmacito A. (2021): »Green and Furry Friends to the Rescue: Plants and Pets Parenting During the Covid-19 Pandemic,« in: *Evolution, Medicine, & Public Health*, 9/1, 287–288. doi: 10.1093/emph/eoab023

De Waal, Frans (2016): *Are We Smart Enough to Know How Smart Animals Are?*, New York: W. W. Norton & Company.

Easter, Michael (2021): *The Comfort Crisis: Embrace Discomfort to Reclaim Your Wild, Happy, Healthy Self*, New York: Rodale Books.

Fletcher, James Bowman (2025): »Metabolism and Mushrooms: An Interview with Mio Tsuneyama,« in: *Union Magazine*, https://unionmagazine.com/metabolism-and-mushrooms-an-interview-with-mio-tsuneyama/, accessed August 8, 2025.

FLUFFFF studio (2021): »*Elysia | Visions on Human/Nonhuman Cohabitation*,« on: YouTube, FLUFFFF, https://www.youtube.com/watch?v=IChC9KXDQoU, accessed May 3, 2025.

Frichot, Hélène (2018): *Creative Ecologies: Theorizing the Practice of Architecture*, New York: Bloomsbury Visual Arts.

Frichot, Hélène (2019): Dirty Theory: Troubling Architecture, Baunach: AADR – Art Architecture Design Research.

Garland, Alex, dir. (2018): *Annihilation, based on* »Annihilation« *by Jeff Vandermeer*, England: DNA Films.

Gilbert, Scott F./Sapp, Jan/Tauber, Alfred I. (2012): »A Symbiotic View of Life: We Have Never Been Individuals,« in *The Quarterly Review of Biology* 87/4, 325–341. doi: 10.1086/668166

Griffiths, David (2015): »Queer Theory for Lichens,« in: *UnderCurrents: Journal of Critical Environmental Studies* 19, 36–45. doi: 10.25071/2292-4736/40249

Gruber, Christiane (2021): »Like Hearts of Birds: Ottoman Avian Microarchitecture in the Eighteenth Century,« in: *Journal18* 11. doi: 10.30610/11.2021.1

Guiab, Justin (2024): »*This Family Built A House On A Remote Island To Live With Nature And Animals | Palawan, Philippines*,« on: YouTube, Design Anthology, https://www.youtube.com/watch?v=qA27k6qQomA, accessed November 12, 2024.

Guiab, Justin (2025): Interview with the authors, Palawan – New York – Washington, D.C., May 11, 2025.

Haraway, Donna (2008): *When Species Meet*, Minneapolis: University of Minnesota Press.

Haraway, Donna (2016): *Staying with the Trouble: Making Kin in the Chthulucene*, Durham: Duke University Press. doi: 10.1215/9780822373780

Holl, Steven (n.d.): »Porosity,« in: *Steven Holl Architects*, https://www.stevenholl.com/words/porosity, accessed May 21, 2025.

Hwang, Joyce (2013): »Living Among Pests,« in: *Volume, Everything Under Control: Building with Biology 35/1*, 60–63.

Ingraham, Catherine (2006): *Architecture, Animal, Human: The Asymmetrical Condition*, New York: Routledge.

Kahn, Andrea (1996): »Overlooking: A Look at How We Look at Site or... Site as ›Discrete Object‹ of Desire,« in: Katerina Rüedi/Sarah Wigglesworth/Duncan McCorquodale (eds.), *Desiring Practices: Architecture, Gender and the Interdisciplinary*, London: Black Dog Publishing Limited, 174–185.

Kristeva, Julia (1982): *Powers Of Horror: An Essay On Abjection*, New York: Columbia University Press.

Lacaton, Anne/Vassal, Jean-Philippe (2024): *Lacaton & Vassal – It's Nice Today: On Climate, Comfort, and Pleasure*, Berlin: Ruby Press.

Laugier, Marc-Antoine (1753): *Essai sur l'architecture*. – English translation: An Essay on Architecture, transl. by Wolfgang and Anni Herrmann. Los Angeles: Hennessey & Ingalls, 1977.

Malterre-Barthes, Charlotte (2021): »*A Global Moratorium on New Construction*,« https://charlottemalterrebarthes.com/practice/research-practice/a-global-moratorium-on-new-construction, accessed November 23, 2024.

Margulis, Lynn/Sagan, Dorion (1997): *Microcosmos: Four Billion Years of Microbial Evolution*, Berkeley, CA: University of California Press. doi: 10.2307/jj.2711625

Mertins, Detlef (1996): »Transparency: Autonomy and Relationality,« *AA FILES* 32, 3–11.

Morton, Timothy (2017): *Humankind: Solidarity with Non-Human People*. Brooklyn: Verso Books.

Ratschen, Elena et al. (2020): »Human-Animal Relationships and Interactions During the Covid-19 Lockdown Phase in the UK: Investigating Links With Mental Health and Loneliness,« *PLOS ONE 15/9*. doi: 10.1371/journal.pone.0239397

Rendell, Jane (2010): *Site-Writing: The Architecture of Art Criticism*, London: IB Tauris.

Saeidi, Sareh/Anderson, Matthew (2021): »Manifesto for Kind Architecture,« in: *Safe Space Zine, no. 6: A Queer Practice of Architecture*, Oslo, Norway: Mahe Cordier-Jouanne.

Strugar, Sarah (2025): Email correspondence with the authors, Palawan – New York – Washington, D.C., June 11, 2025.

Tsing, Anna (2015): *The Mushroom at the End of the World: On the Possibility of Life in Capitalist Ruins*, Princeton, NJ: Princeton University Press.

Tsuneyama, Mio (2023): »*The Berlage Keynotes: Studio MNM*,« on: YouTube, BKTUDelft, https://www.youtube.com/watch?v=7WW3Y9ma3kk, accessed November 12, 2024.

Vimal, Ruppert (2022): »The Impact of the Covid-19 Lockdown on the Human Experience of Nature,« in: *Science of The Total Environment 803*. doi: 10.1016/j. scitotenv.2021.149571

Wigglesworth, Sarah (1996): »Practice: The Significant Others,« in: Katerina Rüedi/Sarah Wigglesworth/Duncan McCorquodale (eds.), *Desiring Practices: Architecture, Gender and the Interdisciplinary*, London: Black Dog Publishing Limited, 274–287.

Wolfrum, Sophie (2018): »Porous City – From Metaphor to Urban Agenda,« in: Sophie Wolfrum et al. (eds.), *Porous City: From Metaphor to Urban Agenda*, Basel: Birkhäuser, 8–11.

Zimmer, Carl (2012): »Mammals Made by Viruses,« in: *National Geographic*, https://www.nationalgeographic.com/science/article/mammals-made-by-viruses, accessed May 22, 2025.

Dimensions of Architectural Knowledge, 2024-08 𝄐
https://doi.org/10.14361/dak-2024-0812

From Companion Mounds to Ruderal Ecologies. Reconstructing Land as a Medium of Resistance in Berlin's Housing Estates

Robin V Hueppe

Abstract: This paper examines two artificial mounds – landscape features embedded within mass housing neighborhoods in former East and West Berlin – as sites through which to reconsider land as a medium of subtle and discursive resistance against institutional control. Berlin's history of unruly urban ecologies converges at every layer of these former waste and rubble landfills, from the deepest stratum to the plants casting their roots into the topsoil covering the physical vessels of past memories and trauma. Based on the comparison and production of the Lübarser Höhe adjacent to Märkisches Viertel in the northwest (formerly West Berlin) and the Kienberg near Marzahn in the east (formerly East Berlin), the paper uses a land(scape)-oriented methodology that blends archival research, oral history interviews, and contemporary site analyses. Seeds, plants, animals, and people appropriated the byproducts of modernist urbanization to produce counter-spaces shaped to their collective desires, transforming the mounds into rich, ruderal ecologies. Today, they represent significant places of encounter between newcomers and long-standing residents, children and insects, and wind and kites. This approach reinforces the shift from strictly building-oriented spatial studies of modernist housing estates towards an enmeshed emphasis on the land and landscapes, able to facilitate a just climate future in Berlin.

Keywords: Berlin; Mass Housing; Landscape; Rubble; Ruderal Ecology; Appropriation; Post-War History.

Corresponding author: Robin V. Hueppe (ETH Zurich, Switzerland); hueppe@arch.ethz.ch; https://orcid.org/0000-0001-9499-8016

Temporarily divided and subsequently unified, Berlin has a long history of rebellion against the institutional exercise of power over urban space and land. There are movements against territorial enclosures through clandestine fence cuttings, market speculation via uncompromising squatting, or the absence of public services, which demand the enforcement of human rights (e.g., Sontheimer and Wensierski 2018; Gruppe Panther & Co. 2021). Beyond the human perspective, the city's history between World War II recovery and the Wall's separation made it a site of novel ecological collectives on fields and mounds of rubble, as well as appropriated industrial sites and landfill negotiations across the Wall (e.g., Sukopp 1990; Gandy 2022; Stoetzer 2022). This story of ruderal resistance (rudus, Lat.: rubble) is unveiled through a land(scape)-oriented methodology exploring two mass housing estates in former East and West Berlin, Marzahn and Märkisches Viertel. The approach involves a multi-temporal investigation into the accumulated layers of two adjacent and accompanying mounds, Kienberg and Lübarser Höhe, each serving as a nexus to understand the estates comparatively and the land features as intersecting companion phenomena. The housing estate and the mound are mutually dependent; neither would exist without the other.

Although the architectural discussion against the paradigmatic myth of mass housing as »failed« has prevailed since the early 1990s (e.g., Bristol 1991), the stigma against inhabitants and architecture persists. Particularly in countries across Europe and North America, widespread criticism of modernist, post-war neighborhoods persists at the national and municipal levels (Harnack 2017; Mack 2023). While architectural history has recently shifted its perspective on this criticism – highlighting the value of buildings for preservation as cultural heritage – recent studies reveal the ensuing challenge to question the dominance of buildings and their construction (cf. Urban 2018; Braun 2019). This shift in focus is significant because much of the life growing in these neighborhoods, from maple trees and water sedges to raccoon families and beaver lodges, has occurred between the buildings in expansive communal spaces of encounter, simultaneously capable of addressing an aggravated climate crisis. These mass housing landscapes have become increasingly relevant as biodiversity in those spaces has increased and flourished over time, contrasting with the decay and decline often seen in aging built structures. This angle highlights the reciprocal relationships between housing estates and the long-term human transformation of their land(scape). It does so by delving into a pre-construction history and considering more immediate and forward-looking events, such as environmental protests by residents after completion.

The land(scape)-oriented methodology that comparatively and relationally explores one housing estate in former East and one in former West Berlin from the ground up consists of three interfering temporalities (AGE). *Assembling* (A) operates on a slow-moving, geo-climatic level, accounting for the pre-construction era that renders the land as already layered and complex before the arrival of modernist city planning. *Governing* (G) describes a medium-length period in the development of macropolitical state systems between the end of World War II (1945) and German reunification (1990), thus scrutinizing the disruptive impact of mass housing construction on formerly agricultural land. Lastly, *enmeshing* (E) includes a more immediate timescale of events and spatial appropriation in the sense of an ontological meshwork of continuous, interwoven, and future-oriented becoming (cf. Barad 2007; Ingold 2011). While each step comes with its own set of methods, the situated tools of *enmeshing* are hypothetically most relevant for the study of resistance in housing estate landscapes. They focus on how the land(scape) eventually becomes a medium for multispecies collectives, including humans, to resist the institutional power of state-owned housing companies, senates and »politburos,« or municipal cleaning services. They include a mix of archival research, oral history interviews, empirical data gathered during field research, and a secondary literature review focused on the history of both case studies. For example, oral history interviews with allotment gardeners and long-standing residents, as well as empirical data, served as primary sources, subsequently cross-referenced for verification with aerial photography from the German Federal Archives (1945-1996) and secondary literature. Other archival research centered on an independent newspaper, the *Märkische Viertel Zeitung*, and the private collection of Eveline, a first-generation resident who provided a Super 8 film roll after prior interviews (for more information, cf. Hueppe 2025).

Berlin offers two distinct spheres for studying the role of land, where two very different approaches to developing the post-war periphery have stood in opposition for over four decades. While the East German Democratic Republic (GDR) operated under a single-party socialist system with a centrally planned economy, the Federal Republic of Germany (FRG) adopted a democratic capitalist framework, characterized by a parliamentary republic and a free market, complemented by social welfare. While they cover only five percent of the city's surface, today, more than one-fifth of Berliners live in the housing estates that both states constructed from the mid to the late twentieth century. Besides providing a significant supply of affordable housing in a capital plagued by a housing shortage, the estates also contribute to the housing and integration of newcomers from conflict-torn territories (Hunger 2021: 95–96). The case study neighborhoods, Märkisches Viertel and Marzahn, were built within approximately one decade each, from 1963 to 1974 in West Berlin and 1977 to 1989 in East Berlin, as densified successors to the garden city concept.

Like many of Berlin's more famous and well-researched rubble mounds, such as the Teufelsberg, East Berlin's Kienberg started as a landfill for remaining war rubble and demolition debris from inner urban areas in 1969 (Gutsche 1969). Following the vision of a later dismissed 1946 master plan for Berlin by Hans Scharoun and Reinhold Lingner in which rubble mounds were envisaged to emphasize the glacial plateau edges and natural eleva-tions of Berlin's topography, it became a convenient location for the disposal of some of Marzahn's excavated soil and construction site rubble. Hans-Georg Büchner, East Berlin's Director of Technology at the Publicly Owned Enterprise for Green Space Construction (VEB Grünanlagenbau), wanted the

> »[e]xcavated material and debris from the Marzahn construction to be de-posited as fuel-efficiently as possible [...]. Following Lingner's vision, elevated points in the surrounding landscape were to be intentionally raised to create a harmoniously graded integration of infrastructure and topography« (Büch-ner 2015: 33, author's translation).[1]

Unlike Marzahn, the master plan of West Berlin's Märkisches Viertel did not incorporate the adjacent mound due to its location in a different district. Thus, it developed independently as a landfill site in the 1950s under state admin-istration. When West Berlin became a territorially confined island within East Germany in 1948, the municipal waste management services (Berliner Stadtreinigung/ BSR) pressured the Senate to find new sites for the disposal of the growing household waste (Park 2004: 44). The cheaply available mead-owland near the medieval village of Lübars, just north of the future housing

---

1 »Verdrängte Massen und beim Bauen der Wohngebiete anfallender Schutt waren möglichst kraftstoffsparend, [...]. Insbesondere hinsichtlich der Generalneigung des künftigen Kienberges [...] wurden im Lingnerschen Sinne mit den anfallenden Massen Hochpunkte in der nahen Landschaft aufgehöht.«

estate, became one of West Berlin's five main waste disposal sites, simultane-ously serving as a convenient disposal site for construction debris (Schlickeiser 2024). Studying the accumulated matter layer by layer, which makes up both mounds, offers a land(scape)-oriented way to trace the history of resistance in Marzahn and Märkisches Viertel. This stratigraphic reading is particu-larly suited because it studies the history of the discarded in three moments of resistance, revealing subaltern histories emerging from the remnants of allotment garden homes preceding the housing estate, the governance of toxic consumer waste during Berlin's division and the ensuing protest, and the eventual retreat of governance, leaving ruderal ecologies thriving in its shadows. These counter-narratives thus include resistance against evictions, environmental pollution, and an anthropomorphic control of »nature.«

Signs, Gardens, and Dwellers: Enmeshing the Deepest Layer

In both East and West, the first and deepest layer of the mounds (1975 and 1963, respectively) contains the remnants of demolished allotment garden dwellings that preceded the housing estates. Mixed with war rubble, construction debris, household waste, and excavated soil, the traces of allot-ment gardens point to the land's long legacy of gardening practices. During Berlin's modernist planning practices after the war, which often formalized and regulated the land use of formerly unregulated or overlooked areas, allot-ment dwellers lived in a state of informality or semi-legality. As the commu-nities of Marzahn and Wilhelmsruh (later Märkisches Viertel) self-organized within the institutional framework of a planning authority, their ambiguous status as »dweller-gardeners« made it challenging to assume a clear legal stance (Urban 2013; Hilbrandt 2021). The Senator of Urban Development (Bausenator) Rolf Schwedler (in office from 1955 until 1972) understood the terms »allotment gardener« (Kleingärtner) and »dweller« (Siedler) in an ambiguous tension: While he considered allotment gardening a highly use of green space, allotment dwellings were seen as the least valued use of resi-dential land, presumably due to the lack of modern infrastructure and an increased risk of diseases (Hildebrandt/Schlickeiser 1989: 192). Nevertheless, the first resistance arose when allotment dweller-gardeners in both East and West organized protests against the institutional seizure of land. The absence of municipal response to reported injustices prompted autonomous action.

When the West Berlin Senate began discussing the future development of Wilhelmsruh throughout the 1950s, the Reinickendorf District
Planning Department's development framework (Richtplan) still respected
the existing communities. In preparation for a legally binding plan, Senator
Schwedler commissioned the district planning department to map the
existing allotments, which ultimately led to the evaluation of most sections
of the allotment gardens as unhygienic, underdeveloped, and pover-
ty-ridden (Schwedler 1972). By 1960, planners had transformed the density
of the guiding development framework from a single-family garden suburb
to a more profitable, technologically progressive master plan for a housing
estate (Bodenschatz 1987: 237). Additionally, the estate's location, situated
right next to the Berlin Wall, which was built in 1961, allowed West Germany
to demonstrate West Berlin's defiance against East Germany in the context
of its border confinements (Hildebrandt/Schlickeiser 1989: 187). Driven by
national interests rather than local concerns, West Berlin's Senate assumed
control over planning from the district authorities in 1962 and established
Berlin's so-called Guidelines for Urban Renovation. These provided a legal
basis for low-rate land and real estate buyouts from leasing allotment
dwellers and, in many cases, for their eviction and displacement (Wilde 1989:
39). These guidelines were in line with Germany's nation-wide first urban
renewal program (Erstes Stadterneuerungsprogramm), favoring the entire
clearance of historic, »unsanitary« city quarters and the modernization of
urban infrastructure.

The consequences of these measures disproportionately impacted
the most vulnerable. Those living in properties leased from farm-
ers-turned-landlords could not sell their homes at market value but had to
settle for small compensation sums for their built-up homes. Upon vacating,
their precarious leasing contracts demanded the removal of all built structures from the land, leaving those dwellers with little financial security or
alternative. At the same time, one-third of the area consisted of land-owning
dwellers, who had managed to buy the land from the farmer and profited
from either a market-oriented selling price of their plot or from moving to a
more prestigious or better-developed neighborhood in Berlin or elsewhere.
The land-owners who stayed and resisted a buyout because their plot was in
one of the areas foreseen to be integrated into the master plan of Märkisches
Viertel benefited from the modern infrastructure coming with the housing
estate, like a sewage system, central heating, water, and a reliable electricity
grid (Wilde 1989: 47; Thiel 2024). Previously, the inhabitants were largely

disconnected from the electrical grids, most drew drinking water from wells located on their properties, and lacked a connection to the sewage system, relying on outhouses or cesspit toilets (Urban 2013: 223).

Despite previous infrastructure deficiencies, the families had primarily lived self-sufficiently and had a sense of mutual support. Those who protested against eviction, the leasehold protestors, were situated between pride in their independence from public infrastructure and the additional costs attached to its comforts, and a sense of helplessness in the face of the state's legal power and housing companies. Hundreds of allotment dwellers in the Wilhelmsruh area, who held leaseholds, resisted the looming evictions by founding an emergency association for legal action Not- und Prozessgemeinschaft in 1963, arguing that the destruction of allotment homes was unconstitutional. Many members of the emergency association installed large signs on their lots with slogans such as »No new millionaires at the expense of allotment gardeners!« (Wilde 1989: 54, author's translation).[2] Several daily newspapers began to cover the dispute, including a twenty-minute report by the public television channel Sender Freies Berlin (SFB) (Hildebrandt/Schlickeiser 1989: 189). The campaign also attracted the attention of the state-owned housing company GESOBAU, which had been put in charge by the Berlin Senate in 1961 to facilitate the »urban renewal« and first buyouts of 3,000 plots. Besides small compensation amounts, the housing company offered a replacement flat in the new development, which – at 344 D-Mark (915 EUR in 2025) for a 2.5-room apartment, despite rent control and state subsidies – was still unaffordable for many (Autorengruppe »Märkische Viertel Zeitung« 1973; Bodenschatz 1987; Wilde 1989).

Although the emergency association took 70 announced evictions to court, their legal leverage as dwellers on agriculturally designated land was too marginal for the district and federal courts to prevent GESOBAU and the municipality from displacing the families (fig. 1). Only one leasing allotment garden community, Kolonie Fechner, managed to strike a deal with the housing company since the location of their allotments overlapped with planned garden plots in the master plan of Märkisches Viertel. Preserving their buildings instead of demolishing and reconstructing convinced the district to grant housing rights until the end of life without the possibility of selling, bequeathing, or giving away the parcels (Hildebrandt and Schlickeiser 1989: 192–194).

---

2 »Nicht auf Kosten der Dauerbewohner und Kleingärtner neue Millionäre!«

1.
Haus Genzmann, 1971: The last holdout at Märkisches Viertel, later demolished.
© Bernd Hildebrandt and Klaus Schlickeiser, 1989.

2.
Single-family housing in Marzahn spared from demolition. © Author, 2022.

In contrast to planning practices in West Berlin, East Berlin generally refrained from evictions due to a lack of financial resources for replacing homes (Urban 2013: 238). However, clearing the site for redevelopment still foresaw the demolition of 575 dwellings and 35 hectares of allotment garden plots, so that at least 475 out of 931 families had to leave their homes. The »freedom to build« (Baufreiheit) in the GDR building legislations legalized the expropriation of property owners for the public good, given that they could receive an appropriate replacement, mainly in the new high-rise buildings (Rubin 2016: 54–55). Many accepted the replacement offers, which were significantly more affordable than those in West Berlin, with 134 East German marks for an 80-square-meter, 4-room apartment, while the average monthly salary in 1975 was 889 East German marks (Zobel/Zobel 2024). Still, the wave of administrative appeals (Eingaben) from several of the 475 households surged in the summer of 1975. Not only were 339 apartments in single- and multifamily buildings, but also 180 permanent dwellings on allotment gardens, as well as 56 homes in the medieval village of Marzahn, were required to be vacated (Schnitter 1996).

The Ministry for State Security (Stasi/Ministerium für Staatssicherheit) surveyed the resistance of families unwilling to vacate their properties, blaming their »stubborn behavior« on petty bourgeoisie striving for the most lucrative compensation possible, as well as their distrust of the promises made by state authorities (Danicke 1979). The Stasi also recorded concerns of inhabitants of Marzahn's historical village, who feared that preservation and restoration measures would never evolve beyond the planning stage. Particularly in the demolition of Marzahn's historical farmsteads, some of the evictions led to suicides (Fahrner 1986). The partial preservation of the Marzahn village predominantly served as an ornamental contrast to the new construction, picturesque shells stripped of their original functions to symbolize socialist progress. Instead of maintaining its complex village life and small-scale agricultural production, the development intended to feature many buildings hosting gastronomic and cultural facilities. While East Berlin's head architect, Roland Korn, and Director of Construction, Günter Peters, tried to persuade the appealing families through phone calls, their protest eventually led to an adaptation of the master plan in the second building phase (WG 2) that spared a section of 83 homes from the planned 575 units (fig. 2) (Rubin 2016: 54–55).

A few years later, some residents in both Marzahn and Märkisches Viertel not only found themselves in a flat overlooking their previous allotment garden but also brought their agrarian life into the towers, farming pigs on the balconies or keeping birds in bathtubs (Plato and Scholz 2024; Dietmann 2025). The remnants of their dwellings, the bricks, timber, tiles, bitumen sheeting roofs, and zinc tubs, material witnesses of the territorial struggle and displacement, were disposed of at the nearby landfills. While most of the preceding *Kolonien* have since disappeared, more so in West Berlin than in East Berlin, their inhabitants' resistance has also led to the preservation of certain communities, such as the Kolonie Fechner, and the formal integration of allotment dwellings into the housing estates by permanently changing the land use to residential land. Therefore, the allotment garden communities also represent a continuity in Berlin's modernist city planning of the twentieth century, showing the deep interconnection of gardening practices with life in and around the housing estates (fig. 3).

Newspapers, Wall Blockades, and Contract Workers: Enmeshing the Middle Layer

The landfill at Märkisches Viertel, one of five major landfills established in West Berlin in the late 1950s, continued to coexist with completed buildings from the first phases of the master plan throughout the 1960s. In 1972, two years before the completion of the building activity, the housing estate's residents began to protest the landfill's multi-sensory disturbances, including smell, sound, and sight, as well as its planned expansion. Their resistance took various forms, such as motorcades, towels and bedsheets hung from windows as a collective protest, or garbage church services against the landfill site and rent increases (Beck and Reidemeister 1975: 160–163; Park 2004: 83). Although some protests were spatially manifested, scholars have typically studied this resistance in the housing estate through a sociopolitical and art-historical lens, rather than an environmental or spatial one (cf. Reinecke 2022; Vasudevan 2022).

In West Berlin, the newspaper Märkische Viertel Zeitung (MVZ), a print medium created by a self-organized group of students and residents, regularly reported on environmental and territorial issues arising from the continuing landfill operation. One report concerning the growing landfill appeared in the first issue of 1972 under the headline »Werden wir im Müll ersticken?« (Will We Suffocate in Waste?) The article sarcastically claimed that residents could look forward to a rent reduction due to the elimination of garbage collection fees, as they might have their own garbage mountain right on their doorstep (Autorengruppe Märkische Viertel Zeitung 1973: 4, 1972/1). Regularly placing itself in opposition to the housing company's professionally distributed information sheet for residents, the MVZ claimed that the GESOBAU would obscure its decision-making power when reporting on the ongoing landfill operation. Instead, MVZ called for the participatory inclusion of residents in the landfill planning process (fig. 4).

The newspaper filled a gap in critically reporting on public decision-making, motivating residents to become politically vocal. In the second section, MVZ reprinted a dialogue between the Senator for Finance (Finanzsenator) and the delegate of the Reinickendorf Social Democratic district party (SPD/Sozialdemokratische Partei Deutschlands) at a state parliamentary session. The delegate opens by asking if the press releases regarding the landfill expansion in the direction of the Märkisches Viertel are true, and how the expansion contrasts with the previous plans of the Senate to close the landfill soon. In the answer, the Senator refers to a landscape master plan foreseeing the transformation of the landfill into a public park, supposedly commissioned by Senator Schwedler before the landfill extension. Although the municipal cleaning services had proposed a landfill transformation in the 1960s, territorial restrictions on waste disposal, imposed by the Berlin Wall in West Berlin, delayed the original plan. The newspaper editors interpreted the dialogue as a passive public relations strategy of the Senate, presenting citizens with accomplished, unchangeable facts. They continued by highlighting the northeast wind that would carry the smell from the landfill into the entire neighborhood, along with crows, rats, and other »pests.« Their article also addressed other environmental disturbances emerging from the growing mound, such as the noise emissions of garbage trucks and the contamination of surface water running from the landfill through historical water streams into the neighborhood's retention basins, where their children would play (Autorengruppe »Märkische Viertel Zeitung« 1973: 5-6 1972/1).

Due to the resident protest, among other entities provoked by the MVZ reporting, West Berlin expedited a long-term contract (Langfristvertrag) with East Berlin in 1973 to ship waste across the Wall, enabling the landfill to be partially decommissioned and transformed into a public park starting the same year (Park 2003: 98). While the partial coverage and park transformation began east of the landfill, it was eventually extended to the southwest

3.
Allotment garden at Märkisches Viertel. © Author, 2024.

4.
»Will we suffocate in waste?« MVZ, March 1972. © Free University of Berlin, Archives of the Extra-parliamentary Opposition (APO).

5.
»In East and West, it reeks like the pest.« East-German protestors. © Bundesarchiv, Klaus Oberst, 1990.

before the landfill was entirely closed in 1981, and the park completed in 1985 (Schlickeiser 2021: 72).

A lesser-known aspect of this history is the political arrangement of waste exports to the GDR, which also stirred resistance and protest among East Berliners. Enabled by churches, among the few relatively autonomous spaces in the GDR's political field, an ecological movement (Ökologiebewegung) began to lobby against the growing signs of environmental exploitation (Wensierski 1986: 162). By the late 1980s, several waste transports from West Berlin had to return because members of the movement blocked the gates to the landfills of Vorketzin and Schöneiche near East Berlin, where the trucks brought most of the West German waste (Park 2003: 85). When a formerly secret environmental report about the pollutant contamination of groundwater near Vorketzin became public, the West German TV program in 1988 (»Kontraste«) intensified the concerns about waste shipment to the East. On November 2, 1988, environmental groups in West Berlin, such as Robin Wood and Bund für Umwelt und Naturschutz Deutschland (BUND), blocked the Wall's checkpoint Kirchhainer Damm in solidarity with their East German allies, while East Berliners blocked the crossing on the other side (fig. 5) (Park 2004: 193).

Open resistance against state governance in the GDR was rarer than in the FDR. However, protests occurred in more clandestine ways, especially in moments when the state's control over labor forces was particularly severe. Vietnamese contract workers (Vertragsarbeiter) were involved in several tasks on the Marzahn construction site, including the prefabrication of concrete panels. Many who were deployed at East Berlin's Housing Construction Combine (Wohnungsbaukombinat) lived in a residential complex adjacent to the concrete panel factory, which supplied construction materials for buildings and pathways up the Kienberg. Overall, the GDR assigned hundreds of Vietnamese contract workers to Berlin's housing construction combine, illustrating state control and the material products of Vietnamese contract labor. Other deployments at state-owned enterprises included the production of electric appliances and construction tools. The externalized and exploited labor renders the (landscape) architecture as both a product of the world and a world-making structure, unveiling the carceral character of the GDR-Vietnam labor agreement (Tieu/Bentcheva 2023). Despite the systematically overlooked hardships keeping the contract workers in a legal gray zone, many individuals defied the imposed regulations and limitations to preserve everyday liberties outside the racist and eugenic system that would threaten Vietnamese women with forced deportations in case of pregnancy (Weiss 2011: 264). Regular visits between residential complexes were a freedom, but controlled and documented by the Stasi. Despite the permanent surveillance, the Vietnamese community maintained lively networks that operated beyond the rules of movement and authority, for example, by leaving through the main entrance and entering through a window. These networks also helped individuals establish secondary sources of income through the illegal manufacturing and trade of goods, such as leather clothing or blue jeans, which helped fill the production gaps in the GDR economy (Weiss 2011). In some instances, contract workers openly complained to their superiors about their lower salary tier in contrast to their East German colleagues, highlighting their exploitation for the East German reconstruction project. In some instances, they were backed by their colleagues (Plamper 2023: 96–97). The concrete panels that were used to pave the way up the mound Kienberg and the excavated soil of the monitored residential complex are physical vessels for the histories of Vietnamese labor and exploitation. However, their material reality is also imbued with the everyday resistance of Vietnamese communities defying the East German drive to control and police their contract labor.

6.

Bird sanctuary at Lübarser Höhe (Vogelschutzgebiet). © Robin V Hueppe, 2022.

Ruderality, Collectives, and Gardeners (again): Enmeshing the Top Layer

After Marzahn and Märkisches Viertel transformed the rubble and waste landfills into parks by 1985, the necessary technical requirements of waste compaction, venting, and settling, paired with a lack of financial resources, led to a hands-off maintenance and management strategy of the District Parks and Garden Departments. As discarded byproducts of the modernist dream, a mix of technical, economic, administrative, and security concerns required the sites' planned and partial neglect. As seen on many ruderal sites in Berlin, this receding level of control allowed for a steady increase in species diversity on the mounds (Gandy 2022: 21). The absence of pesticides, leftover deadwood, and reduced mowing and weeding enabled ruderal plant growth, offering a rich habitat for pollinators, fungi, and earthworms.

In West Berlin, the landfill's early years of waste and soil accumulation in the 1950s already brought pioneering diaspores – plant dispersal units like seeds carried along with the waste – such as heat-loving tomatoes, tobacco, or squash. The afforestation with pioneer tree species, such as ash, maple, poplar, black locust, and black alder, on the former landfill was accompanied by ruderal, low-growing herbs of the Sisymbrium genus and later by higher-growing herbaceous perennials. These plant communities would transform the covered landfill into Berlin's most significant bird-nesting habitats within a few years, also attracting insects, fungi, and various mammals (fig. 6) (Sukopp 1990: 339–342; Tietze 1988). On Kienberg in the East, similar tree species, including oak, chestnut, and ash, were planted by volunteers from Marzahn. The communal efforts to plant saplings helped residents identify with their neighborhood and the land by watching the trees grow taller over time in the sense of a »green affect« (Mack 2021). However, the relatively thin topsoil layer of 25 cm and still partially contaminated sublayers impeded the process of ecological succession, challenging management and maintenance, as the growth of certain plants pushed out others (Hauser 2020: 219; Samstag 2024).

While the relatively low financial investment in park maintenance at Lübarser Höhe has remained consistent since the 1980s, the mound now provides a bird sanctuary around one of the two ponds at its base. Located adjacent to Märkisches Viertel but under the jurisdiction of the neighboring Reinickendorf district, the Public Parks Department manages the mound with minimal intervention. The transfer of green space maintenance from the Public Parks Departments (Gartenämter) to commercially operating state-owned companies, such as Grün Berlin GmbH, weakened Berlin's Parks Departments all over the city, leading to a low-budget, hands-off strategy on the remaining public green spaces (Flierl 2019: 14). To fill the vacuum of a formal design program and more intensive care, residents of Märkisches Viertel historically appropriated West Berlin's Lübarser Höhe with self-made pastimes and plays (Albrecht 1983). These ranged from winter activities such as sledding and skiing to exploiting the windy elevation for paragliding, flying kites, and model airplanes. Specific uses, such as paragliding, seemed inherent to both West and East elevations, as they provided optimal training grounds on windy days in a city whose topography offers only a few natural elevations.

Initially, due to financial constraints, East Berlin's Parks Department also left the Kienberg to itself after its completion in the late 1980s, followed by further neglect during the period of reunification, due to unclear maintenance responsibilities (Samstag 2024). As in West Berlin, this period created vibrant habitats for an array of tree species, fungi, insects, and mammals, including deer, foxes, and badgers, all of which appreciated the disturbed but soft soil, green moss, and plentiful bark. In a subtle way, these multispecies collectives resisted the lack of care by reclaiming the heavily transformed waste landscape. Simultaneously, humans adopted the mound as a primary site for outdoor activities such as hiking, cycling, paragliding, or flying model airplanes. However, collective habitat-shaping did not always remain without conflict. When a temporary construction fence for the 2017 International Garden Exhibition on the mound Kienberg in Marzahn created undisturbed conditions, native beavers returned to Marzahn's river valley at the mound's foot after they had gone extinct in the region. Their presence benefited the ecosystem by forming new wetlands (Treblin 2022). While Grün Berlin GmbH, a formerly West German state-owned non-profit organization that assumed management of Marzahn's Kienberg, protected trees with wire mesh, some individuals saw their tree-gnawing habits as such a nuisance that the beaver's growing presence ultimately led to the autopsy-confirmed killing of a beaver (Dassler 2020). This incident illustrates how the hierarchies between native and non-native, welcome and unwelcome non-human activities are historically contingent. At times, biodiversity, referring to the benefits of the beaver for the local ecosystem, and biosecurity, such as the preservation of a specific landscape aesthetic by preventing the spread of beavers, intersect and legally contradict each other. This tension makes beavers more than passive objects of law but active participants in shaping territorial arrangements around the mound Kienberg (cf. Ojalammi/Blomley 2015).

The identification of unwelcome plants has similarly marked the history of plant sociology, where artificially defining native and non-native species falls together with ideologies of excluding ideas of belonging, blurring the terrain between plants and people (Hauser 2020; Gandy 2022; Stoetzer 2022). Examining domesticated companion species, such as sheep, reveals how humans relate to and make sense of their habitats through a species-to-species relationship. Many of the first gardener-dwellers brought their pigs to their new balcony, and other residents were fascinated by the stark contrast between the agro-industrial land history and the novel architectural modernity. East Berlin's newspapers portrayed this contrast by showing shepherds and sheep roaming around the construction sites, coining the becoming rubble mound Kienberg a new gate to the surrounding landscape (fig. 7) (Unlabeled Footage of Märkisches Viertel 1972; Hahlweg 1981). More recently, some residents argue that particular species, such as Columba livia, or rock doves, often reduced to »common pigeons,« share the struggle of stigmatization with the residents of mass housing estates. A neighborhood-specific website for Märkisches Viertel features an article that empowers the birds by raising awareness among other residents about their rich history. As the author highlights, the species feels exceptionally comfortable between the towers of the estate since they imitate the cliff structures of their original habitats (Trautsch 2025).

In this light, Lübarser Höhe and Kienberg have become refuges for both long-standing and recent species, including humans, to dwell in the overlooked remnants of Berlin's modernist urbanization. The mounds render artificial hierarchies between native and non-native, welcome and unwelcome activities, not as fixed »natural« facts but historically contingent and in flux. Once again, the mounds resist the human drive to categorize and label, as the uncertainty of their exact origins and compositions renders this endeavor futile. This impossibility of a taxonomized origin implies an openness to multiple origins, with nobody and nothing »belonging,« to them as their very core consists of countless »elsewhere.« This tolerance emerging from incomplete initial design programs lacking predefined uses, paired with partial governing absence after their covering, enabled the (human) inhabitants of these landscapes to identify with the mounds and neighborhoods as new homes. In the 1970s and 1980s, observers and critics criticized the unwelcoming »barren plains« between buildings. Today, plant growth

and the transformation of mounds have contributed to a temporal awareness that impacts the changing recognition of these landscapes, leaving
green space among the most appreciated qualities among both recent and
long-standing residents. Some recent Syrian residents of Märkisches Viertel
consider the neighborhood's parks and mounds among its most remarkable
attributes (Amad 2024). Renate, who moved to Märkisches Viertel in 1970
with the first generation of residents, also enjoys the space between buildings
the most. The *Platanus x hispanica* tree, a hybrid of Platanus orientalis and
Platanus occidentalis, which she had observed growing over the past fifty
years from her window, gave her a sense of passing time. She also used to
own an allotment garden on the slopes of the Lübarser Höhe mound, where
she and her husband spent their summers and hosted parties for friends
and neighbors. When the Berlin Wall fell, right next to the mound and her
garden, the constant crushing of concrete left a layer of fine particles on her
lawn. Every weekend, she cleaned up the white concrete dust, settling over
everything like toxic snow (Schaaf 2024).

7.
»A Gate to the Landscape,« 1981. © Wulf Olm/Bezirksmuseumsarchiv Marzahn-
Hellersdorf.

Ruderality After Trauma

Three moments of resistance have touched this story from the beginning: Allotment gardening as a past practice buried *under* yet still present *above* the mounds' slopes; a violent separation of the city into two parts continuously facing protests; and the final collapse of the division and governance retreat that leaves the dust of the Wall's demolition and the regrowing ruderal ecologies to the care of the gardener – a soft resistance emerging from the cracks in institutional management. Over time, the mounds acquired the character of a *Brache*, an urban fallow, typically described as disused industrial sites reclaimed by vegetation after heavy industry left European regions in the late twentieth century. Landscape architects of the 1980s and 90s created an aesthetic tension by showcasing the productive past against its fading and ecological regeneration, transforming industrial sites into public parks, such as the Parc de la Villette or the Landschaftspark Duisburg-Nord. However, without any (visible) industrial heritage to expose, the two rubble mounds circumvent this aestheticization, sharing the relational characteristics of multispecies appropriation without a post-industrial form. On the edge of Berlin's border towards the city's administrative edge, they are situated within a broader traditional visual culture of landscapes, historically assembled into an imaginative, coherent whole called »nature.« However, this imagination collides with the intensive reality of industrialized agriculture or highly controlled plantation forestry around Berlin. In contrast to that imagination, they maintain the ecological character of formerly enclosed territories, initially securing and protecting the already established, then opening up to those who administered and accounted for them, until subversive appropriation becomes central to their existence.

These are the layered histories emerging from a land(scape)-oriented methodology, tracing the trauma of displacement and erasure from the deepest layer in the buried rubble to the ruderal ecologies that have since grown on the two mounds. Despite the disruptions in the mounds' land history, a traceable continuity of protest and resistance is etched into the land's many layers. Therefore, this contribution aims to demonstrate how – despite the power and influence of housing companies, ministries, senates, and planning departments – the land simultaneously becomes a medium for multispecies alliances, including humans, to resist in diverse ways. More tangibly, allotment dwellers resisted buyouts by staying and negotiating their right to the land with much more powerful institutions, while others used a landfill as a cause for protesting their tenant rights. In a more abstract sense, the history of land becomes a medium to revisit the history of migrant contract-worker resistance, going beyond a one-sided representation of powerlessness. As regularly seen in counter-movement histories, some oppositional activity eventually transitions to formal planning processes. Today, formalized successors to informal alliances working toward peaceful coexistence, such as the GESOBAU »Beettinchen« garden for social work with marginalized groups, rely on the financial support and land ownership of the state-owned housing company. As seen with the church's role during the GDR's ecological movement, there are historical precedents for the institutional involvement in the seemingly independent organization of counter-movements. In many instances, progress emerges through the translation of bottom-up protest into policies and laws, complicating the antagonism between governance and resistance. While undeclared gardening on empty plots once stood in conflict with unambiguous land use plans, it has evolved into a planning tool that fosters community outreach and cohesion in social neighborhood work.

Kienberg and Lübarser Höhe are significant biotopes for the present and growing Berlin, adjacent to the city yet relatively undisturbed. As the movement of matter and beings enabled the mounds to come into existence, they neither fit into the visual culture of pastoral landscapes nor into the more recent idea to turn this tradition toward the city as a landscape. Discarded material brought the diaspores of pioneering plants and herbs, which were similarly discarded and discriminated against, like the buildings and their residents from the 1970s onwards. The change in the collective appreciation of the mounds as an infrastructure and their assigned meaning to the public over time is significant, transitioning from material deemed worthless, an environmental threat, and reminders of displacement in the beginning, toward a unique environmental quality today, despite decreasing remnants of soil pollution. Thus, their emergence resonates with Berlin's distinct history of resistance and the emergence of urban ecology as a discipline. In a broader sense, the landscapes of the two mass housing estates might be future-oriented spaces for the entire city, deeply connected to the land through the entanglements of their multispecies inhabitants within and around the buildings.

The exploration of the two rubble mounds through the land(scape)-oriented methodology led to findings that add complexity to post-war housing history. The material histories of waste disposal after the rise of construction and consumerism are intertwined with the social histories of addressing the post-war housing crisis. In other words, the history of devaluing and discarding things such as rubble and consumer products converges with a much more problematic history of devaluing people, relocated in thousands to Berlin's peripheries. Their history is also context-specific in that institutional control resulted in friction at almost every step along the way, making the two rubble mounds suitable examples of counter-activity in the emergence of Berlin's housing estates. At first, the State of Berlin turned former agricultural land into a disposal site to accumulate matter considered worthless, leading to the first resistance of inhabitants of that land, effectively disagreeing with the price tag of 1300 German Marks attached to their homesteads (Wilde 1989: 54). As the mounds of waste grew, so did the environmental movements, the perception of limits to post-war growth, and the consciousness of the violence in labor exploitation, again leading to cooperating resistance between East and West Germans, citizens, and non-citizens. Reimagining the companion mounds as ruderal ecologies can inform the reimagination of housing estates at large: Instead of reducing them to the one-sided history of building design and construction technologies that fail to reclaim the neighborhoods from a stigmatized public image, reimagining modernist housing estates through their landscape features renders them as different places, capable of addressing the crisis of a warming planet and urban housing shortages simultaneously.

Considering the changing practices and consequences for architectural knowledge in academic terms, this research puts land and landscape first when approaching Berlin's post-war housing estates. For architectural pedagogy, this implies a design approach that requires thought and practice in interdependent meshes, leaving behind the ideological dichotomies and spatial fragmentations introduced by modernism. This research assembles an argument for the exceptional quality of these landscapes as they are, without the need for intervention, by outlining the history of resistance as it relates to the two mounds, the housing estates, and Berlin as a whole. It seeks to restore the connection between interior living spaces and their external counterparts, which nurture both ecological and social relations. Drawing from situated and relational approaches to the environment, constructing such a dense inhabitation mesh of mass housing estates calls for critical densification that acknowledges that abundant open space does not equal the necessity to build, that open space is not empty space, and that both not-building, building-elsewhere, or care-management are considerable alternatives in the design repertoire.

In professional terms for (landscape) architectural practitioners, this contribution highlights notions of hands-off maintenance and care over interventionist design or the process of these notions as a design objective itself. Engaging with the multi-layered land under any given site forces designers to engage a deeper temporality that might reveal unforeseen historical details shaping multispecies life around the site, often embedded in the collective consciousness of residents. Land(scape)-oriented research also renders the invisible visible, legal forces that divide and shape the built environment, where architectural design alone remains almost powerless as the last member in the chain of architectural creation. Although rarely operating without institutional frameworks, practitioners could facilitate better opportunities for multispecies collectives to shape future development by entering the design process at an earlier stage of politics, law, and finance. Resonating with this conclusion, the field is currently shifting on a broader level, and notions of architects as public servants and civic advocates are gaining more widespread acceptance.

Revisiting and rewriting the quotidian lives of housing estates is crucial, as they are often self-organized, resistant, and sometimes in collaboration with a governing entity, such as a state-owned company. Such an understanding might push academic and professional practice, along with the land itself, toward a mediating position between policymakers and inhabitants, neither as service providers nor guerrilla activists. The mounds' history also unveils the immense exploitation of labor involved in the creation of the built environment. As there is almost no way to avoid interfering with a life unconsidered, we can try to become aware of whose stories our project tells and excludes, and consider designing with sensitivity, particularly towards those who are potentially ignored, offended, or exploited. While aesthetics and beauty can sometimes distract from it, building almost always means destroying, just as speaking is always a mode of silencing. Before we speak architecturally, we might consider how the land on which we built already spoke before us, perhaps in different keys and languages, and how we might not only answer softly but remain silent altogether.

Acknowledgments

I thank the generosity of ETH Zurich's Institute of Landscape and Urban Studies (LUS) and the stimulating discussions with my fellow LUS doctoral students and those at the Institute for the History and Theory of Architecture (gta). I am indebted to my supervisors, Tom Avermaete and Maria Conen. Additionally, the anonymous feedback from my peer reviewers and the enormous generosity of their comments were substantial in improving this contribution, including those from the editorial team: Kadambari Baxi, Isabel Glogar, Gabu Heindl, Bernadette Krejs, and Tatjana Schneider.

References

Albrecht, Wolfgang (1983): »Besucher im Freizeitpark Lübars (Reinickendorf).« Photograph, *Berliner Landesarchiv, F Rep. 290 (06)*.

Amad, Said (2024): Interview with author July 17, 2024.

Autorengruppe »Märkische Viertel Zeitung« (1973): »*Märkische Viertel Zeitung*,« Boxfile 1294b, Free University Berlin APO-Archiv.

Barad, Karen (2007): *Meeting the Universe Halfway: Quantum Physics and the Entanglement of Matter and Meaning*, Durham: Duke University Press.

Beck, Johannes/Reidemeister, Helga, eds. (1975): *Wohnste sozial, haste die Qual: ›Jetzt reden wir‹: Betroffene des Märkischen Viertels; mühsamer Weg zur Solidarisierung*, Erstausg., [1.–15. Tsd.]. Rororo-Sachbuch: Politische Erziehung, 6912 780, Reinbek bei Hamburg: Rowohlt.

Bodenschatz, Harald (1987): *Platz Frei Für das Neue Berlin! Geschichte der Stadterneuerung in der ›Grössten Mietskasernenstadt der Welt‹ Seit 1871*, Berlin: Transit.

Braun, Jascha Philipp (2019): *Grosssiedlungsbau im Geteilten Berlin: Das Märkische Viertel und Marzahn als Beispiele des Spätmodernen Städtebaus*, Berlin: Gebr. Mann Verlag.

Bristol, Katharine G. (1991): »The Pruitt-Igoe Myth,« in: *Journal of Architectural Education* 44/3, 163–171. doi: 10.1080/10464883.1991.11102687

Büchner, Hans Georg (2015): »Kienberg und Wuhletal in der Landschaftsplanung bis 1989,« in: *Von der Berliner Gartenschau zu den Gärten der Welt. Geschichte und Geschichten, Teil 1. Vorträge aus den Workshops GARTENKUNST IM DIALOG 2010–2013*, Verein ›Freunde der Gärten der Welt.‹

Danicke, Knut (1979): »Die Situation im Räumungsbereich des Neubaugebietes Berlin-Marzahn und über Stimmungen und Meinungen der Bewohner des Dorfkerns Marzahn,« October 30, 1979. BArch MfS BV Bln AKG 2635, Stasi-Unterlagen-Archiv.

Dassler (2020): »Der Hass auf Tiere ist erschreckend: Der Tod eines Bibers beschäftigt die Polizei in Marzahn-Hellersdorf,« in: *Der Tagesspiegel Online*, September 18, 2020, https://www.tagesspiegel.de/berlin/der-tod-eines-bibers-beschaftigt-die-polizei-in-marzahn-hellersdorf-5729794.html, accessed February 26, 2025.

Dietmann, Rolf (2025): Interview with author December 2, 2025.

Fahrner, Moritz (1986): »Marzahn: Realsozialistisches Beton-Berlin. Wohnungsgigantomanie rund um einen innerstädtischen Dorfanger,« in: *zitty*, February. Stasi-Unterlagen-Archiv (BArch MfS BV Bln Abt II 612).

Flierl, Bruno (2017): *Architekturtheorie und Architekturkritik: Texte aus sechs Jahrzehnten. Grundlagen 55. 1st Edition*, Berlin: DOM publishers.

Gandy, Matthew (dir.) (2017): *Natura Urbana: Ecological Constellations in Urban Space*, Cambridge: MIT Press. doi: 10.7551/mitpress/10658.001.0001

Gruppe Panther & Co, eds. (2021): *Rebellisches Berlin: Expeditionen in die untergründige Stadt*, Hamburg: Assoziation A.

Gutsche, Erich (1969): »*Zuweisung von Gelände zur Errichtung einer Hochkippe*,« August 9, 1969. Rep. 110 3637. State Archive Berlin.

Hahlweg, Bernd (1981): »Landschaftliches Tor Marzahns,« in: *Junge Welt (Berlin)*, December 7. Bezirksmuseum Marzahn-Hellersdorf (Zeitungssauschnitte-Archiv).

Harnack, Maren (2018): »In die Zange genommen. Kritik am Wohnungsbau um 1968,« in: *sub\urban. zeitschrift für kritische stadtforschung* 6 2/3, 173–180.

Hauser, Susanne (2020): »Framing Urban Landscapes: Interview with Susanne Hauser,« in: Gandy, Matthew/Jasper, Sandra (eds.), *The Botanical City*, Berlin: Jovis, 216–220.

Hilbrandt, Hanna (2021): *Housing in the Margins: Negotiating Urban Formalities in Berlin's Allotment Gardens. IJURR — Studies in Urban and Social Change Book Series*, Hoboken: John Wiley & Sons, Inc.

Hildebrandt, Bernd/Schlickeiser, Klaus (1989): *Abschied von der Laube. Die Zeit vor der Entstehung des Märkischen Viertels. Bürger erforschen ihren Ortsteil*, Berlin: Konkret-Werbung Gertrud Großkopf GmbH & Co.

Hueppe, Robin V. (2025): »Assembling, Governing, Enmeshing (AGE): A Land(Scape)-Oriented Methodology for Mass Housing Estates,« in: *Landscape Research*, July 2, 1–15. doi: 0.1080/01426397.2025.2514004

Hunger, Bernd (2021): *Berliner Großsiedlungen am Scheideweg?*, Berlin: Kompetenzzentrum Großsiedlungen e.V.

Ingold, Tim (2011): *Being Alive: Essays on Movement, Knowledge and Description*, London: Routledge.

Mack, Jennifer (2021): »Impossible Nostalgia: Green Affect in the Landscapes of the Swedish Million Programme,« in: *Landscape Research* 46/4, 558–573. doi: 10.1080/01426397.2020.1858248

Mack, Jennifer (2023): »Modernism in the Present Tense: "Dangerous" Scandinavian Suburbs and Their Hereafters,« in: *Environment and Planning D: Society and Space* 41/4, 656–682. doi: 10.1177/02637758231182147

Ojalammi, Sanna/Blomley, Nicholas (2015): »Dancing with Wolves: Making Legal Territory in a More-than-Human World,« in: *Geoforum* 62 June, 51–60. doi: 10.1016/j.geoforum.2015.03.022

Park, Jinhee (2003): »Der »Langfristvertrag« oder das zweifelhafte Glück der Kurzsichtigkeit. West-Berliner »Müllentsorgung« in die DDR,« in: Susanne Köstering (ed.), *Müll von gestern? Eine umweltgeschichtliche Erkundung in Berlin und Brandenburg. Cottbuser Studien zur Geschichte von Technik, Arbeit und Umwelt* 20, Münster: Waxmann.

Park, Jinhee (2004): »Von der Müllkippe zur Abfallwirtschaft: Die Entwicklung der Hausmüllentsorgung in Berlin (West) von 1945 bis 1990.« *With Technische Universität Berlin and Wolfgang König. Preprint, Technische Universität Berlin*, July 22. doi: 10.14279/DEPOSITONCE-615

Plamper, Jan (2023): *We Are All Migrants: A History of Multicultural Germany*, Cambridge: Cambridge University Press.

Plato, Eveline/Scholz, Anne (2024): Interview with author January 8, 2024.

Plato, Werner, and Eveline Plato (dirs.) (1972): *Unlabeled Footage of Märkisches Viertel*, Super 8 Film. Private Archive of Eveline Plato.

Reinecke, Christiane (2022): »Into the Cold: Neighborliness, Class, and the Emotional Landscape of Urban Modernism in France and West Germany,« in: *Journal of Urban History* 48/1, 163–181. doi: 10.1177/0096144220931197

Rubin, Eli (2016): *Amnesiopolis: Modernity, Space, and Memory in East Germany*, Oxford: Oxford University Press.

Samstag, Maximilian (2024): Interview with author July 24, 2024.

Schaaf, Renate (2024): Interview with author July 3, 2024.

Schlickeiser, Klaus (2021): *Lübars – Das letzte Dorf Berlins von 1230 bis heute. Chronik des Bezirkes Reinickendorf von Berlin*, Berlin: Förderkreis für Bildung, Kultur und Internationale Beziehungen Geschichte.

Schlickeiser, Klaus (2024): »Infos Lübars, Hüppe, letters,« October 5, 2024.

Schnitter, Daniela (1996): »*Zur Geschichte des 21. Verwaltungsbezirks Berlin-Marzahn*,« Archiv Bezirksmuseum Marzahn-Hellersdorf.

Schwedler, Rolf (1972): *MV-Plandokumentation: Märkisches Viertel*, Berlin: Kiepert.

Sontheimer, Michael/Wensierski, Peter (2018): *Berlin – Stadt der Revolte. Politik & Zeitgeschichte*. 1st E-Book edition, Berlin: Ch. Links Verlag.

Stoetzer, Bettina (2022): *Ruderal City: Ecologies of Migration, Race, and Urban Nature in Berlin. Experimental Futures*, Durham: Duke University Press.

Sukopp, Herbert (ed.) (1990): *Stadtökologie: Das Beispiel Berlin*, Berlin: Reimer.

Thiel, Dieter (2024): Interview with author July 3, 2024.

Tietze, Wolfgang (1988): »Still Ruht der Müll,« in: *Die Tageszeitung: taz*, October 19, 1988, https://taz.de/!1834515/, accessed November 21, 2024.

Tieu, Sung/Bentcheva, Eva (2023): »Gehrenseestrasse 1: Between the Worlds of Architecture and Politics,« in: L. Kost, ed., *Sung Tieu: One Thousand Times*, Köln: Snoeck, 195–202.

Trautsch, Manuel »Lux« (2025): Interview with author December 2, 2025.

Treblin, Johanna (2022): »Wildnis am Wuhlesee: Ein Paradies für Berliner Biber,« in: *Der Tagesspiegel Online*, June 16, 2022, https://www.tagesspiegel.de/berlin/bezirke/ein-paradies-fur-berliner-biber-8023462.html, accessed February 26, 2025.

Unlabeled Footage of Märkisches Viertel (1972), [Super 8 Film], Directed by W. Plato and E. Plato.

Urban, Florian (2013): »The Hut on the Garden Plot,« in: *Journal of the Society of Architectural Historians* 72/2, 221–249. doi: 10.1525/jsah.2013.72.2.221

Urban, Florian (2018): »Large Housing Estates of Berlin, Germany,« in: Daniel Baldwin Hess/ Tiit Tammaru/ Maarten van Ham (eds.), *Housing Estates in Europe*, Cham: Springer International Publishing, 99–120. doi: 10.1007/978-3-319-92813-5_5

Vasudevan, Alexander (2022): »Tenant Trouble: Resisting Precarity in Berlin's Märkisches Viertel, 1968–1974,« in: *Annals of the American Association of Geographers* 112/6, 1537–1552. doi: 10.1080/24694452.2021.1990008

Weiss, Karin (2011): »Die Einbindung Ehemaliger Vietnamesischer Vertragsarbeiterinnen und Vertragsarbeiter in Strukturen der Selbstorganisation,« in: Zwengel,Zwengle (ed.), *Die ›Gastarbeiter‹ der DDR: Politischer Kontext und Lebenswelt 13* Berlin: Lit, 263–279.

Wensierski, Peter (1986): *Von oben nach unten wächst gar nichts: Umweltzerstörung und Protest in der DDR. Informationen zur Zeit 4274. Orig.-Ausg*, Frankfurt am Main: Fischer-Taschenbuch-Verlag.

Wilde, Alexander (1989): *Das Märkische Viertel*, Berlin: Nicolaische Verlagsbuchhandlung.

Zobel, Evelyn/Zobel, Michael (2024): Interview with author January 15, 2024.

Dimensions of Architectural Knowledge, 2024-08 ∂
https://doi.org/10.14361/dak-2024-0813

Urban Mediations and Collective Architecture: Zuloark and the Case of Campo de Cebada, Madrid

Enrique Espinosa, Enrique Nieto

Abstract: Between 1996 and 2006, Spain saw the emergence of several architectural collectives whose practices challenged both the disciplinary models and the organizational structures that had accompanied the urban growth of the early years following the arrival of democracy in 1975. As this paper will argue, these groups – Recetas Urbanas, Zuloark, and Basurama, among others – acted as laboratories for testing alternative approaches to addressing the various crises that coincided with the arrival of the 21st century and that questioned the dominant models of city-making. Based on the role played by Zuloark in the open public design space of Campo de Cebada, this research delves into the notion of mediation as a means to decenter the architectural object, orienting the practice of architecture toward new alliances with other agents (e.g., public administrations, civil society, citizen movements, etc.). We will show how these mediation processes mobilize »minor knowledges« (Braidotti 2019), unfolding from »intra-actions« (Barad 2007) that form »recursive communities« (Kelty 2008). These in turn promote, build, and care for city fragments with ecological, participatory, and more sensitive principles, thereby opening the possibility for other urban futures.

Keywords: Mediation; Minor Architecture; Intra-Action; Recursive Public; Zuloark.

Corresponding authors: Enrique Espinosa (Universidad de Alicante, Spain); Enrique Nieto (Universidad de Alicante, Spain); enrique.espinosa@ua.es; https://orcid.org/0009-0002-4739-5452; enrique.nieto@ua.es; https://orcid.org/0000-0002-8513-7115 ∂

Introduction. Collective Practices in the Midst of Real Estate, Political, and Ecological Crises.

Between 1996 and 2006, Spain saw the emergence of several architectural collectives whose practices challenged both the disciplinary models and the organizational structures that had accompanied the urban growth of the early years following the arrival of democracy in 1975. At that time, Madrid and Seville acted as urban laboratories, being the most active contexts for this type of practice. In Seville, the work of Santiago Cirugeda from 1996 could be seen as a form of hacking, using scaffolding, debris containers, and ephemeral architectures to challenge the administrative frame-works associated with land use, as well as construction and social regula-tions, fostering citizen empowerment and learning through open-source manuals. In Madrid, three different groups of students from the ETSAM[1], dissatisfied with the lack of cultural and political energy, set up their prac-tices by approaching urbanism through political critique and participation (Laboratorio Urbano 2001–2012), or creating spaces between architecture, territory, thought, and sustainability through workshops, lectures, urban actions, and exhibitions, bridging the gap separating academia and the street (Basurama, 2001–until present; Zuloark, 2001–until present). Our hypothesis is that their emergence can be interpreted as a response to the multiple crises that characterized this period (climate, real estate, profes-sional, and academic). By embracing practices in which mediation processes displaced the centrality of the architectural object and questioned the project itself as the only device for accessing reality, they revealed and helped make possible unprecedented professional alternatives that affected both the ways of making architecture and its material results.

The Spanish case is mirrored in other parts of Europe, where collective practices in architecture experienced a resurgence in the late 1990s and early 2000s (Awan/Schneider/Till 2011; Donat-Cattin 2022; Espinosa Pérez 2024: 34–35), with cases such as Esterni (Milan, 1995), Bruit du Frigo (Bordeaux, 1997), Superuse (Netherlands, 1998), Raumlabor (Berlin, 1999), Coloco (Paris, 1999), Atelier d'Architecture Autogèree (Paris, 2002) or Exyzt (Paris, 2002). While many of these groups began as testing grounds for alternative modes of internal organization, some of them had achieved a certain professional –

---

1 Escuela Técnica Superior de Arquitectura de Madrid (Spain's oldest state school of archi-tecture). Universidad Politécnica de Madrid.

economic – autonomy by the time the dominant city-building methods collapsed with the Great Recession of 2007/2008, caused by the bursting of subprime mortgages in the United States of America and its subsequent effects in Europe, and Spain in particular.[2] The conditions shared by these collectives are: Horizontal organization, medium scale of usually four to a dozen members with a flexible composition – members can join or leave easily, especially during the initial stages – and self-imposed disciplinary agendas aligned with political stances aimed at protecting the commons by questioning certain neoliberal and consumerist city models (Espinosa Pérez 2024: 98, 166, 224). To better understand the scope of the transformations introduced in Spain by an architectural and urban practice linked to collaboration, commons, and free culture, we will use Zuloark and their work in/with Campo de Cebada, Madrid, as a case study. This project interweaves topics brought forward by Santiago Cirugeda, namely city, self-construction, and loopholes in building regulations, with those of Basurama with action, play, materiality, and waste, Staddle3 (Barcelona, 1998 – until present) or Todo por la Praxis (Madrid, 2008 – until present) with activism, manuals, and free culture. This case will help us reveal which of their specific practices have helped drive changes in both the models for professional organization and the role of the architect. The methodology for this research has consisted in an ethnographic practice that has accompanied and lived this process. The authors were part of these processes[3] and have carried out interviews

---

2 The emergence of these collectives in Spain is closely tied to the spread of neoliberal policies promoted by Prime Minister Margaret Thatcher, US President Ronald Reagan, and later, Prime Minister of Spain José Maria Aznar (1996–2004), challenging the sustainability of this model of progress based on unlimited resource consumption. In Spain, this crisis overlapped with two key transformations: The liberalization of professional services (Omnibus Law, 2009), which weakened professional associations and deregulated the field; and the Bologna-driven restructuring of architectural education, which broke with traditional models without offering clear alternatives. At the same time, the environmental crisis placed new responsibilities on architecture, calling for more ethical, supportive, and sustainable practices. Although initially not central, this concern aligned with the collectives' approaches and gained critical support. The 1998 Land Law and the real estate boom (1997–2008) intensified urban growth and changed the organization of studios, while digitalization and school proliferation brought young, low-cost labor into increasingly precarious work environments.

3 Espinosa was a co-founder of the PKMN collective (2006–2016) and collaborated with Zuloark and Basurama on several projects.

with relevant actors, collected participant observations, and lived embodied experiences between 2011 and 2023.

Along the way, we will observe how the notion of mediation appears as a fundamental condition of a spatial practice that enables a design process that is situated, negotiated (Schneider in: Bader et al. 2022: 160), and inclusive of multiple participants. Mediation implies a contemporary architectural competence, amidst design, management, participation, and sociotechnical enrollment,[4] and is fundamental in understanding the transformative potential and scope of these types of practices in a society who had only escaped four decades of repressive dictatorship 25 years earlier. These practices, engaged in an activism committed to its present, designed more fair and equitable futures that moved away from the status quo, still centered on modernist obsessions with growth, resource consumption, exclusionary rationality, or technical solutions as a paradigm of intervention (Espinosa Pérez 2024: 118). In particular, we will focus on how these mediation processes mobilized what Rosi Braidotti (2019) characterizes as »minor or nomadic knowledge.« A kind of knowledge that cannot be detached from bodies and histories, or appropriated by disciplines. We will also see how the notion of »intra-actions« deployed by Karen Barad (2007) is useful for assessing the effectiveness of this knowledge. Particularly within practices of social cohesion, which are also practices of design that make up what Christopher Kelty (2008: 3) called »recursive public,« in this case, those that guard, promote, build, and care for fragments of the city from ecological, participatory principles that are more sensitive to a planet in crisis.

Zuloark: The Building is Not the Battlefield

Zuloark emerged in 2001 in Madrid (ETSAM and CEU architecture schools),[5] as a collective of architecture students eager to approach their career with a playful, proactive, and collaborative attitude:

---

4 This notion of mediation transcends the genealogies linked to art (Fontdevila 2018) or media studies (Galloway/Thacker/Wark 2014).

5 Although most of Zuloark's members began studying architecture at the private CEU university in Madrid in 1998, they continued and completed their studies at the ETSAM (Madrid School of Architecture) in 2001, giving rise to the collective.

»The origin of Zulo lies in realizing from the beginning that in school, projects are completed faster with more classmates compared to doing them alone. And in architecture, where you have long-haul projects [...], doing it with people freed you from your prejudices a bit and you could do it more freely, learning more, having more fun. [...] What brought it all together was leisure and productivity, which meant getting things done but having a good time« (Manuel Pascual and Aurora G. Adalid. Interview conducted by Enrique Espinosa in 2011).[6]

Initially, the group was a loose and growing network of more than twenty people, until it stabilized around about six people in 2009, and twelve in 2025. In 2004, Zuloark won their first competition of national relevance and in 2006 they began a process of professionalization that accelerated in 2009 with their presence as assistant directors for the Spanish Biennial of Architecture and Urbanism.[7] In 2010, they started a line of spatial practices driven by the Inteligencias Colectivas initiative and their participation, with the Gran Vía Gran Obra project, in the 2010 La Noche en Blanco event (fig. 1). These projects involved experiments in public space using open-source logics based on collaborative self-construction and circular economy principles. These initial transversal interests and their convergence in public space, along with a sophisticated mode of participating in civic processes, situated between activism, technical advice, and the weaving and maintenance of peer networks, was put into practice in a more elaborate manner between 2011 and 2017 in Campo de Cebada, a plot of land located in the La Latina

---

6 The quotes in this article are excerpts from interviews conducted by Enrique Espinosa between 2011 and 2023.

7 »In 2007–2008, we started finishing our degree and began to professionalize. During that time, there were debates and splits... and there was a debate about whether to maintain the structure of Zuloark as an amateur project, or whether to professionalize it. That transition coincided with the crisis. At the beginning, we entered competitions in a more conventional way [...]. But starting in 2008, we refocused our practice without losing those aspects of authorship, of how we structure ourselves, of openness, and flexibility... Those transitions are soft. In 2014–2015, a third phase began, in which we tried to make the structure more caring. Manu said at the beginning that there was this ›you sign as Zuloark and you have common resources, a meeting place, and a group that gives you security‹. [...] Our effort since then has been to consolidate that... So there are three phases: the student–activist phase, the beginning of professionalization, and this third phase that allows us to work together.« (Juan Chacón and Manuel Pascual. Zuloark, 2021)

1.
Installation on Gran Vía, Madrid, 2010 (left), and its second life in El Gallinero slum (rigth). Photograph by Zuloark.

neighborhood, the abandonment of which can be seen as one of the urban collapses of the 2008 crisis.

For urban anthropologists Alberto Corsín and Adolfo Estalella (Corsín 2014, 2017; Corsín/Estalella 2016, 2023), activism associated with free culture in Spain – and they refer often to Zuloark and Basurama as two important cases – intersects three agendas around the concept of »freedom«: The philosophy of liberty associated with the hacker ethos of free software, the libertarian aspirations of autonomous movements, and the right-to-the-city demands of grassroots struggles. At this intersection, these scholars propose the concept of »Free/Libre Urbanism,« which envisions a city model at odds with liberal urbanism and top-down institutional planning. It is within this framework that Zuloark and similar collectives operate, challenging disciplinary expectations about what architecture can be or do.

It is important to note that many of these architectural collectives and networks understand their own studios as spaces for self-training, complementing the shortcomings of architecture schools' academic curriculum regarding internal management skills and action in the real city. One of the concepts coined by developmental psychologist L.S. Vygotsky, the »zone of proximal development« (Vygotsky 1934), proposes learning contexts as spaces in which one does not know how to do something, but in which one is able to learn how to do it with help. Zones of proximal development in which learning occurs through the interactions among its members and with the outside world; a learning that we could define as P2P because it does not occur through a deductive »teacher–student« method, but rather through amateurism, interaction, and the search for help among peers. Cases such as Basurama and Zuloark came together and became active during their time at university, and they represent communities whose ways of doing things involve creative and hacker methodologies that encourage group learning and peer recognition (Himanen 2001: 51). The Zuloark collective itself has been explicitly using the notions of »zone of proximal development« since 2002, and its members consider »Zulo« to be »the master's degree I could never have afforded.«[8] This way of organizing the collective, from its earliest logistical experiments, has entailed highly committed communication and solidarity protocols, not without risks. In fact, in that first shared apartment in 2004 in Atocha, it was already established that any professional work carried out by Zuloark must entail a return of 20% of the income to the shared structure:

---

8 Planeta Beta, Radio Círculo Program, Capítulo 1, Zuloark, February 26, 2009.

»The horizontal structure has always existed in Zulo. Is it horizontal? No, actually, if you look at it closely, there are many variations. We call it ›fluid hierarchies‹ [...] We felt very comfortable being reflected in what was happening in the 15M movement or what was happening in La Cebada. It's not so much that we assimilated those structures, but rather that we shared the way of structuring and organizing ourselves, ways in which we felt seen [...].« (Manuel Pascual. Zuloark. Interview conducted in 2021 by Enrique Espinosa).

Within these collectives, the roles of the members rotate. Although members of the collective may recognize certain strengths or unique skills in one another, there is no rigid assignment of tasks and certainly no stratification throughout the different phases of each project. In horizontal, collaborative structures, defining work protocols involves more than just establishing dynamics, rhythms, methodologies, or decision-making guidelines: Between the »hardware« (the team structure and its governance) and production, there is a layer of »software« or sensitive tools that expand and enable better organization, communication, and task completion among team members (fig. 2).

Zuloark has implemented various tools, ranging from internal communications to work organization and information flow, archiving, etc. But above all, they have established three synchronization protocols that involve an important relational dimension. The first is the division of infrastructural tasks, i.e. the underlying design processes, into three areas (governance, economy, and communication), where team members take responsibility and organize autonomously, booking an inter-area meeting (govecom) once a month. The second is »the Tuesday meeting,« systematized since 2015 and limited to one-hour, which allows for organizing project developments, any associated human resources, and calendars.

»How are decisions made? At Tuesday meetings, we've probably voted twice in ten years. So, in reality, decisions aren't made; they're inhabited and settled, as Amador says. That's the key. The same thing happened at La Cebada. It sounds like a cliché, but it's true, I assure you. Tuesday meetings are for getting together, seeing each other, and raising concerns if someone is involved in a project that isn't profitable but ends up being done anyway... It's more about being there.« (Manuel Pascual. Zuloark. Interview conducted in 2021 by Enrique Espinosa).

The third one is the »Zulocongress,« a face-to-face meeting held during the last week of January, which serves both to review the previous year and plan Zuloark's future agenda and work conditions, as well as to celebrate together with the collective's close affective-professional community. These meetings have been key in implementing horizontal organization and self-care strategies, such as extending the workday, vacations, or enhancing the value of certain non-productive jobs (Espinosa Pérez 2024: 85). It is important to note that it is akin to free culture conferences. For anthropologist Gabriella Coleman, these conferences, or »cons« in the hacker communities, are not mere gatherings to optimize the functioning of a community of practice, or even to learn new technical-productive matters. Rather, they are »rituals of confirmation, liberation, celebration, and reenchantment« (Coleman 2013: 48) in which to recognize oneself as a community and value the qualities of one's social and productive life.

We can also look at these collectives and their work tools as labor experiments where, despite the initial precariousness, the work models developed often helped overcome some of the most complicated effects of the crisis in the sector. These cooperative structures have created working conditions that, although by no means highly salaried, have qualitative benefits such as more flexibility, an ethical backbone, or proportionality across the team members' salaries. Thus, the extractivism inherent in any corporate structure aligned with neoliberal capitalism is challenged by increasingly self-aware ways of working, where inspiring terms such as »care« or »good living« are more and more central to the internal debates and decision-making processes. Another revealing aspect is all the analogies that arise between these groups of architects and certain communities linked to free software and culture, characterized by horizontality, open codes and sources, or the sophisticated construction of communication and design tools, which these groups of architects »modulate« (Kelty 2008: 2, 12, 16, 245), explicitly or implicitly.

On Different Notions of Mediation: Campo de Cebada

On September 12, 2010, the streets of Madrid were being cleaned up after the end of La Noche en Blanco event. A few days earlier, in Plaza de Cebada, the French collective Exyzt had built an ephemeral pool with wooden slats and a plastic sheet, in memory of the municipal pool that once occupied the site. This pool, demolished in 2009 by the City Council in order to rebuild it, had

2.
*Collaborative work session for internal organization
at the Zulocongress, Berlin 2015. © Zuloark.*

HEUTE FREITAG
NACHMITTAG WIRD
GEPUTZT.
MATRIOSKA
BERLIN
BARCELONA
MADRID
MAD
MANU P.
MANU D.
ALBERTO
JUANJO

left an urban void, and the new intervention, which included a new facility to be designed by the winning architects of a 2007–2008 competition, had been suspended due to the economic crisis, yet it had also been met with certain public opposition. The exceptional nature of the temporary opening of the building site for the cultural events of La Noche en Blanco triggered debates about the fates of these kinds of plots, an opportunity seized by local architect groups such as Basurama, Zuloark, and Todo por la Praxis, in collaboration with local residents and the Regional Federation of Neighborhood Associations of Madrid (FRAVM). This experience, as well as some other precedents,[9] provided the legal and organizational basis for the community that emerged from the former La Latina pool to present a project to the City Council to claim the use of the land. Thus, on January 21, 2011, the use agreement was signed, and on May 15, Campo de Cebada opened its doors to the public as a public square.

Campo de Cebada was one of the nodes in a network of initiatives that were deployed over 2011, and which, through a series of projects, activated multiple urban concepts aligned with the political sensibilities in the air during and after the 15M movement,[10] e.g. urban commons, neighborhood assemblies, public squares, citizen participation, or environmental awareness. Zuloark was a very active participant in all forums. Furthermore, their infrastructure supported this kind of »non-productive« work and understood it as labor hours even though it was not mediated by a contract with any public or private entity. Zuloark members did not only coordinate and participate in workshops to build urban infrastructure such as dry toilets, bleachers, planters, and benches. They also participated in the weekly assembly, drafted projects with the community members to obtain public subsidies, and mediated between the administration, the local associations,

---

9 It should be noted that, in parallel, between 2008 and 2010, a complex urban process had taken place in the nearby neighborhood of Lavapiés, with the Esta es una Plaza project and its associated organization, which constituted a precedent for the transfer of municipal land for community management and use.

10 The 15M movement in Madrid is a phenomenon derived from the Arab Spring of 2010 and connected to the Occupy movement that swept the world in 2011. It began on May 15, 2011, with a large national demonstration driven by the crisis, austerity policies, and generational despair, and it triggered various encampments in squares such as the Acampada de la Puerta del Sol in the center of Madrid.

and other stakeholders in order to activate the Campo de Cebada space itself.[11] This was highly relevant as it created a middle ground between activist and professional practice. Moreover, participation in this network allowed Zuloark to cement three key pillars for its own future: Firstly, expanding the collective's learning, acquiring tools and contacts that would allow them to understand urban practices that mediate between administration, public space, and citizenship; secondly, forging a dense network of peer agents; lastly, these sophisticated support and guidance projects would eventually crystallize into professional work.

During its six years of existence, Campo de Cebada was a laboratory for collective citizen practices where a range of different experiences were tried and tested, for example construction (workshops for furniture making), environmental awareness (creation of a community garden, and manufacturing with recycled materials), culture (music and fanzine festivals, conferences, singer-songwriter sessions, and theater), and citizen mediation (weekly assemblies, agreements, and alliances between neighbors).

Campo de Cebada became a crucial experience for other projects like Autobarrios (Basurama, 2013), although it cannot be explained without the prior trajectory of the architecture collectives involved, which, beyond activism, free culture, and the commons, is marked by experiences with self-construction and DIY (Corsín/Estalella 2023) (figs. 3 and 4). This set of interests, often composed of non-academic knowledge, expands as a disciplinary field and agenda where other pedagogies and learning spaces are tested (Corsín/Estalella 2016). These include modes of construction that dissent from those of the real estate market, such as open and modular practices (Kelty 2008), in which construction manuals and management guides coexist with protocols for enrolling and transmitting knowledge, similar to the communities around free software described by Kelty, and spaces of affection, participation, and citizen engagement that challenge, as minor architectures (Stoner 2012), top-down models of city planning and materialization.

---

11 »There was always a desire to make reproductive tasks something that was done together [...]. The leap that occurred when we set that fee meant, for example, that those of us who participated in the Campo de Cebada project were surely the only agents in all of Cebada who were being paid for carrying out that project, because Zulo supported us. I mean, the hours we spent in La Cebada were hours of work in Zulo [...]. And that was supported because the structure had already said that here we all earn the same and move forward.« (Manuel Pascual. Zuloark, 2021)

3.
Catalog of open-source chairs built in the Campo de Cebada workshops. © Anna Salom (Zuloark).

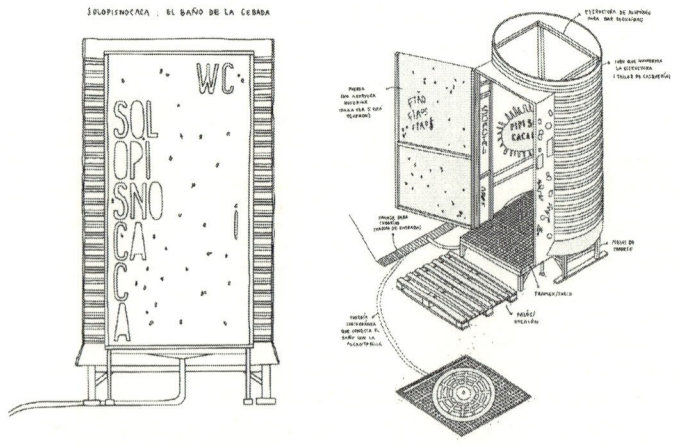

4.
Scheme of the W.C. »Solopisnocaca.« (»Pee yes, poop no«), designed by Zuloark. Cebada Field Design Manual. © Anna Salom (Zuloark).

Overall, Campo de Cebada represents an example – in a real city – of a shift in architects' interest from the design of architectural objects to the design of mediation processes[12] As a result of this, and due to the inclusion of a much more heterogeneous range of agents and the so-called »minor knowl-edges« (Braidotti 2019), there is an emergence of objects of difficult affiliation as well as other types of socio-material assemblages. In summary, three types of mediation are evident in Zuloark's work for, in, and with Campo de Cebada:

First, the Campo de Cebada is a space of material mediation that unites a basic materiality (wood, steel rods, tubes, screws, and basic tools) and an immediacy that escapes the usual lengthy process times of management and construction. Additionally, the materials that make up, are recovered, drilled, or screwed in Cebada are residues of diverse origin and therefore require easily accessible tools and knowledge. Due to their »immediacy,« these materials are treated as opportunities, but they are also useful in driving citizen mediation processes. We could say that their presence is as recognizable as a popular song, inviting the activation of citizen co-de-sign and co-production processes. These experiments transcend the notion of object – furniture or public space – or ecological awareness – through the recovery of discarded material – to become spaces of socialization and building city and citizenship. In this sense, designing and building could be seen as mediation practices, where the results are less important than the debates and the invitation for citizens to participate in the process (fig. 5).

Second, this experience involves an affective or »soft« mediation (Espinosa Pérez 2024: 127) between the particular people with whom Zuloark operates, in their dual role as architects and neighbors. An example that illus-trates this well is one presented by Alberto Corsín (2017) through the words of Manuel Pascual, a member of Zuloark, as well as part of the assembly and the active community of Campo de Cebada. He described the coexistence protocol with Don Antonio, a neighbor whose balcony overlooks the square. Manuel explained how, when the sound of amplified equipment was too loud during an event, Antonio called Manuel directly to have the volume turned down in Campo de Cebada.

---

12 This change is gradual and happens both through ephemeral and urban experiences such as those by Santiago Cirugeda (1996–2002) or the aforementioned Esta es una Plaza (2008–), other ephemeral ones developed in protected contexts such as festivals and biennials, such as the Basurama festivals (2001–2006) or the French Pavilion by Exyzt at the Venice Biennale in 2006, and even more sophisticated experiences such as the one initiated by Raumlabor at the Floating University in Berlin (2018–until present).

5.
Campo de Cebada. Furniture workshop reusing wood from formwork from the CICC, Madrid 2012. © Manuel Domínguez (Zuloark).

Finally, Zuloark's work is part of and catalyzes a network mediation, where municipal technicians, neighbors, politicians, activists, and architects, along with other entities such as assemblies, open-source manuals, celebrations, or urban gardens, become a recursive community (Kelty 2008) that makes and cares for the city.[13] This issue is relevant, as it enables the scaling or transfer to the public administration of certain protocols and generalizable learnings from this specific experience. An example that shows this potential for transfer and modulation is the Operación Herminio project (2014–until present), also by Zuloark, that began with the chance discovery of an unexpected public resource: A conversation between the group and the janitor of a municipal warehouse revealed the existence of a surplus amount of 24 x 4 x 200 cm wooden planks from deteriorated benches from the city streets. This resource, linked with the concept of urban mining, was first used as a material in the design of a prototype for an ephemeral municipal pavilion and ended up giving rise to a protocol for the transfer of construction materials for self-managed citizen projects. It involved different areas and technicians of the municipal administration, as well as different associations and neighbors, and it allowed the construction of urban furniture in Campo de Cebada, and subsequently equip and build infrastructures on plots across the whole municipal allotment network in Madrid.

Discussion: Urban Mediations

Through the case of Campo de Cebada, one can see how the outcomes of the events that took place were not previously described through that special device we call a »project.« Instead, the relational dimension unfolded by the practice itself brought about unforeseen encounters, alliances, and

---

13 »Free software consists of a set of practices for the cooperative and distributed creation of source code, which is then disseminated openly and freely through an astute and unusual use of copyright legislation [...]. Since 1998, the practices and ideas of free software have expanded into new vital and creative spheres: from software to music and film, from there to science, engineering and education [...]' (and here we could add, ›and to the city,‹ as an extra ›modulation‹). [...] A recursive public is a public that is vitally involved in the material and practical conservation and modification of the technical, legal, practical and conceptual means of its own existence as a public; it is a collective independent of other forms of power constituted and capable of addressing existing forms of power through the production of truly existing alternatives.« Chris Kelty in Two Bits (2008).

possibilities. While these potentials were inherent in each participant, they required specific dynamics and kinds of participation to be realized. This is one of the most shared characteristics of the work of all these collectives, and one that shifts the importance of the project to that of mediation processes. The extent to which these processes are able to integrate more and more urgent issues, as well as involve more communities and activate more negotiation processes, will determine how successful the mediation is. Karen Barad's research on the notion of »intra-actions« (Barad 2007) helps us understand the creative potential that arises from the »during« and the kind of creativity inherent in the relational. Barad (2023) challenges the traditional notion of interaction, which assumes that the entities coming into relation exist independently, fully formed, prior to the modes, ethics, and politics that articulate their encounters. This view treats entities as pre-existing and only later entering into relation (Barad 2023: 11). For her, the entities that participate in encounters do not necessarily preexist as such, but rather are completed in intra-actions that only exist within the phenomena (ibid.: 11). This has enormous implications for design practices, as it shifts their centrality from the participants of an encounter or its final outcome to that »intra« (in-between) that separates them and is no longer an unproductive moment, but precisely the event that creates the participants themselves in the process, introducing divergences into their itineraries and opening up possible futures for each of them. It is through the hands and screwdrivers of the participants in Campo de Cebada that a choreography of actions unfolds, which does not conclude with the assembly or even with the beers and celebrations that follow. We would say that the notion of »intra-action« allows us to approach design practices as highly complex processes of »becoming« and as processes of mediation between entities that are co-produced precisely from these practices of being together »through« design. It should also be noted that, obviously, these futures are not infinite. The range of possibilities opened up through mediation is crossed by the agendas, skills, and orientations of each collective and the particularities of each project, hence the differences between them. In the case of Zuloark, we could say that its main goal is oriented towards a complex, participatory, and soft – *»blandengue«* (Pascual 2025: 98) – way of city-making.

For a practice as purposive and focused on the built object as architecture, these considerations surrounding mediation as a process of urban intervention help us understand the importance of the encounter and the »during« that occur in the practice of architecture. This emphasis on the mediating dimension of architectural practice invites us to reconsider the political and ethical dimension of architecture, in contrast to the modernist paradigm, while offering dissident avenues of action with which to expand the spectrum and format of the transformative practices that build cities and citizenship. These avenues of action demand the participation of other types of expert knowledge from outside academia, much more widely distributed and not yet captured by the normative logic of academic practice. These lines of flight – where environmental awareness, inclusivity, autonomy, participation, and lesser knowledges are interwoven with design and technique – enable an overflow of architecture as both a construction project and a built object. In future research, this mediating dimension of architectural practices could be complemented with other perspectives to help us »imagine« its full potential, such as that proposed by Isabelle Stengers and her notion of an »ecology of practices« (Stengers 2005).

It is essential to recognize a certain recursive seed in this mediating condition. The particular experience of Campo de Cebada transcends the notion of temporal and spatial limits that every canonical architectural project implies. In this case, the emotional relationships, construction techniques, and the participation of certain agents go beyond the case study itself to become modulated and distributed in a network and ecology of practices that still survive in Madrid, and in which Zuloark continues to participate today.[14] We previously mentioned Operación Herminio, which was also relevant for the consolidation of the Madrid Network of Community Urban Gardens[15], a popular initiative that emerged informally and illegally in the early 2000s, yet which was not recognized, legalized, or articulated by the City Council itself until 2015 through legal regulations such as land use transfer agreements.[16] This appreciation of Campo de Cebada as a seedling of

---

14 Other experiences after Campo de Cebada that connect with the multimodal condition (Dattatreyan/Marrero-Guillamón 2019) of these spatial practices are Ciudad Escuela or Ciudad Huerto (Corsín/Estalella 2016), situated learning experiences where urban management, construction, Los Madriles (Madrid map of common resources), and care skills are developed, or Sendas Ocultas (Hidden Paths) (2020–present).

15 There are currently 62 municipal community gardens, of about 500, including gardens associated with schools and other municipal infrastructure.

16 Zuloark was one of the key agents in municipal regulation of the transfer of use of community urban gardens, through multiple working groups with the public administration and collaborating with civic entities such as the FRAVM and the Madrid Garden Network.

6.
Campo de Cebada. Aerial view, 2014. © Manuel Domínguez (Zuloark).

multiple urban futures reflects the survival, relevance, and multiple futures of the case addressed here (fig. 6).

Conclusions: What Assertions and Futures Can We Share?

Collective architectural practices emerged in Spain 25 years ago as a response to a very specific context of altered rules through which the discipline had become relevant to the nation's neoliberal growth policies of the 1990s. After all these years and after experiences such as Campo de Cebada, we have some pertinent questions: What do these practices empower us to do, and what futures do they open up? To what extent are the decentering of the object as the final product of architecture and architecture-as-mediation approaches viable alternatives to modernist architectural practices?

The research suggests that mediation was never an »a priori« in the work of Zuloark and other architectural collectives, but, on the contrary, it was an empirical methodology that gradually yielded results. In the interviews conducted, the effectiveness of the program or the form gradually shifted to the effectiveness of the negotiations with the agents involved and with the members of the communities. It is in this sense that the battlefield of the building gave way to a battlefield that is always open and produced collectively. This is a change of perspective with major repercussions on professional practices and on the tools of architecture. However, it should be noted that this type of change requires a high level of commitment and involvement on the part of the institutions, the positive assumption of certain levels of uncertainty, as well as an availability of time, which is not always the case. For this reason, this type of practice also requires lasting and stable alliances that guarantee the viability of these mediations over time.[17]

---

17 A full article would be needed to analyze in depth how these practices have evolved, how they operate now, and what their prospects are. Regarding the concept of mediation, we find it relevant to recognize that many members of these groups have been involved in other practices related to civic design or academia, sometimes leaving these groups and sometimes combining their work: for example, one member of Zuloark and another from Basurama work at a social innovation NGO (Demsoc); four members of Zuloark have worked or are working in academia; two members of Basurama have been part of the municipal administration in Madrid; and Santiago Cirugeda not only designs but also coordinates a construction company that promotes collaborative self-construction for social and solidarity economy organizations.

Within the practice analyzed, we recognize surprising learnings that involve knowledge beyond the disciplinary, in a similar vein to that used by concerned feminist climate thinkers such as Barad, Stengers or Braidotti. This is what happens, for example, when we focus on the relevance of conversation as a way of convening and mobilizing shared matters of interest, more than architectural practice itself promotes. This presence undoubtedly slows down and hinders certain types of productive efficiency in favor of other forms of effectiveness, as we have seen. In this path to »minorness,« one can call on many different authors and concepts, such as Erin Manning's »minor gesture« (Manning 2016) or Donna Haraway's »sympoiesis« (Haraway 2016). Yet the results of the kind of mediations that conversations produce are not easily grasped, since we cannot relate to the magnitude of the problems that climate change or the real estate crises introduced through formulas based on the problem–solution equation, but rather through a progressive change of attitude, oriented towards a better being with the problem, as Haraway invites us to do, as a way of keeping up with the times.

Collectives such as Zuloark have developed sophisticated routines to keep the conversation alive, continuing to change together. For this, the construction of care protocols and internal organization takes on particular significance. This relational and interpersonal dimension inherent to any practice of mediation explains the vocation of many of these collectives for teaching or caring for labor conditions. What types of organizations for architectural production can weave together futures, care, learning, and collaboration? This research emphasizes the importance of these case studies, organized based on ethics more attuned to the types of problems emerging from the consideration of a planet in crisis. These collectives, in different ways, challenge the logics of capitalist extractivism.[18]

On the other hand, this research also reveals the de facto incorporation of environmental awareness into the agenda of collective practices, which seems to happen gradually, diversely, and without any turning back. Notions such as »circularity« first appear as the material need to work with what is available,

---

18 For example, new projects are evaluated and agreed upon to ensure that ethical principles and the collective's position prevail over profit-making; regarding working conditions, salary differences between more experienced and younger members are moderate, following the principles of cooperative models, while equal rights and participation in decision-making are fundamental.

with what is free, as Santiago Cirugeda describes.[19] However, gradually, the practice of collectives such as Basurama or Zuloark incorporates this feature through sophisticated protocols that involve public administrations, local communities, and other agents. These interdisciplinary transfers involve multiple moments of friction with academia and institutions, but they represent a determined commitment to addressing the planetary repercussions of urbanization processes. At least one uncomfortable question remains to be investigated: *How can this environmental awareness be scaled?*

Some of the clearest repercussions of this type of shift at the core of architectural practices, as we inherited them from the 20th century, can be found in the educational field. We would say that, as a whole, collective architectural practices have consolidated some special lines of pedagogical research in architecture schools, forced today to be sensitive and strategic in the face of the paradigm shifts brought about by digitalization, the real estate crisis, and climate change. These then transfer to the office certain concerns, such as the object not being the only possible result of the processes in which architecture intervenes, horizontality in decision-making processes, cooperativism as an alternative to conventional office organization, the critique of the problem–solution equation, the increasing focus on processes or the ethical implications of architecture as a practice.

Finally, we recognize that the collection of these practices forms a network, a community, and a recursive public that creates, reproduces, and nurtures a way of making an open, inclusive, participatory, and collaborative city, which gradually consolidates and grows. This is made possible thanks to the mediating nature of these collective practices: It is from the ability to speak different languages and enlist various participants that this network of practices becomes recursive and gains agency to change the city and the spatial protocols and practices that govern its renewal.

---

19 »It may be hacking, [but] I'm much more interested in the alternative use of things. And now that we are so involved in the circular economy: We have been moving materials for twenty-two years. Before, we did it because of precariousness. Before, we used materials that were lying around in municipal warehouses, in junkyards, or in construction sites that were thrown away... We started using them because we didn't have a damn thing. Now there is an ecological, energetic, sustainable vision. But twenty-two years ago, I hadn't even heard of sustainability. [...] We did things with the tools we had. And we continue doing them. We have moved more than two million euros in materials. Everything is appraised, listed, and everything.« Santiago Cirugeda. Urban Recipes (Espinosa Pérez/Sánchez-Laulhé 2025: 150)

Funding

The research presented in this paper is part of the Research Project »The good arts of living with others through design (PID2024-158514NB-I00),« funded by MICIU/AEI/10.13039/501100011033/FEDER, EU

References

Awan, Nishat/Schneider, Tatjana/Till, Jeremy (2011): *Spatial Agency: Other Ways of Doing Architecture*, London/New York: Routledge.

Bader, Markus/Kafka, George/Schneider, Tatjana/Talevi, Rosario (2022): *Making Futures*, Leipzig: Spector Books.

Barad, Karen (2007): *Meeting the Universe Halfway: Quantum Physics and the Entanglement of Matter and Meaning*, Durham (NC), London: Duke University Press.

Barad, Karen (2023): Cuestión de materia. *Trans/Materia/Realidades y performatividad queer de la naturaleza*, Barcelona: Holobionte Ediciones.

Braidotti, Rosi (2019): *Posthuman Knowledge*, Cambridge: Polity Press.

Coleman, E. Gabriella (2013): *Coding Freedom: The Ethics and Aesthetics of Hacking*, Princeton, Oxford: Princeton University Press.

Corsín Jiménez, Alberto (2014): »The Right to Infrastructure: A Prototype for Open Source Urbanism,« *Environment and Planning D: Society and Space* 32/2, 342–362. doi: 10.1068/d13077p

Corsín Jiménez, Alberto. (2017): »Auto-Construction Redux: The City as Method,« *Cultural Anthropology* 32/3, 450–478. doi: 10.14506/ca32.3.09

Corsín Jiménez, Alberto/Estalella, Adolfo (2016): »Ecologies in Beta: The City as Infrastructure of Apprenticeships,« in: *Infrastructures and Social Complexity. London:* Routledge, 159–174.

Corsín Jiménez, Alberto/Estalella, Adolfo (2023): *Free Culture and the City*, Ithaca, London: Cornell University Press.

Dattatreyan, Ethiraj Gabriel/Marrero-Guillamón, Isaac (2019): »Introduction: Multimodal Anthropology and the Politics of Invention,« *American Anthropologist* 121/1, 220–228. doi: 10.1111/aman.13183

Donat-Cattin, Natalie (2021): *Collective Processes: Counterpractices in European Architecture*, Boston/Berlin: De Gruyter.

Espinosa Pérez, Enrique (2024): *Learn, Make, and Hack together. Minor Collaborative Practices from Architecture in a Free Spanish Culture 1996-2021*, Alicante: Universidad de Alicante.

Espinosa Pérez, Enrique/Sánchez-Laulhé, José (2025): »Recetas Urbanas (Urban Recipes): Hacking Architectural and Urban Codes,« *Technology|Architecture + Design* 9/1, 142–155. doi: 10.1080/24751448.2025.2475721

Fontdevila, Oriol (2018): *El arte de la mediación*, Bilbao: Consonni.

Galloway, Alexander R./Thacker, Eugene/Wark, McKenzie (2014): *Excommunication. Three Inquiries in Media and Mediation*, Chicago: The University of Chicago Press.

Haraway, Donna J. (2016): *Staying with the Trouble: Making Kin in the Chthulucene*, Durham (NC), London: Duke University Press.

Himanen, Pekka (2001): *The Hacker Ethic And The Spirit Of The Information Age*, New York/Toronto: Random House.

Kelty, Christopher M. (2008): *Two Bits: The Cultural Significance of Free Software*, Durham, London: Duke University Press.

Manning, Erin (2016): *The Minor Gesture*, Durham, London: Duke University Press.

Pascual, Manuel (2025): »La plaza blandengue,« *Arquitectura 389*, 98–103.

Stengers, Isabelle (2005): »Introductory Notes on an Ecology of Practices,« *Cultural Studies Review 11/1*, 183–196. doi: 10.5130/csr. v11i1.3459

Stoner, Jill (2012): *Toward a Minor Architecture*, Cambridge (MA): MIT Press.

Vygotski, Lev S. (1979 [1978]): *El desarrollo de los procesos psicológicos superiores*, Barcelona: Editorial Crítica.

Vygotsky, Lev S. (1962 [1934]): *Thinking and Speech*, Cambridge: MIT Press.

Dimensions of Architectural Knowledge, 2024–08 ⊖
https://doi.org/10.14361/dak-2024-0814

Spatial Activist Research as Embodied Praxis

Esra Can, Maria Alexandrescu, Andrew Belfield, Jakleen Al-Dalal'a, Lara Scharf, Doina Petrescu

Abstract: We propose learning from situated, collective, and reflexive action in response to intersecting and interconnected global crises by asking: »What do embodied knowledge(s) that emerge from activist research bring to spatial practice?« Adopting a feminist and decolonial lens on architectural knowledge production, we outline a shared approach to *embodied praxis*, defined as reflexive embodied knowledge production and action towards emancipatory socio-spatial transformation, that can inform spatial practice in times of polycrisis. Drawing on lived experience at the intersections of architecture, research, and activism, we invite four spatial activist-researchers working across contested sites to reflect on the ways in which embodied praxis can operate as a methodology for architectural knowledge production and spatial practice grounded in care, solidarity, and justice.

Keywords: Embodied Praxis; Embodied Knowledge; Activist Research; Practice-based Research; Reflexivity; Spatial Practice; Polycrisis.

Corresponding authors: Esra Can (School of Architecture and Landscape, University of Sheffield), Maria Alexandrescu (School of Architecture and Landscape, University of Sheffield), Andrew Belfield (School of Architecture and Landscape, University of Sheffield), Jakleen Al-Dalal'a (Department of Geography, University College London), Lara Scharf (School of Architecture and Landscape, University of Sheffield), Doina Petrescu (School of Architecture and Landscape, University of Sheffield); e.can@sheffield.ac.uk; https://orcid.org/0000-0001-5067-2153; malexandrescu1@sheffield.ac.uk; https://orcid.org/0000-0002-6536-4716; andrew.belfield@sheffield.ac.uk; https://orcid.org/0000-0003-4617-2142; j.al-dalal'a@ucl.ac.uk; https://orcid.org/0009-0003-3638-7219; lascharf1@sheffield.ac.uk; https://orcid.org/0009-0000-8545-8536; d.petrescu@sheffield.ac.uk; https://orcid.org/0000-0002-3794-3219 ⊖ Open Access.

Introduction

Policymakers are increasingly invoking the concept of »polycrisis,« to describe how interconnected global risks converge and amplify one another, producing effects greater than the sum of their individual impacts (Tooze 2022; Jayasuriya 2023). While these overlapping crises – climate breakdown, political instability, economic inequality, and housing insecurity – are global in scope, they are experienced unevenly across geographies (Ruwanpura et al. 2025). In urban and architectural contexts, the disruptions caused by polycrisis manifest through settler colonialism, displacement, land financialization, and extractivism, leading to environmental degradation, segregation, gentrification, housing precarity, and even urbicide (Fawaz et al. 2012). The destructive reach of polycrisis is not only material but also epistemic, as local knowledge systems that enable us to thrive together are often erased. Where compounding socio-ecological urgencies reflect a world which needs to change, how we produce architectural knowledge must also shift towards cultivating alternative, situated knowledges that are grounded in context and oriented toward justice. This calls for (re)new(ed) approaches to both research and practice that recognize that the ontologies and methodologies seeking knowledge production for socio-spatial justice cannot be neutral or apolitical.

Building on the work of architectural practices that have sought to use the skills and spatial intelligence of spatial agency (c.f. Awan et al. 2011), we argue that knowledge production in architecture must respond critically to the unequal dynamics shaping how spaces and knowledges are made. This means confronting the asymmetries not only of spatial production but also of who gets to know, speak, and design.

We understand polycrisis as a structural condition and adopt a feminist and decolonial lens that accounts for the asymmetries it upholds. In this context, architecture must move beyond esthetics to engage with resilience, justice, and collective survival. Traditional, top-down models give way to participatory, activist, and decolonial practices that center those most impacted. As disciplinary boundaries blur, new forms of knowledge emerge, positioning architecture as a vital site for imagining and enacting more just and livable futures. For this, we turn to embodied praxis, which we define as a mode of reflexive, **embodied knowledge** and action rooted in lived experience and collective struggle, capable of responding to polycrisis by generating emancipatory socio-spatial change. These insights emerge through ongoing dialogue among researchers and communities committed to co-producing knowledge by centering agency, resilience, and resistance.

Background and Methodology

This paper emerged from a collective recognition among activist researchers of the urgent need to articulate a shared position on the value of activist research in architecture.[1] To examine how activist, participatory, and practice-based research can reframe architectural knowledge production as a transformative, collective endeavor, we ask: *What do embodied knowledge(s) that emerge from activist research bring to spatial practice?* With this question, we explore embodied knowledge production not only as a mode of theorization and practice, but also as a vital site for building solidarities of survival in the face of ongoing crises.

Part 1 of this paper frames embodied praxis by identifying the situated and embodied character of knowledge production in struggles for socio-spatial justice. In Part 2, we present four reflections based on the co-authors' research, which examine the ways activist and/or practice-based research was informed by, and gained strength from hands-on experiences in four different contexts of crises. Rather than being comparative, they are supported by prompts for co-writing a collective discussion focusing on how embodied praxis as a methodology can inform spatial practice in the future, presented in Part 3.

---

1 This paper builds on insights developed during the »Situating Engaged/Practice-based Research as Activism(s)« workshop, organized by the Lines of Flight (LoF) Research Group at the School of Architecture & Landscape, University of Sheffield, in February 2024. The workshop brought together early career researchers and activist scholars to reframe research through the lens of activism, in conversation with the school's long-standing commitment to social justice. The workshop was chaired by Esra Can and Andrew Belfield, and included research presentations from Esra Can, Thomas Moore, Alex Axinte, Ana Mendes de Andes Aldama, Andrew Belfield, Jakleen Al Dalal'a, Maria Alexandrescu, and Lara Scharf, with responding statements from Gabu Heindl, Doina Petrescu, and Emre Akbil. The documentation of the event can be found at [https://linesofflight.wordpress.com], accessed October 4, 2025.

Part 1: Theoretical Orientation: Embodied Praxis in Relation to Spatial Activist Research and Embodied Knowledge

Our collective orientation links embodied knowledge and activist research to articulate *embodied praxis* as a form of spatial practice. We claim a feminist and decolonial lens in approaching architectural knowledge production, recognizing its reciprocal relationship with the ways we live, shape and inhabit spaces, neighborhoods, cities, and territories. From this reciprocal relationship, embodied praxis emerges as a reflexive approach and situated (Haraway 1988) form of knowing and doing that is deeply embedded and entangled in specific contexts. It builds on Feminist spatial practices' understanding of the body as a site of embodied knowledge for »practicing otherwise« (Petrescu 2007; Schalk et al. 2017). Embodied praxis disrupts the academic location of knowledge production by prioritizing the multiplicity of perspectives and knowledges, particularly from the marginalized and minoritized communities, which emerge from collective struggles. By centering embodied knowledge produced through the lived experience of the activist researcher, engaged spatial practitioner, and/or active inhabitant, spatial practice can become more attuned to respond to crises through ways grounded in care, solidarity, and justice.

The situated and reciprocal relationship between spatial production and knowledge production supports thinking beyond the often extractive and exploitative conditions of normative architectural knowledge production. This shifts the sites of knowledge production toward lived and intersectional experiences, revealing the disproportionate effects of crisis on marginalized subjects (Harding 1991) and communities around the world, especially, but not only, in the Global South. While these communities are directly impacted by the ongoing economic dependencies, resource exploitation, and environmental breakdown, they are often the ones that continue to do the care work for local ecologies and vulnerable subjects. This embodied care work for »living together as well as possible« is also where they ground their capacity to resist, offering a critical opening for activist research and spatial practice to learn from (Tronto/Fisher 1990: 41). This emphasis on embodied work and situated knowledge to think within, against, and beyond crisis is inherently political. Scholars have shown that, in the context of polycrisis, architecture's most radical potential lies in creating both material and epistemic spaces, where marginalized communities can assert knowledge, agency and alternative futures (Awan et al. 2011; Escobar 2018; Miraftab 2022). These interconnected spaces of action and knowledge have been seen in contexts such as Karachi, where tools of spatial knowledge production such as mapping and documenting could align with and activate community knowledges in shaping infrastructures (Hasan 1999), or in the form of »autonomous territorial plans« that embody the territorial knowledges of Indigenous and Afro-descended peoples in Latin America, incorporating local values and ecological management beyond political boundaries (Escobar 2018).

Articulation of knowledge is more than a cognitive process; Latour describes it as always being an embodied practice which requires engagement with the genealogy of the conditions and instruments that frame such reporting (Latour 2004). More recently, the »embodied turn in social sciences« (Thanem/Knight 2019), has argued that all research is embodied, and »asks for reflexivity, an exploration, attention to and non-judgmental awareness of self in addition to attention, exploration and non-judgmental awareness of others' experiences« (Leigh/Brown 2021: 2). Yet, for activist, participatory, and practiced-based research the assumption of a neutral, non-judgmental observer, detached from the context they find themselves in, falls short. Feminist thought (c.f. Harding 1991; Grosz 1994; Braidotti 1994) has long emphasized the role of embodied, lived experience that is necessarily differentiated across intersectional political, social, and historical dimensions as the basis of any knowledge.

Dominant architectural and urban research and practices, and their »neutral methods,« often reinforce the very systems of capitalism, colonialism and patriarchy and reproduce the same unjust power relations which underlie crisis, further embedding these structures into the everyday lives of marginalized communities, often in violent ways (Patrick 2017: 747). In response, Shafique (Shafique 2025) calls for »dirty research,« bridging the gap between theory and action by emphasizing *reciprocity* for genuine parity in research that attends to the socio-spatial dynamics shaping the »ground« and leads towards meaningful research co-inquiry. We suggest that spatial practices would benefit from a generative relationship between knowing (embodied, situated and critical) and doing (practice, intervention and organizing). This echoes the pedagogical praxis based on action and reflection that Paul Freire developed in *Pedagogy of the Oppressed* (Freire 1970). He suggested that knowledge emerges through dialogue, critical reflection and action, together posing an empowering liberatory process, which informs our position that knowledge emerging from embodied action can be transformative for architecture as a discipline and practice, and can empower the communities and contexts in which it unfolds.

Embodied praxis aims for a socio-spatial change within everyday lived experiences. By making structural inequalities visible in the processes of spatial production, it expands our capacities for sensing and understanding diverse forms of agency. The lived experiences merge the researcher and »researched« positions in a shared confrontation of diverse forms of (in) justice, creating emancipatory openings for both. From decolonial and feminist perspectives, we approach these openings revealed through embodied praxis as incubators of collective subjectification (Petrescu 2005), from which to develop new epistemologies and emancipatory practices that are in constant dialogue with the context in which they emerge. We explore this in the next section through four reflections from different activist research and spatial practices in contexts with distinct contestations.

Part 2: Embodied Praxis Reflections

makāna: resisting and rebuilding amid constraining contexts in Amman, Jordan. | Jakleen Al-Dalal'a

In 2021, *makāna* was established as an interstitial movement based in Amman, emerging from a belief in the power of grassroots agency. Co-founded by two researcher-activists together with two architects and two urbanists. It was born from the ethos of a decolonial, Southern and feminist doctoral research, tackling the critical question of how alternative ways of participation can be practiced within constraining contexts, rather than remaining on the fringes as a critique of dominant paradigms of city-making. This research emphasized doing as a means to imagine alternatives, aligning with Peter North's call to develop our power to create the world we want to see« (North 2014: 1058). Embodied knowledge emerged through direct collaboration with local grassroots actors and participation including community gardeners, youth groups, and neighborhood organizers in their conversations and struggles.

The learning generated throughout these collaborations informed action, establishing a politicized, care-based accountability toward public participation practices. Inspired by Southern scholars (cf. Miraftab 2022; Ortiz 2022), we co-created spaces of solidarity in diverse venues, including community centers, community gardens, public parks, and informal public settings across Amman. Bringing together those who are usually at the margins of the research process, such as women-led collectives, stateless groups, and youth networks operating without formal organizational status. This work became especially urgent in the context of Jordan's restrictive civic space, where laws regulating public gatherings, foreign funding, and association registration often curtail political expression and limit the operation of independent civil society actors. In response, we adopted a relational approach grounded in care to build translocal alliances by collaborating with regional networks of urban practitioners, solidarity economies, and other grassroots collectives beyond Amman. This approach allowed different conversations, dialogues, and practices to flourish and facilitated new networks resisting the co-optation of care into the patriarchal-racial-capitalist accumulation agenda. Following Miraftab (2022), by challenging restrictive systems such as forced evictions, urban displacement, and privatization of public space. These alliances included collaborations with grassroots organizations, such as Yalla Nel'ab and CLUSTER from Cairo, and local practitioners like architects, planners, and community organizers from ARINI and MMAG, co-hosting monthly public workshops and events in community centers, informal spaces, and university venues between 2021 and 2024. Across these gatherings, we collectively mapped neighborhood struggles, shared lived experiences of exclusion, and co-designed participatory actions addressing community priorities in East Amman, particularly in Hashemi and Jabal Al Natheef. Some of these initiatives continue through community steward-ship and are documented on makāna's public channels.

Through these practices, *makāna* promoted advocacy, forged connec-tions, expressed solidarity, supported local initiatives, and worked toward progressive social change. Translating solidarity into tangible actions by collaboratively producing contextually relevant knowledge with and for grassroots struggles. This took shape through diverse formats aimed at the public: facilitating workshops, hosting open discussions, leading collabora-tive mapping sessions, and curating exhibitions, both in community spaces and online platforms such as websites and social media (see makāna 2022: Instagram and LinkedIn @makana.jor) (fig. 1).

Positioned at the intersection of activism and research for just urban places, *makāna* became a living platform engaging with issues of social and spatial justice, self-organization, experimentation and imagination in advo-cating for participatory urban practices in Jordan. *makāna* created spaces

1.
Workshops with grassroots organizations and local communities at makāna.
Photograph by Jakleen Al-Dalal'a, 2022.

for dialogue and alternative social infrastructures that challenge top-down, formalized modes of city-making. Offering a vision of urban development rooted in solidarity, empowerment, and the right to the city. This case articulates embodied architectural knowledge production as integral to participative activist spatial practice, in response to the structural crises shaping Amman's urban space.

Civic Co-learning as Activist Research in Poplar, East London, UK | Andrew Belfield

»Climate Companions« (CC) was a two-year participatory research project exploring the transformative potential of design-driven civic pedagogies in nurturing agency toward more resilient urban futures. It was nested within an existing R-Urban hub (Petcou/Petrescu 2015) supporting its members (4 non-profit associations and 10 resident food growers) to open up to new networks and citizens. This co-inquiry responds to our unfolding ecological and climate crisis, grounding its urgency within learners' everyday experiences of the city, as a form of consciousness building through civic learning. Civic Pedagogies are situated and embodied practices, utilizing the neighborhood as the site of knowledge production and exploration, with the aim to catalyze local action and agency (Antaki/Belfield/Moore 2024). The process was iterative, working with a citizen co-design group of 10 local residents, alongside another 20 civic associations, non-profits, artists, and educators, to develop and trial two »festivals of learning.« The first was in September 2022, before collectively reflecting and co-designing a second, which responded more directly to local needs in June/July 2023.

The research became the site of activism, setting up a process with the intent of »nurturing agency and capabilities for action« within participants. Situated and embodied knowledges were co-created through the collective inquiry. Rather than creating binaries of »researcher« and »participant,« the term co-learners was adopted, as recognition of the diverse community of practice (Wenger 1999) assembled to learn together without an ingrained hierarchy. Co-learning became a collective practice and research method, embedded within a place and learning through the body. The pedagogies trialed were situated and embodied; learning was primarily through action (by doing), from place (via urban exploration) and through togetherness (by building social relations and networks) (fig. 2). This process supported the valorisation of situated knowledges; rooted in experience and embraced its

2.
Learning through togetherness – Companions Digest, discursive dinner and celebration of the Climate Companions 2022 program. Photograph by Andrew Belfield, 2022.

»partial« positioning by sharing subjectivities within the group. By learning through the body, the collective made sense of our surrounding lived world, how everyday life at the scale of the neighborhood interfaced with our contemporary crises, and through small actions, committed to their transformation.

Climate Companions recognizes the innate activism of emancipatory learning, by making »change« in different capacities. This materializes through »small acts« of hope, by altering individual habits, learning new skills, or by expanding networks and alliances of grassroots groups who steward the hub. By diversifying these voices and the alliances that govern the hub, you ensure local needs and urgencies are foregrounded throughout the process. Agency was nurtured individually, by raising consciousness and is realized as »achievement« by sharing knowledge between co-learners (Biesta/Tedder 2007). In parallel, civic agency is formed through the collective capacity of R-Urban as a space where climate action is taken. Architectural research and knowledge can respond to our climate crisis by instrumentalizing the collective; by initiating processes of co-learning with the intent of generating new capabilities for citizen action in the neighborhood. By centering situated and embodied learning practices, researchers may act as allies for communities seeking change and nurturing capabilities which were previously obscured and raising collective consciousness.

In this case, »embodied praxis« was the shared method of learning and unlearning toward equitable futures in the neighborhood in which the participants live and work. The »doing« of this praxis produces new knowledge for spatial practices by stepping back, relinquishing researcher control and engaging as a co-learner with others. This »dirty« research process (Shafique 2025) builds reciprocity by blurring the roles and identities of researchers and citizens, helping to alter subjectivities toward neighborhood spatial transformations.

Activating Embodied Knowledges for Emancipatory Territorial Practice in Famagusta, Cyprus | Esra Can

The crisis that gave rise to grassroots urban activism in Famagusta was multi-layered. This divided city is shaped by the consequences of the post-conflict condition in Cyprus, which became the pretext of segregation, militarization, and territorial partition rooted in colonialism. The resulting status quo led to an urban development shaped by the financialization of city-making (Can

3.
Participating in a bicommunal gathering of Famagustians across the Cypriot division within the fenced-off district of Varosha. Photograph by Esra Can, 2023.

2023), where the absence of participatory and transparent decision-making processes has exacerbated everyday challenges. This institutional neglect, or structural uncaring, has facilitated the expansion of development and enclosures, risking the integrity of Famagusta's urban eco-culture.

Conducting spatial activist research in this context necessitated embracing a plurality of interwoven roles: a spatial practitioner, an urban activist and a researcher, each role continuously blurring into the next. This fluidity enabled reconfiguration of relationships through the generative cross-contamination of skills, methods and knowledges. Embodying the city's everyday urban controversies as an architect and as a Turkish Cypriot raised in a neighborhood shaped by infrastructures of division meant that the research agenda had extended much beyond knowledge production toward urban action. A multilayered researcher subjectivity emerging from these interwoven roles enabled the city, its ecologies, and spatial thinking to be positioned as active agents within the research. I collaborated with architects and urbanists across the territorial divide, fostering collective imaginaries of a shared urban future and resisting the dominant narratives of territorial separation (see *Hands-on Famagusta*[2]). Being a member of an urban activist network[3] contributed to shaping collective care and solidarity grounded in counter-militarist, counter-developmentalist, environmentalist, and decolonial advocacy, foregrounding eco-cultural sites as connective elements of coexistence (fig. 3). Through a reflexive research praxis, these entangled roles coalesced into an interdependent ecosystem of knowledge production.

With these interdependent roles, a plurality of knowledges and agencies were shaped through interactions and collective experiences. Petrescu suggests that revealing micro-agencies of participants compose a shared and collective agency towards enacting change (Petrescu 2005). Central to the transformative dimension was becoming the initiator of new connections, initially by building transversal networks of solidarity, and then for the spatial actions which extended beyond human participants. The »reconstituted relationships and existential dimensions of people,« as Lopes De Souza also observed in the autonomous spatial praxis of Latin American social movements (2016: 1298), gave way to new networks of interspecies care

---

2 Hands-on Famagusta project promotes a unified urban future for Famagusta, opening up the reconstruction process as a means for collective peacebuilding.

3 Famagusta Initiative urban activist network is a grassroots group advocating for local ecologies and peacebuilding in Famagusta.

4.
Building collective counternarratives by inventorization of trees, with aici a fost o pădure/aici ar putea fi o pădure. Photograph by Maria Alexandrescu, 2023.

and solidarity with expert citizens. On the ground, this new, situated, and transformative mode of spatial action challenged not only the financialized development but also the conventional understandings of what architecture and urbanism can do.

Two key premises emerged from the embodied praxis developed within this contested context. First, architecture was extended as an embodied territorial practice, where territory is not a fixed ground but a »transversal process« (Tan 2020) shaped by human and more-than-human entanglements beyond infrastructures of division. Defying the imposed borders and enclosures by thinking and doing architecture with care materialized as the recognition of interdependence between bodies, ecologies and territories, which opened up its space to a variety of actors and positions. Second, activating embodied knowledge fostered generative spaces and alliances across urban activists, expert citizens, ecologists, and spatial practitioners that fundamentally shifted how the crisis condition was approached. Together, they account for a more embedded role for spatial praxis, in actively navigating the crises by responding not only to how it is lived but also to the ways it is collectively resisted.

Maidan Research, Park Activism in Bucharest, Romania | Maria Alexandrescu

This research inquiry begins with the Romanian maidan, a situated social-ecological landscape whose meaning shifted from referring to an open space to something akin to a wasteland. The issues faced by Bucharest's maidans spaces reveal multiple crises intertwining local and planetary scales: the financialization of housing and land, (green) gentrification, and struggles for the rights to urban nature, to life in the city in a postsocialist context.

During the fieldwork, I came across a call from *aici a fost o pădure / aici ar putea fi o pădure*, a grassroots citizens' movement fighting for one of Bucharest's many contested parks, Parcul IOR. The privatization of 12 ha of this park meant that what once was a park became *maidanized*, becoming a feral landscape (Alexandrescu/David 2024). Since 2022, this area has increasingly been the target of tree poisoning, arson, and illegal tree felling, presumably to circumvent existing legislation protecting green space in order to eventually build on it. Neighbors of the park have been mobilizing for its protection and recuperation for over 10 years. Responding to this urgency, I joined this struggle, shifting my position from that of a situated observer (Haraway 1988) to one taking part in what Solomon and Kaika describe as »skin-in-the-game« methods, referring to the »sustained practices of intense physical and emotional labor« (Solomon/Kaika 2024: 1505). Such methods challenge the expectations of the time, labor, and boundaries of research, but produce embodied knowledge that is able to respond to the crisis at hand. Understanding how crisis, as a structural condition, affects all aspects of urban nature, city life, and how it might be tackled across multiple scales toward a more just city.

Working in solidarity with the activist group for two months, the fall of 2023 was spent organizing around its defense, mapping its remaining vegetation, and discussing what its future could be. (fig. 4) The body – both individual and collective – was a key site of knowledge production, whether in the memories of those who have passed through this park every day and continue to do so; in the bodies of the volunteers who inventoried the trees, embracing each one in measuring it; or in our shared coming together on the park site. The embodied knowledge resulting from these forms of engagement challenged official and developer narratives about the park and empowered and mobilized the park's neighbors by valorizing their knowledge and lived experience. The activist's sustained presence around the site became a way of caring for this landscape, mobilizing more-than-human latent commons (Tsing 2015) to prefigure shared visions for its future. This opened possibilities for collectively reimagining this landscape's future beyond preexisting urban forms such as parks or nature reserves (aici a fost o pădure / aici ar putea fi o pădure 2024). While these are yet to be negotiated and enacted, the experience shows how collective embodied knowledges can provide a different grounding for rethinking urban nature that can challenge existing city-making processes and mobilize around alternative visions driven by citizens.

Part 3: Discussion: Reconfiguring Scale, Tending Collective Reflexivity, Infrastructuring Embodied Praxis

Across these four reflections, embodied praxis emerges as a means of engaging with the deeply political dimensions of crisis as they manifest within distinct context-specific ways. This shifted our understanding of what constitutes social and spatial justice activism combining situated knowledge and practice. The modes of engagement varied, ranging from building grassroots alliances and shaping climate and spatial justice advocacy movements (*makāna*, Climate Companions, Famagusta's urban activism, *maidan*), forming community-led neighborhood hubs (Climate Companions), establishing partnerships with local spatial practices (*makāna*), and supporting initiatives for alternative forms of urban governance and decision making (Famagusta's urban activism).

These *diverse modes of engagement* are grounded in the researchers' own embodied ambivalences, necessitating ongoing negotiation of positionality on when to witness, participate, facilitate or lead within socio-spatial activism. Such embodied praxis contributes to a reimagining of spatial practice: one that privileges cultivation of relations, building alliances, and enacting solidarities over physical interventions. In this section, we trace this shift by reconfiguring scale, tending to collective reflexivity and infrastructuring embodied praxis as a mode of transformative engagement.

Embodied praxis generates relational spaces embedded within and shaped by the specific contexts they operate in, where social, political and spatial dimensions are negotiated through lived, situated action. A key element of this negotiation is articulating links between *scales*, whether scales of urgency, scales of action, or scales of agency. These scales are often necessarily determined but not limited by how the crisis as a structural condition is experienced within different contexts. For example, the operation of *makāna* was initially a form of micro-agency, scaling up to respond to urgencies of capitalist paradigms of urban production. Similarly, the scale of urgency often influences the scale of action. Climate Companions sought to link the planetary scales of the ecological and climate crises with the everyday scales of the neighborhood. Similarly, living in a divided city such as Famagusta has a very palpable impact on the everyday life of people, experienced in part through the intentional uncaring resulting from the financialization of city-making, but also in the urgency to contest this condition. Situated encounters of polycrisis that embodied praxis account for, forges diverse solidarities across scales and sites, allowing for a spatial practice which challenges the abstract, nested scalar configurations of (colonial) power (Tsing 2012) and actively works to reconfigure their constraints. As spatial practitioners, we bring this ability to think in multi-scalar terms to other communities, as much as we learn from multiple sites to work together for a wider socio-spatial justice.

If embodied praxis is to work relationally between scales, the relations must be built and maintained through embodying pluralities, both as individuals and as part of collectives. Such praxis follows a *feminist ethics of care and reciprocity* (Tronto/Fisher 1990) and works to build alliances from and with the margins and allows for the emergence of *collective subjectification* (Petrescu 2005). In the case of Climate Companions, the researcher and participants shifted their roles to becoming co-learners, »learning to act« by/ through »doing« to collectively realize alternative modes of civic pedagogy. In the case of *maidan*, the collective embodied knowledge developed through sustained practices of intense physical and emotional labor as a way to challenge institutional claims to knowledge and mobilize solidarities. For *makāna* and urban activism in Famagusta, the frame of the research extends beyond knowledge production to serve as a catalyst for building solidarities, and alliances. Embodied praxis in the context of activist research can be thought of as a mode of *knowledge co-production* (Perry 2022) oriented to transformative change, one that requires a negotiation of the boundaries of knowledge production and enclosure within and beyond different systems of knowing and doing, their institutions, and power structures. A care-full shift in spatial practice toward modes of embodied praxis relies on these moments of negotiation for *tending collective reflexivity*. These practices are needed to navigate power relations and resist knowledge extractivism, instead by empowering and building capacity for action through grounded research.

Embodied praxis can be a form of *generative*, feminist, decolonial spatial practice that produces relational spaces of collective reflection and action, such as in the case of *makāna* and Famagusta's urban activism. These spaces might be thought of as *infrastructures for future resistance* (Shantz 2009) operating beyond the conventional forms of activism such as contesting, negotiating and protesting. In the case of makāna, this infrastructure exists through creating spaces not only for collaborative reflection but also as infrastructural space for caring practices, including healing, maintaining, recovering, and making peace. In Famagusta, architectural infrastructures become the medium to build care and solidarity in the collective imagining of new ways of moving and acting. Such infrastructural spaces operate on multiple temporal scales and are able to generate multiple forms of solidarity in a given context. By centering the care and maintenance of infrastructural place, embodied praxis enables engaged spatial practices to nurture collective reflection, build solidarities, and grow capacity for action amid conditions of polycrisis.

Conclusion

In this paper, we put forth *embodied praxis* as an approach to architectural knowledge production that attends to the specificities of place, body and experience, challenging us to think of architecture and urbanism not merely as technical professions, but as practices capable of cultivating spaces of care, solidarity, and justice. Embodied knowledge emerges in the back and forth of doing and reflecting – reworking spatial practice through more equitable methods, shared responsibilities, and orientation toward supporting collective and shared agencies. Building a reflective praxis through situated and embodied architectural research invites us to, in Haraway's terms, »stay with the trouble,« forming unanticipated coalitions for »making oddkin« as »we require each other in unexpected collaborations and combinations« (Haraway 2015: 4). Embodied praxis thus becomes a transformative mode of engagement, grounded in the lived experience of structural conditions and capable of enabling socio-spatial change. Learning from spatial contestations and relational ecologies, we suggest a feminist, decolonial, and Southern agenda for spatial practice (Vasudevan/Novoa 2022), shifting the role of the architect/urbanist from the isolated/outsider position to engaged participants in generative collectivities.

This study suggests that reconfiguring scale, tending to collective reflexivity and infrastructuring embodied praxis could transform spatial practice towards not only being responsive but generative. Embodied praxis is transformative across individual, collective, and planetary scales, reconfiguring how and where spatial interventions take place. By centering lived experience as a site of counter-knowledge and collective world-making, embodied praxis contests dominant narratives and mobilizes a coalition of engaged citizens and spatial intelligence toward collective futures. The knowledge produced through embodied praxis does not simply address crisis but actively prefigures more just and caring spatial futures through spatial action.

The diversity of reflections presented in this paper highlights the potential of collective subjectification emerging from embodied praxis. One which incorporates multiple histories, experiences and imaginations in the making of more just and equitable urban futures and is the basis for an emancipatory spatial practice. The spatial production through embodied praxis differs from normative approaches in generating different configurations in response to structural crisis, whether through emergent collectivities, situated epistemologies, or new ways of working together. Future spatial practice can learn from these relational spatial configurations by further expanding the understanding of the material and immaterial relations which sustain them, so it may better address, resist, and ultimately prefigure transformative futures beyond the conditions of crisis.

References

aici a fost o pădure / aici ar putea fi o pădure (2024): »*TITANII NU DORM. Ziarul celor 12 ha retrocedate din parcul IOR*,« aici a fost o pădure / aici ar putea fi o pădure. https://aiciarputeafiopadure.org/titanii-nu-dorm-ziar/, accessed July 10, 2025.

Alexandrescu, Maria/David, Andreea (2024): »*RO_ Urban Feral Landscapes_ Maidan*,« MADE IN Knowledge Atlas. https://madein-platform.com/knowledge-atlas/urban-feral-landscapes/, accessed October 1, 2024.

Antaki, Nicola/Belfield, Andrew/Moore, Thomas (2024): »Radical Urban Classrooms: Civic Pedagogies and Spaces of Learning on the Margins of Institutions,« *Antipode 56/5*, 1509–1534. doi: 10.1111/ anti.13039

Awan, Nishat/Schneider, Tatjana/Till, Jeremy (2011): *Spatial agency: Other Ways of Doing Architecture*, London: Routledge.

Biesta, Gert/Tedder, Michael (2016): »Agency and learning in the lifecourse: Towards an ecological perspective,« *Studies in the Education of Adults 39/02*, 132–149. doi: 10.1080/02660830.2007.11661545

Braidotti, Rosi (1994): *Nomadic Subjects: Embodiment and Sexual Difference in Contemporary Feminist Theory*, Cambridge: Cambridge University Press.

Can, Esra (2023): *Instituting Hayat: Disruptive Care and Stasis Urbanism in Famagusta*, Doctoral dissertation, Sheffield: University of Sheffield.

Escobar, Arturo (2018): *Designs for the Pluriverse: Radical Interdependence, Autonomy, and the Making of Worlds*. Durham (NC): Duke University Press.

Fawaz, Mona/Harb, Mona/Gharbieh, Ahmad (2012): »Living Beirut's Security Zones: An Investigation of the Modalities and Practice of Urban Security,« *City & Society 24/2*, 173–195. doi: 10.1111/j.1548-744X.2012.01074.x

Freire, Paulo (1970): *Pedagogia do Oprimido.– English translation: Pedagogy of the Oppressed*, transl. From the second edition by Myra Bergman Ramos, Harmondsworth, England: Penguin, 2017.

Grosz, Elizabeth (1994): *Volatile Bodies: Towards a Corporeal Feminism*, Bloomington: Indiana University Press.

Hasan, Arif (1999): *Understanding Karachi: Planning and Reform for the Future*, Karachi: City Press.

Haraway, Donna J. (1988): »Situated Knowledges: The Science Question in Feminism and the Privilege of Partial Perspective,« *Feminist Studies 14/3*, 575-599. doi: 10.2307/3178066

Haraway, Donna J. (2015): *Staying with the Trouble: Making Kin in the Chthulucene*, Durham: Duke University Press.

Harding, Sandra G (1991): *Whose Science? Whose Knowledge? : Thinking from Women's Lives*, Ithaca: Cornell University Press.

Jayasuriya, Kanishka (2023): »Polycrisis or crises of capitalist social reproduction,« in: *Global Social Sciences Journal 2/2*, 203-211.

Latour, Bruno (2004): »How to Talk About the Body? The Normative Dimension of Science Studies,« *Body & Society 10/2–3*, 205–229. doi: 10.1177/1357034X04042943

Leigh, Jennifer/Brown, Nicole (2021): *Embodied Inquiry*, London: Bloomsbury Publishing.

Lopes de Souza, Marcelo (2016): »Lessons from Praxis: Autonomy and Spatiality in Contemporary Latin American Social Movements,« *Antipode 48/5*, 1292-1316 doi: 10.1111/anti.12210

Miraftab, Faranak (2022): »Southern Theories Centre on Practices and Experiences of Subordinate Groups Wherever They Are,« in: Oren Yiftachel/Nisa Mammon (eds.), *TheoriSE: Debating the Southeastern Turn in Urban Theories*, Cape Town: African Centre for Cities, 102–108.

North, Peter (2014): »Book Review Symposium: JK Gibson-Graham, Jenny Cameron and Stephen Healy, Take Back the Economy: An Ethical Guide for Transforming Our Communities,« *Sociology 48/5*, 1057–1059. doi: 10.1177/0038038514544487

Ortiz, Catalina (2022): »Cardinal Insubordination,« Oren Yiftachel/Nisa Mammon (eds.), in: *TheoriSE: Debating the Southeastern Turn in Urban Theories*, Cape Town: African Centre for Cities, 72–77.

Patrick, Lyana (2017): »Indigenist Planning,« *Planning Theory & Practice 18/4*, 647–650.

Perry, Beth (2022): »Co-Production as Praxis: Critique and Engagement from within the University,« *Methodological Innovations 15/3*, 341–352. doi: 10.1177/20597991221129773

Petcou, Constantin/Petrescu, Doina (2015): »*R-URBAN or how to co-produce a resilient city,*« ephemera theory & politics in organization 15/1: 249–262.

Petrescu, Doina (2005): » Losing Control, Keeping Desire,« in: Peter Blundell Jones/Doina Petrescu/Jeremy Till (eds.), in: *Architecture and Participation*, London, New York: Spon Press: 42–70.

Petrescu, Doina (ed.) (2007): *Altering Practices: Feminist Politics and Poetics of Space*, London/New York/Abingdon: Routledge.

Ruwanpura, Kanchana N/Cederlöf, Gustav/Ramasar, Vasna (2025): »Decolonising Polycrisis: Southern Perspectives on Interlocking Crises,« *Environment and Planning A: Economy and Space*. doi: 10.1177/0308518X251345308

Schalk, Meike/Kristiansson, Thérèse/Mazé, Ramia, eds. (2017): *Feminist Futures of Spatial Practice: Materialism, Activism, Dialogues, Pedagogies, Projections*, Baunach: AADR, an imprint of Spurbuchverlag.

Shafique, Tanzil (2025): »Dirty research: a call towards decolonial urban knowledge production,« *City 1—14*. doi: 10.1080/13604813.2024.2447687

Shantz, Jeffrey (2009): »Re-Building Infrastructures of Resistance,« *Socialism and Democracy 23/2*, 102–109. doi: 10.1080/08854300902904949

Solomon, Debra/Kaika, Maria (2024): »Methodological Rift: Applying Infrastructure Activism's ›Skin in the Game‹ Embodied Art Research Methods to Urban Green Infrastructure Planning,« *Environment and Planning E: Nature and Space 7/4*, 1504–1525. doi: 10.1177/25148486241256622

Tan, Pelin (2020): »Surpassing Disaster: Territories, Entanglements and Methods,« in: Armina Pilav/Mark G. H. Schoonderbeek/Heidi Sohn/et al. (eds.), *Mediating the Spatiality of Conflicts: International Conference Proceedings*, Delhi: BK Books: 45–58.

Thanem, Torkild/Knights, David (2019): *Embodied Research Methods*, London: SAGE Publications, Ltd.

Tooze, Adam (2022): »Welcome to the World of the Polycrisis,« *Financial Times*, October 28, 2022, https://www.ft.com/content/498398e7-11b1-494b-9cd3-6d669dc3de33, accessed July 10, 2025.

Tronto, Joan C./Fisher, B. (1990): »Toward a Feminist Theory of Caring,« in: Emily K. Abel/Margaret K. Nelson (eds.), *Circles of Care*, New York: SUNY Press.

Tsing, Anna Lowenhaupt (2012): »On Nonscalability,« *Common Knowledge* 18/3, 505–524. doi: 10.1215/0961754X-1630424

Tsing, Anna Lowenhaupt (2015): *The Mushroom at the End of the World: On the Possibility of Life in Capitalist Ruins*, Princeton: University Press.

Vasudevan, Raksha/Novoa E., Magdalena (2022): »Pluriversal Planning Scholarship: Embracing Multiplicity and Situated Knowledges in Community-Based Approaches,« *Planning Theory* 21/1, 77–100. doi: 10.1177/14730952211000384

Wenger, Etienne (1999): *Communities of Practice: Learning, Meaning, and Identity*, Cambridge: Cambridge University Press.

Dimensions of Architectural Knowledge, 2024-08 ⊖
https://doi.org/10.14361/dak-2024-0815

Repair as Practice: Expanding Architectural Approaches to Climate Justice in Southern Africa

Jhono Bennett

Abstract: The built environment contributes over 40% of global carbon emissions. Yet, architectural knowledge and practice remain shaped by Western, extractive, and technocratic paradigms that fuelled this crisis and still conceal their colonial entanglements while perpetuating systemic inequality. Towards which, this paper advances the concept of *reparative urbanism* as a spatial design approach that centers justice, care, and relational practice in the face of the growing climate crisis. Drawing on my position as a South African practitioner-scholar and two case studies – Liz Ogbu's healing-centered design practice in the United States and 1to1 – Agency of Engagement's grassroots work in Johannesburg – I explore how a reparative approach offers a means to operate as both material and relational practice.

Rather than an endpoint, repair is presented as a sustained architectural process: creative, imperfect, and politically engaged. It speaks to everyday acts of maintenance in informal settlements, long-term community partnerships in contexts of spatial injustice, and design processes that acknowledge systemic harm while cultivating futures of dignity and belonging. Through a concise analysis of two practices, the paper explores how repair has the potential to disrupts cycle of disposability embedded in mainstream planning and instead enables adaptive infrastructures, multi-authorship, and collective governance.

The paper proposes five interconnected practice principles for reparative design: acknowledging histories of spatial harm; co-authoring knowledge through long-term partnerships; embedding care and deliberation in design; activating local infrastructures through community-led planning; and sustaining networks of solidarity across geographies. In doing so, it argues that architecture and urbanism must move beyond sustainability metrics to embrace repair as climate justice – redefining architectural agency not by what it produces, but by how it sustains the relationships, systems, and communities it touches.

Keywords: Repair; Climate Justice; Southern Africa; Spatial Practice; Reparative Urbanisms.

Corresponding author: Jhono Bennett (University of Cape Town); jhono.bennett@ucl.ac.uk; https://orcid.org/0000-0002-3901-7040 ⊖

Introduction

Since 1751, the effective beginning of the industrial revolution, the world has emitted over 1.5 trillion tonnes of CO_2, with nearly half of these emissions originating from the United States and the European Union (Institute for European Environmental Policy, 2020). The built environment sector alone accounts for over 40 percent of global carbon emissions, with 30 percent attributed to building operations (United Nations Environment 2024; WEF 2022). At the same time, rising global inequalities exacerbate spatial injustices, leading some urban scholars to frame these disparities as a form of »climate apartheid« (Brisman et al. 2018).

As a South African architect and researcher working at the intersection of practice and academia, my perspective on these global crises is deeply informed by the specific urban realities of post-apartheid cities. Having co-founded 1to1 – Agency of Engagement[1] in Johannesburg, a design-based social enterprise that collaborates with grassroots urban movements on issues of spatial justice, I have spent much of the past decade navigating the tension between formal architectural practice and the lived experiences of communities facing systemic precarity. This has profoundly shaped my reading of climate injustice: For me, the climate crisis is inseparable from histories of segregation, dispossession, and and coloniality, and it is within this nexus that reparative approaches to spatial practice emerge as critical. Africa, for instance, contributes less than four percent of global carbon emissions, yet faces climate policies that restrict its industrialization and technological development (UNEP 2021). Meanwhile, European nations, particularly the UK, amassed wealth through colonial resource extraction, and these exploitative dynamics persist in modern waste disposal and industrial practices. For example, an estimated 64 percent of the EU's electronic waste – equivalent to 2.5 billion smartphones annually – is exported to African countries like Ghana and Nigeria, where it is processed informally under hazardous conditions (Basel Action Network 2022). Agbogbloshie, Ghana, one of the world's largest e-waste landfills, exemplifies the consequences of

---

1 1to1–Agency of Engagement is a Johannesburg-based, non-profit, design-led practice founded in 2010 to support community organizations, social movements, and residents in co-design processes that address spatial inequality. For further information, consult: https://1to1.org.za, accessed October 5, 2025.

these environmental injustices, exposing local residents to toxic pollutants in unregulated settings.

These double standards highlight the broader structural inequalities embedded in climate discourse, wherein formerly colonized regions bear the greatest burdens yet wield minimal influence over global policy frameworks (Hickel 2020). Africa's minimal per capita carbon emissions – just one tonne annually compared to Europe's 7.1 tonnes (Friedlingstein et al. 2022) – stand in stark contrast to the continent's severe climate disruptions, including food insecurity, water shortages, and economic instability. As African cities undergo rapid urbanization under the compounded pressures of climate change and historical exploitation, they continue to grapple with entrenched environmental and socio-economic inequities.

Urbanization patterns beyond the Western world further underscore these shifting global dynamics. Rapid urban growth in regions such as Africa and Asia is not only surpassing that of Europe and North America but is also unfolding under unprecedented socio-economic conditions. Towards which, Africa's median age is approximately 19.7 years, making it the youngest continent demographically (Median Age in Africa 2000–2030 2020; Paice 2021). Meanwhile, between 2011 and 2013, China used more concrete than the United States did throughout the entire 20th century – highlighting a dramatic realignment in global construction trends (Chen 2014; Swanson 2015). These patterns reflect deeper global asymmetries, often along structural inequalities that shape how built environments are produced and inhabited on a global scale. In this context, spatial practices must be critically re-evaluated, particularly those that claim to address climate and development challenges.

Across the built environment there is a pressing need for climate-resilient, context-sensitive design approaches that enable architects and planners to meaningfully engage with uneven development and entrenched disparities (Raworth 2017). Yet the values underpinning dominant architectural knowledge systems remain overwhelmingly Western and Eurocentric, often failing to account for the legacies of extraction, economic exploitation, and political domination that continue to structure contemporary global inequities (Mbembe 2017). Beyond questions of material use and energy efficiency – both central to the climate crisis – architectural education and practice must also contend with foundational issues of social and spatial justice.

The dominance of Western/Eurocentric knowledge systems has increasingly been challenged by calls for decolonization in architectural curricula, aligning with Aníbal Quijano's theorization of coloniality of power, which

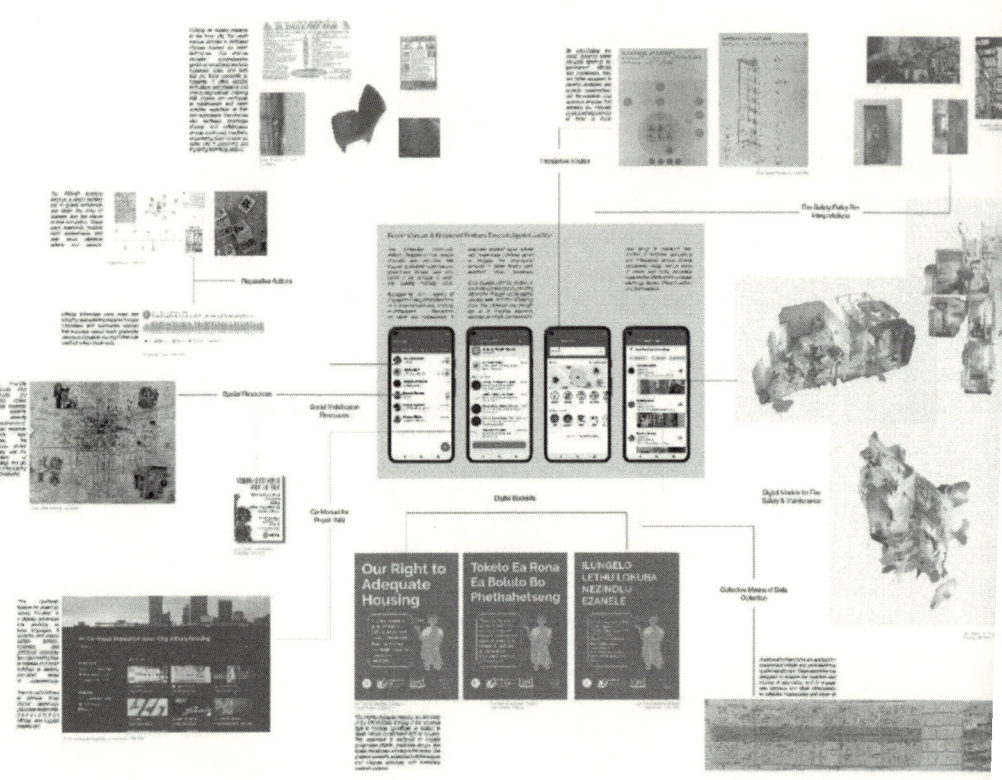

1.

Repair Manual: Reparative Spatial Practices, by author, 2024.

describes how colonial structures have historically – and continue to – shape knowledge production and value systems (Quijano 2000). Until these epistemological hierarchies are addressed, the knowledge systems that frame how we even understand crises like climate change will continue to perpetuate exclusionary frameworks that marginalize extra-Western practices and spatial knowledge. Scholars such as Walter Mignolo and Achille Mbembe have further demonstrated how dominant paradigms reinforce educational inequities and dismiss indigenous and alternative knowledge systems (Mignolo 2011; Mbembe 2017). Furthermore, such models often fail to reflect the contemporary realities of global architectural practice, which increasingly involve iterative, collaborative design and co-production processes that better represent how built environments are shaped in practice (Till 2009).

This paper contributes to the growing discourse on reparative urbanisms by arguing that reparative spatial design (fig. 1) – enacted through architectural processes not limited to, but inclusive of, architects – offers a meaningful response to the intensifying conditions of the looming climate apartheid (Alston, 2019). It proposes that reparative design operates across multiple scales, from the interpersonal to the global, by integrating multi-authorship, systemic intervention, and relational practices that challenge exclusionary forms of urbanism. Drawing from settler colonial contexts and architectural practices – specifically the work of Liz Ogbu's Studio O and 1to1 – Agency of Engagement, this research explores how reparative approaches developed in places like South Africa can inform a broader, globally relevant framework for spatial practice. Considering the escalating climate crisis and its entanglement with colonial legacies, the paper calls for urgent shifts toward spatial justice-oriented models of design and governance, and offers a conceptual framework for an emergent practice principles through the idea of reparative architectural practice.

The Missing 'e' of Climate Justice

With cities across the globe experiencing rapid growth, adopting a more grounded perspective on social and spatial justice has become increasingly critical to addressing decarbonization efforts. This involves protecting vulnerable populations from the adverse effects of climate change, safeguarding them from its disruptive impacts, and facilitating the transition toward an equitable post-carbon society. In South Africa, this challenge is particularly acute: Rapid urbanization collides with the country's deeply unequal spatial legacy, where informal settlements on floodplains or in fire-prone areas disproportionately bear the brunt of climate hazards. Rising sea levels threaten coastal communities in Cape Town's low-lying townships, while heat waves and increased flooding compound existing infrastructural deficits in Johannesburg and Durban. These overlapping pressures highlight how climate emergency and urbanization are inseparably entwined in contexts shaped by apartheid-era land use and persistent socio-economic inequality.

Towards this, Climate Urbanism offers a crucial framing for how architects, urbanists, and planners can situate their role addressing the global climate crisis, positioning cities as central actors in this unfolding challenge. As articulated by Long and Rice (2019), climate urbanism underscores the role of cities as vital sites for climate action, emphasizing the protection of infrastructures, services, and economies from climate-related hazards. For example, investments in stormwater systems in Durban's eThekwini municipality or the City of Cape Town's water resilience strategy demonstrate how urban governments mobilize adaptation measures. Yet these same strategies often reproduce inequality by privileging well-resourced neighborhoods over marginalized ones.

This foundational perspective requires a more nuanced and located understanding, particularly when its underlying assumptions and the political narratives driving its adoption are critically examined. Scholars in the field of climate urbanism have identified that mitigation and adaptation efforts often produce distributional impacts that exacerbate existing social and economic inequalities (Hughes/Hoffmann 2020). For instance, flood-buffering infrastructure in Cape Town's wealthy suburbs frequently receives more investment than informal settlements along rivers, where residents face recurrent flooding without adequate protection. Such examples illustrate that climate adaptation can reinforce, rather than alleviate, urban divides. For this reason, architects, planners, and urbanists must go beyond one-size-fits-all approaches. Instead, they must develop responses that are adaptive, inclusive, and transformative, acknowledging the distinct challenges and opportunities presented by different urban areas in different parts of the world (Watson, 2014; Bhan, 2019). Scholars increasingly argue for including marginalized communities such as shack-dwellers' movements (e.g., Abahlali baseMjondolo in South Africa or Shack/Slum Dwellers International globally) in decision-making around adaptation. Yet Jonathan Silver, a geographer working on African urban infrastructures, critiques climate justice efforts for privileging top-down adaptation strategies over grassroots practices already at work in marginalized neighborhoods (Silver 2023). For example, while state-led relocation schemes often fail, community-driven upgrading initiatives – like the participatory flood-mapping in Cape Town's Khayelitsha or the co-produced maintenance of drainage systems in Dar es Salaam – offer more context-sensitive, resilient solutions.

In this light, the notion of »climate colonialism« has been suggested to frame the current era as a continuation of long-standing environmental injustices (Sultana 2022). The climate crisis emerges here as a manifestation of deeply embedded global inequalities, where technocratic sustainability frameworks obscure the legacies of colonialism, extractivism, and uneven industrialization. For example, large-scale renewable energy investments in South Africa's Karoo region often exclude local communities from decision-making, echoing extractive land-use patterns while being promoted as »green« solutions. This tendency to sideline politics in favor of technical fixes is evident across many less developed contexts. In Mozambique, for instance, post-cyclone reconstruction prioritized foreign investment projects while sidelining local rebuilding practices – reinforcing dependency and marginalization. Such cases underscore that adaptation strategies must not only address immediate hazards but also confront historical injustices.

These concerns are framed within the broader scholarship on »climate apartheid,« which describes the global phenomenon of inequality and segregation intensified by climate change (Long/Rice 2019). While recently coined, the concept is deeply rooted in historical legacies of exploitation, racism, and the unequal distribution of resources and risks associated with climate hazards (de Shalit 2011). Climate apartheid highlights how ongoing systems of oppression – namely settler colonialism, racial capitalism, and neoliberal governance – magnify the crisis and make injustice visible in urban form. In South Africa, apartheid's legacy of spatial segregation means that low-income communities remain concentrated in peripheral or risk-prone areas. Housing policies continue to reinforce these patterns by reproducing mono-functional settlements on cheap, vulnerable land rather than integrating communities into safer, better-serviced urban fabrics.

This process of dispossession and systemic violence is not confined to the past but continues to shape present-day realities, particularly in the management of disaster risk and housing provision. For example, informal settlement residents in Cape Town's Philippi or Johannesburg's inner city face repeated evictions in the name of »risk mitigation,« even though such measures rarely address the root causes of vulnerability. Climate change magnifies these injustices, rendering such communities more expendable in the face of environmental hazards (Tuana 2019).

To address these injustices, the concept of »climate justice« is offered as a supportive frame for action toward fairness and equity in the distribution of both the benefits and burdens of climate change (Jasrotia 2016; Macquarie 2023). For spatial practitioners, this means embedding equity into design and planning decisions: Ensuring, for instance, that flood infrastructure is co-designed with informal settlement residents; supporting community-managed water storage projects in drought-prone areas; or creating participatory planning processes that redistribute state resources toward the most vulnerable. These actions highlight the central role of architects and planners not as neutral problem-solvers, but as actors accountable to histories of harm and capable of shaping reparative futures. Climate justice thus insists that those most affected by climate change must be at the center of decision-making, and that design practice itself must evolve into a tool of redistribution and solidarity.

Repair as Architectural Practice

Humanities scholar Elizabeth Spelman's characterization of repair as »the creative destruction of brokenness« provides a foundational insight, supporting a view of repair that extends beyond the act of fixing an object toward a dynamic process of urban, architectural, and social renewal (Spelman 2003). Spelman highlights the creativity inherent in repair, illustrating that the process transcends mere reconstruction. Destruction becomes a catalyst for transformation, enabling growth and new possibilities.

In my own work, I work with repair as a sustained spatial practice of care that works through systemic brokenness to reconfigure relationships, infrastructures, and environments in ways that address both material and social inequities. In this sense, repair is not simply about restoring a building or a city to a former state, but about actively engaging with histories of harm and the lived realities of those excluded from conventional development. Rather than aiming for seamless restoration, this approach challenges conventional ideas of repair by valuing the layered conditions as expressions of care and history. It advances an iterative, reparative practice that simultaneously interrogates how reparation functions as a mode of spatial justice.

An example of which I offer is the iterative maintenance of Johannesburg's Slovo Hall (fig. 2). These traces narrate layered histories of survival, collaboration, and endurance rather than erasing them. Extending this understanding, repair becomes more than a material act – it becomes a critical lens for addressing broader socio-spatial challenges. For spatially marginalized groups, repair is relational: It is about sustaining connections to place, rebuilding networks of solidarity, and exercising agency in contexts where formal planning often ignores or displaces them. For instance, the everyday acts of fixing electricity lines, digging drainage ditches, or reinforcing homes in informal settlements are not only technical responses but political practices of autonomy and resilience (Simone 2008).

Rather than a one-time fix, repair should be understood as a long-term intervention that disrupts cycles of disposability embedded in dominant models of urban development. In contexts where infrastructure is deliberately under-maintained or withdrawn – as in many townships and inner-city housing blocks in South Africa – repair resists abandonment by sustaining value, continuity, and social presence. It celebrates the *how* of making, foregrounding cycles of iterative making and remaking as creative and social acts, rather than privileging the one-off, aesthetically oriented celebration of a finished structure or building. This perspective foregrounds repair as a generative practice: iterative, creative, and capable of responding to environmental precarity and social fragmentation (Berger/Irvin 2023). Towards which, urban scholar Gautam Bhan conceptualizes repair as a relational practice, underscoring the potential for localized, context-specific solutions to catalyze broader transformations within urban ecosystems (Bhan et al. 2018). This is particularly vital in southern cities (Watson 2014), where narratives often label certain places uninhabitable due to violence, poverty, or infrastructural collapse. Scholars such as AbdouMaliq Simone have emphasized the capacity of residents in such contexts to transform their environments through everyday acts of maintenance, adaptation, and relational repair (Simone 2008). Bhan extends this, framing repair as an inherently southern practice – less about technical correction than about cultural and political intervention rooted in situated knowledge and resilience (Bhan 2019). Examples include community-managed sanitation systems in Nairobi's Mathare settlement, or the incremental upgrading of stormwater channels in Dar es Salaam led by resident associations (Bhan et al. 2017).

These inclusive and equitable reparative practices invite a rethinking of how spatial practitioners engage with cities – both in terms of material form and the social systems that shape them. Medellín's long-term investment in neighborhood-scale infrastructure co-designed with residents demonstrates how repair and social inclusion can shift urban governance. Similarly, Cape Town's »Reblocking« projects – where informal housing layouts are reorganized collaboratively to allow for drainage and service access – show how participatory repair practices strengthen both physical and social resilience.

Central to this shift, as Castán Broto et al. (2021) and Ortiz (2022) argue, is moving away from top-down planning toward participatory and collaborative modes of practice where historically marginalized voices are central to outcomes. Understanding repair as a relational practice deepens this reorientation, offering a lens to view ongoing maintenance, adaptation, and transformation in relation to climate change. It foregrounds multi-authorship, emphasizing that resilient cities are shaped collectively through diverse knowledge systems, lived experiences, and community practices. This orientation has significant implications for climate adaptation. Reparative practices can be seen in co-designed flood management in Cape Town's Philippi settlement, where residents map vulnerabilities and build retention ponds; in incremental housing upgrades in Johannesburg's inner city, where residents repair and adapt buildings in defiance of eviction threats; and in community land trusts in US cities such as Boston, where residents collectively manage land and housing to resist displacement. By recognising the social dimensions of vulnerability, such practices contribute to physical resilience and the healing of communities fragmented by inequality. They foster dignity, belonging, and agency in places long denied them.

Looking at two practices in settler colonial contexts,[2] the work of organisations such as 1to1 – Agency of Engagement offers insight into these principles. Through a multi-scalar, participatory design approach, 1to1 provides a compelling alternative to conventional planning models – centering collaboration and long-term engagement. Similarly, Studio O, led by Liz Ogbu in the United States, integrates reparative methodologies into architectural processes, working with communities to address inequality and foster healing. Both reject prescriptive solutions in favour of adaptive processes rooted in co-authorship, care, and relationality.

---

2 *Settler colonial contexts* refer to countries where colonial structures established enduring racialised land dispossession and spatial inequality, such as South Africa, the United States, Canada, and Australia.

Liz Ogbu's work in Akron, Ohio, addressing displacement caused by the Innerbelt highway, illustrates this. Through grief-sharing workshops, story-telling, and collective reimagining of the site, Ogbu helped residents process loss and secure resources to reconnect fractured urban space (Greenspan 2018). This process-centered repair demonstrates how design can serve both material and emotional needs. In South Africa, 1to1's long-term involvement in Slovo Hall exemplifies repair as sustained practice. Built, adapted, and maintained over more than a decade, the Hall reflects a co-produced legacy where architecture is bound to ongoing community life. Repair is as much about sustaining relationships and governance structures as maintaining bricks and mortar. Importantly, practitioners deliberately displaced their professional privilege, working outside remuneration and sharing author-ship with community members.

Together, 1to1 and Studio O show how architectural practices that do not solely focus only on built products as their primary offering can serve as a sustained act of reparative urbanism. Their work is not rhetorical but iterative, grounded in trauma, power, and collaboration. Whether through participa-tory mapping, storytelling, or co-produced infrastructure, they demonstrate that repair addresses not only places but the relationships and systems that shape them – and affect spaces long after the involvement of professionals.

Conclusion: Reparative Architectural Practices

Through my long-term involvement in spatial practice as co-founder – and now advisor – of 1to1, my exploration of reparative approaches to systemic injustice has led to a critical understanding: Repair is not an endpoint but a process. It is a sustained, ongoing journey that embraces imperfection and acknowledges structural inequities without assuming the possibility of abso-lute resolution (Berger/Irvin 2023c). This understanding calls for a collective commitment to interrogating and transforming the systems we inhabit. Framed as a continuous and reflexive engagement, repair urges a departure from conventional problem-solving toward methods rooted in curiosity, care, humility, and learning. Within this framework, physical infrastructures and socio-political obstacles are no longer seen as static barriers, but as oppor-tunities for transformative and creative responses – an enactment of ethical responsibility through design.

2.

Slovo Hall in repair (1to1, 2010 – 2022). Photographs by author.

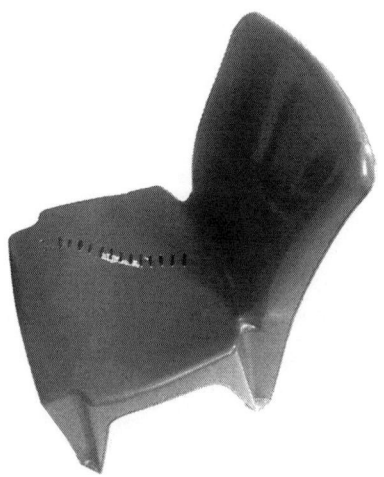

3.

An artefact of grassroots repair from inner-city Joburg. Photograph (cutout) by author.

Crucially, the concept of repair extends beyond the material, encompassing the moral and social fabrics torn by histories of colonialism, enslavement, and structural racism (Ganguly 2023). While some harms may never be fully repaired, the act of engaging with the socio-technical dynamics of systemic brokenness retains deep symbolic and political value. Repair becomes a way of working through systemic inequality, often maintaining rather than restoring (fig. 3), while signalling an ongoing commitment to justice. The notion of repair as a »double bind« – simultaneously necessary and impossible – reveals its layered complexity. Public acts of reparation, such as South Africa's Truth and Reconciliation Commission, demonstrate that repair is not about returning to an idealised past, but about constructing ethical futures within the limits of what can be redressed (Krog 2009; Ganguly 2023).

In this light, repair demands continuous reflection, adaptation, and context-sensitive action. It fosters a critical balance between historical awareness and future aspirations within cultural and communal spheres. This includes working alongside young people, responding to evolving socio-political conditions, and embedding care within the practice of spatial design (Berger/Irvin 2023a). Acknowledging the limits of reparative intervention does not diminish its value; instead, it reinforces the need to embrace repair as a grounded, justice-oriented practice – an essential foundation for broader systemic transformation. Recognising that the complete undoing of past harm may be impossible, reparative action becomes an expression of humility, solidarity, and resilience. In architecture and urbanism, this translates into a departure from singular, technocratic solutions in favour of layered, situated responses to deep-rooted inequality. Reparative frameworks acknowledge that spatial interventions may not erase injustice, but they can enable new relationships, expand agency, and cultivate a sense of belonging.

Here, reparation is not limited to material restitution; it operates as a symbolic and political practice to heal collective wounds through cultural and social processes (Berger/Irvin 2023b; Kemper/Rutten 2023). It insists on acknowledging harm, affirming dignity, and supporting collective futures rooted in self-determination and liberation. Rather than positioning repair as a form of improvement in the developmental sense, this approach sees it as the sustained maintenance of dignity and coexistence within fractured urban contexts. Against the backdrop of colonial legacies, modernist planning, and donor-driven development – each of which has marginalized vulnerable communities – reparative urbanism offers a critical alternative.

Designers such as Markus Berger and Kate Irvin describe repair as a form of empowerment and agency that resists environmental degradation and socio-political fragmentation (Berger/Irvin 2023d). Their work reframes repair as a generative design ethos – one that expands the capacity of design to imagine and construct more just ecological, social, and spatial futures.

This perspective necessitates a critical reassessment of spatial methodologies. It compels practitioners to ask who benefits from spatial interventions and how these decisions impact marginalized communities. The racialised geographies shaping Liz Ogbu's work in the United States and 1to1's work in Slovo Park reveal a shared commitment to relationality, equity, and lived experience as central to the design process (Ogbu 2019; Tissington 2012). These practices reject dominant paradigms that treat space as neutral or static, instead recognising spatial production as socially embedded and politically active.

For the discipline of spatial design, this relational orientation opens new pathways for how we build and inhabit cities. It demands a shift from simply constructing buildings to cultivating environments that foster social cohesion and respond to spatial inequality. In this context, repair becomes a layered and multifaceted practice – encompassing informality, infrastructural adaptation, and the co-production of urban life. It values local knowledge, supports collective governance, and challenges the technocratic, extractive tendencies of mainstream planning. The tools and methods of spatial repair must emerge from within communities themselves, shaped by their own histories, practices, and aspirations.

In response, this paper proposes a reparative framework for architectural practice that reorients the field toward climate justice and spatial equity. Rather than optimising for efficiency or performance alone, reparative design entails an epistemological shift: One that views architecture as a negotiated, care-based process rooted in context, history, and community. Drawing from the practices of Studio O and 1to1, I outline five interlinked practices that embody this reparative orientation: Acknowledging and situating architectural work within histories of spatial harm; co-authoring spatial knowledge through long-term, horizontal partnerships; embedding care and deliberation into design methods as integral processes; activating local infrastructures through adaptive, community-led planning; and sustaining networks of solidarity across disciplines, scales, and geographies.

These principles offer an expanded framing of architectural agency in an era of intersecting crises. While reparative urbanism cannot deliver perfect solutions – particularly in the face of climate apartheid – it affirms a politics of presence, humility, and responsibility. Under this lens, architecture is no longer defined by what it produces, but by how it engages, repairs, and sustains the relationships and systems it touches.

References

1to1 – Agency of Engagement. (2019): »A Reflective Engagement: 2010–2018,« Johannesburg: 1to1 – Agency of Engagement. https://1to1temp2020. wordpress.com/2019/02/01/a-reflective-engagement-2010-2018/, accessed September 12, 2025.

Alston, Philip (2019): »Climate change and poverty: Report of the Special Rapporteur on extreme poverty and human rights (A/HRC/41/39),« Geneva: United Nations Human Rights Council. https://www.ohchr.org/en/documents/thematic-reports/ahrc4139-climate-change-extreme-poverty-and-human-rights-report, accessed September 12, 2025.

Berger, Molly/Irvin, Kate (2023): »Repair: Sustainable Design Futures,« London: Routledge.

Bhan, Gautam (2019): »Notes on a Southern urban practice,« Environment & Urbanization 31/2, 639–654. doi: /10.1177/0956247818815792

Bhan, Gautam/Srinivas, Smita/Watson, Vanessa, eds. (2018): »The Routledge Companion to Planning in the Global South,« London: Routledge.

Brisman, Avi/South, Nigel/Walters, Reece (2018): »Climate apartheid and environmental refugees,« in: Kerry Carrington/Russell Hogg/John Scott/Maximo Sozzo (eds.), The Palgrave Handbook of Criminology and the Global South, Cham: Springer International Publishing, 301–321. doi: 10.1007/978-3-319-65021-0_16

Castán Broto, Vanesa/Boyd, Emily/Ensor, Jonathan (2021): »Reparative climate justice and development futures,« Journal of the British Academy 9/S1, 141–165. doi: 10.5871/jba/009s1.141

Chen, Xiangming (2014): »Steering, speeding, scaling: China's model of urban growth and its implications for cities of the global South,« in: Susan Parnell/Sophie Oldfield (eds.), The Routledge Handbook on Cities of the Global South, London: Routledge, 155–172.

Crysler, C. Greig/Cairns, Stephen/Heynen, Hilde, eds. (2012): The SAGE Handbook of Architectural Theory. London: SAGE.

Cuff, Dana (1991): Architecture: The Story of Practice. Cambridge, MA: MIT Press.

Dutton, Thomas A. (1991): Voices in Architectural Education: Cultural Politics and Pedagogy. New York: Bergin & Garvey.

Fremstad, Anders/Paul, Mark (2019): »The impact of a carbon tax on inequality,« Ecological Economics 163, 88–97. doi: 10.1016/j.ecolecon.2019.04.016

Friedlingstein, Pierre/Jones, Matthew W. /O'Sullivan, Michael et al (2022): Global Carbon Budget 2022. Earth System Science Data 14/4, 1917–2005. doi: 10.5194/essd-14-1917-2022

Ganguly, Pritika (2023): Reparation and Its Limits: Symbolism in Justice and Healing, Manchester: Manchester University Press.

Hickel, Jason (2020): Less Is More: How Degrowth Will Save the World. London: William Heinemann.

Hughes, Sara/Hoffmann, Matthew (2020): »*Just urban transitions: Toward a research agenda.*« Wiley Interdisciplinary Reviews: Climate Change 11/3, e640. doi: 10.1002/wcc.640

Institute for European Environmental Policy (IEEP). (2020): »*More than half of all CO_2 emissions since 1751 emitted in the last 30 years.*« https://ieep.eu/news/more-than-half-of-all-co2-emissions-since-1751-emitted-in-the-last-30-years/, accessed September 12, 2025.

Jasrotia, Rakesh (2016): »Climate justice: A voice for the global South,« *Environmental Policy and Law 46/2*, 78–83. doi: 10.57749/fjqf-gm87

Long, Joshua/Rice, Jennifer L. (2019): »From Sustainable Urbanism to Climate Urbanism,« *Urban Studies 56/5*, 992–1008. doi: 10.1177/0042098018770846

Mbembe, Achille (2017): »*Critique of Black Reason,*« Durham (NC): Duke University Press.

Mignolo, Walter D. (2011): »*The Darker Side of Western Modernity: Global Futures, Decolonial Options,*« Durham (NC): Duke University Press.

Ogbu, Liz/Bouie, Jamelle (2022): »*On Repair*« [Video], Charlottesville: UVA School of Architecture, https://www.youtube.com/watch?v=bkkSoon8GFw, accessed September 12, 2025.

Paice, Edward (2021): »*Youthquake: Why Africa's demographic edge matters,*« London: Headline.

Quijano, Aníbal (2000): »Coloniality of power, Eurocentrism, and Latin America,« *Nepantla: Views from South 1/3*, 533–580.

Raworth, Kate (2017): »*Doughnut Economics: Seven Ways to Think Like a 21st-Century Economist,*« London: Random House Business.

Silver, Jonathan (2023): »Infrastructure, adaptation and politics in African cities,« in: Adriana Allen/ Sarah Colenbrander (eds.), *Urban Infrastructures in a Changing Climate*, London: Routledge, 75–92.

Simone, AbdouMaliq (2004): »People as infrastructure: Intersecting fragments in Johannesburg,» *Public Culture 16/3*, 407–429. doi: 10.1215/08992363-16-3-407

Spelman, Elizabeth V. (2003): »*Repair: The Impulse to Restore in a Fragile World,*« Boston, MA: Beacon Press.

Statista (2020): »*Median age in Africa 2000–2030,*« https://www.statista.com/statistics/1226158/median-age-of-the-population-of-africa/, accessed September 12, 2025.

Sultana, Farhana (2022): »The unbearable heaviness of climate coloniality,« Political Geography 102, 102684. doi: 10.1016/j.polgeo.2022.102684

Swanson, Ana (2015): »*How China used more cement in 3 years than the U.S. did in the entire 20th century,*« Washington Post, March 24, 2015, https://www.washingtonpost.com/news/wonk/wp/2015/03/24/how-china-used-more-cement-in-3-years-than-the-u-s-did-in-the-entire-20th-century/, accessed September 12, 2025.

Till, Jeremy (2009): »*Architecture Depends,*« Cambridge, MA: MIT Press.

Tissington, Kate (2011): »*A Resource Guide to Housing in South Africa 1994–2010: Legislation, Policy, Programmes and Practice,*« Johannesburg: Socio-Economic Rights Institute of South Africa (SERI). https://www.seri-sa.org/index.php/research/all-publications/resource-guides, accessed September 12, 2025.

Tuana, Nancy (2019): »Climate apartheid: The forgetting of race in the Anthropocene,« *Critical Philosophy of Race 7/1*, 1–31. doi: 10.5325/critphilrace.7.1.0001

United Nations Environment Programme
(UNEP) (2024): *2024 Global Status Report
for Buildings and Construction*, Nairobi:
UNEP, https://globalabc.org/sites/default/
files/2025-03/Global-Status-Report-2024
_2025.pdf, accessed September 12, 2025.

Watson, Vanessa (2014): »The case for a
Southern perspective in planning theory,«
International Journal of E-Planning Research
3/1, 23–37. doi: 10.4018/ijepr.2014010102

World Economic Forum (2021): *Net-Zero
Challenge: The supply chain opportunity*,
https://www.weforum.org/publications/
net-zero-challenge-the-supply-chain-
opportunity/, accessed September 12,
2025.

Dimensions of Architectural Knowledge, 2024-08 ⊖
https://doi.org/10.14361/dak-2024-0816

Mapping Territorial Resistance – Transformative Heritage in Bogotá

Alissa Diesch

Abstract: This article explores Bogotá's urban transformation, framed within the concept of crisis as a catalyst. Drawing on the city's history from an indigenous territory to a modern megacity, it examines how different kinds of crises overlap and endure over time. The analysis uses former villages and their plazas as a starting point, showing how the (post)colonial structures, indigenous spatial practices, and rapid urbanization intersect to shape contemporary urban spaces. By integrating decolonial theory, critical cartography, and participatory action research, the study redefines crisis as a turning point that can foster resilience, adaptation, and transformation. It advocates for a shift from a problem-centered view to an urban transformation based on local communities, cultural heritage, and historical continuities as critical resources for reimagining urban futures. Through this, the article proposes new roles for architects and urbanists, proposing »transformative heritage« as an agent in the process of urban renewal.

Keywords: Bogota; Critical Cartography; Heritage; Participatory Action Research; Postcolonial Space; Urban Transformation.

Corresponding author: Alissa Diesch (Universidad del Norte, Colombia); alissa.diesch@t-online.de;
https://orcid.org/0000-0002-0230-7933 ⊖ Open Access.

Introduction

Global megatrends – the effects of climate change, political, economic and societal disruptions and transformations – currently discussed in Europe and North America as poly-crisis, are hitting cities in the Global South on top of long-lasting, silenced crises outside the spotlight. Here, »crisis not only is acute but also characterized by persistence« (Appelhans 2024:305). Taking the example of Colombia, acute crises range from unstable economic and political prospects, environmental disasters – namely droughts and floodings – to systematic killings of community leaders, forced internal and transnational migration, as well as health issues due to neglected tropical diseases. In a bigger framework, persisting post-colonial structures and effects such as immense social-ethnical disparities, the decade-long armed conflict, including narco-industries and politics, as well as the continuing economic dependence on extractivism, are of striking influence. All these crises have a strong spatially related agency. They are about spatial conflicts and have propelled on-going rapid urbanization including dynamics that defy Western urban theories. In this article, the Colombian capital – Bogotá – will be analyzed as a space where crises constitute and evolve.

Crisis here will be understood not only as a state of misery but, closer to its original Greek meaning, *krisis*, as a turning point of a malfunctioning situation. Uncovering effective, culturally evolved structures and systems supports the overdue shift of the dominant problem-centered view of cities of the Global South to a more differentiated and empowering narrative (King 2006; Robinson 2022; Roy 2009) – without denying existing challenges and the need of structural transformation (Appelhans 2024). The role of architects and urbanists in this context concerns specific spatial analytical approaches, theoretically informed (de)construction and analysis of narratives and how they are related to and nourished by urban practices and imaginaries (Silva 2006; Huffschmid/Wildner 2013), as well as advanced communication and moderation abilities (Heindl 2024). Reflections on norm and deviation of urban ideals (Chandokes 199; Kraft 2016) are embedded in broader considerations about decolonial knowledge production (Bhambra 2014; Kerner 2012; Mignolo 2011; Quijano 1992).

Due to the rapid urbanization between 1950-1990, Latin America today has an urbanized population of more than 80% and the highest rate of inhabitants of megacities (United Nations, Department of Economic and Social Affairs, Population Division 2019). Bogotá is a paradigmatic example of these dynamics, representing annual growth rates of up to 5-7% during that period (WPR 2023) while performing pragmatic problem-solving in urban planning and policies. The rapid conquest and colonization by the European powers during the 16th century, along with the exuberant and capital-driven urbanization of the 20th century, represent two profound ruptures for Latin America, both of which continue to shape its urban spaces. Many of these spaces are characterized by the simultaneity of different cultures and historical periods leading often to conflicts, segregation and hybridization (Huffschmid/Wildner 2013). From an architectural and urban design perspective, the characteristic square *plazas* of colonial urban foundations in the the former Spanish colonies will be analyzed as such places. These plazas continue to influence centrality and the understanding of public space to this day.

The genesis of Bogotá (fig. 1) is commonly, even in academic literature, told as the story of a city (»Santafe de Bogotá«) founded by Spanish conquerors in the 16th century, that expanded mono-centrically and explosively in the 20th century. While this describes the two most important turning points in its history, it is sidelining the agency of communities, structures and dynamics active since pre-Hispanic times. The Muisca, the Indigenous group continuously inhabiting the high plains of Bogotá for more than 1200 years, for a long time have been referred to as extinct and merged into the mestizo society (Diesch/Niviayo/Yopasá 2018). Only since 1991 have the first local communities been formally recognized as Indigenous groups, also due to their uninterrupted presence and agency in the territory. Their strong though mainly ignored influence on colonization and urbanization is lately getting more scientific attention, increasingly also authored by researchers of the Muisca communities (del Castillo 2019; Durán 2004; Fernandez 2014; Goubert 2019; Niviayo 2017).

After decades of a problem-centered urbanistic perspective on the city with a focus on quick and technology-driven solutions, in the last two decades, academic attention has been put on the urban cultural-historic background of the present-day megacity, too. Especially, the historic center »La Candelaria,« the Spanish foundation and later colonial city, has received scientific consideration (Mejía 2000; Escovar/Mariño/Peña 2004). Individual research works have examined urban development aspects on a territorial scale with a critical historical contextualization before colonization (Calderón 2016), providing also important map material, and a new framing

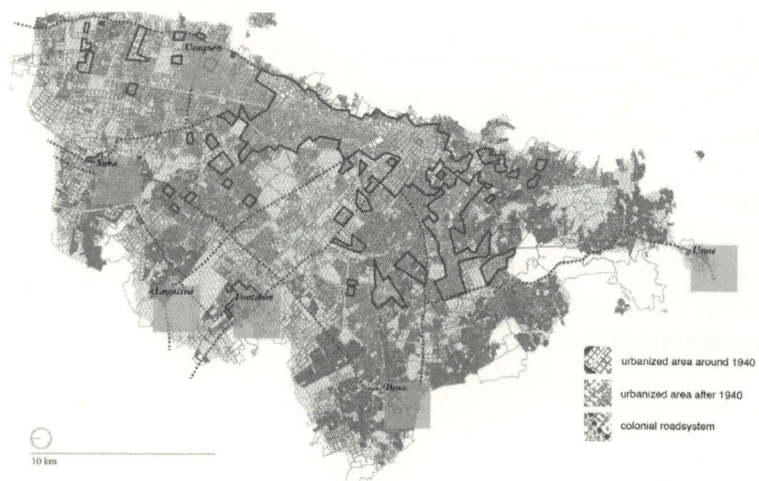

1.

Map of Bogotá showing urbanization between 1940 and 2020 and the examined former villages in the urban periphery. Image by the author.

2.

Aerial picture of the plaza of Bosa, a former village / »Pueblo de Indio,« part of Bogotá in 2014. Image by the author based on a map from https://mapas.bogota. gov.co/, accessed October 5, 2025. The marked buildings have operative and representative functions and are of different historical backgrounds: The colonial church building represents the Catholic church, the presumable republican town house hosts a metropolitan administrative unit, and the building of the Muisca community is a place of gathering and reception.

of the pre-European territory of the high plains of Bogotá as a complex human-environment system of trans-scalar shaping (Rodriguez 2019).

The focus of this article is on the process of conurbation of formerly rural centralities into the megacity. These places have been nodes of slightly clustered, dispersive settlements in a network of the Muisca empire, were reshaped as densified »Pueblos de Indios« (Indian villages) around a characteristic central plaza during the time of Spanish colonization in the 16th century and became individual villages and centers of municipalities around the Colombian capital before turning functionally, politically, and morphologically into parts of the mega city during the 20th century (fig. 2).

Material and Methods

This research followed a culture-based, decentralized, and locally informed approach. Using the plazas of the six former villages as entry points, it explored Bogotá's periphery and its metropolitan transformation through a set of qualitative methods (fig. 3) synthesized in different mappings compiled in an atlas (Diesch 2024). The explorations ranged from gathering, classifying and processing historic plans and archive material from various sources, including gray literature and primary sources, to diverse forms of participatory action research (PAR) (Fals Borda 1978). PAR, informed here by critical cartography (Turnbull 1993; Corner 1999), is understood as a means to represent and localize different layers of knowledge, especially the perspective from which this knowledge has arisen. »[T]he place of ›the utterance‹« (Spivak 1998: 82) is highlighted, facilitating the relation between place, knowledge and power (Roy 2015) in a decolonial sense. Through mapping and linked theorization, »new geographies of theory« (Roy 2009) emerge revealing postcolonial structures and enabling integrative measures.

Based on heterogeneous historic plan material, a uniform typo-morphological plan synopsis was created, making visible the forma urbis (Moudon 1997) around the historic plazas and their transformations over time (Solà Morales 1997). The newly developed set of maps now reveals spatial continuities and transformations that were previously unreadable, enabling entirely new interpretations. These cartographic representations were correlated with sets of maps at larger scales and over broader temporal frameworks (Calderón 2016; Diesch 2022) and the results of PAR.

**transdisciplinary
multi-method approach**
- architectural-urbanistic analysis   *individual*
- archieves, primary sources   *disciplinary research*
- mental maps   *participatory -*
- photography and   *artistic research*
  social cartography   *with students*

walkscapes, performative mappings   *participatory -
in-depth research
with local communities*

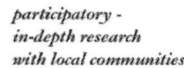

3.

Overview of research methods and sites of analysis. Image by the author.

The concept of PAR has been developed and theorized in Latin America under the influence of critical geography (Santos 1978) and liberation pedagogy (Freire 1970), underscoring the transformative and empowering aspects of participatory knowledge creation. Especially notable is social cartography (Diez 2012; Vélez/Rátiva/Varela 2012) – collectively created maps that include conventionally unrepresented aspects such as personal relations and vanished places and linkages, that are widely employed to gather spatialized data while strengthening the sense of local belonging and agency of communities.

For the analyzed examples here, different forms of maps were created with university students in Bogotá to represent informed external perspectives, and with representatives of selected local initiatives from three of the villages, for internal perspectives.

In each case, mapping was designed as a site- and context-specific process with and for the participants, fostering transdisciplinary settings. Artistic and performative approaches helped soften conventional hierarchies, which were blurred, enabling new forms of knowledge and experience exchange. In line with a decolonial approach, this can amplify previously overheard voices and disrupt dominant structures of knowledge production (Bhambra 2014; Kerner 2012).

One source of mappings with students was individual mind maps, where students were asked to draw their ideas and concepts related to the names of the former villages, today city districts in Bogotá. Another source of collective mappings was the interdisciplinary student research group »Fotografía y Cartografía social[1].« Here, social cartography was combined with photography as a subjective-visual act of selection, omission, contextualization, and representation (Tagg 1988; Pink 2013) that allowed for the expression of perceptions without the need to verbally define concepts and definitions. It was used on-site as a first step (Casasbuenas/Diesch 2017). In a second step, cooperative selection, localization, and conceptualization of photographs articulated collective imaginaries and evaluations of the local heritage of each of the places in maps and short texts (Diesch 2024).

Participatory walks with representatives of three local initiatives (Diesch 2020) – a heritage group consisting of peasants and students, an academic-pedagogy collective and an indigenous community – constituted »walkscapes« (Careri 2009). By roaming the territory in question, space is perceived and created, and the character, meaning, and relationships (Certeau 1988)

---

1 https://miradas.poligran.edu.co/index.html, accessed October 5, 2025.

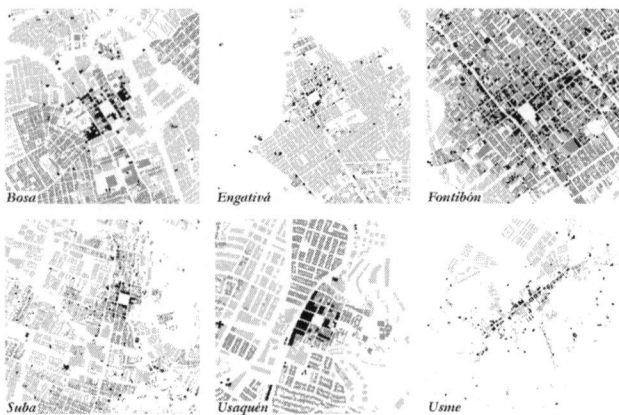

4.

Plan synopsis of the sites 1940 (black) - 1980 (gray) - 2020 (light gray). The urbanistic typology of the square colonial plazas sticks out as the centers of the historic village (in black). Image by the author.

5.

Impressions from the plaza of Bosa. Images by Luis Ramos (top and bottom center), Maria Fernanda Corredor (left center), Roger Niño (right center) taken in the framework of the student research group »Fotografía y Cartografía social« coordinated by Maria José Casasbuenas, Politecnico Grancolombiano and Alissa Diesch, Universidad la Gran Colombia 2015-2018, all the other images by the author.

of different places are transmitted performatively (Wolfrum/Brandis 2015). Just like in photography, selection, omission, and context can be surfaced in a non-verbalized way. In the intense exchanges during the on-site research and follow-up meetings with cartographic and photographic material, situations of actual transdisciplinary knowledge generation were achieved (Diesch 2024).

Results

All the information extracted from the different sources was spatialized into cartographic form. A broad set of different maps – compiled in an atlas – brings together knowledge from diverse sources, initiating a hermeneutic dialogue and prompting further inquiry (Cavalieri 2019), in line with the iterative nature of abductive research.

Synthetic typo-morphological maps for 1940, 1980, and 2020 (fig. 4) reveal the persistence of both colonial urban design principles and Indigenous land-use patterns (Diesch 2022). The historic colonial plazas remain spatially-typologically central, functioning as reference and meeting points equipped with representative architecture (Diesch 2024): They act as »significant places [that] do not lose their importance. [...They] offer an open tableau for constantly changing social and urban use. They are at the same time places of conciseness and contingency« (Wolfrum 2015: 18). The specific urban layout of the colonial plazas has largely remained unchanged, proving to be a robust framework for changing realities in the last 500 years. Qualitative findings – from academic publications, gray literature, (social) media, personal observation, students' mind maps, and participatory walks with local heritage initiatives (Diesch 2024) – demonstrate that these plazas continue to embody and related to pre-Hispanic, colonial, contemporary, rural, and urban spatialities (fig. 5). As such they create »third spaces« (Bhabha 1994).

In addition, the plan synopsis reveals that, beyond the clearly delimited colonial-founded village cores, there exists – to varying extent across cases and especially prevalent near rivers and wetlands – a continuity of rural typologies and land use patterns characterized by a dispersed settlement structure (fig. 6). These correspond closely to archeological patterns, attributed to pre-Hispanic Muisca settlements (Boada 2006; Herrera 1998). The plans illustrate their presence in the transforming rural-urban fabric until the 1980s and show how they continue to influence the morphological structure of the contemporary metropolis. This suggests a continuity

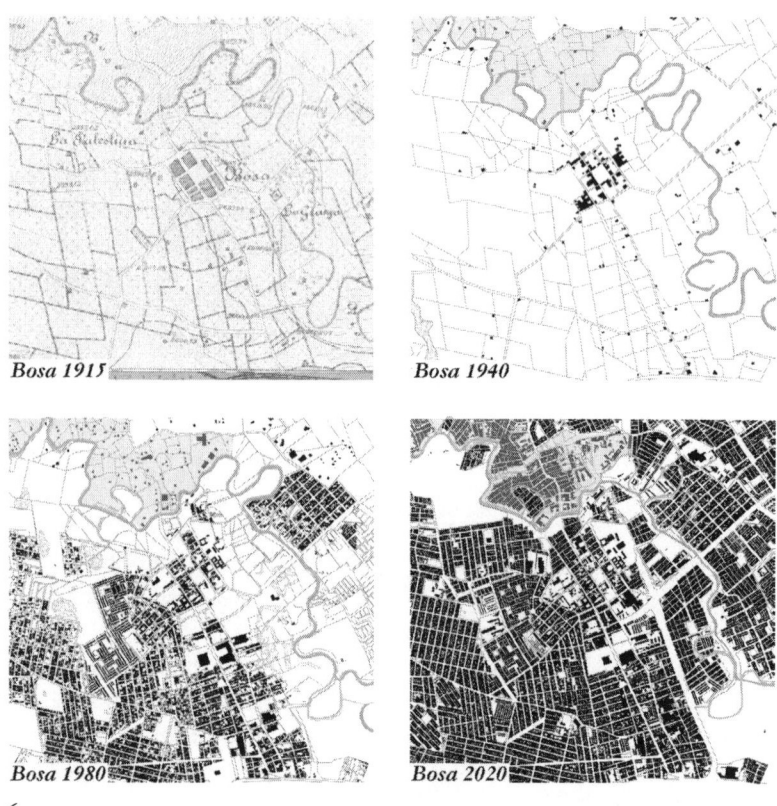

6.
Indigenous settlement structures in the transforming city, top-left in each of the maps. Marked with a hatching as mixed cultivation areas in a map from 1915 (Estado Mayor General. Carta Militar de Colombia. 1:25.000, from: Universidad Nacional de Colombia (http://cartografia.bogotaendocumentos.com/mapa, accessed October 5, 2025) and typo-morphologically identified by comparison with archeologically proven Muisca settlement patterns in maps in different phases of urbanization, here highlighted as shaded area. Image by the author.

of Indigenous socio-spatial relations to the territory. When contextualized with additional historic map material, (gray) literature, and in-depth participatory research with local Muisca community leaders, the evidence supports the assumption of continued, territory-bound practices (Diesch 2021).

Discussion

The Dilemma of Formal Recognition

The findings show that each of the plazas represents and continuously reproduces multiple simultaneously existing spaces – referencing pre-colonial, colonial and post-colonial times, expressing Indigenous, rural and urban characteristics, which elude the simplifying dialectic of colonial ideology and modern technocratic thinking. These spatial, discursive and functional continuities encounter ruptures and transformations, whereby the reading, interpretation, creation, and appropriation of spatial-material traces depend heavily on differing social perspectives: Residents from the surroundings of the plazas, farmers, indigenous people, other inhabitants of Bogotá, planners, and scientists perceive and evaluate the plazas differently and form changing relationships. The interpretative and performative range is far more complex and contradictory than the dichotomous division of urban/rural, indigenous/European, or modern/traditional. From the perspective discussed here, the plazas appear as highly polyvalent spaces in the urban fabric – spaces that have actively shaped both historical and current dynamics and hold significant potential as agents for future urban transformations.

They are simultaneously historic and contemporary places with an effective agency for the current metropolis. As a recognizable urban typology, they act as a symbol (Eco 1968), whose signification has drastically changed from spaces of submission to places of community, gathering and exchange. In this »seizure of the sign« (Bhabha 1994: 193), the current »mestizo« society has deconstructed implicitly the logic and authority of the colonial system in a gradual and ongoing process (fig. 7). This powerful transformation has not been made explicit so far and reflections in the present decolonial discourse in Latin America are still pending.

Their official recognition as »componentes del patrimonio construido« (components of built heritage) (Decreto 190 de 2004, Art. 125) at the metropolitan level in Bogotá; however, it follows a mere preservationist approach and

7.

Example of third spaces. A graffito at the door of the local Muisca community space at the plaza of Suba: The urban Indigenous community, rooted in their ancestral territory, academically educated, and bearers of ancient wisdom, continues the tradition of corn cultivation and the use of petroglyphs – symbolized in a graffito of the »Tunjo,« a water deity. The community space at the colonial-founded plaza highlights the plaza's continuous significance as a central urban site – now appropriated to assert Indigenous presence in the territory. Photograph by the author.

reduces their heritage value to the urban layout rooted in colonial rule and selected historic buildings representing state and church power. This framing limits their broader significance as historical centralities (Carrión 2003) by omitting the simultaneous presence of more diverse historical traces and transformations on a material, social and discursive level. The plazas are not static, they are embedded in a permanent dynamic that continually generates new »third spaces,« where multiple temporalities and spaces emerge (King 2009). A purely chronological perspective only partially reveals their character, as what appears to be the past continues to actively shape the present and the future. A transversal reading, focusing on this simultaneity and thus on the space offers deeper insight. Such a reading reveals their architectural capacity as concise structures with a high contingency (Wolfrum 2015), enabling drastic shifts in significance and highlighting their potential as catalysts for urban renewal. Their generic, repetitive appearance makes them a rhetorical figure in the urban space that can turn out to be a powerful symbol of community-led change, unleashing transformative dynamics.

For the high plains of Bogotá, Calderón (2016) points out that today's territory is the result of many interlocking phases, emphasizing that these historical layers are not just an inert substrate, but rather an active principle that is still effective today. The traces of the past in the present city are not silent witnesses, but rather spaces that still characterize the metropolis today. The palimpsest character of the territory (Corboz 2001 [1983]) manifests itself in different ways, and the impact of these spaces depends on their meaning and interpretation, which can be turned into an active measure for urban renewal. These considerations call for a new understanding of heritage, a shift from a mere preservation of historic structures to empowering the transformative agency of significant places and structures.

Continuous Territorial Presence

Indigenous infrastructures and territorial systems have been systematically dismissed for centuries, usually reducing human intervention to isolated settlements and framing natives as simply adapting to or taking advantage of so-called »natural environments« as Heckenberger and Góes Neves (2009) exemplify this in the Amazon. Recent studies reveal that in the high plains of Bogotá as well, complex systems of water management, settlement and agricultural structures were carefully developed and expanded over centuries, transforming the entire territory that has often been labeled as

8.

Indigenous settlement structures highlighted as shaded areas in original map
material: 1915 (Estado Mayor General. Carta Militar de Colombia. 1:25.000,
from: http://cartografia.bogotaendocumentos.com/mapa, accessed October 5,
2025) –1940 (Instituto Geográfico Militar y Catastral. Cundinamarca. Carta
preliminar. 1:10.000, from: Universidad Nacional de Colombia http://cartografia.
bogotaendocumentos.com/mapa, accessed October 5, 2025) –2007 (Martinez et
al. 2007; this map shows current residences of Muisca families). Tight relations
between the place of dwelling and the river become evident. Shadings by the author.

natural (Rodriguez 2019). A decolonial perspective calls for a reframing of these cultural achievements (Hernández 2020), a reevaluation of socio-spatial continuities and, hence, the derivation of new insights that support their integration into contemporary planning. A significant yet underrepresented heritage value of these systems lies in their trans-scalar multifunctional logic which – beyond their historical relevance – offers a form of culturally rooted framework for future planning.

Cross-referencing written sources and the developed cartographic data reveals previously overlooked continuities. Several colonial sources refer to the refusal of the Muisca – among others in Usaquen (Zambrano et al. 2000) – to abandon their original places of residence, settlement and lifestyle in favor of relocation to the colonial urban structures around the plazas, despite drastic coercive measures such as torture and the burning of dwellings. Maps from the early 20th century show typical pre-colonial Muisca settlement structures in various of the examined places (figs. 6 and 8), emphasizing the endurance of Indigenous settlement structures. Additionally, academic work, mostly authored by community members, evidences continuity in Indigenous, territorially related cultural practices throughout the 20th century (Durán 2004; Fernandez 2014; Niviayo 2017). These practices coincide with the described settlement patterns, underscoring the strong relationship between spatial organization and cultural practices. The analysis of the spatial transformation points out the reciprocal impact urbanization and communities have had: Urbanization has affected habits and cultural self-awareness of the communities (Durán 2004; Niviayo 2017) and the mapped-out Indigenous typologies along the river – though highly altered – have molded the basis for contemporary urban structures that are still home to Muisca families (Diesch 2021) (fig. 8). These structures represent third spaces, they are simultaneously rural, indigenous, urban and modern but in a new, consciously and commonly crafted way. This leads to the assumption that, on the one hand, socio-spatial structures have been maintained throughout colonial and post-independence periods; and on the other, that territorial relations and spatial configurations, or, more simply, architecture, have been used as spatially articulated resistance to colonization measures and capitalist urbanization processes (Diesch 2021). These socio-spatial structures, proven to be resilient even throughout critical ruptures, today represent a call to reactivate such interlinked systems – technically and culturally – as part of a broader, culture-based urban design strategy.

Disruptive Appearance

Urbanization has acted as a catalyst for the literal »uncoverings« of Bogotá's Indigenous past and ongoing presence. Around the year 2000, physical excavations for infrastructure and housing projects revealed archeological evidence in Engativá (Muñoz 2004) and Usme (Urrea 2011), indicating pre-colonial significance of these sites. Likewise, land-title processes in Bosa uncovered long-suppressed Indigenous roots and enduring territorial relationships of the current inhabitants (Durán 2004). These examples illustrate how archeology here shifts from merely digging in the past towards a relational, interdisciplinary practice with territorial and transformative perspectives (Heckenberger/Góes Neves 2009). Community initiatives have taken these clashes and the conflicts they expose as a starting point to claim their right to co-create the city. By drawing on the history of their places, they were developing action-related, community-based concepts of heritage (Diesch 2020). While the rapid and uncoordinated urbanization of Bogotá reflects crises of the 20th century, these grassroots responses reveal a spatial-temporal collision of crises. Here, accumulated ruptures appear as turning points – in the Greek sense of »krisis« – enabling a reframing of the present and creating new possibilities for future city-making.

This reframing implies new responsibilities for architects and urbanists. Rather than relying on conventional top-down solutions, professionals need to explore how these initiatives can become transformative actors in processes of urban transformation. This requires a careful balancing – avoiding both the delegation of responsibility onto under-resourced grassroots initiatives and the paternalistism of top-down approaches (Heindl 2024). Architecture then comprises discursive and functional linkages with large-scale human-environment-relations that can be reactivated by integrating these communities into future planning. In this light, the »tabula plena« (Roberts 2016) becomes a basis for actively engaging past eras in present-day interventions, fostering a creative dialog across centuries. Significant sites such as the plazas and the layered territorial dynamics of Bogotá's periphery can be activated through »horizontal« relationships (Viganò 2019). Recognizing the rhythms and traces of the past becomes essential to sustain the evolving »dance« of urbanism (Solà-Morales 1997).

In all these cases, spatial analysis and mappings have been essential tools: They help to disentangle complex realities, reveal interrelated dynamics, and transform them into agents of urban transformations. Under this lens, the spaces, relations, and dynamics presented here can be seen as counterprojects of coexistence, »radically different systems, alternative world visions, and as such they may legitimise positions currently marginalized by mainstream thinking or dominant discourses« (Viganò/Pietropolli 2024: 73). The role of architectural thinking – recognizing these principles as active assets and a creative resource for urban design – is crucial for developing the skills needed to transform cities into sustainable urban spaces.

Conclusion

Understanding crisis as a potential turning point – a way out of a malfunctioning situation – the described ruptures, clashes and outcomes offer insights for new opportunities in urban design. However, while strategies that demonstrate community resilience must be recognized, they should not be overburdened with expectations (Appelhans 2024). The role for architects and urban designers is to uncover the underlying socio-spatial structures – a decolonial perspective helps to identify and name them – and to develop context-sensitive frameworks and strategies for transformation. This article illustrates how unraveling complex urban constellations and reframing them through spatial and cultural analysis can generate empowering starting points for urban transformation – rooted in local context and communities' practices rather than in problem-driven, technological solutions.

Using the example of rapid urbanization as a consequence of poly-crisis, where ruptures of different times and contexts spatially clash, the shifting meanings and appropriations of originally colonial plazas and the continuity of Indigenous spatial practices in the territory call for a new notion of heritage. Based on the relationship among significant places, territorial structures, and active communities, heritage becomes a means of »exploring and proposing [a] counterproject« (Viganò/Pietropolli 2024: 73). *Transformative heritage* a concept based on an expanded creative and relational understanding of heritage enables the uncovering of rooted site-specific as well as structurally ignored trans-scalar places, structures and interactions (Diesch 2024).

Through a wide set of participatory methods, this research highlights the agency of communities as key actors in the making of the city. This recognition enables the empowerment of overlooked organizational principles and socio-cultural significance to places and territories that continue to shape urban spaces. Alongside material traces, conventional recognition and overall known relations, these principles, communities and networks are relational, spatial, and discursive resources for future design strategies. While these systems may appear fragmented, subtle and complex, they have proven resilience as they have endured through colonization and urbanization. Recognizing their structuring logic allows planners to draw on them as cultural assets. In this sense, spatial analysis becomes a tool not only for diagnosis but also for the discovery of latent capacities for renewal.

Transformative heritage calls for new relational and design-driven paradigms: Inherent transformative structures and narratives can replace rigid dichotomies and open new pathways for action. Through existing discursive references, social structures and paradigmatic architecture can support new narratives, while triggering cooperative transformation processes. For this to be effective, planners and decision-makers must be trained to recognize and integrate these rooted practices into formal systems and understand them as bases for design-driven projects (Aschner/Forero/Sarmiento 2025). This includes shifting institutional frameworks to support community-led design, culturally rooted urban strategies, and multi-scalar approaches to territorial transformation. Ultimately, this article advocates for urbanism as a practice of co-creation – where local knowledge, community agency, spatial practices, and heritage are understood as active, relational resources for designing resilient urban futures.

References

Appelhans, Nadine (2024): »The academic publishing system in crises: absences in international urban studies,« *Geographica Helvetica 79/3*, 305-309. doi: 10.5194/gh-79-305-2024

Aschner, Juan Pablo/Forero, Michael Andrés/Sarmiento, Alma (2025): Decolonizing creative education in the global south, *Design Studies 98*, 101316. doi: 1016/j.destud.2025.101316

Bhabha, Homi (1994): *The Location of Culture*, London, New York: Routledge.

Bhambra, Gurminder (2014): »Postcolonial and Decolonial Reconstructions,« in: *Connected Sociologies*, London: Bloomsbury Academic, 117–140. doi: 10.5040/9781472544377.ch-006

Boada, Ana María (2006): *Patrones de asentamientos regional y sistemas de agricultura intensiva en Cota y Suba*, Bogotá: Banco de la Republica.

Calderón, Arturo (2016): *Territorios Simultáneos. Formas de territorialización de la Sabana de Bogotá (Dissertation)*, Barcelona: Universidad Politécnica de Cataluña.

Careri, Francesco (2009): *Walkscapes. El andar como práctica estética*, Barcelona: Editorial Gustavo Gili.

Casasbuenas, María José/Diesch, Alissa (2017): »Fotografía y cartografía social. Aproximaciones al patrimonio urbano de Bogotá,« in: Paulina León/María Fernanda Troya (eds.), *Mapear no es habitar*, Quito: FLACSO, Arte Actual, 185-203.

Cavalieri, Chiara (2019): »Atlas(es) Narratives,« in: Chiara Cavalieri/Viganò Paola (eds.), *the Horizontal Metropolis. a Radical Project*, Zürich: Park Books, 69–77.

Certeau, Michel ([1980] 1988): *Kunst des Handelns*, Berlin: Merve.

Chandoke, Neera (1991): The Post-Colonial City, *Economic and Political Weekly 26 /50*, 2868–2873.

Corner, James (1999): »The Agency of Mapping: Speculation, Critique and Invention,« in: Denis Cosgrove (ed.), *Mappings*, London: Reaktion Books. 213-300.

del Castillo, Lina (2019): »Surveying the Lands of Republican Indígenas: Contentious Nineteenth-Century Efforts to Abolish Indigenous Resguardos near Bogotá, Colombia,« *Journal of Latin American Studies 51*, 771–799. doi: 10.1017/ S0022216X19000294

Diesch, Alissa/Niviayo, Iván/Yopasá, Jorge (2018): »We Were Considered Extinct and Our Cultural Heritage Was Denied,« in: Jörg Schröder/Maurizio Carta/ Sarah Hartmann (eds.), *Creative Heritage*, Berlin: Jovis, 74–75.

Diesch, Alissa (2020): »Claiming the Future by Pronouncing Local Heritage,« *European Journal of Creative Practices in Cities and Landscapes: The Matter of Future Heritage*, 01, 77–90.

Diesch, Alissa (2021): »Transformación morfológica y cultural de la periferia de Bogotá,« *Quaderns de Recerca en Urbanism QRU 12 (2021)*, 78–96.

Diesch, Alissa (2022): *Atlas Uncovering Territories in Bogotá*, Hannover: Abteilung Regionales Bauen und Siedlungsplanung, Leibniz Universität Hannover. doi: 10.15488/11902

Diesch, Alissa (2024): *Bogotás ländliches Erbe* (Dissertation), Munich: TUM. doi: 10.14459/2024md1725528

Diez, Juan Manuel (2012): »Cartografía Social. Herramienta de intervención e investigación social compleja. El vertebramiento inercial como proceso mapeado,« in: Juan Manuel, Diez/Beatriz, Escudero (eds.), *Investigación e intervención desde las ciencias sociales, métodos y experiencias de aplicación*, Comodoro Rivadavia: Universitaria de la Patagonia, 9–25.

Durán, Carlos (2004): *El Cabildo Muisca de Bosa: el discurso de un nuevo movimiento social, étnico y urbano* (Doctoral dissertation), Bogotá: Universidad de los Andes.

Eco, Umberto (1972 [1968]): *Einführung in die Semiotik*, München: Wilhelm Fink Verlag.

Escovar, Alberto/Mariño, Margarita/Peña, César (2004): *Atlas histórico de Bogotá, 1538-1910*, Bogotá: Instituto Distrital de Patrimonio Cultural.

Fals Borda, Orlando (1978): »Über das Problem, wie man die Realität erforscht, um sie zu verändern,« in: Helmut Ornauer/ Heinz Moser (eds.), *Internationale Aspekte der Aktionsforschung*, München: Kösel, 78–112.

Fernandez, Mauricio (2014): *La resignificación cultural mediante la acción colectiva frente a la expansión urbana. Un estudio diagnóstico sobre la problemática del territorio del cabildo indígena muisca-Bosa periodo 1999-2013*, Thesis, Bogotá: Universidad del Rosario. doi: 10.48713/10336_8680

Freire, Paolo (1970): *Pedagogía del Oprimido*, Montevideo: Tierra Nueva.

Goubert, Beatriz (2019): *Nymsuque: Contemporary Muisca Indigenous Sounds in the Colombian Andes*, Dissertation, New York: Columbia University.

Heckenberger, Michael, Góes Neves, Eduardo (2009): Amazonian Archaeology, *Annual Review of Anthropology 38*, 251–266. doi:10.1146/annurev-anthro-091908-164310

Heindl, Gabu (2024): Interview by Jesko Fezer, Benjamin Foerster-Baldenius, Frauke Gerstenberg, Gabu Heindl, Christof Mayer, Alex Nehmer: »Ohne imaginatives Denken kommen wir aus den gegenwärtigen Verhältnissen nicht heraus,« in: *ARCH+ 258 Urbane Praxis*, 66–77.

Hernández, Felipe (2020): »Modern Fetishes, Southern Thoughts,« *Dearq 29 (2021)*: 40–53. doi: 10.18389/dearq29.2021.01

Herrera, Marta (1998): »Los pueblos que no eran pueblos,« *Anuario de Historia Regional y de las Fronteras 2–3–4*, 13–45.

Huffschmid, Anne/Wildner, Kathrin (2013): *Stadtforschung aus Lateinamerika. Neue urbane Szenarien: Öffentlichkeit – Territorialität – Imaginarios*, Bielefeld: transcript.

Kerner, Ina (2012): *Postkoloniale Theorien. Zur Einführung*, Hamburg: Junius.

King, Anthony (2009): *Postcolonial Cities*, Binghamton (NY): State University of New York. https://booksite.elsevier.com/brochures/hugy/SampleContent/Postcolonial-Cities.pdf, accessed May 31,2019.

Kraft, Sabine (2016): The Future will be Decided in the Cities, *ARCH+ Planetary Urbanism: The Transformative Power of Cities* 223, 12–13.

Mejía, Germán (2000): *Los años del cambio. Historia urbana de Bogotá 1820-1910*, Bogotá: Universidad Javeriana.

Mignolo, Walter (2011): *The Darker Side of Western Modernity. Global Futures, Decolonial Options*, Durham (NC): Duke University Press.

Moudon, Anne (1997): »Urban morphology as an emerging interdisciplinary field,« *Urban Morphology 1*, 3–10.

Muñoz, Jhon (2004): *Humedal Jaboque, evolución geomorfológica y geológica; y su relación con las culturas prehispánicas* (Thesis), Bogotá: Universidad Nacional.

Niviayo, Iván (2017): »El rostro, la tierra y la ciudad: reflexiones sobre la etnicidad de los muyscas de Suba,« in: Fredy Reyes/Pablo Gómez (eds.), *Territorios y memorias culturales muiscas: Etnografías, cartografías y arqueologías*, Bogotá: Usta.

Pink, Sarah (2013): *Doing Visual Ethnography*, Los Angeles, London, New Delhi, Singapore: Sage.

Quijano, Aníbal (1992): »Colonialidad y modernidad/racionalidad,« *Perú indígena*, 13 (29), 11–20.

Robinson, Jennifer (2022): *Comparative Urbanism: Tactics for Global Urban Studies*, Oxford, Wiley.

Rodríguez, Lorena (2019): »La construcción del paisaje agrícola prehispánico en los Andes colombianos: el caso de la Sabana de Bogotá,« *Spal 28/1*, 193–215. doi: 10.12795/spal.2019.i28.09

Roy, Ananya (2009): »The 21st-Century Metropolis: New Geographies of Theory.« In: *Regional Studies 43/6*, 819–30. doi: 10.1080/00343400701809665

Roy, Ananya (2015): »Who's Afraid of Postcolonial Theory?,« in: *International Journal of Urban and Regional Research 40/1*, 200–9. doi:10.1111/1468-2427.12274

Santos, Milton ([1978] 1990): *Por una geografía nueva*, Madrid: Espasa-Calpe.

Silva, Armando (2006): *Imaginarios Urbanos*, Bogotá: Arango.

Solà-Morales, Manuel (1997): *Las formas del crecimiento urbano*, Barcelona: Ediciones UPC.

Spivak, Gayatri (1994): »Can the Subaltern Speak?,« in: Patrick Williams/Laura Chrisman (eds.), *Colonial Discourse and Post-Colonial Theory: A Reader*, New York, Harvester/Wheatsheaf. 66–111.

Tagg, John (1988): *The Burden of Representation. Essays on Fotographies and Histories*, Minneapolis: University of Minnesota Press.

Turnbull, David (1993): *Maps Are Territories: Science Is an Atlas: A Portfolio of Exhibits*, Chicago: University of Chicago Press.

United Nations, Department of Economic and Social Affairs, Population Division (UN) (2019): *World Urbanization Prospects: The 2018 Revision*, New York: United Nations, https://population.un.org/wup/assets/WUP2018-Report.pdf, accessed September 19, 2019.

Urrea, Tatiana (2011): *Usme. Historia de un territorio*, Bogotá: Metrovivienda.

Vélez, Irene/Rátiva, Sandra/Varela, Daniel (2012): »Cartografía social como metodología participativa y colaborativa de investigación en el territorio afrodescendiente de la cuenca alta del río Cauca,« *Cuadernos de Geografía | Revista Colombiana de Geografía* 21/2, 59–73.

Viganò, Paola (2019): »A Radical Project. Projects: Urbanism as a Research Tool.« In: Chiara Cavalieri/Paola Viganò (eds.), *The Horizontal Metropolis: A Radical Project*, Zürich: Park Books, 118–129.

Viganò, Paola/Pietropolli, Tommaso (2024): »How Will We »Occupy« Space and Land? Counterprojects of Coexistence,« in: Jeffrey Huang/Dieter Dietz/Laura Trazic/Korinna Zinovia Weber (eds.), *Transcalar prospects in climate crisis. Architectural research in re/action*, Zürich: Lars Müller, 66–74.

Wolfrum, Sophie (2015): *Platzatlas. Stadträume in Europa*, Basel: Birkhäuser.

Wolfrum, Sophie/Brandis, Nikolai, eds. (2015): *Performative Urbanism. Generating and Designing Urban Space*, Berlin: Jovis.

World Population Review (WPR) (2023): *World Population Review*, https://worldpopulationreview.com/world-cities/bogota-population, accessed August 24, 2023.

Zambrano, Fabio/Castelblanco, Carolina/Sánchez, Laura/Hoyos, Juan Felipe/Benninghoff, Federico/Ruiz, Manuel (2000): *Comunidades y Territorios. Reconstrucción Histórica de Usaquén*, Bogotá: Impresol.

CONTRIBUTORS

Biographies

Jakleen Al-Dalal'a

is a trained architect, researcher, and activist based in the UK. She is currently a Postdoctoral Research Fellow at University College London, working on the *CHRYSES* project on mapping environmental and health crises. She completed her PhD at the University of Sheffield, where her research focused on rethinking public participation in planning in Amman, Jordan, through Southern, feminist, and decolonial lenses. Jakleen is co-founder of the *Southern Theorising Group* and *makāna Collective*, both platforms that bring together research, activism, and pedagogy around spatial and social justice. Her work combines participatory methods, critical pedagogy, and urban research to explore commons, care, and grassroots city-making. She has taught at the University of Sheffield, Manchester Metropolitan University, and Applied Science University in Jordan, and is a member of the *Urban Commons Research Collective*.

Maria Alexandrescu

is a landscape architect and researcher interested in environmental histories of situated urbanized natures as common grounds for reimagining and reclaiming the right to life in the city. Maria is currently an ESRC-funded PhD candidate at the School of Architecture and Landscape, University of Sheffield, finishing their thesis entitled *Common maidan futures: caring for resilience in Bucharest's marginal and peripheral landscapes*, which addresses the role of marginal and peripheral landscapes in the climate crisis through the Romanian *maidan*, a situated landscape figure located in the Global East.

Alvie Augustin

is in the final stages of completing their master's degree in spatial planning at the Technical University of Vienna, building on a foundation in socioeconomics. They are a qualitative urban researcher, youth worker, and activist. For their master's thesis, they are currently collaborating with genderqueer youth in Vienna, exploring the intersections of public and digital spaces in the construction of youthhoods and materializations of social marginalization. Their research emphasizes collective, participatory, and power-critical methods that prioritize community and solidarity beyond traditional academic outputs.

Kadambari Baxi

is Professor of Practice at Barnard College, Columbia University, New York. Her architecture and media practice designs exhibitions as public pedagogy on vital socio-political issues. Recent projects exploring climate justice, reproductive healthcare, labor exploitation on construction sites, and transboundary pollution were exhibited at the *Frieze Art Fair* and *Unison Sculpture Garden* in New York; at the *Architecture Biennale* and *Triennale* in Seoul and Oslo, and at the Art Institute Institute of Chicago and Beiqiu Museum in Nanjing. Combining interactive media, moving images and architectural visualizations, her exhibitions integrated collaborations with scientists, artists, human-rights organizations and public-health experts.

Andrew Belfield

is the Architecture Agency Fellow at the School of Architecture and Landscape at the University of Sheffield and co-director of the London-based critical design practice *public works*. His research supports just neighborhood transitions by utilizing design-based approaches, which center citizen agency in built environments. This has been explored through his practice-based PhD research, *Climate Companions: Civic Pedagogies through Design and Critical Spatial Practice* (2025).

Jhono Bennett

is a South African architect, urbanist, and educator whose work engages with inclusive design, spatial justice, and the ethics of practice in post-apartheid contexts. He co-founded *1to1 – Agency of Engagement* in 2010, a Johannesburg-based design social enterprise that develops collaborative, multi-scalar interventions addressing systemic spatial inequities. Jhono is a Senior Lecturer at the University of Cape Town and also teaches across city and design programs at University College London (UCL) and the University of the Arts London (UAL). He earned his doctorate at the Bartlett School of Architecture, UCL, as part of the *TACK / Communities of Tacit Knowledge* network. His research explores the relational dimensions of spatial design, focusing on inclusive methodologies, critical positionality, and planning within South African cities. His doctoral work, in particular, advanced reparative, Southern

Urbanism-informed approaches that confront entrenched socio-spatial bias through situated practice.

Ana Bisbicus

studied architecture at the Berlin University of Arts and the Glasgow School of Art. They live and work between Berlin and Cali, Colombia. In their work, Ana operates at the intersection of artistic research and education, as well as the curation and design of spaces. Together with Sarah Hachem, they founded *habi practice* ﺣﺒﻲ in 2024. Together, they develop anti-racist and anti-colonialist educational formats for spatial planning. From 2019 to 2024, they were part of the *fem_arc* collective in Berlin until its dissolution. There, together with Océane Vé-Réveillac, they designed, among other projects, the exhibition architecture for the show *Wor(l)ding Dreamers* at Galerie im Turm, Berlin, in 2024. Since December 2024, Ana has been a research associate at the Chair of Architecture Cities Economies.

Armelle Breuil

is a French-trained architect from the ENSA Paris-Val de Seine, a climate and social activist, and an architectural educator for youth. After obtaining a Permaculture Design Certificate she founded the office *ACT!*, as Breuil believes the time for talking about the ongoing ecological collapse is over; it is time to *ACT!*. Her climate and social activism engagement focuses on the building industry, she co-founded the Norwegian branch of the *Architects Climate Action Network (ACAN)*, and is the international coordinator for the UK branch. She is one of three core members of both *Safe Space Collective* and *JAM Collective*, a collective focusing on empowerment through workshops for youth and self-publishing.

Esra Can

is a researcher, architect, and activist who explores the transformative potential of architecture and urbanism in contested and socio-ecologically precarious contexts. Her PhD in Architecture and Design Action from the University of Sheffield, titled *Instituting Hayat: Disruptive Care and Stasis Urbanism in Famagusta, Cyprus*, developed a feminist and decolonial framework for studying urban activism. Her work unfolds across care as disruptive practice, contested spaces, and socio-ecological justice, mobilizing participatory action research, co-design, and civic pedagogy. A co-founder of transborder collectives in Cyprus, including *Archis Interventions_Cy* and *Imaginary Famagusta*, she has co-produced projects engaging diverse publics in envisioning shared urban futures. Her publications and collaborations contribute to debates on Southern theorization, spatial justice, urban commoning, and eco-feminist imaginaries.

Alissa Diesch

is an architect and urbanist, and a graduate of TUM. Her doctoral thesis *The Rural Heritage of Bogotá*, was supervised by Sophie Wolfrum (TUM) and graded *summa cum laude*. She has over 10 years of research experience covering diverse topics about cities and territories in Europe and Latin America, with a focus on culture-based urban transformation, urban and territorial heritage, territorial innovation, critical cartography, creative cities, artistic research, and circular design. Currently, she is Professor and a DAAD Long-Term Lecturer at the Faculty of Architecture, Urbanism, and Design at the Universidad del Norte in Barranquilla, Colombia, with a focus on sustainable development. From 2018 to 2024, she was an assistant Professor at the Chair of Territorial Design at Leibniz University in Hannover (LUH), working for the EU Innovation Alliance »Circular Design,« among other projects. From 2015 to 2018, she was an assistant Professor and leader of the Research Group *Habitat Sociocultural* at Universidad La Gran Colombia in Bogotá.

Natalya Dikhanov-Juswigg

applies research-driven design to environmental and social issues, also drawing on living principles from our nonhuman counterparts. Her background includes salvaged-object design, urban farming, and design-build projects. Dikhanov-Juswigg began collaborating with and mobilizing students and experts from various fields with the 2011 UMD Solar Decathlon winner, *WaterShed*, and organizing an interdisciplinary maker session with *REFUNC* (Den Haag/Berlin) and Salvaging Creativity (York, PA). After earning her B.Sc. from the University of Maryland, Dikhanov completed a M.Sc. in Architecture at TU Berlin. Her critical investigative work has addressed the revitalization of mined indigenous land, water injustice in California's Central Valley, and access to reproductive healthcare in the US via a traveling exhibition. As the cofounder of the studio *FLUFFFF* (2020), her work has garnered awards from the Graham Foundation, the AA Visiting School, the LA+ Journal, and she participated in the *ARCH+ Cohabitation* exhibition at silent green Kulturquartier, in Berlin.

Beverly Engelbrecht

completed her preliminary studies at the Leipzig School of Design, subsequently studying architecture at the Bauhaus-Universität Weimar (Germany). She has worked for various architectural firms in Germany and abroad, including Miller & Maranta Architekten in Basel (Switzerland). She was a long-standing member of the interdisciplinary, and collaborative workspace collective *Studio Wägetechnik e. V.* in Weimar. From 2021 to 2023, Engelbrecht was a research and teaching assistant at the Chair of Design and Housing at the Bauhaus-Universität Weimar. Since 2022, Beverly Engelbrecht has been working on her dissertation, *Counter Architecture of Sex Work. The Example of Potsdamer Straße in West Berlin* (1961-1989). Since 2023, she has been a recipient holder of the Thüringer Graduiertenförderung scholarship of the Bauhaus University Weimar and an associated fellow of the DFG Research Training Group 2227, *Identity and Heritage*.

Enrique Espinosa

is a Professor at the University of Alicante. He holds a PhD in architecture from the University of Alicante (2024) and a master's degree in architecture from Universidad Politécnica de Madrid (2009). He is a member of the *TRANS* and *PLAYA* research groups at UPM and UA. He was a co-founder of the *PKMN* collective from 2006 to 2016 and has led *Eeestudio* since 2016. His practice has won the Arquia Proxima Prize (2014) and has been nominated for the Mies van der Rohe Award (2013, 2022). His research focuses on the intersection of collective practices and learning, the construction of disciplinary peripheries, open and hacker culture, and the landscapes of ecology and rurality. He is the co-author, with Colaboratorio, of *Post DomestiCity: Re-thinking Urban Obsolescence* (Actar, 2022) and *Open City: Re-thinking the Post-industrial City* (Actar 2020).

Rui Ferreira dos Santos

is completing a PhD in architecture at TU Braunschweig, exploring the lost and found in matters-of-space – from urban politics and policies to democratic facilitation and stage design. After brief detours and disillusionment with urban planning and management in international development contexts (Egypt, Nepal), Ferreira dos Santos embarked on a longer doctoral journey to explore collective and situated responses to the urgencies, frictions, and contradictions of the (Mis)Anthropocene, Capitalocene, Plantationocene, and Chthulucene. His research now focuses on terrestrial mediations, speculative pragmatism, and composting practices. He seeks to entangle spatial practices with feminist, queer, and post-growth struggles (degrowth, buen vivir, eco-swaraj, ecosocialism), grounding these explorations poeto-politically through intersectional care, critical hope, and situated invention.

Isabel Glogar

is a Senior Researcher and architect working in the fields of housing and urban studies with a focus on collaboration, urban transformations and (climate) just cities. She teaches and researches as Postdoctoral Researcher at the Professorship of Urban Design at Technical University of Munich (TUM) and is Head of the Research Group *Cooperative Planning, Collaborative Housing and Neighborhoods*. She taught at the TU Wien and the Hochschule Campus Wien. Currently, she is a Laura Bassi Fellow at TUM and researches collaborative transformation and reuse; as part of her research she is a Visiting Scholar at ETH Wohnforum at ETH Zurich. In Vienna she works with her office *Ofhaus - Office for Housing and Urban Studies* in the field of architecture, housing and urban research. She is the author and co-editor of publications including »TOUCH.01. Collaborative Housing« (2024) and »A Collaborative Approach for Urban Design Education in Light of the Climate Emergency« in the *Dimensions Journal of Architectural Knowledge* (2023).

Lýdia Grešáková

is a sociologist, publicist, and activist focusing on feminist values, pro-climate spatial practices, and housing estate transformations. She researches marginalized voices in Central and Eastern Europe, connecting local stories to global contexts. She is a member of *Spolka*, a Slovak nonprofit studio for architecture and sociology that emphasizes feminist spatial practice and its communication. Previously, she was a research fellow at K LAB at TU Berlin, where she contributed to projects on critical mapping and socio-environmental transformation.

Lis-Mari Gurák Hjortfors

is a Sámi ethnologist and anthropologist from Sápmi in Sweden. She is a Lule Sámi person and lives in the municipality of Gällivare in Koskullskulle, near Malmberget and Gällivare. She is a PhD student and researcher in Sami Studies at the *Várdduo - Centre for Sámi Research*, Umeå University. She is interested in Sámi-related perspectives. Lis-Mari is also a curator, writer, poet, and storyteller, and works to protect Sápmi as well as Sámi and Indigenous history and culture. She curates exhibitions, writes articles, gives presentations about Sámi and Norrbottnian culture and history. She has published numerous articles.

Sarah Hachem

is an artist, spatial practitioner, researcher, and writer whose work interrogates the norms that organize space, pedagogy, and belonging. She co-founded *habi practice* ↩ with Ana Bisbicus, a power-critical, anti-racist, queer-feminist collective working across architecture, art, research, and teaching. Their work unfolds through seminars, studios, and workshops at Dekoloniale, the University of the Arts Berlin, the University of Siegen, Weißensee Academy of Art, and the University of Applied Sciences Erfurt, tracing how coloniality and relational structures shape the spaces we inhabit and imagine. She is part of the *Entity of Decolonization* and has also worked in stage design and curation. Her studies span architecture at the University of the Arts Berlin, the post-MA program Decolonizing Architecture at the Royal Institute of Art in Stockholm, and the MA Art History in the Global Context at the Free University of Berlin.

Lindsay Harkema

is an architect, educator, and organizer based in NYC. She is the founder of the award-winning shared practice *WIP Collaborative (WBE)*, a feminist design collective that engages the public realm by creating vibrant, inclusive spaces informed by local communities and context. Harkema's design, research, and teaching projects center equity, adaptability, and embodiment in the built environment, exploring how shared spaces can be transformed through design to create opportunities for positive change. She advocates for collaborative design processes and equitable labor practices that challenge the notion of singular authorship. Harkema has taught at Barnard College, Cornell University, the City College of New York, Syracuse University, and The New School. She is a licensed architect in New York and is NCARB certified.

Gabu Heindl

is Professor and Head of the Department ARCHITECTURE CITIES ECONOMIES | Building Economy & Project Development at the University of Kassel since 2022. Before that, she was Unit Master at the AA in London, Visiting Professor at University of Sheffield, and Professor of Urban Planning at TH Nürnberg. As an architect and planner, she runs the Vienna-based studio *GABU Heindl Architektur*. Her focus lies in housing, public space, wealth distribution and divisions of labor, and in justice regarding migration and the climate crisis. Her recent publications include the collaborative anthology *Building Critique. Architecture and its Discontents* (2019), and her books *Stadtkonflikte* (2020, 2022) and *Nonsolution* (with Drehli Robnik 2024).

Robin V Hueppe

is a doctoral fellow at the Institute of Landscape and Urban Studies at ETH Zurich. He earned degrees in architecture, urban design, and city planning from Rice University and TU Berlin with the support of Fulbright and DAAD fellowships. Further grants and fellowships supported research stays at the Universidade de Lisboa, Tongji University in Shanghai, and the Canadian Centre for Architecture in Montreal. Formerly an adjunct Professor at the University of Houston, Robin has published in journals such as City, Culture and Society, Pidgin, and OASE, among others. Robin also co-founded *Deux*, a design and research collaborative, and has worked in design firms across Houston, Berlin, and Lisbon.

Husos arquitecturas

established in Madrid in 2003 by Diego Barajas (Bogotá, CO) and Camilo García (Cali, CO), the studio operates between Spain and Colombia, blending research and design, theory and practice. Selected as one of ten studios in Europe for the Royal Academy Dorfman Prize 2024, its work is part of the permanent collections of the FRAC Centre in Orléans and the History Museum of Rotterdam. Husos has received the Holcim Awards for Sustainable Construction (Gold, Europe). The studio's projects have been showcased at the *Venice Biennale* (Central Pavilion), the *International Architecture Biennale Rotterdam* (IABR), the *Oslo Architecture Triennale*, Matadero Madrid, the Tápies Foundation, the *Bienal de Quito*, the Witte de With Museum, Archilab, Ecovisionarios, and *PhotoEspaña*, among others. The founders co-authored *Urbanisms of Remittances: (Re)productive Houses in Dispersion* (Caniche 2017), which won the Fundació Sabadell Prize in 2019 and is included in the Banco Sabadell Art Collection.

Sadie Imae

is a co-founder of *FLUFFFF* studio, where she utilizes storytelling and design to study the intersection of women's health, women's work, and cross-species collaborations. Coming from a background rooted in making, her work and research emphasize the material expression of architecture. Imae entwines physical making with the digital, illustrating distant and not-so-distant futures as feasible realities that question the role of architecture while advocating for others. Her advocacy work includes design, research, and production for the traveling exhibition Early Women of Architecture in Maryland, supported by the Baltimore Architecture Foundation, and Maternal Health Infrastructure, a prototype for Unite for Health's Maternal Care micro-clinic in Cameroon. Imae has instructed architecture students at Morgan State University and the University of Maryland, and currently teaches at the Pratt Institute.

Bernadette Krejs

is an architect and researcher based at the Vienna University of Technology. Her work is situated in a transdisciplinary research field between architecture, housing, and visual culture. She is editor and author of numerous books, such as *Instagram-Wohnen* (2024), *Lorde for Architecture Students* (2023), and *Vienna: The End of Housing (as a Typology)* (2021). She is part of the queer-feminist collective *Claiming*Spaces* and co-founded the activist research practice *Palace of Un/Learning*, where she collaborated with various institutions, including the *Fundació* Mies van der Rohe Barcelona, the *Oslo Architecture Triennale*, the *Design Academy Eindhoven* and *DAZ – Deutsches Architektur Zentrum* Berlin.

Enrique Nieto

is an architect who graduated from ETSAM in 1994. He received his PhD from the University of Alicante in 2012. He is Professor of Architectural Projects at the University of Alicante and Head of the Research Group *Architectural Projects: Critical Pedagogies, Ecological Policies and Material Practices* (PAPCPEPM). He is currently co-directing a national research project entitled *The good arts of living with others through design*. As a professional, his work has been recognized by the European Union Prize for Contemporary Architecture – Mies van der Rohe Award, the Spanish Biennial of Architecture, and the Urbanism or Architecture Awards of the Region of Murcia. His most recent books include: *¡Prescindible organizado!: Una agenda docente, afectiva y disidente para el proyecto arquitectónico* (2022), and *Emergences of the poshuman. Architectural and pedagogical challenges from a disciplinar margin* (2021).

Alina Paias

is a spatial designer and occasional architecture worker, writer, curator, and researcher based in Rotterdam. Paias investigates the systems of architectural production by engaging with a broad range of philosophies. She was an associate curator for the 2024 *International Architecture Biennale Rotterdam (IABR)* and the sole curator of *Taking More Than What's There to Give* at VI PER Gallery in Prague and at the *Lisbon Architecture Triennale* with the support of the LINA platform. She is a member of the editorial team for *Footprint*, the Delft Architecture Theory Journal, and was a participant in the 2025 edition of the Bauhaus Lab program in Global Modernism Studies at the Bauhaus Dessau Foundation. Her latest published work is »Making a/one-self: Afro-Brazilians and more-than-double Architectures of the Black Atlantic,« in *Noetics Without a Mind* (2024), written in collaboration with Léa Alapini.

Doina Petrescu

is a Professor of Architecture and Design Activism at the University of Sheffield. Her research concerns urban commons, resilience, co-production, feminism and politics of space. Her publications consist in authored, edited and co-edited volumes including *Architecture Otherhow* (forthcoming), *LiveAct* (2023), *Urban Commons Handbook* (2022), *Architecture and Resilience* (2018), *The Social (re)Production of Architecture* (2017), *Learn to Act* (2017), *R-Urban Act* (2015), *Agency: Working with Uncertain Architectures* (2009), *Trans-Local Act* (2009), *Altering Practices: Feminist Politics and Poetics of Space* (2007), *Urban/ACT* (2007), and *Architecture and Participation* (2005). Petrescu is also co-founder, together with Constantin Petcou, of *Atelier d'Architecture Autogérée (AAA)*, an internationally acclaimed collective practice which conducts actions and research on participative architecture, resilience and cities co-produced transformation.

public works

is a nonprofit critical design practice, set up in 2004 that works across architecture, art, and performance. The collective seeks out community-driven development opportunities to nurture and promote the rights of communities, environments, and ecologies. As of this writing, the collective has eleven members, and they are based in London, UK. The contribution to this journal was written by Andy Belfield, Andreas Lang and Rhianon Morgan Hatch.

Andy is the co-director of *public works*, a researcher, and an educator. He is currently the Architecture Agency Fellow at the University of Sheffield, focusing on civic pedagogies and climate learning.

Andreas is a spatial practitioner and educator. He is the founding director of *public works* and Course Leader of the M Arch: Architecture Master's program and Reader in Situated and Ecological design Practices at Central Saint Martins.

Rhianon is a co-director of *public works*, working as an architect, researcher, and educator. Her practice explores critical spatial practice, focusing on the intersection of the social and environmental, believing in a future fueled by togetherness and abundance.

Karin Reisinger

is a lecturer at the Academy of Fine Arts in Vienna and a senior scientist at the University of Applied Arts in Vienna. Her two projects, »Two Ore Mountains: Feminist Ecologies of Spatial Practices« and »Stories of Post-extractive Feminist Futures,« funded by the Austrian Science Fund (https://www.mountains-of-ore.org), focus on intersectional feminist and interspecies research with mining communities in Malmberget/Gällivare in Northern Sweden, within Sápmi, and Eisenerz in Austria, and their practices of care and dealing with loss. Together with four practitioners from Gällivare, Reisinger contributed to the *International Architecture Biennale Rotterdam (IABR)* with a *Listening Station on Practices of Hope amidst Extractive Violence*. She curated the exhibition *City of Care* in Eisenerz (2024) and *Fences Insects Embroideries in Vienna* (2022). Recent publications include »Doing Material Positionality while Listening to the Prolonged Coloniality« in *Architectures of Colonialism* and »Two Mining Areas: Spaces of Care amid Extraction« in *Architecture and Culture* 11/3 (both 2024).

Lara Scharf

is an architect, urban designer, and researcher, currently undertaking an ESRC-funded PhD and working as a Teaching Associate at the MA Urban Design at the Sheffield School of Architecture and Landscape, University of Sheffield. Originating from Cyprus, her research, practice, and teaching explore the role of spatial practice in contexts of urban conflict and inequality. Her PhD, *Radical Spatial Futures*, investigates how radical imagination is convoked through critical spatial practice in contested settings around the globe. She is also part of a number of research-based collectives, including *Imaginary Famagusta*, a bi-communal initiative advocating for the role of spatial practice in reconciliation processes, the *Urban Commons Research Collective* and *Lines of Flight* research group.

Tatjana Schneider

is a researcher and educator focused on critical spatial practices for the common good and resistances to exploitative productions of space. She's taught at the Universities of Sheffield, Strathclyde, and Braunschweig, and co-founded *Glasgow Letters on Architecture and Space*. Her publications as author and editor include *Spatial Agency. Other Ways of Doing Architecture* (2011) and *Making Futures* (2022). Current work centers on architecture's role in climate breakdown, including the project *Architecture is Climate*. In 2021, she ran for mayor of Braunschweig.

Vio:la Wagner

is a student of architecture at the Technical University of Vienna and of cultural science at the University of Arts Linz and is a member of the inter-sectional feminist collective *Claiming*Spaces*. As a trans activist, Vio:la is involved in Austria-based organizations such as *Trans Femme Fatale* and *Venib*, a group for non-binary individuals. Wagner's work focuses on increasing visibility for non-binary and trans realities, creating trans spaces, and community work. Notable efforts include founding »Trans and Non-Binary Youth« Vienna and organizing regular meetups for trans people in Vienna and Linz.

ZAS*

is an association of young architects and city residents. Through actions and new narrative approaches, ZAS* rethinks the existing city and proposes alternative visions that go beyond those shaped by conventional, formalized planning processes. Rather than merely opposing official urban planning, ZAS* reimagines the existing city and formulates transformative counter-projects. With the »Speculative Ideas Competition Stadthotel Triemli,« ZAS* successfully challenged a long-standing planning decision, paving the way for the continued use of the residential towers next to the Triemli Hospital in Zurich. In the fall semester of 2024, ZAS* led an experimental guest studio at the Department of Architecture at ETH Zurich and initiiated the »Ämtli für Städtebau« [Small Ministry for Urban Planning]. The authors for this contri-bution are Milena Buchwalder, Ella Eßlinger, Sonja Flury, Jens Knöpfel, Blanka Major, Meghan Rolvien as part of ZAS*.